RIVAL PRAISES

RIVAL PRAISES

Ovid and the Metamorphosis of the Hymnic Tradition

Celia M. Campbell

THE UNIVERSITY OF WISCONSIN PRESS /
WISCONSIN STUDIES IN CLASSICS

Publication of this volume has been made possible, in part, through the generous support and enduring vision of Warren G. Moon.

This book will be made open access within three years of publication thanks to Path to Open, a program developed in partnership between JSTOR, the American Council of Learned Societies (ACLS), University of Michigan Press, and The University of North Carolina Press to bring about equitable access and impact for the entire scholarly community, including authors, researchers, libraries, and university presses around the world. Learn more at https://about.jstor.org/path-to-open/space

The University of Wisconsin Press
728 State Street, Suite 443
Madison, Wisconsin 53706
uwpress.wisc.edu

Copyright © 2024
The Board of Regents of the University of Wisconsin System
All rights reserved. Except in the case of brief quotations embedded in critical articles and reviews, no part of this publication may be reproduced, stored in a retrieval system, transmitted in any format or by any means—digital, electronic, mechanical, photocopying, recording, or otherwise—or conveyed via the Internet or a website without written permission of the University of Wisconsin Press. Rights inquiries should be directed to rights@uwpress.wisc.edu.

Printed in the United States of America
This book may be available in a digital edition.

Library of Congress Cataloging-in-Publication Data

Names: Campbell, Celia M. (Celia Mitchell), 1987- author.
Title: Rival praises : Ovid and the metamorphosis of the hymnic tradition / Celia M. Campbell.
Other titles: Wisconsin studies in classics.
Description: Madison, Wisconsin : The University of Wisconsin Press, 2024. | Includes bibliographical references and indexes.
Identifiers: LCCN 2023050489 | ISBN 9780299348748 (hardcover)
Subjects: LCSH: Ovid, 43 B.C.–17 A.D. or 18 A.D. Metamorphoses. | Ovid, 43 B.C.–17 A.D. or 18 A.D.—Criticism and interpretation.
Classification: LCC PA6519.M9 C345 2024 | DDC 873.01—dc23/eng/20231218
LC record available at https://lccn.loc.gov/2023050489

For
A, B, AND C

CONTENTS

Acknowledgments		ix
List of Abbreviations		xi
Introduction: The Nature of Praise		3
1	Amorphous Control? Resolving the Question of Cosmic Authority within the World of the *Metamorphoses*	14
2	Divining Praise: Jupiter, Apollo, and Poetic Primacy	45
3	Rivaled Affection and Affectation: Diana, Apollo, and Delian Disguise	88
4	Ovid's *Lavacrum Dianae*: The Huntress Muse of the *Metamorphoses*	134
5	The Hymnic Battle for Helicon: Reflections over Contested Grounds	173
6	Calliope's Hymn: Musing on the Nature of Love	201
	Conclusion: Amor's Winged Words	229
	Notes	237
	Works Cited	281
	Index	303
	Index Locorum	313

ACKNOWLEDGMENTS

A first book owes a particular set of debts. This work has been long in the making, and although the debts of gratitude I would like to enumerate could run proportionately long, I will rein in my effusions (sharply). First and foremost: thank you to Virginia Lewis, Laurel Fulkerson, and John Marincola for believing in my ability to undertake an Ovidian project. It may not have been the book I intended to write, but it is the book I needed to write, and so I thank everyone at the University of Wisconsin Press who made this a reality. I owe a great deal to the classics faculty at the University of Oxford, especially Matthew Leigh, for giving me a scholarly foundation to keep building upon; I owe even more to all the wonderful and learned people I have worked with at NYU, Fordham, UVa, and FSU for their help, kindness, and inspiration amid that building process. I am tremendously thankful for the support and encouragement of my current colleagues in Candler Library, who bolstered me through difficult beginnings. To my brilliant friends Calloway Scott, Jessica Carey-Webb, and Antonia Halstead (who are also brilliant scholars), mere thanks are nowhere near enough. Similarly, this would have been impossible without the support and perspective of Giandamiano Bovi. Thanks always to Andrew Beswerchij. And last (but not least): my family deserves all gratitude for their love, patience, and support.

ABBREVIATIONS

Ancient authors and texts have been abbreviated largely following the conventions of the *Oxford Classical Dictionary* (4th ed.). Journal titles have been abbreviated according to the conventions of *L'Année philologique*. Ancient editions referred to by the entire surname of the editor can be found in the bibliography. The following abbreviations are used in the text and notes:

Anth. Pal. = *Anthologia Palatina*

Barchiesi = Barchiesi, A. 2005–7. *Ovidio: Metamorfosi*. Vol. 1, *Libri I–II*; Vol. 2, *Libri III–IV*. Translated by L. Koch. Rome.

Bömer = Bömer, F. 1969–86. *P. Ovidius Naso Metamorphosen: Kommentar*. Heidelberg.

D-K = Diels, H., and W. Kranz, eds. 1952. *Die Fragmente der Vorsokratiker*. 6th ed. Berlin.

FGrHist = Jacoby, F., ed. 1923–69. *Die Fragmente der Griechischen Historiker*. Leiden.

GP = Gow, A. S. F., and D. L. Page, eds. 1968. *The Greek Anthology: The Garland of Philip and Some Contemporary Epigrams*. 2 vols. Cambridge.

K-A = Kassel, R., and C. Austin, eds. 1983–. *Poetae Comici Graeci*. Berlin.

LIMC = Ackermann, H., and J. R. Gisler, eds. 1981–97. *Lexicon Iconographicum Mythologiae Classicae*. Zurich.

L-P = Lobel, E., and D. Page, eds. 1955. *Poetarum Lesbiorum fragmenta*. Oxford

M-W = Merkelbach, R., and M. L. West, eds. 1967. *Fragmenta Hesiodea*. Oxford.

OF = Bernabé, A. O., ed. 2004. *Orphicorum et Orphicis similium testimonia et fragmenta: Poetae Epici Graeci. Pars II. Fasc.1.* Leipzig.

OLD = Glare, P. G. W., and C. Stray, eds. 2012. *Oxford Latin Dictionary.* 2nd ed. Oxford.

Pf. = Pfeiffer, R., ed. 1949–53. *Callimachus.* Vol. 1, *Fragmenta*; Vol. 2, *Hymni et epigrammata.* Oxford.

Rosati = Rosati, G. 2009. *Ovidio: Metamorfosi.* Vol. 3, Libri V–VI. Translated by G. Chiarini. Rome.

SH = Lloyd-Jones, H., and P. Parsons, eds. 1983. *Supplementum Hellenisticum.* New York.

S-M = Snell, B., and H. Maehler, eds. 1975. *Fragments of Pindar.* 2 vols. 4th ed. Leipzig.

Stephens = Stephens, S. A. 2015. *Callimachus: The Hymns.* Oxford.

SVF = von Arnim, H., ed. 1903–5. *Stoicorum veterum fragmenta.* Stuttgart.

Rival Praises

Introduction

The Nature of Praise

Let me begin with a statement that represents the overall thesis of this book, albeit in its most polemical and dramatic form: Ovid's *Metamorphoses* is programmatically designed as a Callimachean *Hymn to Venus and Amor*. Of course, this statement can hardly be left to breathe for a bit before its oversimplification clamors for qualification, for caveating, for more detailed explanation. However, the essence stands: Ovid's *carmen deductum* proclaims its Callimachean allegiances early and paradoxically, and unfurls a world history that is, at heart, a monumental tribute to the power of love. Love—as primordial element, as son of Venus, as active participant in the lineage of the Julio-Claudians—is responsible for the evolution, and revolution, of Ovidian epic. More guardedly, this literary study recenters the significance of the hymnic tradition for reading and interpreting the first pentad of the *Metamorphoses*, the portion of text that deals most concertedly with the gods. Primarily, this significance is shown broadly via the thematic lens of divine rivalry, a mode of interaction native to hymnic material. In tracing the networks of allusion Ovid makes to hymns and hymnic features, I show how Ovid's epic divinities are competitively concerned with the issues of identity and control as determined by praise, love, and love of praise.

OVID'S GODS

Ovid's epic gods are present from the beginning of his poem. The consummate work of a consummate storyteller yet begins with a divine invocation of breathtaking brevity: *di* ([you] gods, *Met.* 1.2).[1] The gods receive a mere two letters acknowledging the poet's call for assistance with his new task of describing bodies changing into new forms—a task he describes twice with reference to himself (*coeptis . . . meis*, "my beginnings" 1.2–3; *mea . . . tempora*, "my times," 1.4). The disproportionality of the divine presence Ovid invokes to his own self-reference raises questions from the *Metamorphoses'* very beginning about Ovid's treatment of and involvement with the gods. Unlike the gods of Homeric epic, who come to have the *Homeric Hymns* as an external guide for understanding the formation of their Olympian order and the consolidation of its power—an almost aetiological set of glosses to parsing their Olympian identities—Ovid's gods come with no such overt companion text to divine personality and psychology.[2] Ovid himself, perhaps the most marked proemial presence, comes with the companion texts of his elegiac corpus. These are works that go quite a distance in lending logic and perspective to Ovid's development and trajectory as a poet, and to his growth and assumption of various roles and powers. But again, there is no parallel guide to understanding the Ovidian divinities, for whom the first pentad of the *Metamorphoses* provides the greatest stage (or arena) for the gods.

In these five books, the Olympians, in their Ovidian iteration, appear as the primary characters who drive and determine action. Hymns, as poems praising the gods, provide a natural trove of material relevant to these textual appearances. In their form as verbal offerings to the gods and expressions of divine praise, hymns help shape perceptions of divine identity, agency, and personality.[3] One especial quality of hymns is their capacity to "locate," to orient the reader to the sanctity of the gods. We can understand this hymnic capacity to "locate" in a strictly physical, geographical sense of the word (i.e., identifying important cult sites and areas of worship) but we can also note a more diffuse understanding held in "location," as an act of positioning or contextualizing, whether that is in relation to other gods, with reference to specific attributes, or within spheres of responsibility. In this understanding, hymns can serve generally to locate gods within the mytho-literary matrix of divine power.

But how do we locate the elusive Ovidian gods within the narrative matrix of the *Metamorphoses*? A body of *Ovidian Hymns* never (to the best of our knowledge) presented itself as enticing subject matter to any mischievously enterprising pseudepigrapher. Part of my purpose with this study is to provide one answer to this question, and this is where Callimachus comes in. Specifically, I suggest that Callimachus offers one solution to Ovid's overtly

Introduction

lacunose and elusive approach to the Olympian order within the *Metamorphoses*, in the form of his poetry book of *Hymns*. Although it is tempting to situate the Callimachean hymns simply as a companion text, along the lines of the correspondence between the *Homeric Hymns* and Homeric epic, the picture is rather more complex. It is additionally tempting to position Ovid's use of the six Callimachean hymns as an expedient outsourcing of mythological material, making Callimachus (paradoxically and anachronistically) an independent creative contractor of the Ovidian narrative machine; a clever cross-referencing to a literary kindred spirit.[4] However, the relationship between Ovidian epic and the Callimachean hymns is more symbiotic. By relying upon Callimachus' *Hymns* to form a sustained pattern of meaning for the opening narrative unit of his epic, Ovid invests in a mutual identification of form, as he assimilates his epic to the narrative dynamism and learned polyphony of the Callimachean hymnic collection. The following chapters reveal the continuous seam of meaning derived from Callimachus' hymns for the first pentad of the *Metamorphoses*, showing that allusion to this body of work provides a meaningful and sustained narrative pattern that permits this interpretive styling of affiliation.

THE *METAMORPHOSES* AND CALLIMACHUS' *HYMNS*

The import of this investigation of hymnic influence, grounded in the Callimachean hymns, reaches simultaneously in two productive directions. First, it provides a more systematic and nuanced reckoning with the *Hymns* as source texts for Ovid in ways previously unexamined. Second, this more systematic reckoning allows us to recognize Ovid as a reader of the Callimachean hymns in a specific way: namely, that he experienced them as a self-conscious collection. Cumulatively, examining both how the Callimachean hymn collection poses a distinct microcosm of influence to *Metamorphoses* 1–5, and the ways Ovid deliberately adapts and manipulates this collective influence, represents a new frontier of understanding for Ovid's Callimacheanism. One especial way this collective influence becomes experienced is in looking at the role of the Muse. The way Callimachus assimilates the goddesses he individually hymns to Muses becomes a model for the competitive relationships and identity games Ovid constructs between his own Olympian goddesses and the Muses themselves. The issue of overlapping identities between goddess and Muse that Ovid inherits from the Callimachean hymnic collection provides one persistent axis of inquiry for this study.

6 Introduction

Although I am looking at what amounts to the Ovidian reception of the *Hymns*, in one sense, this study necessarily also aims to encourage further efforts in reading Callimachus' *Hymns* as a comprehensive collection. While the individual *Hymns* command a rich bibliographical tradition, together, the poems garner proportionately less attention.[5] Manuscript tradition preserves the *Hymns* in only one order: *Zeus, Apollo, Artemis, Delos, Bath of Pallas,* and *Demeter*. Taking his known editorial interests and responsibilities into consideration, Callimachus himself stands as the most likely candidate for the compilation, arrangement, and editing of the *Hymns*. Although I have no opinion here on the question of whether he turned his attentions to the *Aetia* for a second time, creating a more expansive second edition[6]—evidence of an editorial spirit that would certainly appeal to the Ovidian sensibility—I do subscribe to the (reasonable) assumption that Callimachus is the original arranger and editor of the six-poem poetry book of *Hymns*.[7] However, only one English monograph has taken a comprehensive view of these poems (Michael Brumbaugh's *The New Politics of Olympos*).[8] A natural consequence of these individual treatments of the *Hymns* is the fact that their *collective* influence—as a self-conscious, authorially arranged volume—is easily overlooked. This is assuredly the case when it comes to viewing their inspiratory impact upon Ovid's epic, which also occasionally suffers from the limited perspectives of episodic treatment.

Ovid's Callimacheanism

Ovid's Callimachean bona fides are well-established: from the very beginning, Ovid professes to be writing a poem that displays a programmatic Callimachean allegiance.[9] The influence of Callimachus upon Ovid is a central preoccupation of Ovidian scholarship, and Ovid has long been studied as a "Hellenistic" poet or, even more directly, as a "Callimachean" poet.[10] Both Callimachus and Ovid are indisputably poets' poets. Noting a shared revelry in dense allusivity, sophisticated wordplay, elaborate displays of learning, and narrative misdirection is only the beginning when painting the picture of aesthetic affiliation between these erudite literary luminaries—one of Rome, and one of Alexandria. Ovid is not shy in revealing the depth and breadth of his Callimachean affect: the *Aetia, Hecale, Iambs, Ibis,* and epigrams all find adapted expression within Ovidian poetic programming across his entire oeuvre (although the *Fasti* deserves especial notice for its Callimachean indebtedness). As such, Callimachean literary influence is

Introduction

fairly the Hydra of Ovidian scholarship: a seemingly inexhaustible source of new readings, with a correspondingly immense bibliographic record. And yet, the *Hymns*—despite their existence as an entire, extant Callimachean collection—do not occupy a prominent place in the bibliography that enriches an overall understanding of Ovid's poetics. As far as the *Metamorphoses* is concerned, the *Hymns* are discussed in their roles as mythological sources; that is, their relevance and influence is largely confined to places where the same narrative material is treated.[11] Ovid's myth of Actaeon in Book 3 has long been tied to the Callimachean version of the myth in the *Bath of Pallas* (*Hymn* 5).[12] The myth of Erysichthon told by Achelous in Book 8 is discussed alongside the source material of Callimachus' sixth hymn, the *Hymn to Demeter*.[13] The *Hymn to Delos* is also one identifiable source for the tale of Latona and the Lycians in *Metamorphoses* 6.[14]

In their role as mythological sources, then, Ovid's own mythological debts to and divergences from the *Hymns* are dutifully recorded. However, the literary substance of intertextuality and allusion, along with the poetic intrigue of Ovid's recognition and repurposing of this one expressed mythological tradition, become subsidiary.[15] Instead, the focus is more mechanical, laying out the narrative facts of the details Ovid reprises or discards. Such a strategy is understandable, given the immensity of the *Metamorphoses* and the encyclopedic array of mythological sources Ovid consults, compares, combines, and contests; it is also appreciable for understanding Ovid's continuity in or breaking with mythological tradition, which allows us to develop our sense of Ovidian poetic innovation. And yet, at this stage in scholarship on the *Metamorphoses*—over half a century since Brooks Otis' *Ovid as an Epic Poet*, to use one benchmark—there is room for more intensive, nuanced interpretive work to be done.[16] The collection of Callimachean hymns offers the locus for this work.

The *Metamorphoses* and the Hymnic Tradition

While the poetic collection of Callimachean hymns provides the central focus of my discussion of Ovid's engagement with the hymnic tradition, it is not the exclusive focus. I am also concerned with integrating the source material (albeit more limited) from the Roman hymnic tradition more contemporary to Ovid into the picture of his poetic influences. By necessity, too, some time will also be spent with the wider tradition of hymns and other embedded hymnic material, especially the *Homeric Hymns*. Happily, a renewed interest in the *Homeric Hymns* themselves has led to a concomitant interest in their reception, and recent scholarship on Ovid and the *Homeric Hymns* provides a new platform for thinking about hymnic influence upon Ovidian epic.[17] However, the importance of the *Homeric Hymns* to the *Metamorphoses* has been recognizably influential since Stephen Hinds' 1987 landmark study of Ovidian genre, a work that stands as a crucial source for my own thinking on *Metamorphoses* 5 and the hymn of Calliope, a portion of the epic where Ovid overtly moves into hymnic territory. Alessandro Barchiesi's 1999 piece "Venus' Masterplot: Ovid and the *Homeric Hymns*," a pioneering study on Ovid's collective use of the *Homeric Hymns*, has also shaped my thinking about the role of Venus and Love within the epic—thinking that eventually led to the somewhat sensational framing of Ovid's foray into an epic universe as indebtedness to the Callimachean hymnic spirit.[18]

However, there is also cause to frame more broadly Ovid's interest in hymns—including more "contemporary" iterations—in litero-cultural terms: namely, as reproducing one aspect of Augustan essentialism, embodying the learnedness of the age. Experimenting with hymnic material allows for a powerful blend of tradition and innovation, as became the defining sensibility of the Augustan age: a promise to return to traditional roots, yet in quietly revolutionary form.[19] The first overt example of a hymn within the tradition of Latin heroic epic was a recent innovation, pioneered by Virgil's construction of the Salian hymn to Hercules found in the *Aeneid* (8.285–305).[20] However, epic and hymns have long been formally connected by the theory that suggests the *Homeric Hymns* were purposefully designed to inaugurate the longer performative recitals of Homeric epic.[21] More recently, Christopher Faraone has put forth a new understanding of embedded genres in hexametric verse, including hymns. As a case study for seeing how hymns can be absorbed by the overarching, hexametric epic narrative, he reconsiders the Chryses episode at the beginning of the *Iliad* as an epichoric hymn.[22] Rethinking the potential of relationships between epic and hymns from the very beginning of the recorded epic tradition can allow a broadening of perspective on how epic can encompass hymns and hymnic material within its hexametric fabric. The ability of epic—the flexibility of hexameter—to absorb other generic material enables Ovid's program of the *Metamorphoses*, as he attempts to override, by overwriting, not just the Epic Cycle but *all* epic cycles.[23] Ovid's accommodating of hymnic material and influence within the *Metamorphoses* is one way for the poet to stake this new sense of the

Introduction

neo-traditional that came to define the Augustan legacy, and to further innovate his expression of epic.

COMPOSITION, COMPETITION, AND HYMNIC RIVALRIES

When considering Ovid as a composer of epic, it is difficult to decouple innovation from competition. This difficulty is insistently felt in moments where Ovid deliberately trades on hymns as known fixities in the literary consciousness, as in the case of Calliope's hymn to Ceres in *Metamorphoses* 5. On a metatextual level, rivalry is omnipresent: poetic creation and authorship are naturally competitive, responsive acts in the ancient world. Augustan works especially practice a studiously calibrated intensity of self-awareness when it comes to the literary tradition at large. Authors choose moments at will either to guard or flaunt competitive voices. Only part of this inescapable Augustan textual-relational awareness can be written off as a parrying cultural reflex of the "belatedness" of the Latin literary tradition;[24] claiming generic territory and pushing generic boundaries, displaying a fashionable learnedness, and cultivating a similarly learned readership made writing an even more directly and inherently competitive act in the Rome of the late Republic and early Empire. Ovid's works are unmistakable products of this competitive culture of literary production.

Competition and rivalry, as thematic modes of interaction, are also native and consequential to hymnic material. The fight for τιμή that motivates the hymnic enterprise and narrative momentum ensures this dynamic. For example, the narrative *Homeric Hymn to Hermes* is a full-scale example of enacted hymnic rivalry: the baby Hermes challenges the power and authority of his older brother Apollo in a competitive effort to stake out his own defining attributes and Olympian status. In essence, the *Homeric Hymn to Hermes* is a tale of sibling rivalry—a rivalry that ultimately needs the mediation of Father Zeus. The hymn is therefore especially notable for the ways it already meditates, both self-consciously and playfully, on the hymnic form itself: after creating the lyre, Hermes' first song is a hymn to himself, embedding a hymn within a hymn. Even this hymn is foretold by the hymnic address Hermes makes to the turtle that will become the lyre, which speaks wittily to Hermes' simultaneous usurpation of power over his brother Apollo's property, the hexametric genres of both poetry and prophecy.[25] The hymnic form is inescapably intertwined with the narrative theme of competition. Within the collection of *Homeric Hymns*, the sense of rivalry between the brothers Hermes and Apollo that needs the adjudication of Zeus also en-counters the seam of possible rivalry between Apollo and Zeus himself, hinted at by the *Homeric Hymn to Apollo*.[26]

This triangulation of rivalries presents one relational model I explore within *Metamorphoses* 1, but transferred between Jupiter, Apollo, and Cupid. The *Homeric Hymn to Aphrodite* also explores divine rivalries in narrating how the threat Aphrodite poses to Zeus is neutralized; the axis of divine identity explored revolves around Zeus, the head of the Olympian order, despite the fact there is no narrative *Homeric Hymn to Zeus*. Ovid's response to this relationship between Zeus and Aphrodite, and their modes of puta-tive world domination, provides a different, more comprehensive thread of emphasis throughout the epic. This Ovidian thread is explored most con-centratedly at the beginning and end of this study, bookending in related ways in chapters 1 and 6 how Ovid metes out controlling praise to these competing forces of might and love. Just as competition shapes one sense of the Homeric collection, when we turn to Callimachus, we can also immedi-ately observe that his allocation of hymnic praise invites suspicion of rivalry as a theme: a brief look at the dedicatees of *Hymns* 2–4 (the *Hymn to Apollo*, *Hymn to Artemis*, and *Hymn to Delos*) cannot help but raise questions about how the relationship between the Delian siblings will be played out. This Callimachean sequence of hymns finds a very perceptive reader in Ovid and constitutes a large portion of my discussion of sibling rivalry as a defin-ing influence upon the characters of the *Metamorphoses*, especially within chapter 3. Hymns provide fertile ground for acknowledging, exploring, and exploiting the fundamentally competitive spirit and instinct of the Olym-pian order precisely because of their status as metaphorical gifts of praise, and the reciprocities of delight and good favor they intend to establish be-tween worshipper and divinity, as exemplified by χάρις.[27] Praise needs spe-cific targets, and so the gods need their specific facets of divine ownership defined, to accrue mortal and poetic praises in proper proportion. Rivalry, as an interactive dynamic, provides an interstice of opportunity for these divine markers of identity to be challenged, manipulated, and redrawn in fundamentally telling ways. One especial nexus for investigation that focuses directly on competition is the singing contest of *Metamorphoses* 5 that inte-grates a number of competitive interactions: the overarching contest between the Muses and the Pierides, but also the embedded contests within their own song offerings, between Olympians (in the case of Calliope) and Olympians and Giants (in the case of the Pierides). Fittingly, this contest is the focus of two chapters (4 and 5). From an authorial standpoint, introducing competition creates a space of maneuverability that can be controlled through conceptual acts of assimilation, differentiation, and imitation. Becoming "known" as a god is an enterprise of negotiation. The reader of the *Metamorphoses*, after encountering the unelaborated *di* of the invocation, is justified in wondering: who will Ovid's gods *be*? Understanding competition as a window into the urgently relational expressions of divine identity helps answer this question, on the levels of both the mythological and the literary.

The Literary Focus on Hymns

At this point, I should emphasize that this study focuses on the latter approach.[28] As a literary study, this is a text-based work of traditional philological inquiry and analysis. On the broadest level, two long-standing critical interests in Ovidian poetics motivate my lines of philological inquiry and analysis: the set of intertextuality and allusion, and narratology.[29] Despite my dependence on hymns, a genre with a defining set of religious and cultic identities and purposes, because of the literary nature of my approach, I am not engaging with hymns as strictly religious texts, nor with their performance as religious acts.[30] To focus on the primary body of hymnic work under focus, it is of course without doubt that the questions surrounding the performative context and history of the Callimachean hymns constitute an important and fruitful aspect of their understanding (and a major point of their differentiation from the *Homeric Hymns*), but such questions lie outside of my present interest.[31] As I hinted at earlier, my concern with the Callimachean poetry book of six hymns is based on its identity as a poetic text arranged and edited by the authorial design of Callimachus, subsequently used in its written form by Ovid to further his own poetic agenda. This definition sets clear expectations of how I view and use the *Hymns* within my analyses of the *Metamorphoses*; it is not intended to minimize or trivialize the overall status of hymns as powerful expressions of the relationship between humans and the divine. Rather, I am concerned with what Ovid's vantage point affords, that is, the literary nature of hymns, and the identifiable features and expressions of this generic form.

These identifiable features therefore also act as guiding principles to choose best the material that showcases Ovidian poetic innovation, in drawing out the overarching, navigatory theme of competition for praise. To elaborate previous mention of the "locational" ability of hymns, two perennial preoccupations of hymns are names and territory. When praising a god, these are two elemental considerations of divine identity that need to be addressed. Typically, epithets and the earthly home of the god, their cult seat, form part of the opening of the hymn. Although these two elements receive various forms of attention, ranging from mere inclusion to a full aetiological narrative, they are necessary ingredients for understanding divine identity, and therefore, canonical targets for hymnic praise. In light of these fundamental hymnic features, my literary focus is often trained narrowly on names, naming conventions, and etymology, and—more expansively—upon the idea of territory and geography. I focus on territory as one marked zone of competition, and untangling geographical complexities shapes much of my discussion of Jupiter's identity in chapter 2 and the contest of the Muses and Pierides in both chapters 5 and 6. In these chapters, the idea of poetic territory is raised to an importance almost parallel with divine rivalry itself, as ownership is called into question as a consequence of these rivalries. With this concentration, I come into contact with one of the recognizable narrative patterns of the first pentad: the idealized landscapes that become home to acts of sexual and physical violence.[32] Diana's grotto in Book 3 perhaps stands as the foremost example of these idyllic *loca amoena* (3.155–62), which I do discuss as it relates to Diana's divine identity in chapter 4. The nexus of landscape, body, sexualization, and idealization brought together by the commonplace of rape in the Ovidian *locus amoenus* has been of especial impact in opening scholarly conversation about the "embodied" landscapes of Ovid. This focus has in turn further encouraged symbolic readings of the landscape, as their pristine environs first mirror, and then belie, the virginal nature of the figures they tend to enclose.[33] Instead of only treating poetic territory symbolically, I am interested in the ways the poetic geography of the first pentad can be read as an encoded reflection and index of hymnic praise. Conversely, hymnic intertextuality and allusion can also provide a map for the complex geopoetic spaces of the first pentad, specifically in the case of Callimachean allusion.[34] Investigating the poetic territory of the first pentad in service of the rivalries that determine divine identity allows for a staking of new interpretive ground regarding Ovid's handling of geography and the natural world.

REINVIGORATING HYMNIC INFLUENCE
UPON THE *METAMORPHOSES*

The following chapters move collectively to reorient perception of the first pentad of the *Metamorphoses* by highlighting Ovid's underappreciated poetic dependency on hymns to craft his especial mosaic of epic divine identity, and, in concert, the reliance of epic identity upon the shaping forces of praise and love. One persistent, significant part of poetic dependency is represented by Callimachus' *Hymns*, which play a collective influence in forming a continuous thread of structural, narrative, and thematic significance within the first five books of the *Metamorphoses*. However, to understand how hymns, as expressions of praise, operate as critical influences and intertexts, I direct their analysis through the specific thematic lens of rivalry, a mode of interaction that has perceptibly shaped hymnic collections and their expressions of divine interaction and identity. The details drawn from etymological and geographical reference, illuminated by philological readings, collectively coalesce to provide a new background for the opening of Ovid's epic. And this background is one that professes, to a certain degree, its own identity as affiliated with Callimachean hymns, but this time dedicated to Ovid's patron powers of Love.

1

Amorphous Control?

Resolving the Question of Cosmic Authority within the World of the Metamorphoses

One overarching context for interpreting the inner workings of Ovid's epic universe is to explore the dynamic he creates between two determining factions of power: the forces of love, via Cupid/Amor (in conjunction with his mother, Venus) and Jupiter, king of the gods.[1] This competitive relationship, essential to understanding the world of Ovid's epic, makes symbolic contact between forces internal and external, personal and political. In other words, we see love (the established patron and controlling power of Ovid's elegiacally determined poetic world) interact with Jupiter's imperial power, representative of the forces that control the world Ovid himself occupies. Here, I examine the narrative evidence provided throughout the first pentad for the interplay between Cupid/Amor and Jupiter that speaks to this issue of cosmic control, and interrogate its purposefully ambiguous presentation. This narrative evidence comes from passages that rely on the hymnic tradition, and so, rely on a genre that is determinedly invested in the twinned concepts of praise and power, shaping focus on the presence of rivalry and the effacement or displacement of praise. In bringing to light the hymnic influence upon Ovid's constructed relationship between Cupid/Amor and Jupiter, we first see how Ovid borrows the structure of competitive exchange that exists between the independent traditions of hymning Eros and Zeus in their roles as masters of the cosmos. When Ovid applies this structure of competitive exchange to his epic, he thereby creates a tension for his readers about who is in ultimate control of his poetic cosmos. We can then see how Ovid complicates, or makes precarious, this developed notion of competitive tension by looking at specific textual intervals where the poet chooses to sidestep narrative opportunities to praise Jupiter and instead promote the forces of love. As Ovid performs this elision of praise, he simultaneously sets up an alternate hymnic lineage of exchange and inspiration that creates how Jupiter and Amor perform their powerful identities within his epic.

PROEMIAL PARTNERSHIPS

Ovid's epic begins ostensibly with a partnership, rather than a rivalry. The poet introduces a joint effort between his own motivation and the inspiration of the gods: his *animus* has compelled him to assume this theme of change, and he calls upon the gods (*di*) to first breathe life (*aspirate*) into his compositional efforts (*coeptis*), and then to lead them down (*deducite*) in a continuous song from the first origin of the world to Ovid's own time. Ovid himself dominates this four-line proem. The compositional initiative are his undertakings, his beginnings (*meis . . . coeptis*); he will provide the temporal end-point ("my times," *mea tempora*).[2] However, the gods are charged with the active forces of inspiration and the guidance of Ovid's song down along its unending path. Ovid also gives a reason for his invocation: the gods themselves have previously influenced his *coepta* by change (*nam uos mutastis et illa*, "for you have changed even these," 1.2). Through this qualification of *coeptis*, Ovid reinforces a sense of mutual investment, and alludes to a previous poetic relationship. However, the way that Ovid sets up (and sets out) his epic as a joint enterprise has raised questions about narrative authority and control: is the governing body in charge of the poem human or divine?

As James O'Hara has discussed, the question of control raised by the proem also has implications for understanding the world set out within the poem. By ascribing generating force to both his own *animus* and the gods, Ovid signals a participation in traditional debates about the nature of the gods. Ovid reveals his literary consciousness about these arguments in the allusive reference he makes to the query Nisus poses to Euryalus in *Aeneid* 9: *dine hunc ardorem mentibus addunt / Euryale, an sua cuique deus fit dira cupido?* ("Do the gods give this passion to our minds, Euryalus, or does man's own ominous desire become a god for him?," *Aen.* 9.184–85).[3] Nisus' question forms part of the epic tradition of speculation about the nature of the gods: whether the gods act (and can be read) as characters in their own right, or if psychological factors of human personality and behavior are promoted to the level of divine personification. At heart, Nisus' question can be read as being about both the nature of the gods and the nature of transformation, and the transformative role *cupido* plays. This Virgilian couplet, beginning with *di* and ending with *cupido*, can therefore also stand as an interpretive bridge between the elegist Ovid and the epicist Ovid: it allows Ovidian readers to remember that at the opening of the *Amores*, the would-be epicist was purportedly foiled by a laughing Cupid, who stole a foot away, subsequently rendering the poet an elegist (*Am.* 1.1.1–4). Ovid now redresses these epic ambitions with the *Metamorphoses*—but in a way that nevertheless recalls Cupid's transformative intervention at the beginning of the *Amores*. The proemial aside of *nam uos mutastis et illa* unfailingly points to Cupid, who is the only god known responsible for any changes in Ovid's poetic *forma*. The knowledge of Cupid's specific role in rerouting Ovidian poetics sets him up in further juxtaposition to the generalized *di* of the invocation and marks out a further relationship with Ovid's own *animus*.[4] Cupid forms a connecting bridge between the poet's *animus* and the invoked *di*.

Ovid's reader has reason to return to this question about the nature of the gods almost immediately. As promised, the starting point of *prima origo mundi* ("the first origin of the world") leads to a cosmogony, where the universe is ordered by a force described as *deus et melior . . . natura* ("a god and better nature," or "a god, an even better nature," *Met.* 1.21). Initially, this descriptive divide seems to map neatly onto the proem's split governance of *di/animus*, this time more overtly as one totalizing creative force.[5] However, this force is subsequently described in sequence as *quisquis fuit ille deorum* ("whichever of the gods that being was," 1.32); *mundi fabricator* ("the fashioner of the world," 1.57) and *ille opifex rerum, mundi melioris origo* ("that worksman of things, the origin of a better world," 1.79). If Ovid's proem begs the question of authority, his cosmogony begs the question of identity. Who is the creator? If we consider the traditional generic placement of cosmogonic material, and how Ovid describes this divinity, we can begin to see that Ovid creates a fundamental, productive tension or instability to motivate and give momentum to one divine rivalry within his epic: the competition for control between Jupiter and Cupid/Amor.[6]

The Demiurgic Creator: Whose Mind, Whose Matter?

First, let us spend some time thinking about the models for the ways Ovid talks about his divine creator. Initially, Ovid ascribes the ordering of the universe to a divinity (*deus*) and/or an originating power (*natura*). This conjunction points not to mythology, but to philosophy.[7] The use of both *deus* and *natura* hints first at a Stoic conception of the universe, where *natura* and a god (Zeus) coexist as named understandings or manifestations of the universe's creative power.[8] However, the subsequent terms *fabricator* and *opifex* point squarely to the figure of the demiurge from Plato's *Timaeus*.[9] Plato's δημιουργός ("demiurge," "maker") is also named a τεκταινόμενος ("framer," "joiner"), terms that Cicero renders in his translation (adaptation, really) as *fabricator* (*Tim.* 6.3) and *artifex* (*Tim.* 6.7).[10] In Cicero's closely related work *de Natura Deorum*, Velleius refers to this Platonic demiurge as both *opifex* and *aedificator* (*opificem aedificatoremque mundi Platonis de Timaeo deum*, "worksman and builder of the world, the god according to Plato's *Timaeus*," 1.18.5–6). The Stoic and Platonic conceptions are, however, united by the metaphor of the craftsman. In Cicero's record, Zeno's definition of nature expands from being a "craftsmanlike fire" (*ignem . . . artificiosum*, *Nat. D.* 2.57.3; cf. the Stoic πῦρ τεχνικόν) to being a craftsman itself: *natura non artificiosa solum sed plane artifex ab eodem Zenone dicitur* ("nature is not only craftsmanlike, but clearly a craftsman, according to that same Zeno," *Nat. D.* 2.58.2). Therefore, in each description of the universe's creative force, Ovid seemingly emphasizes the figure of the craftsman.

When we look back to this figure in Plato, we can see that before he introduces the δημιουργός with this specific name, he uses the descriptor ποιητής καὶ πατήρ ("maker and father," *Tim.* 28c).[11] "Father" can be interpreted as a brief nod to Hesiod's *Theogony*, where Hesiod emphasizes genealogical descent in his mythological account of cosmic order and creation; Plato acknowledges this formulation, before providing a wholly separate derivation of creation.[12] These two identifiers, however, are separate from the creator's descriptive position as a craftsman. Similarly, Ovid's *deus et melior . . . natura* is a distinctly separate formulation from the later, technical phrasing of *fabricator mundi* and *opifex rerum*, concepts that are only bridged by supplying the Stoic use of the craftsman metaphor. If Ovid's account of creation, in terms of its assignation, is meant to develop in a way that mimics the staged unfolding of the Platonic demiurge's identity, it leans into an initial indebtedness not to Hesiodic cosmogonic poetry, but to Stoic philosophy. However, both the Stoic *deus/natura* and the Hesiodic πατήρ would point to the same divine entity: Zeus.[13] Even so, the emphasis in both the *Timaeus* and in Ovid's cosmogony is on the identity and role of the creator as a craftsman.

Although Ovid's indebtedness to the demiurge of the *Timaeus* is clear (both in its original formulation and in the Ciceronian translation) there are other potential models of demiurgic thought to be considered. Increasingly, scholars are thinking more widely about sources Plato may have used in setting forth his figure of the demiurge, and cross-referencing Platonic works for further evidence of engagement with other traditions.[14] One such tradition that poses a potential model of demiurgic thought is the material of Orphic cosmogonies. In particular, there is a god known as Protogonos (also called Phanes), who, in some accounts, is responsible for the generation and design of the cosmos, and therefore can earn the title of demiurge (*OF* 120–43b; 147–49; 153–58; 168; 171–73; 240–41; cf. also 12).[15] The evidence of these Orphic cosmogonies is interpretively fraught to the degree that Protogonos cannot be *consistently* attributed with demiurgic activity. However, the power of world creation can be firmly attributed to Zeus, who is recorded as swallowing Protogonos, and by doing so, absorbing the capability of world-generation and ordering (*OF* 240–41; cf. also *OF* 243.1–2, 14.1–2b; 31). A demiurgic Zeus, this time Orphic, could therefore also fit the identity of Ovid's *deus*. The picture becomes more complex, however, when we consider an observable set of similarities between Protogonos/Phanes and Eros.[16] In the case of some evidence, this is less a set of similarities than pure identification: Phanes also receives the name Eros. However, in the *Birds*, the Eros of Aristophanes' ornithogony, a mock or parodic cosmogony (*Av.* 694–99 = *OF* 64), bears traceable resemblance to the Orphic Protogonos: both gods are resplendent, gold-winged beings hatched from an egg. Here, Eros does perform a demiurgic function. The ability to connect Protogonos and Eros therefore necessarily connects Eros and Zeus: a secure point of demiurgic activity within the Orphic tradition (unlike Protogonos' own contested ability) is Zeus' absorption of Protogonos, which gives him the ability to (re)create and (re)order the cosmos. An affiliation between Zeus and Eros in the act of world-building is also a feature of the cosmogony of Pherecydes of Syros. Of his account, Proclus records that the god Zas (Zeus) becomes Eros at the critical moment where he is about to assume the role of demiurge (μέλλοντα δημιουργεῖν, "on the cusp of acting as a demiurge," *in Ti.* 32c [B3]). Pherecydes' Eros as demiurge subsequently influences the philosophical accounts of Acusilaus, Parmenides, and Empedocles,[17] but the exchange of identity between Zeus and Eros would naturally appeal to the Ovidian sensibility: at the outset of his epic, Ovid is ostensibly poised to exchange his own identity from an elegiac poet to an epic poet, and to transfer allegiance from his long-standing commitment to

Love to the god of epic, Jupiter. The blurred boundaries of identity between Zeus and Eros precisely at the juncture of demiurgic activity in both the world of Orphic cosmogonies and Pherecydes establishes both a relationship and an envelope of potentially exploitable tension: a choice of attribution for the act of world-ordering, and for the role of divine craftsman. Eros (Amor), too, becomes a candidate for Ovid's *deus et melior . . . natura*.

Looking to the wider Platonic corpus, an Aristophanic Eros modeled on the Orphic Protogonos neatly paves the way for seeing Orphic influence upon Aristophanes' praise of love in the *Symposium*, in awareness of the initial creative indebtedness Aristophanes displays in outlining the cosmogony of the *Birds*. In the *Symposium*, the physicality of the primitive humans Aristophanes describes contains especial resonance with the features of Protogonos. The perception of Orphic influence within this dialogue is not limited to Aristophanes' speech, but has additionally been touched upon regarding the speeches of both Diotima and Alcibiades.[18] However, the Orphic fabric of connectivity between Zeus and Eros being explored here also illuminates part of Agathon's praise of love. To expand our purview further, even the wider consideration of form plays a role here in shaping how we understand this strain of influence. Altogether, the *Symposium* can be read as a hymn to Eros, a series of praises of the god (cf. Pl. *Symp.* 177a–d for the topic proposal). The outset of Agathon's speech especially refocuses this notion of praise (Pl. *Symp.* 195a). Similarly, within the tradition of evidence for Orphic texts, the repeated passages that pertain to Zeus' demiurgic role are quoted as part of a "Hymn to Zeus."[19] Although this is a specific designation for a constituent part of the existing body of Orphic material, Meisner has recently argued for a whole-scale repositioning of the extant Orphic material as "theogonic hymns," which further entrenches a sense of generic connectivity.[20] Part of the praise of Zeus within this Orphic "Hymn to Zeus" is his position as both born first and last. Zeus' absorption of Protogonos allows this paradox of birth order, a fact hinted at by the phrase πρῶτος γένετο. In Agathon's portion of the Platonic "Hymn to Eros," his praise of Eros first challenges Phaedrus' view that Eros is the oldest of the gods (178b), instead identifying him as the youngest (πρῶτον μὲν νεώτατος θεῶν, ὦ Φαῖδρε, "firstly, Phaedrus, he is the youngest of the gods," Pl. *Symp.* 195a). Within the *Symposium*'s praise of Eros, then, we see the god as simultaneously the oldest and youngest, akin to the Orphic Zeus. Agathon's signaling of this paradox is perhaps also hinted at by the placement of this new

Amorphous Control?

identifying aspect: he is the youngest (in other words, the last-born) "firstly" (πρῶτον). Agathon further brings his praise of Eros into contact with Zeus, and specifically, with Zeus as demiurge:

> καί μὲν δὴ τήν γε τῶν ζῴων <u>ποίησιν</u> πάντων τίς ἐναντιώσεται μὴ οὐχὶ Ἔρωτος εἶναι σοφίαν, ᾗ γίγνεταί τε καὶ φύεται πάντα τὰ ζῷα; ἀλλὰ τὴν τῶν τεχνῶν <u>δημιουργίαν</u> οὐκ ἴσμεν, ὅτι οὗ μὲν ἂν ὁ θεὸς οὗτος διδάσκαλος γένηται, ἐλλόγιμος καὶ φανὸς ἀπέβη, οὗ δ᾽ ἂν Ἔρως μὴ ἐφάψηται, σκοτεινός; (Pl. *Symp.* 197a)

> [Again, who will deny that the creation of all animals is the wisdom of Eros, by whom all animals are born and begotten? But do we not also know in the craftsmanship of the arts that he of whom this god becomes teacher turns out to be notable and illustrious, but he whom Eros leaves untouched remains in the shade? (trans. R. Allen)]

The identification of Eros as a ποιητής in the sense of "creator" first brings the role of the demiurge into the picture; this is the same designator later used to introduce the demiurge of the *Timaeus*. The metaphorical use of "craftsman" as an identification with ποιητής is activated by the literal use of δημιουργία. Just as Agathon himself is a ποιητής in the sense of "poet," but here employs the broader meaning of the now typically winnowed definition to indicate "creator," the literal meaning of "creating" is easily extended to the metaphorical and cosmic, given his description of Eros' creative responsibility over all life forms. The duality of ποιητής in this context is subsequently reinforced by Eros' later invocation as a κόσμος (συμπάντων τε θεῶν καὶ ἀνθρώπων κόσμος, "ornamentation to all gods and men," Pl. *Symp.* 197e), another term with multiple signifiers within this context of creation.[21] Eros' creation of all life indicates a contact with the typical responsibility of Zeus; as later explored in the etymologies of the *Cratylus*, Zeus is so named because of his authorship and gift of life (Pl. *Cra.* 396a–b). In this passage, Agathon not only praises Eros as a demiurge, but does so in a way that is informed by Zeus' Orphic role. Approaching the *Timaeus* with this reading of Agathon's speech also reaffirms Eros' viability for the role of demiurge, which lends Ovid's use of the craftsman metaphor greater accrued significance.

Praising Zeus or Eros? Creative Exchange in Hymning the Cosmic Creator

Examining the relevance of Orphic theogonic hymns, the cosmogony of Pherecydes, and the Platonic texts beyond the *Timaeus* show how the figure of the demiurge has a mythologically exploitable identity, reaching toward both Zeus and Eros. This tension of attribution provides a further point of entry into the documented hymnic tradition of competition between Zeus and Eros. The rerouting of Zeus' praise to the glory of Eros is a textual strategy of immense relevance to Ovid's construction of his epic universe. We can locate one aspect of Ovid's strategic inspiration in how Callimachus exploits this tradition of exchange. To understand this tradition, we return to Plato's *Symposium*, which displays a persistent reflection of and engagement with Hesiod that establishes how a text in service of the praise of Zeus (the *Theogony*) can be used a touchstone to instead establish and embellish praise of Eros.[22]

Hesiodic riffing (or, indeed, selective quotation of) is an especial feature of Phaedrus' speech, which, in turn, stands as one model for Callimachus' *Hymn to Zeus*. As Andrew Ford describes,

> The first of Callimachus' *Hymns* thus stands revealed at its end as a song mimicking a sympotic speech, a toastmaster's discourse, full of high sentence, a bit oblique, indeed at times humorous. In *To Zeus*, then, the tradition of hexameter hymns proves to be a feint: this performer utters no opening invocation but begins as would an *arkhôn logou* at a drinking party.... When viewed in light of mythographic discourse, the antecedents of Callimachus' song include not only Pindaric epinician and Plato's *Phaedrus* but, even more directly, the speech on Eros that Phaedrus makes in the *Symposium* to inaugurate its feast of speeches.[23]

Callimachus' use of the overall sophisticated aesthetic of the *Symposium*—its learned, sometimes humorous mode of manipulating mythographic sources—to model his *Hymn to Zeus* engages in a more general, overarching way with the idea of rerouting divine praise, this time from Eros to Zeus. Callimachus is aware of how Zeus' Hesiodic primacy and glory is diverted to prop up an agenda of praising Eros, and so, inserts himself into this tradition of a successive exchange of hymnic praise, ostensibly closing the loop through his sympotic praise of Zeus. The modeled relationship Ford identifies between the *Hymn to Zeus* and the *Symposium*, however, is only one layer of the interaction between praise of Zeus and Eros Callimachus literarily exploits. Callimachus taps further into this tradition in the way he begins to set up praise of the god, asking about how to appropriately hymn Zeus:[24]

πῶς καί μιν, Δικταῖον ἀείσομεν ἠὲ Λυκαῖον;
ἐν δοιῇ μάλα θυμός, ἐπεὶ γένος ἀμφήριστον.

(Callim. *Hymn* 1.4–5)

[But how shall we hymn him, as Dictaean or Lycaean?
My heart is in doubt, for the birth is contested. (trans. Stephens)]

Callimachus' question is framed geographically: should Zeus be called "Dictaean" (Cretan) or "Lycaean" (Arcadian)? The poet confesses that his θυμός is in doubt, claiming that the birth of the god is contested. Scholars have noted how Callimachus' sentiment of doubt echoes a line from Antagoras' hymn to Eros (ἐν δοιῇ μοι θυμός, ὅ τοι γένος ἀμφίβοητον, "my heart is in doubt, in that your birth is celebrated everywhere," Antag. fr. 1.1. Powell).[25] The poet preserves γένος ("birth"), in a move that might prove surprising when applied to Zeus, but he makes a telling substitution in altering the crucial adjective.[26] Martijn Cuypers suggests that Callimachus' swapping of ἀμφιβόητος for ἀμφήριστος (related to the verb ἐρίζω) evokes Eris, the power of similar name but opposite force. She further suggests that the Hesiodic distinction between "good" and "bad" Eris informed Antagoras' delineation of "good" and "bad" Eros.[27] Just as the Hesiodic discussion of Eris is packaged within a continuous "hymning" of Zeus and related conceptualizing of "good" kingship, Callimachus returns the focus to Zeus, but not without the meaning accrued from textual contact with Antagoras' Eros. The idea of competition denoted by ἀμφήριστος likewise summarizes the potential literary context of Antagoras' hymn, composed as an Academic rejoinder to the Stoic hymning of Zeus as the rational personification of the originating principle, the deity celebrated in Cleanthes' *Hymn to Zeus*.[28] By quoting Antagoras' hymn, Callimachus allusively introduces an element of competition between Zeus and Eros as generating world-forces. He reminds his readers how each god was the recipient of hymnic praise in their form as these originating principles (Stoic and otherwise).[29]

Amorphous Control?

This juxtaposition of hymnically praised primordial power can now be read against the creator of the *Metamorphoses*. As previously discussed, Ovid's *deus et melior . . . natura* occupies a distinct register of Stoic thought that accords nicely with the role occupied by the Stoic Zeus in the exchange of hymnic praise just traced, from Cleanthes to Antagoras to Callimachus. It could equally describe Eros as demiurge, in an extension of his role as a Hesiodic primordial principle expressed via Pherecydes and the tradition of Orphic theogonic hymns. If we return to the Ovidian text, the activity of this figure is described with *litem . . . diremit* ("he dissolved/imposed a decision upon the strife," 1.21). The initial act of cosmic ordering is categorized as a separation of warring elements, described overall as a *lis*—a word with a distinct judicial meaning, but also capable of meaning simply "strife" or "quarrel."[30] Ovid's use of *lis*, which can translate the Hesiodic ἔρις, further grounds his demiurgic figure in the contentious attributive space between Zeus and Eros, in light of Cuypers' argument that Callimachus' replacement of Antagoras' ἀμφιβόητος with ἀμφήριστος acknowledges how the two Erotes in Antagoras' hymn may have paralleled the two Hesiodic Erides.[31] Beyond this very technical allusion, however, that grants Ovid a similarly sensitive reading of Callimachus as Cuypers, the judicial context of *lis* within the Ovidian poetic world can also point to either Jupiter or Cupid/Amor. Conventionally, or even stereotypically, Jupiter as the king of gods and men is a dispenser of justice—but we have already seen Love play this role in the *Amores*, from the moment Ovid pointedly asks how he gained legal sway over Ovidian song (*quis tibi, saeue puer, dedit hoc in carmina iuris?*, "Who, savage boy, gave this jurisdiction over my poems to you?," *Am.* 1.1.5).

THE ELEMENTS OF COSMOGONIC IDENTITY:
METAMORPHOSIS AND ALLEGORY

This section moves from hymnic exchanges of power to focus on elemental identities, and how Jupiter and Cupid as makers are tied to physical expressions of the cosmos. The tension created by the opportunity to identify either Jupiter or Cupid/Amor as Ovid's divine creator also reinforces the implicit divide of inspiration in the proem. Unlike Antagoras and Callimachus, Ovid's own θυμός (rendered by the Latin *animus*) is not in doubt, but leads him to speak of transformations, guided expressly by *di*, but, as discussed, with implicit emphasis on Cupid. The implicit presence of Cupid/Eros continues to be evoked by hinting at Cupid/Eros as the potential demiurgic figure who unites and differentiates the world of chaos. The juxtaposition between *di* and Cupid, then, can be internally informed by awareness of the tradition of hymnic alternation between Zeus and Eros. The competing issues of proemial authority and creator identity can also be parsed by looking at not only recalling Cupid's poetical transformative agenda in *Amores* 1.1, but the more literal transformative powers at work in the *Metamorphoses*. In the proem, Ovid uses the verb *muto* to describe the altering of both appearances (*mutatas . . . formas*) and his own work (*mutastis et illa*). It is therefore noteworthy that the first active, descriptive use of the verb *muto* in the *Metamorphoses*, where agency and purpose is directly ascribed, belongs to Jupiter.[32] To avoid Juno's suspicion, he changes Io into a cow: *coniugis aduentum praesenserat inque nitentem / Inachidos uultus mutauerat ille iuuencam* ("he had sensed the impending arrival of his wife and so, he had changed Inachus' daughter, lookswise, into a gleaming heifer," 1.610–11). The relationship of this *mutauerat* to the verbs of the proem is suggestively hinted by the following qualification, *bos quoque formosa est* ("even as a cow, she is beautiful," 1.612), given the semantic ties between *forma* and *formosa*. The linguistic shift required to make *formosa* from *forma* is hinted at by the preceding *bos*.[33] The vocabulary employed surrounding Io's transformation adds to its exemplary status: while *forma* is implicitly present within *formosa*, the locus for Io's transformation is her *uultus*, while Juno then first looks at her *species* (*speciem Saturnia uaccae / quamquam inuita, probat*, "Saturn's daughter, albeit begrudgingly, approvingly rates the appearance of the heifer," 1.612–13). Each of these physical terms play significant roles in the world building of the cosmogony (*unus erat toto naturae uultus in orbe*, "there was one face of nature to the world's totality," 1.6; *nulli sua forma manebat*, "nothing was keeping a handle on its own form," 1.17; *magni speciem glomerauit in orbis*, "he rolled its appearance into a large globe," 1.35). Cumulatively, this suggests Io's metamorphosis, under the direction of Jupiter, also holds especial creative significance.

The potential cosmogonical resonances of this episode are strengthened in two ways. First, Jupiter and Io's physical union is a concise reflection of the Homeric *hieros gamos*, itself only one trace of the tradition surrounding the elemental union of sky and earth (*cum deus inducta latas caligine terras / occuluit tenuitque fugam rapuitque pudorem*, "the god hid the broad earth by introducing a shroud of fog, halted her flight, and snatched away her chastity," 1.599–600; cf. Hom. *Il.* 14.342–52). Secondly, Jupiter explains the genesis of Io's new form to Juno as "earth-born" (*Iuppiter e terra genitam mentitur*, "Jupiter feigns she was born of the earth," 1.615), a product of spontaneous generation in a way that echoes the earlier creation of animal forms in Book 1 (cf. *sponte sua*, 1.417). By linking this episode of metamorphosis to the proem and cosmogony, Ovid suggests Jupiter as a cosmogonic god—but this is also complicated by the issue that Jupiter here is a cosmogonic god because he is in love, at work transforming the object of his beloved. Io's metamorphosis also looks back to the second creation, after the flood. Her identity as the daughter of a river-god plays into a recollection of this second generative tale, given the post-diluvian creation's emphasis on the elemental mixing of water and fire (1.416–37).[34] With the famous paradox of *discors concordia* (1.433), Ovid reminds the reader of the initial act of separation, not mixture, performed by the demiurgic being (cf. *discordia semina*, 1.9). With the mixture of fire and water, we can perceive an allegorical representation and foreshadowing of the mythological narratives of love that will follow, of gods kindled with desire in pursuit of nymphs, the constituent river divinities, including Jupiter's programmatic love for Io.[35]

The allegorical mixing of fire and water that maps onto these love stories replicates one mode of demiurgic power: unification. As Claude Calame describes Eros in his role as demiurge, "The generating and demiurgic power of Eros thus seems to possess two complementary aspects: it is an agent both of unification and differentiation."[36] Separation is the first act of the Ovidian demiurge. The four warring elements are separated and bound into harmonious placement. This strikes an ironic chord when Jupiter's first actions in the epic are measured against the original cosmogonical process: the flood Jupiter sends in retribution against humanity's wickedness functionally returns the world to chaos, erasing the boundaries between elements (*iamque mare et tellus nullum discrimen habebant; / omnia pontus erat, deerant quoque litora ponto*, "and now the sea and land was bearing no distinction: all was sea, shores absented themselves from the sea," 1.291–92). The recently ordered cosmos reverts to chaos. Jupiter, however, first considers using his lightning bolts to set the world aflame. While pondering his options, the god recalls (*reminiscitur*) there will come a time when land, sea, and heaven shall be ablaze (1.253–58), causing him to set aside his bolts (*tela reponuntur*, 1.259).[37] Many scholars have recognized this as a foreshadowing of Phaethon's disastrous ride, which Ovid will narrate in Book 2. Phaethon's charioteering results in a world conflagration that was read allegorically as an *ecpyrosis*; the flood therefore provides the elemental opposite return to chaos, a nod to (especially Stoic) cycles of destruction and regeneration.[38] Hovering in the philosophical background here, however, as Jupiter turns to flood, could be the Stoic notion of the cosmos *as* Eros. If we read Jupiter's decision against this cosmic conception, there is also the momentary presentation of a Jupiter not yet ready to give the world over to the fire of Eros, a world the love poet Ovid is much more familiar with.[39] Once again, a tension of primacy between Zeus and Eros is evoked, and one traceable to a cyclical exchange of praise within the hymnic tradition.

Jupiter's setting aside of his thunderbolts as he opts for flood additionally summons a specific set of contextual scenarios in which the god lays down his fabled weapons. Ovid famously exploits one such scenario at the opening of *Amores* 2.1. At the beginning of this new book of elegies, in which he reintroduces himself and his elegiac themes, the poet remembers (*memini*, 2.11) composing a Gigantomachy, with Jupiter and his bolt in hand. This work becomes fatally interrupted when his *amica* slams her door:

> in manibus nimbos et cum Ioue fulmen habebam,
>> quod bene pro caelo mitteret ille suo.
> clausit amica fores: ego cum Ioue fulmen omisi;
>> excidit ingenio Iuppiter ipse meo.
> Iuppiter, ignoscas: nil me tua tela iuuabant;
>> clausa tuo maius ianua fulmen habet.
>
> (Am. 2.1.15–20)

> [In my hands, I was holding stormclouds and, along with Jupiter, a
>> thunderbolt-
> the sort he well dispenses on behalf of his heavens . . .
> My girl slammed the door! I dropped the bolt, along with Jupiter;
> Jupiter himself disappeared at the expense of my inspiration.
> Jupiter, forgive me! Your weapons can profit me not at all;
> a closed door has a bolt stronger than yours.]

In a clear thematic replay of *Amores* 1.1, love displaces Jupiter, forcing aside his weapons. As Julia Hejduk reads, "the humorously understated 'I beg your pardon, Jupiter!' implies that Jupiter the Lover would of course understand why he was unceremoniously dropped, being subject himself to the electrifying power of forbidden love."[40] Later, in *Amores* 2.5, the poet describes the disarming charms of a kiss as "just the sort that could shake the triple-forked weapons from an angered Jove" (*qualia possent / excutere irato tela trisulca Ioui*, 2.5.51–52). When Ovid again reminds his readers that love has the power to cause Jupiter to set aside his weaponry, he is also saying that love has the power to displace part of Jupiter's divine identity.[41] Jupiter's decision to return the world to chaos by flood, not flame, is therefore also accomplished in a way that circumstantially evokes exchange between rule by might or power, and rule by love. At the beginning of a cycle of destruction and creation, the report of *tela reponuntur* creates a momentary slippage between Jupiter Tonans and Jupiter Amans that renews the tension of hymnic primacy between Zeus or Eros as demiurge.

THE TORCH AND THUNDERBOLT: *AMOR*, *VIS*, AND *IOVIS*

If we continue our investigation further into the narrative and look at additional markers of divine identity, we can see that the elemental identities belonging to Jupiter and Amor just discussed can be further refined in mutually implicated and reflective ways. The shifting sense of universal control between Zeus and Eros, thunderbolt and torch, power and love, also subtly generates the narrative conditions that continue until made explicit by the dangerously gnomic statement in *Metamorphoses* 2 after Jupiter once again sets aside his identifying weapons (and more) in amorous pursuit of Europa: *non bene conueniunt nec in una sede morantur / maiestas et amor* ("not well do sovereignty and love come together, nor do they linger long in one seat," 2.846–47).[42] Despite its brevity, Ovid's statement reveals a great deal of conceptual work in his poetic brokering of divine identity. The combination of *maiestas* and *amor* naturally leads to thinking about Jupiter and the god Amor. The reader has already seen a Jupiter who exercises his *maiestas* in heading the council of the gods (1.163–252), quickly followed by a Jupiter in love, as he pursues Io (1.588–600). The kindling of Jupiter's passion for Europa now reflects anew upon both identifying presentations of the king of the gods. To scrutinize Ovid's gnomic statement carefully, the uneasy sharing of *una sedes* first hints at the meaning of *sedes* as a seat of cult worship (cf. *OLD* s.v. 5a). The focus on a space of worship makes the tension Ovid allusively builds between these divinities more explicit. By bringing this divine competition into a spatial dimension over a site of praise and divine command, Ovid emphasizes its territorial aspect and scale, from the cosmic to the cultic. Once again, a conflict over a seat of cult worship begs the question of who controls Ovid's poetic universe.

The uneasy convergence of *amor* and *maiestas* in the *Metamorphoses* can be further illuminated by looking at the figure of Maiestas in the *Fasti*. Within this text, the Muse Polyhymnia describes the birth and role of Maiestas herself within a wider narrative of cosmogony and the Olympian succession myth (*Fast.* 5.25–46). As Polyhymnia relates, after Saturn's fall and the defeat of the Giants, Maiestas moves into a new, distinct role and sits beside Jove, granting him his sceptre (*assidet inde Ioui, Iouis est fidissima custos / et praestat sine ui sceptra timenda Ioui*, "from that time she sits beside Jove in council, the most loyal guardian of Jove, and she hands over, without force, Jove's scepter, of ordained fearsomeness," *Fast.* 5.45–46). Previously, the goddess was herself flanked by Pudor and Metus (*consedere simul Pudor et Metus*, "once Pudor and Metus made their homes beside her," *Fast.* 5.29), now she becomes the companion of Jupiter, attending him in his *sedes*. The acceptance of Maiestas' scepter shows the provenance of one of Jupiter's accessories of divine power and identity. This is the scepter illustrative of Jupiter's command as he summons the divine council in the opening of the *Metamorphoses* (*sceptroque innixus eburno*, "resting upon his ivory scepter," 1.178). It also appears as an instrument of Jupiter's self-proclaimed divinity as he pursues Io (*sed qui caelestia magna / sceptra manu teneo*, "but I am he who holds the great heavens, scepter in hand," 1.595–96). And finally, it is set aside in his pursuit of Europa (*sceptri grauitate relicta*, "with dignity and scepter abandoned," 2.847). However, when Jupiter's accession is ratified by the scepter, but described as *sine ui*, we should be wary, given the usual twinned status his powerful accessories receive: the scepter and the thunderbolt.[43] As for the thunderbolt, we learn from an earlier book of the *Fasti* that Jupiter had received these weapons at the time of the Gigantomachy (*fulmina post ausos caelum adfectare Gigantas / sumpta Ioui: primo tempore inermis erat*, "Jove assumed his weaponry after the Giants dared to assay the sky; in earlier times, he was unarmed," *Fast.* 3.439–40; cf. *Met.* 1.151–55). Prior to this combat, the *iuuenis* Jupiter was unarmed. As he looks at a statue of this deity on the Capitoline, Ovid explains the identity of the "unarmed" god as Veiovis, or "young Jupiter." (*Fast.* 3.437–48). Combining these two passages from the *Fasti*, we can make a loose equation of identity, based on the turning point of the Gigantomachy: Veiovis plus Maiestas equals Iovis. Ovid concludes his thoughts on etymologizing Veiovis, the "young Jupiter," from the prefix *ue-* and Iouis with the expression *uis ea si uerbi est* ("if this is the force of the word," *Fast.* 3.447). This phrasing further underscores the *uis* found within Iouis.[44] The use of *uis . . . uerbi* to denote the act of etymologizing should therefore alert the suspicions of the learned reader when Maiestas cements Jupiter's status as king with the gift of the scepter *sine ui*: to quote the crucial lines again, *assidet inde Ioui, Iouis est fidissima custos / et praestat sine ui sceptra timenda Ioui* (*Fast.* 5.45–46). The stately parade of *Ioui, Iouis, Ioui*, multiplying the appearance of *ui/s*, suggests that the phrase is not nearly so innocuous as it looks.[45] With remembrance of the thunderbolt that helped secure his win over the Giants, perpetually paired with the scepter, the reader understands that Iouis is not truly Iouis without *uis*. The permanence of *uis* within Iouis speaks to its immanence, whether or not Jupiter wields the external expressions of this power, the thunderbolt and scepter.

It is worth lingering a little more on the Capitoline's statue of Veiovis. The *Fasti*'s depiction of the young god raises other points of contact between Jupiter and Amor that stand in the background of the epic competition posed in and by the world of the *Metamorphoses*. In short, Ovid's description of Veiovis may not be so innocent as it first appears. Of the cult image, Ovid says, *fulmina nulla tenet* (*Fast.* 3.438), ostensibly describing the god's lack of arms (*inermis, Fast.* 3.440). However, Aulus Gellius records that the statue held arrows (*sagittas tenet*), furthermore identifying them as objects of harm (*ad nocendum, NA* 5.12.11). If we keep in mind that the prefix *ue-*, used by Ovid as a diminutive, can also have the force of a privative, this arrow-wielding statue can also depict an "anti-Jupiter."[46] A young, arrow-sporting anti-Jupiter is one working Ovidian definition of Cupid, as we will see. Just as Jupiter has his thunderbolts, Cupid has his arrows; as Jupiter has his scepter, Cupid wields his torch.[47] Both gods are equipped with flame and weaponry, and, in the Ovidian world, both vie for a sense of sovereignty. To understand the split sovereignty wrought by this competition, we must remember that the Ovidian world is also the Roman world. If we return anew to Ovid's aphorism about *maiestas* and *amor*, the significance of this identification gains currency. The two opposing forces cannot linger (*morantur*) alongside each other. The anagrammatic appearance of *Roma* in *amor* (both appearing in *morantur*) reinforces the indivisibility of the two in their embedded Ovidian context, regardless of the ostensible progression of world development as Ovid's epic unfolds.

DISPLACING JUPITER: THE CASE OF HALICARNASSUS

Ovid's gnomic statement about the inability of *maiestas* and *amor* to coexist harmoniously can be read as the most targeted commentary on the interplay of Jupiter and Amor. This conceptualization concretizes the fact that the two are involved in a cycle of exchange, channeling directly the instability instigated by Ovid's play upon the potential identity of his demiurge. As the first pentad proceeds, however, the sensitive Ovidian reader might be tempted to revise an understanding of the competitive exchange of praise and primacy between Jupiter and Amor instead to an eclipsing of praise. An overt eclipsing of Jupiter's praise by the young upstart Amor would be a radical move indeed, given the inescapable political dimensions the epic gods have attracted by the imperial period. In effect, the promotion of Cupid at the expense of Jupiter is tantamount to Ovid's "personal" (poetic) divinity, responsible for the inward facing role of inspiration and motivation, eclipsing the ruler of the gods, and so, the external body responsible for exercising imperial power. However, this is not to say that Ovid shies entirely away from such a dynamic. One such mythological space that begins to introduce such a possibility is the moment Ovid does make (indirect) reference to Jupiter's birth.

Despite Ovid's promise in the proem to present what amounts to a world history, there is a surprising lack of explicit theogonic material. On one hand, the complete absence of theogonic narrative in the first book also gives readers the clue that Ovid will consistently resist one established epic trope—genealogical catalogs. Overwhelmingly, Ovid rejects the rigid linearity of genealogy as a narrative organizing principle. On the other hand, this lack is also indicative of Ovidian epic's more complex relationship with hymnic material. Birth narratives are stock fodder for hymns. From the beginning, Ovid's casual approach to divine introductions within the fabric of his ostensible world history vexes the issue of a sustained relationship with hymnic material; his side-stepping of birth narratives seems to abrogate any engagement with the narratives designed to promote the "knowability" (and therefore, praisability) of the divine. It is too easy, or glib, to conclude that Ovid avoids these mythological data points to frustrate the expectations of the reader, and/or to bury the depth of his use of hymnic material. Without assigning intention to Ovid, the salient point here is that when divine origins *are* mentioned, they are worthy of scrutiny.

Amorphous Control? 31

We can now turn directly to Jupiter and his birth as a type of case study for understanding how Ovid strategically deals with this issue of praising the king of the gods. Jupiter is first introduced obliquely in Ovid's description of the Golden Age. Acorns from "his" tree provided nourishment (*et quae deciderant patula Iouis arbore glandes*, "and the acorns which had fallen from Jove's spreading tree," 1.106), before his reign over the earth officially begins (1.113–14).[48] The first mention of his birth comes in Book 4, in a fashion similarly oblique. Alcithoe, one of the Minyeides, rapidly cycles through and discards a list of narratives she deems too "common" for her learned sororal audience:

Poscitur Alcithoe, postquam siluere sorores;
quae radio stantis percurrens stamina telae
"uulgatos taceo" dixit "pastoris amores
Daphnidis Idaei, quem nymphe paelicis ira
contulit in saxum (tantus dolor urit amantes);
nec loquor ut quondam naturae iure nouato
ambiguus fuerit modo uir, modo femina Sithon.
te quoque, nunc adamas, quondam fidissime paruo,
Celmi, Iovi largoque satos Curetas ab imbri
et Crocon in paruos uersum cum Smilace flores
praetereo dulcique animos nouitate tenebo."

(*Met.* 4. 274–84)

[Alcithoe is asked, after the sisters fell silent.
And she, running the threads through on her upright loom with her shuttle,
said, "I pass over silently those common tales, the loves
of the Idaean shepherd Daphnis, whom a nymph wrought into stone
in a fit of jealous rage: so great is the pain that scorches lovers.
Nor do I speak of Sithon, as once by a novel law of nature, was made
changeable, now man, now woman.
You also, now adamant, once most loyal to infant Jove,
Celmis, and the Curetes created from rainfall,
and Crocus, with Smilax, transformed into small flowers,
I will pass over summarily in silence, and cradle your minds
with tales alluring in newness."]

32   Amorphous Control?

After summarily dismissing the story of Idaean Daphnis, Alcithoe passes over the story of Sithon. She then briefly mentions Celmis and the Curetes, who play mythological roles in the infancy of Jupiter. The tale that Alcithoe decides to tell instead, further dismissing the two metamorphoses of Crocus and Smilax, is the story of Salmacis and Hermaphroditus, and the aetiology of the gender-bending Carian spring. Alison Keith has shown how Alcithoe's mythological rejections can be traced to the presence of Dionysiac imagery,[49] extending the rebellion the sisters display against the new god into a systematic narrative presence—a new god who receives hymnic praises at the opening of the book (4.11–30). However, as is consistent with much Ovidian poetic practice, there are multiple agendas at work. One layer of allusion is often designed as a red herring, diverting attention from yet another embedded layer of allusion. In this case, Alcithoe's ostensible refusal to engage in celebrating Bacchus, expressed through her narrative rejections, also masks a refusal to celebrate Jupiter. This refusal is packaged in the presentation of the myth that subtly privileges the sway the powers of love hold over its geographical setting. Alcithoe's circumventing of Jupiter's praise is not only indicated by her stated passing over of Celmis and the Curetes, but the choice of myth and narrative priorities she reveals in her relating of the meeting between Salmacis and Hermaphroditus. Concerning Alcithoe's version of this myth, Allen Romano has challenged the view that Ovid was unaware of the Halicarnassus inscription that features, in elegiac couplets, the myth of Salmacis. I would like to suggest, like Romano, that Ovid was indeed aware of this inscription's myth, but that he puts it to substantially different effect.[50] This lengthy elegiac inscription begins with an address to "Aphrodite of the Reeds," and then asks about the special nature of Halicarnassus:

"ἔννεπέ μοι, Σχοινῖτι, φίλον τιθάσε[υμα φέρουσα]
    Κύπρι, μυροπνεύστων ἐμπελάτειρα Πό[θων],
τῆς Ἁλικαρνάσσου τί τὸ τίμιον; οὐ γὰρ ἔγωγε
    ἔκλυον ἢ τί θροεῖ γαῦρα φρυασσομένη;"
"γηγενέων μεγάλαυχον ἐτέκνωσε στάχυν ἀνδρ[ῶν]
    Ἀκραίου πάρεδρον κυδαλίμοιο Διός
οἳ πρῶτοι κοίλην ὑπὸ δειράδα θέντο νεογνὸν
    παῖδα Ῥέης κρύφιον Ζῆν᾽ ἀτιταλλόμενοι
Γαίης ἀμφ᾽ ἀδύτοισιν, ὅτε Κρόνος ἀγκυλομήτης
    οὐκ ἔφθη λαιμῷ θέσθαι ὑποβρύχιον.

Amorphous Control?

Ζεὺς δὲ πατὴρ Γῆς υἷας ἀγακλέας ὀργειῶνας
θῆκεν, οἳ ἀρρήτων πρόσπολοί εἰσι δόμων.
Οὔδ᾽ ἄχαριν μόχθοιο παραὶ Διὸς ἔ[σ]χον ἀμοιβὴν
ἔργων ἀντ᾽ ἀγαθῶν ἐσθλὰ κομιζόμενοι."

(col. I. 1–14)

["Tell me, Schoinitis, dear tamer of our cares, you, Kypris, who bring close to us Desires scented with myrrh, what is it that brings honour to Halicarnassus? For I have never been told this. What words does she utter when she proudly boasts?"

"She brought forth an illustrious crop of earth-born men, to lodge beside mighty Zeus of the Height, who first in secret placed the new-born child of Rhea, Zeus, beneath the hollow ridge, caring for him, in the shrine of Gaia, when Kronos of the crooked counsels had failed to get him into the depths beneath his throat in time. And Zeus made the sons of Ge his honoured priests, who care for his awesome house. Nor was the reward they got from Zeus one of ingratitude, for they got good things in return for their good deeds."[51]]

With this inscription, the Carians have appropriated the myth of Zeus' birth for their own regional purposes, putting it toward honoring Halicarnassus itself. The Carians' appropriative use of fundamentally Hesiodic material to (re)present their autochthonic nature rests on a surprising mythological innovation: an honorific effort to illustrate Halicarnassus as the nurse of the infant Zeus.[52] Within Alcithoe's narrative, Zeus' birth first registers with references made to the Curetes and then the explicit phrase *paruo . . . Ioui*. Her specification that Hermaphroditus was (presumably born) and raised on Mt. Ida (*Naides Idaeis enutriuere sub antris*, "the nymphs nursed him under the Idaean caves," 4.289) subsequently reminds readers of Zeus' birth on Crete, exploiting the homonym of Ida as both a Phrygian and Cretan locale.[53] *Enutriuere*, not a common verb (nor one seen before the Augustan era), is also reminiscent of the inscription's use of ἀτιτάλλω to describe the care of the "earth-born men" for Zeus, a care that also occurs within the space of a cave. Alcithoe descriptively engineers the care of Hermaphroditus to recall Zeus' similar infant experience. The detailed illustration of Salmacis' pool as bereft of reeds, rushes, and sedge (*non illic canna palustris / nec steriles uluae nec acuta cuspide iunci*, "not in that place were there marshy reeds, nor barren sedge, nor sharp-pointed rushes," 4.298–99) appears in further dialogue with the inscription's recondite epithet of Aphrodite, *Schoinitis* ("of the reeds," "in the marsh"). Ovid's descriptive export of this epithet shows his attentiveness to the mythological presentation of Caria that he (via Alcithoe) chooses not to follow.[54]

There are other reasons to see competing presences in this Carian locale. The site that became the major Carian sanctuary of Aphrodite first supported a cult of Zeus. Within this region, Zeus was the initial focus of more worship than the Aphrodisian goddesses. This cultic focus shifted in the late Hellenistic period, when the local goddess first became identified with Aphrodite. The goddess then received the increase in cult worship that would inspire the city's new name of Aphrodisias.[55] Correspondingly, Salmacis' activities (bathing, combing her hair, admiring her reflection, lounging amid soft foliage, picking flowers; cf. 4.308–15) clearly ally her with Aphrodite.[56] Salmacis' hymnic entreaty to the young Hermaphroditus privileges this Carian lineage and focus of worship, rather than the Zeus-centric account detailed in the "Pride of Halicarnassus" inscription: *puer o dignissime credi / esse deus, seu tu deus es, potes esse Cupido* ("boy, most worthily believed of being a god—if you indeed are a god, you are Cupid," 4.320–21). Salmacis' inclusion of the further detail of the blessedness (*fortunata*, 4.323) of Hermaphroditus' nurse (*et quae dedit ubera nutrix*, "and the nurse who gave you her breast," 4.324) solidifies the subtle chain of reference to Zeus' birth that runs from the narrative framing of the myth and its beginning. The god hailed here in Halicarnassus by Salmacis is Cupid, not Zeus. Salmacis' praise of Hermaphroditus is functionally a hymn to Cupid, and one that supplants the praise of Zeus that shapes Halicarnassus' special identity, as especially revealed in the elegiac inscription.

Although a minor thread within the narrative, the overt effacement of Zeus from the Carian myth is further evidence for the Ovidian resistance to engage with straightforward hymnic praise of the king of the gods, as he instead sets up a hymnically derived tension between Zeus/Eros and Jupiter/Cupid. Ovid uses a hymn to Cupid to replace the elegiac inscription in praise of Zeus, only after he feints toward Zeus' own mythology. The diversion from Bacchic myth and material is one layer of Ovid's game with the reader, designed as a smokescreen for the further embedded poetic sleight of hand that toys with both reader expectation and the literary tradition: the signaled eclipsing of Zeus by Eros.

Replacing Jupiter: The Case of Venus' Territory

By embedding a hymn to Cupid in Salmacis' praise of Hermaphroditus, itself embedded within an internal narrative, Ovid distances himself from a direct radicalization of the hymnic tradition and an overt diversion of praise from Jupiter to Cupid. Alcithoe's song, however, can be read as a strategic antecedent to another embedded narrative, one that belongs to the hymnic genre. Alcithoe's participation in Ovid's resistance to a committed praise of Jupiter sets up, in brief, the narrative conditions of Calliope's hymn to Ceres. In this hymn, the true search for hymnic praise and the staking of divine identity is explored not via Ceres but through Venus. Although Calliope's hymn will broaden the focus of discussion here to include Venus, which will necessitate some delving into her own hymnic appearances separate from Cupid/Amor, the way Ovid constructs the hymn and packages the powers of Venus together with Cupid still speaks to the ultimate vying for mastery between Jupiter and the forces of love. As such, the following discussion takes into consideration the different layers of textual reliance that construct hymnic authority: first, the reliance of Venus' "hymn" to herself and her son upon the question of divine territory revealed in the *Homeric Hymn to Demeter* and the Callimachean *Hymn to Zeus*, and second, the reliance of the Callimachean *Hymn to Zeus* on the *Homeric Hymn to Aphrodite*. These layers of textual reliance stack together to show an accumulated lineage of meaning from the hymnic tradition, a primary chain of inspiration illuminated through other subsidiary texts from the epic tradition.

The ways in which Calliope's hymn provides evidence of this rivalrous dynamic between Jupiter and Amor also reveals some of Ovid's epic architecture. Venus' obsession with rivalry and territory, desires that define divine identity in the *Metamorphoses*, crystallizes and recapitulates the prevailing Olympian dynamic at this structurally critical moment in the epic. Venus' address to her son within Calliope's hymn completes the trajectory of the tension between Jupiter and Amor developed across the first pentad by confirming not only their divine rivalry, but Cupid's mastery. Ovid's use of the hymnic form to do so further confirms the literary origins of this rivalry: the competition between Jupiter and Amor that he borrowed from the cyclic exchange of primacy and praise between the two gods staged within the hymnic tradition. The territorial networks of rivalry that animate Calliope's hymn to Ceres will be discussed at greater length in chapter 5, but here, the

36   Amorphous Control?

dominance of Love (exemplified in the forces of both Venus and Cupid) will focalize and reaffirm the threads of divine competition Ovid has spun out between creation and rule by might versus love.

The passage of central focus for this discussion is Venus' address to her son, expressing her desires.

> "arma manusque meae, mea, nate, potentia" dixit,
> "illa, quibus superas omnes, cape tela, Cupido,
> inque dei pectus celeres molire sagittas,
> cui triplicis cessit fortuna nouissima regni.
> tu superos ipsumque Iouem, tu numina ponti
> uicta domas ipsumque regit qui numina ponti.
> Tartara quid cessant? cur non matrisque tuumque
> imperium profers? agitur pars tertia mundi.
> et tamen in caelo (quae iam patientia nostra est!)
> spernimur ac mecum uires minuuntur Amoris.
> Pallada nonne uides iaculatricemque Dianam
> abscessisse mihi? Cereris quoque filia uirgo,
> si patiemur, erit; nam spes adfectat easdem.
> at tu pro socio, si qua est ea gratia, regno
> iunge deam patruo."

(*Met.* 5.365–379)

> ["my arms and my hands, my son, my executive power," she said
> "take up those arrows, the ones with which you conquer all things, Cupid,
> and launch those swift missiles into the chest of a god—you know,
> the one to whom the newest lot of the triple kingdom fell.
> You conquer the gods, and Jupiter himself; the powers of the sea
> you subdue, and you have subdued even the god who lords over them:
> why does Tartarus remain uncultivated? Why not advance our empire, yours
> and mine? A third part of the world is at stake,
> and still we are spurned in the heavens, despite its sufferance of us,
> and the forces of love dwindle alongside my own. Don't you see how
> Pallas and archeress Diana have withdrawn from me? The daughter
> of Ceres, too, would be a virgin, if permitted; she assays the same hopes.
> But you—if you possess any pride in our joint kingdom—join
> the goddess to her uncle."]

This passage also provides the basis for Barchiesi's influential discussion of the *Homeric Hymns* within the *Metamorphoses*. Within his reading, Venus' words here reveal her "masterplot" for the epic: a universe under Cupid's rule (and so, a poetic metaverse under Ovid's rule). Venus' ambitions are reinforced by the poetic maneuvers of her speech: she uses material from her own *Homeric Hymn* (cf. 6–35) to allusively annex the "territory" of the hymn to Ceres, itself a repeat of the *Homeric Hymn to Demeter*.[57] However, the poetic implications of Venus' expansionist ambitions reverberate beyond the *Homeric Hymns*. In discussing this passage, Barchiesi's focus is on the literary interplay between the Homeric hymns to Demeter and Aphrodite and its Ovidian legacy. The machinations of the Ovidian Venus causes a collision between the strategies of Zeus and Aphrodite for divine order: within the Ovidian version, Proserpina's kidnapping is the plan of Venus, not Jupiter.[58] To add to the complexity of the dynamic identified by Barchiesi, I suggest that the Ovidian Venus' address to her son can be considered a hymn to Cupid, and that it is meant to further efface Jupiter, replacing his praise with expressions of love's supremacy. By redirecting praise of omnipotence from Jupiter to her son, Venus looks back to the opening books of the epic and reinforces one identity of Jupiter: a Jupiter whose deeds are defined not by majesty or displays of kingly justice, but of erotic appetites and the pursuit of pleasure. With Venus' words, this becomes the prevailing identity of the Ovidian, epic Jupiter established by the first pentad.

Within this passage, Venus displays a concern for physical territory as evidence of Love's dominion.[59] Venus' regard for physical territory is a mutation of Dis' concern for his kingdom that occasions his unusual visit to the upper world (5.356–63). His reconnaissance mission replays Jupiter's concern for Arcadia after the destruction wrought by Phaethon (2.401–8). Espying the god beyond the confines of his traditional space, Venus is given cause to consider her own territory, and how she might expand it beyond the realms of sky, land, and sea—a set of territories that are commonplace in hymnic addresses that praise the universality of the goddess' power.[60] Within her address to Cupid, Venus conceptualizes the seen god of the unseen world as the physical embodiment of his domain, equating physical space and divinity. Dis is not named, only identified as the god to whom the final lot of the triple kingdom fell. Poseidon receives the same conceptual treatment. Venus' equation between kingdom and divinity is a blurring of boundaries only Jupiter seems to escape, called by name (*Iouem*, 5.369).

38   Amorphous Control?

Venus' query of *cur non matrisque tuumque/ imperium profers?* is further revelatory of her agenda, as her use of *imperium* occupies a distinctly territorial sense.[61] As part of John Richardson's investigation of how *imperium* shifted in meaning from a simple sense of "power" to encompass the geographical sense of "empire," he notes a comparatively rare example from the *Res Gestae*, used after the gates of the temple of Janus were closed: *cum [p]er totem i[mperium po]puli Roma [ni terra marique es] set parta uictoriis pax* ("when throughout the whole empire of the Roman people, by land and by sea, peace had been established by victory," *Res Gestae* 13).[62] With peace secured for the Romans over land and sea, the gates were closed; Venus wishes to expand her *imperium* beyond land and sea to Tartarus.[63] Richardson cites Venus' usage as an example of "power in a general sense . . . when tendering advice," but, with wider consideration of context, it is more apt to see Venus using *imperium* precisely in its meaning of empire.[64] Venus' expansionist vision is crystallized by this meaning of such a weighted word. Venus, not Jupiter, is the divinity who upholds the priority of imperialist expansion.

Venus' expression at being slighted in the heavens (*et tamen in caelo . . . spernimur*, 5.373–74) also targets Jupiter specifically. The heavens are his share of the triple kingdom, the mythological model of divine allocation Venus follows when setting her mind to expansion (*triplicis . . . regni*, 5.368). The tripartite model of division effected by the drawing of lots is a tradition stemming from Homer (*Il.* 15.187–93). The opposing tradition comes from Hesiod (*Theog.* 881–85; cf. also 111–13). The myth of lot-drawing also appears in the *Homeric Hymn to Demeter*, when Helios tells Demeter where her child has gone, and who is responsible. He ends with a statement of Hades' divine honors:[65]

> οὔ τοι ἀεικὴς
> γαμβρὸς ἐν ἀθανάτοις πολυσημάντωρ Ἀϊδωνεύς,
> αὐτοκασίγνητος καὶ ὁμόσπορος· ἀμφὶ δὲ τιμὴν
> ἔλλαχεν ὡς τὰ πρῶτα διάτριχα δασμὸς ἐτύχθη
> τοῖς μεταναιετάει τῶν ἔλλαχε κοίρανος εἶναι.
>
> (*Hymn. Hom. Dem.* 83–87)

[Among the gods Aidoneus is not an unsuitable bridegroom,
Commander-to-Many and Zeus's own brother of the same stock.

Amorphous Control?

As for honor, he got his third at the world's first division
and dwells with those whose rule has fallen to his lot. (trans. Foley)]

The relationship between Zeus' strategizing and the division of lots is made concrete in a different hymn, Callimachus' *Hymn to Zeus*. The poet draws a direct line between the god's plans and the honors he receives:

ἀλλ' ἔτι παιδνὸς ἐὼν ἐφράσσαο πάντα τέλεια·
τῷ τοι καὶ γνωτοὶ προτερηγενέες περ ἐόντες
οὐρανὸν οὐκ ἐμέγηραν ἔχειν ἐπιδαίσιον οἶκον.
δηναιοὶ δ' οὐ πάμπαν ἀληθέες ἦσαν ἀοιδοί·
φάντο πάλον Κρονίδῃσι διάτριχα δώματα νεῖμαι·
τίς δέ κ' ἐπ' Οὐλύμπῳ τε καὶ Ἄϊδι κλῆρον ἐρύσσαι,
ὃς μάλα μὴ νενίηλος; ἐπ' ἰσαίῃ γὰρ ἔοικε
πήλασθαι· τὰ δὲ τόσσον ὅσον διὰ πλεῖστον ἔχουσι.
ψευδοίμην, ἀΐοντος ἅ κεν πεπίθοιεν ἀκουήν.
οὐ σε θεῶν ἐσσῆνα πάλοι θέσαν, ἔργα δὲ χειρῶν,
σή τε βίη τό τε κάρτος, ὃ καὶ πέλας εἶσαο δίφρου.

(Callim. *Hymn* 1.57–67)

But when you were still a child you devised all things in their completion. And so your siblings, although they were older, did not begrudge you heaven to hold as your allotted home. Ancient poets are not always completely truthful: they claim that a lot assigned homes in a threefold division to the sons of Cronus, but who would cast lots for Olympus and Hades, unless he was utterly foolish? For one casts lots, it seems, for things that are of equal value, but these are very far apart. I would tell fictions of the sort that would persuade the ear of the listener. Lots did not make you king of the gods, but the deeds of your hands; your force and might, which you have set beside your throne. (trans. Stephens)]

Although the nature of Zeus' plans is not specified in the hymn beyond their completion, the subsequent focus on the opposition between Olympus and Hades draws greater attention to the role of Hades, and therefore greater likelihood to the suggestion that Callimachus is not only reacting to the Homeric tradition in the *Iliad*, but also the tradition found in the

Homeric Hymn to Demeter.[66] Along these lines, Susan Stephens notes that the use of the rare designator διάτριχα (*Hymn* 1.61) could be attributed to its appearance in the *Homeric Hymn* (*Hymn. Hom. Dem.* 86).[67] The Ovidian Venus' conceptual use of the triple kingdom to construct and justify her imperialist plan thereby reverses the poetic circumstances of the *Hymn to Zeus*. Ovid's focus on territory forges a new literary lineage between the *Homeric Hymn to Demeter*, Callimachus' *Hymn to Zeus*, and Venus' hymn to Amor within the Muse Calliope's hymn to Ceres.

However, Callimachus' hymn also reveals a focus that gestures toward the framing concerns of the *Homeric Hymn to Aphrodite*.[68] This focus is made more meaningful by the two hymns' shared delineation of power (whether poetic or divine) that looks to the Muses. The hymnist claims that the poets of old do not tell the truth, citing the absurdity of drawing lots for territories as different as Olympus and Hades. He contrasts this foolishness with a statement about his own poetics: that he would lie persuasively (*Hymn* 1.65).[69] As is readily understood, his claim echoes various expressions of the Muses' power.[70] However, the direction Callimachus proceeds in, further qualifying the act of lying, can be read as exploring powers beyond the tradition of Muse-like fiction. "Lying persuasively" is also in accordance with the powers of Aphrodite twice cited in the *Homeric Hymn*, of deception and persuasion (πεπιθεῖν φρένας οὐδ' ἀπατῆσαι, *Hymn. Hom. Ven.* 7 and 33).[71] This emphatic formulation similarly places Aphrodite in the expressive territory of the Muses.[72] Through this shared similarity, the fictive agenda set forth by the *Hymn to Zeus* can also be seen to resemble the defining points of Aphrodite's divine influence of charm.

This general background between the two hymns, meeting over the shared power of the Muses, leads to a more focused point of connection. Callimachus claims that Zeus was made king by his deeds (ἔργα δὲ χειρῶν, "the works of his hands," *Hymn* 1.66). This phrase looks back to the nourishment of the infant god by the Panacrian bees (ἔργα μελίσσης, *Hymn* 1.50)[73] and anticipates the poet's hymnic *envoi*: τεὰ δ' ἔργματα τίς κεν ἀείδοι; / οὐ γένετ', οὐκ ἔσται· τίς κεν Διὸς ἔργματ' ἀείσει; ("Who would sing of your deeds? There has not been, there will not be; who shall sing of the deeds of Zeus?," *Hymn* 1.92–93).[74] The image of the bee's nourishing work, a well-known poetic symbol, is transmuted into the work of Zeus, before the concept of "work" is re-enshrined as the impossibly illustrious act of singing Zeus' praises at the hymn's close. Work and song are intertwined in defining

Amorphous Control?

41

the hymn's theme and momentum.[75] The plurality of the works at the hymn's end (ἔργματα . . . ἔργματ') also underscores the near redundancy of the phrase ἔργα δὲ χειρῶν ("handiwork of hands"). The focus on Zeus' deeds as responsible for his kingship and hymnic status brings Callimachus' hymn surprisingly into contact with the *Homeric Hymn to Aphrodite*, the only hymn that self-professedly focuses on the *deeds* of the goddess (not the goddess herself) as the subject of the hymn: Μοῦσά μοι ἔννεπε ἔργα πολυχρύσου Ἀφροδίτης ("Muse, tell me of the *deeds* of Aphrodite, rich in gold," *Hymn. Hom. Ven.* 1; cf. ἔργα . . . ἐϋστεφάνου Κυθερείης, 6).[76] After her powers of deception and persuasion are introduced, the again-cited "works of golden Aphrodite" (9) are rapidly contrasted with the "work of Ares" (10), the craftwork and women's work (12–15) of Athena, before Hestia's immunity to her works (ἔργ' Ἀφροδίτης, 21) is explained. Altogether, ἔργα appears seven times in the first twenty-five lines of the hymn. This emphasis should be read against the Callimachean emphasis in the *Hymn to Zeus*.

In the *Homeric Hymn*, the beguiling "deeds" of Aphrodite are what Zeus is militating against by causing her to fall in love with Anchises, another divine plan that stands beside his union of Persephone and Hades. Callimachus' marked insistence upon the authority given to Zeus by his plans and deeds in his first hymn therefore can be read as a focused commentary upon Zeus' latent presence and relationship to the divine order in the *Homeric Hymns*, especially the pair of the hymns to Demeter and Aphrodite. He replaces the myth of territorial division found in the *Homeric Hymn to Demeter*, redirecting a definition of hymnic divine identity by deed away from the Homeric Aphrodite to his Zeus; as such, he responds in turn to the Homeric Zeus who takes retributive measures to shore up his authority against the forces of Aphrodite. Callimachus borrows the modality of Aphrodite's power (persuasion, deception) for the hymnic voice he uses to communicate his commentary, and to emphasize the mastery of his Zeus over the goddess of love—a goddess who is not gifted her own hymn within his collection. Mitigating the challenge that Aphrodite poses to Zeus' divine authority underlines further Callimachus' poetic strategy in refashioning Antagoras' *Hymn to Eros* for the praise of Zeus at the hymn's opening.

Ovid's Venus makes a sequel to this sensitively delineated hymnic rivalry. The Ovidian Venus unpicks the Callimachean refashioning of a hymnic Zeus to suit her own praises and the praises of Amor. If Callimachus sought to redirect a hymnic model of deeds-based authority to Zeus in a way that could be read as programmatic, Ovid is now here to establish Love, in the forms of Venus and Cupid, in firm control of hymnic territory and tradition, and therefore as the Olympian authority to be reckoned with. Far from orchestrating its events, Jupiter fades into the background of this myth.[77] Venus' address to Cupid recognizes this agenda and traffics in specific textual details that underscore Ovid's "hymn" as a continued installment in the hymnic exchanges of power between Zeus and Amor.

HANDIWORK AND CRAFTSMANSHIP: THE GLOBE OF CUPID

One detail of this narrative portion allows us to bring our discussion full circle. The closeness of mother and son is humorously suggested by the opening of Venus' address, *arma manusque*. Previously within the *Metamorphoses*, *manusque* always follows a physical body part, be it fingers or shoulders (*digitosque*, 1.500; *umerique*, 1.741, 4.658, 4.592; *umerosque*, 2.354); *arma* therefore easily denotes both body part and weaponry.[78] Calling Cupid her "arms and hands" with both active understandings of *arma*, as she embraces him, is another Ovidian blend of the physical and metaphorical. Giving Cupid the agency of her actions, her formulation is tantamount to calling the winged god her "handiwork"—which he is, and also, what he does. Cupid's biddability here, as he complies immediately and uncomplainingly, aligns with Virgil's responsive Cupid, but acts in extreme juxtaposition to the scene of literary inspiration for the Virgilian Venus' address to her son: the opening of the third book of Apollonius' *Argonautica*, where Eros is depicted as an unrepentantly greedy little hellion. Aphrodite, entreated by Athena and Hera to convince Eros to enchant Jason with love for Medea, professes her inability to control him (Ap. Rhod. *Argon.* 3.91–99); to guarantee the use of Eros' arrows, Aphrodite resorts to bribery with a toy once belonging to Zeus, a wondrous ball (*Argon.* 3.131–44).

The nature of this toy returns us to the Ovidian passage. The toy is a little globe—that is, an image of the cosmos.[79] Apollonius evokes here the image of the cosmic Eros, but one negatively transformed by the petulance and caprice of the young god. The passing of the toy from Zeus to Eros is a crucial aspect of this vignette.[80] Eros' ownership of a cosmos once under Zeus' guardianship evokes again the Hellenistic interest in the competing visions of world-creation and maintenance, and the competitive interchange between Zeus and Eros as demiurgic forces. By giving the cosmos to

Eros, Apollonius lends a different worldview to the second half of his epic. In a vein similar to the *Homeric Hymn to Aphrodite*, Apollonius turns to a literary experiment of how Eros can compete generically with Homeric *kleos* as a governing ethos for his epic poem. Ovid, rather, presents his reader with a Cupid automatically and generously responsive to his mother's plea, as her plan is the literal equivalent to the Apollonian Aphrodite's symbolic bribe: the cosmos. Unlike the cosmic toy of Apollonius' Eros, however, the Ovidian universe at stake is never explicitly described as under Jupiter's total dominion. Apollonius' symbolic cosmos becomes the real Ovidian world, one always poised for Cupid's control. Ovid's return to the image of the globe as evoked through the Apollonian allusion also brings full circle the presentation of the demiurge in Book 1. Within the context of the first book, the demiurge's identity is purposefully ambiguous, suggesting the mythological and philosophical powers attributable to both Zeus and Eros in order to generate the conditions of tension and instability Ovid desires to exploit and explore between Jupiter and Amor. With the allusion to the globe as it appears in Apollonius, we arrive once again at a depiction of the cosmos under the artistic direction of the demiurge. As Peter Kelly explains, Ovid's "most detailed representation of the cosmos as artifact can be seen in his description of the armillary sphere of Archimedes in *Fasti* Book 6" (cf. *globus, Fast.* 6.278); Kelly compares this description to the cosmogony of *Metamorphoses* 1, uniting the passages through the idea of craftsmanship.[81] He further connects Ovid's use of the *Timaeus* and the craftsman metaphor in the *Metamorphoses* with this passage of the *Fasti* by calling attention to the connection Cicero himself makes between Archimedes' armillary sphere (akin to a globe) and the demiurge of the *Timaeus* (*Tusc.* 1.63.1–5). In this passage, Cicero draws an explicit parallel between Archimedes and the demiurge, the sphere and the cosmos. With these parallels in mind, the cosmos as the purview of Cupid, as suggested by Ovid's reliance upon the Apollonian encounter of Aphrodite and Eros, can be extended now to claim, retrospectively, an identity of the demiurge as Cupid. Overall, Venus' formulated strategy works to erode Jupiter's might with a delicately learned insidiousness, as she leaches his presence and praises from her literary playbook.

CONCLUSION

From the very beginning, Ovid raises the question of cosmogonic responsibility. He sets into a motion a complex tension of cosmic control and direction—a tension given structure from applying knowledge of the competitive cycling of power exchanged between Zeus and Eros within the hymnic tradition.[82] Ovid's understanding and use of the hymnic tradition can be read expansively, inclusive of Plato's *Symposium* as a hymn to Eros and the Orphic cosmogonies as theogonic hymns. These more panoramic understandings of the hymnic form that shape the overarching narrative tension between the competing forces of love and sovereignty are also balanced on a more detailed level by literary reference to the tradition of the Homeric and Callimachean narrative hymns. As the first pentad progresses, we can see how this initial tension, expressed with an ambiguity indicative of cyclic exchange, becomes channeled more directly into the dynamic allocation of praise: less an exchange than acts of diversion, circumventing, and supplanting. Jupiter and Cupid are the divine polarities upon which Ovid's cosmic determinacy is strung, setting up these forces as the first order of divine rivalry, and the arena of their competition as nothing less than the universe.

2

Divining Praise

Jupiter, Apollo, and Poetic Primacy

The competition between Jupiter and Amor that constitutes one axis of understanding for Ovid's divinities brings to the fore the friction between the epic tradition and the Ovidian tradition, and the gods that occupy their respective positions at the head of each: Jupiter, as the epic king of gods and men, and Amor, the deity who presides over the elegiacally committed poet. When Ovid turns to writing epic, conflict necessarily ensues. The productive, creative tension that results provided the content for chapter 1. In chapter 2, we turn to a new divine rivalry: the competition between Jupiter and Apollo. Similarly, this rivalry also comes with an overarching interpretive context. This new overarching context expands beyond the realm of the literary: understanding the set of interactions between Jupiter and Apollo also bridges perspective between Ovidian poetics and the Augustan world. Given Apollo's role as the god of poetry, there is still a prevailing context of literary concern illuminated by investigating this new divine competition, but this time, there is also a more explicit political dimension that arises. Jupiter's position at the head of the Olympian order makes him a prime candidate upon which to map imperial identity—in other words, a prime candidate for Ovid to imagine as an analogue of Augustus, when he chooses to use his epic as a means to reflect (or distort) political realities. However, the divine analogue selected and relentlessly cultivated by Augustus himself also participates actively within the world of the *Metamorphoses*: Apollo, the son of Jupiter. What happens, therefore, when these two gods interact within Ovid's epic space? By deliberately setting Apollo and Jupiter in conflict, Ovid creates a literary thread of commentary that also has significant political ramifications and repercussions.

46 Divining Praise

Chapter 2 has interrelated aims, which cumulatively advance new perspectives on the opening books of the *Metamorphoses*. First, I read a set of ecphrases to frame the competition between Jupiter and Apollo. By investigating how Ovid uses place, space, and (dis)location to introduce these divinities, this mutually implicated pair of descriptions sets up a foundation for the most prolonged inquiry of the chapter: the relationship between Jupiter and Arcadia that Ovid constructs to convey his ideas about poetic praise, and therefore, his ideas about the praise of Jupiter versus Apollo. This relationship is explored through a detailed examination of Ovid's rerouting of the Callimachean landscape of the *Hymn to Zeus* to the Thessalian environs of Book 1, and, in relation, through the symbolic figuring of praise within these landscapes. To examine the nature of Ovidian praise when it comes to Jupiter versus Apollo, I discuss the symbolic presence of praise as it appears in two forms: first, water as the symbolic equivalence of praise, as motivates one reading of the *Hymn to Zeus*, and second, the laurel as the embodiment of praise within *Metamorphoses* 1. Looking at the laurel as an emblem of praise also refocuses a reading of the Apollo and Daphne myth upon praise instead of love. This refocusing lends the myth a new interpretive dimension: not only can it tell us about the rivalry of Cupid versus Apollo, as tends to be the focus of interpretation, but also, the rivalry of Apollo versus Jupiter. After detailing and analyzing Ovid's poetic strategy of geographic displacement and postponement as it pertains to Arcadia and the praise of Jupiter, I discuss the way the myth of Callisto can be read to internally confirm the purpose of this poetic strategy. Finally, I turn to two more parallels of power and identity between the gods: the competitive primacies of first battles and of first love, appropriate polarities for an Ovidian epic. Overall, through each of these three main sections, I illuminate how Ovid uses the hymnic tradition to build an internal understanding of praise for his epic world and how this understanding impacts the competitively staked divine identities of Apollo and Jupiter.

A GAME OF THRONES: WHOSE PALATINE? WHOSE PALACE?

Ovid fully introduces Jupiter to the fabric of his epic when he describes the heavens, in the prelude to the council of the gods. When Ovid elaborately details the heavens, he comes to a descriptive climax when he calls them a celestial Palatine (*hic locus est quem, si uerbis audacia detur, / haud timeam magni dixisse Palatia caeli*, "here is the place, which, if such a boldness of

Divining Praise 47

phrase is permitted, I would have no trepidation in naming the Palatine of the great heavens," 1.175–76). However, there is a notable change made to this scene: instead of seeing Palatine Apollo ensconced there, the reader encounters Jupiter Tonans (*Tonantis*, 1.170). Jupiter Tonans was housed in the new temple on the Capitoline vowed by Augustus—one that was already (problematically?) drawing traffic away from the temple of Jupiter Capitolinus (Jupiter Optimus Maximus; cf. Suet. *Aug.* 91.2).[1] Ovid's thwarting of expectations when it comes to the allocation of divine space and divine appearance not only effaces the physical, sacred space of the Capitoline, but the appellation of Jupiter Capitolinus. Should his reader then take this to mean Jupiter Palatinus is an imposter, or a trespasser? Certainly, the reader could question whether Jupiter even has a divine home in Ovid. Furthermore, the reader now has direct cause to question the relationship Ovid constructs between Jupiter and Apollo.

Let us consider more closely the passage that leads to this surprise star appearance on Heaven's "Palatine," which is also the poem's first landscape ecphrasis:

est uia sublimis, caelo manifesta sereno;
Lactea nomen habet, candore notabilis ipso.
hac iter est superis ad magni tecta Tonantis
regalemque domum. dextra laeuaque deorum
atria nobilium ualuis celebrantur apertis.
plebs habitat diuersa locis; hac parte potentes
caelicolae clarique suos posuere Penates.
hic locus est quem, si uerbis audacia detur,
haud timeam magni dixisse Palatia caeli.

(Met. 1.168–76)

[There is a highway, visibly bright in the clear heavens;
it is called the Milky Way, remarkably so by its very brightness.
By this way there is traverse to the complex of the great Thunderer,
his kingly home: along the right and left, the halls of the celebrated gods
are thronged, doors flung open. Lesser gods live elsewhere.
In these parts the powerful and distinguished of heavens' dwellers
situate their own household shrines; here is the place, which,
if such boldness of praise is permitted, I would have no trepidation
in naming the Palatine of the great heavens.]

Divining Praise

Again, the presence of Jupiter Tonans presiding from the shining marble of this heavenly Palatine proves unexpected. Obviously, it is the specification of *Palatia* that most directly summons the idea of Apolline territory to Augustan readers, but additional hints build up to confirm this assumption. As Ovid describes it, the Milky Way (*uia lactea*) is marked by its visible clarity. The vocabulary of brightness that is used calls Apollo more to mind than Jupiter. Twice within the Ovidian corpus, Apollo appears with a use of *manifestus*, as similarly introduces the Milky Way (*sume fidem et pharetram—fies manifestus Apollo*, "take up a lyre and quiver, you patently would become an Apollo," *Her.* 15.23; *haec ego cum canerem, subito manifestus Apollo / mouit inauratae pollice fila lyrae*, "When I was to sing these things, suddenly Apollo epiphanized, strummed the strings of his golden lyre with a thumb," *Ars am.* 2.493–94). In the epiphany from the *Ars amatoria*, one layer of allusion evoked is the Apolline epiphany that opens the Callimachean *Hymn to Apollo*. This allusion comes in the form of a translingual pun: *manifestus* equals *Delius*, as derived from δῆλος (cf. ὁ Δήλιος . . . φοῖνιξ/ ἐξαπίνης, Callim. *Hymn* 2.4–5).[2] This Apollo of the *Ars* also arrives bedecked in laurel (*laurus . . . laurus*, 2.495–96), the accessory that most powerfully summons Apollo's Delphic aspect. Apollo's epiphanic appearance signals a further investment in this feature of hymnic presentation: to attuned readers, Apollo simultaneously registers as the Delian and Pythian god, uniting the two versions of the god the *Homeric Hymn to Apollo* presents (the Delian and Pythian).

Ovid names the Milky Way the *via lactea*, rewriting the Greek Γαλαξίας or γάλακτος κύκλος (γάλα, "milk"). He transforms the circular image of the Greek technical expression into a road, a conceptual shift that further allows his Romanizing analogy of Heaven's space.[3] The road up the Palatine would lead to the presence of the laurel outside the house of Augustus, marking its doors, and "the snow-white threshold," as Virgil describes the housing complex, "of shining Phoebus" (*niueo <u>candentis</u> limine <u>Phoebi</u>*, Virg. *Aen.* 8.720).[4] Within this Virgilian description, *candentis* also glosses *Phoebi* (φοῖβος, "bright, radiant").[5] Ovid's Milky Way, *candore notabilis ipso*, possesses a brightness more illuminating of Apollo than Jupiter.[6] Through these textual reminiscences, *manifesta* and *candor* conjure the presence of Apollo as Delius and Phoebus within the space of the *uia lactea*. These appearances compound to suggest the eventual presence of Apollo Palatinus, but there is another cult title of Apollo also embedded in this passage that has escaped attention: Apollo Galaxios.

Apollo Galaxios is associated with the Theban rite of the Daphnephoria and a Boeotian cult site called the Galaxion.[7] According to ancient evidence, the Theban laurel-bearing procession ended at the Apolline cult center known as the Galaxion, so-called due to the god's presence manifesting as the abundance of milk borne by local cattle. The Theban Daphnephoria, ending at the Galaxion, can therefore also be aptly evoked by the Ovidian *via lactea* that leads to the laurel-graced, shining domain of Palatine Apollo. The imaginative route of the Daphnephoria that can map onto the Milky Way also understandably summons the presence of laurel, which anticipates (and is ratified by) the myth of Daphne that ends with a similar, explicit flash-forward in time, within Apollo's hymn to the laurel:

> cui deus "at quoniam coniunx mea non potes esse,
> arbor eris certe" dixit "mea; semper habebunt
> te coma, te citharae, te nostrae, laure, pharetrae.
> tu ducibus Latiis aderis, cum laeta Triumphum
> uox canet et uisent longas Capitolia pompas;
> postibus Augustis eadem fidissima custos
> ante fores stabis mediamque tuebere quercum.
> utque meum intonsis caput est iuuenale capillis,
> tu quoque perpetuos semper gere frondis honores."
>
> (Met. 1.557–65).

> [To the tree, the god said, "well, since you can't be my wife—
> surely, you'll be my tree! Always you'll adorn my hair,
> you, my lyre—you, my quiver, laurel;
> you'll be there for the Latin generals, when joyous voice
> sings out of triumphs; you'll be the most loyal guardian
> of Augustus' doors, where you'll stand before the entrance,
> looking after the oak placed in the middle,
> and just as my head is ever-youthful with hair unshorn,
> so you, too, will always bear the honor of being evergreen."]

Apollo's speech to the laurel, designating its position of honor outside Augustus' door, also serves to confirm the earlier sense of Apolline displacement, when Jupiter instead occupied Apollo Palatinus' seat of power.

This act of Apolline displacement, and the struggle over power and identity it sets up between Apollo and his father Jupiter, is revisited after the

50   Divining Praise

boundaries of both book division and world (re)creation. By recalling this
displacement in a pendant scene, Ovid further confirms and builds the com-
petitive dynamic between the two gods, while he establishes this mode of
rivalry as an element that belongs to each iteration of his poetic world. As
the flood stands as one narrative border, so too does the conflagration of
Phaethon, a myth that spans the first two books. The second book begins
with an ecphrasis, a description of the house of the Sun:

> Regia Solis erat sublimibus alta columnis,
> clara micante auro flammasque imitante pyropo,
> cuius ebur nitidum fastigia summa tegebat,
> argenti bifores radiabant lumine ualuae.

> (*Met.* 2.1–4)

> [The palace of the Sun, exalting in its high columns,
> sparkled with pure gold and metal imitative of flame,
> the highest gables of which sported an ivory gleam,
> and the double doors scattered forth silver light.]

This ecphrasis is complementary to the spatial, territorial expression of
competition found in the Milky Way ecphrasis, for it provides a narrative
parallel to Jupiter's enthroning within an Apolline space.

While the Milky Way ecphrasis seeks to make a statement about ground-
ing Ovid's epic within its historical reality, creating an atmospheric link
between the defining landscape of Rome and its visual display of an espe-
cially Roman power, the ecphrasis of the palace of the Sun instead grounds
Ovid's epic within the illustrious epic tradition. Along these lines, Barbara
Weiden Boyd has illuminated the many ways that the narrative of Phaethon
relies upon the *Odyssey* as an intertext, with Telemachus acting as a model
for Phaethon.[8] However, Knox states of the ecphrasis, "Ovid's sun palace
has no psychological connection with the experience of Phaethon, who
does not even pause to consider it."[9] Although Peter Knox details the many
literary models (both Greek and Roman) for this ecphrasis, there is one
model for Ovid's sun-palace that has gone unnoticed: Telemachus' awe-
struck assessment of Menelaus' palace in *Odyssey* 4.

> φράζεο, Νεστορίδη, τῷ ἐμῷ κεχαρισμένε θυμῷ,
> χαλκοῦ τε στεροπὴν κὰδ δώματα ἠχήεντα

Divining Praise 51

χρυσοῦ τ᾽ ἠλέκτρου τε καὶ ἀργύρου ἠδ᾽ ἐλέφαντος.
Ζηνός που τοιήδε γ᾽ Ὀλυμπίου ἔνδοθεν αὐλή,
ὅσσα τάδ᾽ ἄσπετα πολλά· σέβας μ᾽ ἔχει εἰσορόωντα.

(Hom. Od. 4.71–75)

[Look, son of Nestor, obliging my wishes,
and see the flash of bronze ringing throughout the halls,
the gleams of gold, electrum, silver, and ivory.
This hall's interior is of the sort that must belong to Olympian Zeus,
in all its unutterable plenty: majestic awe holds me, beholding.]

Both descriptions are dominated by a list of precious metals and their dazzling visual effect: the Ovidian palace of the Sun shimmers from a combination of gold, *pyropus* (either a bronze and gold alloy, or a reddish bronze), ivory, and silver, while the Homeric Menelaus' palace flashes with bronze, gold, electrum, silver, and ivory. Ovid emphasizes the active, permeating nature of the palace's metallic gleam (*micante, flammasque imitante, nitidum, radiabant*), while Telemachus' wondrous awe is expressed by his breathless enumeration of four materials within the same line (*Od.* 4.73). The word of illumination Homer uses (στεροπή) is most associated with the flash of lightning, and therefore appropriate for a hall Telemachus deems reflective of Olympian Zeus.[10] Ovid therefore borrows the metallic materiality of the palace Telemachus thinks is worthy of Zeus, but instead, makes it the palace of the Sun, an aspect of Apolline divinity.[11] Finding the Sun in "Zeus'" palace visually redresses the power shift of seeing Jupiter in Apollo's Palatine seat. Ovid underscores this exchange of divine territory by exploiting the gods' shared aspect of brightness, emblematized by the lightning-bolt of Jupiter and the light itself of the sun.[12] Within the context of the Ovidian myth, the overlapping of the terminology of brilliance also prepares for the moment of ultimate showdown between the light of the Sun and Jupiter's lightning bolt, as the Sun's out-of-control chariot is curbed by a use of the lightning bolt. Ovid acknowledges the shared space of divine identity but firmly enthrones Sol in a palace visually and materially indebted to one Telemachus states as embodying the glory of Zeus.

The shared set of precious metals firmly link these two descriptions, but Ovid also marks his poetic debt to Homer by receptively adapting Telemachus' experience of his dazzling surroundings into his specific mode of narrative framing. Telemachus begins his speech to Nestor's son with the imperative of φράζω, the root verb that gives us *ecphrasis* (ἐκφράζω; ἔκφρασις). He subsequently ends his speech with his sense of marvel, as typically accompanies an ecphrasis (σέβας μ' ἔχει εἰσορόωντα, "majestic awe holds me, beholding," *Od.* 4.75). Ovid transforms Telemachus' description into an actual ecphrasis. As such, Telemachus' psychological response to the majesty of his surroundings is responsible for Ovid's use of ecphrasis; recognition of the Homeric intertext therefore provides the psychological connection Knox deems missing. The ecphrasis of Sol's palace offers a pendant to the Milky Way ecphrasis by countering the replacement of Apollo with Jupiter with Sol in a palace literarily assigned to Zeus. Although the dramatic incursion of Jupiter into Apollo's Palatine space has occasioned plenty of commentary, Ovid's balancing act in the opening of *Metamorphoses* 2, accomplished more subtly through literary (rather than topographical) means, has garnered no corresponding attention. It is significant for understanding the persistent relationship of rivalry Ovid builds between Jupiter and Apollo, and specifically how space and territory are used and manipulated to reveal that relationship.

Jupiter and Arcadia

As we can see from these ecphrases and their reciprocal sense of divine space and belonging, Ovid's strategy for constructing competition and power-play between Jupiter and Apollo rests significantly on the concept of location—or, more accurately, dislocation. It is with this strategic lens in mind that we can begin to approach in more detail the question of the relationship between Jupiter and Arcadia and begin to further assess Ovid's diversion of praise away from the epic king of the gods at the poem's outset. Ultimately, I suggest that the rivalry Ovid sets up between Jupiter and Apollo, another iteration of a struggle for praise, primacy, and control, explains the displacement and postponement of the Arcadian landscape as a place of mythological prominence in the opening of the epic. Arcadia is a region of great importance to the god, as is well known within material that creates Jupiter's mythological identity. Consequently, Ovid's tampering with Arcadian myth can be extended interpretively to act as a tampering with Jupiter himself, together with his importance and identity. In short, the Ovidian refusal to grant Arcadia epic prominence can be read as resistance to praising Jupiter. Tracing this resistance represents a new understanding of Ovid's relationship to imperial power, and can reshape thinking about how Ovid

Divining Praise 53

uses hymns, the traditional texts of praise, to communicate his discomfort with navigating the ever-encroaching concept of imperial praise. In this light, Arcadia also bears significance for Ovid and Augustus in a different way. If we look to the new standard for Roman epic set by Virgil, we can see that when Virgil incorporates the Arcadian figure of Evander into his epic with especial innovative attention and designates him to give Aeneas the tour of early Rome (and therefore, access to a Roman future), he functionally crafts Arcadia as an imaginative antecedent to Rome.[13] Receptively picking up on this Virgilian configuration, Ovid frequently presses Arcadia into service as an idealized proto-Rome within the *Fasti*.[14] Ovid's abundant use of Arcadian myth in the *Fasti* indicates that the program of observable postponement and suppression of Arcadian importance in the *Metamorphoses* is part of a work-specific agenda. The appearances of Arcadian myth within the epic's first book, and crucially, within its first programmatic love episode, have not been systematically tackled or explored in any way that can illuminate Ovid's poetic purpose to a consistent degree. One aim for this chapter is to provide a reading that explains Ovid's treatment of Jupiter as focalized through Arcadian myth. I suggest that there is a literary logic to Ovid's resistance to presenting a continuous Arcadian suite of myth within the epic's first book, a resistance that he encodes within the choices he *does* make with how his narrative proceeds, both mythologically and geographically. This comprehensive geographical inquiry reinforces the consistent and competitive parallels drawn between Jupiter and Apollo that are also circumscribed by territorial concerns.

With this in mind, we can now turn to examining the opening appearances of Jupiter and Arcadia in the *Metamorphoses*, and how they build a sense of epic identity. As briefly detailed in the previous chapter, Jupiter first appears to the reader as a name in Ovid's description of the Golden Age. Acorns from "his" tree provided nourishment for the first humans (*et quae deciderant patula Iouis arbore glandes*, "and the acorns which had fallen from Jupiter's spreading tree," 1.106), before his reign over the earth officially begins (1.113–14).[15] The first myth Jupiter directly appears in is the tale of Lycaon, the Arcadian king who dishonours the god by attempting to serve him a human sacrifice. Jupiter himself narrates the story of Lycaon, his misdeeds, and his punishment and transformation to the assembled council of the gods, using Lycaon's actions exemplarily to indicate the wickedness of the human race and to call for their destruction. His narration says just as much about himself as it does about Lycaon. As Jupiter begins the narrative of Lycaon's misdeeds to the assembled gods, he describes himself with an assertion of absolute kingship: *qui fulmen, qui uos habeoque regoque* ("[I] who possess the lightning bolt, and both have and rule you," 1.197).[16] Such a forceful assertion is soon juxtaposed with his relating that the signs of his divinity he provides to Lycaon give insufficient proof, and the Lycaon himself proceeds to perform his own test of divine veracity. What were these signs? Thunder and lightning? An eagle? In short, something that would identify Jupiter *as* Jupiter? Lycaon's mistrust of divine appearances is further complicated by the descriptive mechanisms of the narrative's framing, where the gods are deliberately compared to Roman senators (1.199–205). This characterization makes further explicit the Romanization of the space of heavens begun earlier in the narrative, culminating with the phrase "Heaven's Palatine" (1.168–76). The gods, unsettlingly, are depicted as performing within a political and behavioral context that is recognizably *human*.[17] Jupiter's self-identification as a king, confirmed by the later use of *rex superum*, provides a point of dissonance within this context. An assertion of kingship understandably clashes with the Romanized presentation of the gods participating in a senatorial assembly. The narrative commitment to presenting Jupiter as a king is critical, for it represents one acknowledgment of his stereotypical mythological role, preserving a crucial aspect of his divine identity. It is also noteworthy given Lycaon's response to the god's appearance.[18] At this early stage in the epic, and after Jupiter's own proclamations of kingship, the Arcadian king's refusal to acknowledge Jupiter as a god baldly problematizes a dictum of Jupiter's divinity and responsibility that is both mythologically defining and literarily programmatic: that kings come from Zeus, stated by the famous Hesiodic dictum and subsequently quoted by Callimachus in his *Hymn to Zeus* (ἐκ δὲ Διὸς βασιλῆες, "kings come from Zeus," Hes. *Theog.* 96; cf. Callim. *Hymn* 1.79).[19] Hymning Zeus is an act that functionally inaugurates one strand of the hexameter epic tradition, if, as Alexander Kirichenko suggests, the *Theogony* and *Works and Days* are read as a sequential, continuous hymn to Zeus: leading the audience through the generation of a world from chaos, and the succession myth that sees Zeus impose a new order of justice and harmony.[20] Ovid's tale of Lycaon does little to establish Jupiter as a truly powerful guarantor of justice.[21] William Anderson notes the details of his "divine clumsiness and inelegance," a phrase stopping just short of calling it "incompetence."[22] One corroborating detail is the fact that Jupiter's lightning-bolt destroys Lycaon's palace, but not Lycaon himself (*ego uindice flamma / in domino dignos euerti tecta Penates*, "with my punishing bolt I overturned the house upon its household gods, deserving of such a master," 1.230–31). Jupiter's later statement of *occidit una domus* ("one house has fallen," 1.240) then must be taken literally, rather than metaphorically, as Lycaon still lives on, as a wolf. Hardly the avenging weapon one might expect from Jupiter.

Questioning Jupiter's position within the space of Ovid's epic is further prompted by Lycaon's role as an Arcadian king (1.218). Within this episode, there is no direct mention of Arcadia as a region sacred to Jupiter. The narrator does not contextualize Jupiter's visit to this region as one that stems from especial care and concern.[23] Arcadia's sanctity to the king of the gods is both literarily and mythologically commonplace (not to mention archaeologically verifiable); Ovid's elision of geographical affiliation stands out. The narratorial failure to draw attention to this special relationship within the Lycaon episode could lead readers to assume that Ovid here implicitly endorses the mythological version of Jupiter's birth in Crete, rather than Arcadia.[24] However, the prior use of the oak and its acorns to introduce Jupiter unsettles this assumption. By using the gentle periphrasis of *Iouis arbor* instead of *quercus* or *aesculus*, Ovid wants a connection to be made between the god and the primitive diet of acorns. The region and people distinguished by this diet are the Arcadians.[25] An oracular epithet quoted by Herodotus calls the Arcadians "acorn-eaters" (βαλανηφάγοι, Hdt. 1.66.2); according to Apollonius, at one time "only Apidanian Arcadians existed, Arcadians who are said to have lived before the moon existed, eating acorns in the mountains" (Ap. Rhod. *Argon.* 4.263–65). In the *Fasti*, as he explains the origins of the Lupercal, Ovid relates that the land is not only said to be older than the moon, but to predate Jupiter: *ante Iouem genitum terras habuisse feruntur / Arcades, et luna gens prior illa fuit* ("tradition holds that the Arcadians held the lands before the birth of Jove, and that their people are older than the moon," *Fast.* 2.289–90; cf. also *luna credita terra prior*, "a land believed pre-lunar," *Fast.* 5.90). The pre-lunar ancientness of Arcadia is an enduring detail of its mythology, while the acorn is not only a staple of their mytho-historical diet, but a known emblem.[26] Ovid's seemingly anachronistic designation of the oak as belonging to Jupiter is made more sensible by imaginatively layering an Arcadian context upon the Golden Age imagery. The very fact that by the chronological standard of the text,

56 Divining Praise

the tree ostensibly exists "before the birth of Jupiter" and yet is still called "Jupiter's," seems designed to be parsed by the knowledge of Arcadian myth (perhaps specifically from the *Fasti*), and therefore, to connect the metaphorical "birth of Jupiter," his first appearance within the *Metamorphoses*, with Arcadia. And yet, why such subtlety in establishing a relationship between Jupiter and Arcadia?

JUPITER AND ARCADIAN WATERS

To return to a literary origin point of this affiliation, we can see that hymns play a crucial role. In the extant tradition, Callimachus poetically pioneers the Arcadian birth for Zeus, opening his hymn with a question about how to appropriately hymn the god:[27]

> πῶς καί νιν, Δικταῖον ἀείσομεν ἠὲ Λυκαῖον;
> ἐν δοιῇ μάλα θυμός, ἐπεὶ γένος ἀμφήριστον.
>
> (Callim. *Hymn* 1.4–5)

> [But how shall we hymn him, as Dictaean or Lycaean?
> My heart is in doubt, for the birth is contested. (trans. Stephens)]

Callimachus' question is framed geographically: should Zeus be called "Dictaean" (Cretan) or "Lycaean" (Arcadian), actively modifying tradition. His Zeus is intimately tied with the Arcadian landscape in ways that merit some prolonged focus. After the hymnist introduces his poetic theme (*Hymn* 1.1–9), he gives a detailed picture of the Arcadian landscape, and the geomorphic changes wrought by the birth of the god:

> ἐν δέ σε Παρρασίῃ Ῥείη τέκεν, ᾗχι μάλιστα
> ἔσκεν ὄρος θάμνοισι περισκεπές· ἔνθεν ὁ χῶρος
> ἱερός, οὐδέ τί μιν κεχρημένον Εἰλειθυίης
> ἑρπετὸν οὐδὲ γυνὴ ἐπιμίσγεται, ἀλλὰ ἑ Ῥείης
> ὠγύγιον καλέουσι λεχώϊον Ἀπιδανῆες.
> ἔνθα σ᾽ ἐπεὶ μήτηρ μεγάλων ἀπεθήκατο κόλπων,
> αὐτίκα δίζητο ῥόον ὕδατος, ᾧ κε τόκοιο
> λύματα χυτλώσαιτο τεὸν δ᾽ ἐνὶ χρῶτα λοέσσαι.
> Λάδων ἀλλ᾽ οὔπω μέγας ἔρρεεν οὐδ᾽ Ἐρύμανθος,
> λευκότατος ποταμῶν, ἔτι δ᾽ ἄβροχος ἦεν ἅπασα

Divining Praise

57

Ἀζηνίς· μέλλεν δὲ μάλ' εὔυδρος καλέεσθαι
αὖτις· ἐπεὶ τημόσδε, Ῥέη ὅτε λύσατο μίτρην,
ἦ πολλὰς ἐφύπερθε σαρωνίδας ὑγρὸς Ἰάων
ἤειρεν, πολλὰς δὲ Μέλας ὤκχησεν ἀμάξας,
πολλὰ δὲ Καρνίωνος ἄνω διεροῦ περ ἐόντος
ἰλυοὺς ἐβάλοντο κινώπετα, νίσσετο δ' ἀνὴρ
πεζὸς ὑπὲρ Κρᾶθίν τε πολύστιόν τε Μετώπην
διψαλέος· τὸ δὲ πολλὸν ὕδωρ ὑπὸ ποσσὶν ἔκειτο.
καί ῥ' ὑπ' ἀμηχανίης σχομένη φάτο πότνια Ῥείη·
"Γαῖα φίλη, τέκε καὶ σύ· τεαὶ δ' ὠδῖνες ἐλαφραί."
εἶπε καὶ ἀντανύσασα θεὴ μέγαν ὑψόθι πῆχυν
πλῆξεν ὄρος σκήπτρῳ τὸ δέ οἱ δίχα πουλὺ διέστη,
ἐκ δ' ἔχεεν μέγα χεῦμα·

(Callim. *Hymn* 1.10–32)

[In Parrhasia Rhea bore you, where the mountain was especially dense with thickets. Afterwards the place was sacred; nothing in need of Eileithyia, neither crawling thing nor woman approaches it, but the Apidaneans call it the primeval childbed of Rhea. From the moment when your mother produced you from her great womb, immediately she searched for a stream of water in which she might cleanse the afterbirth, and therein might wash your body. But the mighty Ladon was not yet flowing nor was the Erymanthus, the whitest of waters, and the whole of Azenis was not yet irrigated. But thereafter it was to be called well irrigated. For at the time when Rhea loosened her sash, the watery Iaon bore many oaks above it, and the Melas provided a course for many wagons, many serpents made their lair above the Carnion (although it is now wet), and a man was accustomed to walk upon the Crathis and the stony Metope, thirsty. But abundant water lay under his feet. In the grip of helplessness, lady Rhea spoke: "Dear Gaia, you too give birth; your birth pangs are light." She spoke and the goddess, lifting up her great arm, struck the hill with her staff; it was split wide apart for her and a great stream of water poured forth. (trans. Stephens)]

Callimachus' account of Zeus' birth is dense with aetiological learning and etymological play that especially serves to highlight the relationships between the god and water, and water and Arcadia. His recherché designation of the Arcadians as Ἀπιδανῆες (1.14) and Arcadia as Ἀζηνίς (1.20) links the region's lack of water with the absence of the god. Within these designators, the implicit presences of ἀ-πίνειν / ἀ-πῖδαξ ("undrinking" or "springless") and ἀ-Ζήν ("Zeusless," and by extension, "lifeless," with the etymologizing of the *Cratylus* and Chrysippus[28]) or ἀζαίνειν ("to dry up, parch") give an etymologically encoded portrait of the landscape's deprivation.[29] The linguistically expressed lack of water is also complemented by the set of plays upon Ῥείη/Ῥέη and ῥέω ("to flow, stream"), with ῥόον ὕδατος (1.16) and ἔρρεεν (1.18): the goddess with the flowing name, ironically, cannot find a stream in which to bathe her newborn.[30] As Neil Hopkinson further notes, Ῥεία is also etymologized via metathesis from ἔρα ("ground"), and thus "Ῥεα = ἔρα = γαῖα = Γαῖα," an equivalence between goddesses Callimachus depicts in line 32, when a stream of water gushes forth (ἐκ δ' ἔχεεν) after Rhea addresses Gaia (l. 29) and strikes the earth.[31] Kirichenko detects a further etymological note in the birth of this new water source: noting not just etymological equivocations between Rhea and the earth, but specifically the earth that produces water (according to Chrysippus) and the earth and water as primary elements (as in Pherecydes), he suggests that the Callimachean phrasing ἐκ δ' ἔχεεν μέγα χεῦμα also alludes to the tradition of deriving Chaos, in an understanding as the "original water," from χεῖσθαι.[32] Through this etymological play, Callimachus crafts an allegorical layer of meaning within his narrative of Zeus' birth: he also makes it a narrative of the earth producing water.[33] Zeus' birth from Rhea therefore holds the hint of a return of a watery chaos, in an image that renovates the Hesiodic concept of Chaos as a chasm or abyss.

This bears some significance for the narrative choices Ovid has made. Within the *Metamorphoses*, Ovid's use of Jupiter's flood as a new agent of Chaos—of returning the newly ordered cosmos to an originative, watery state—gains significance given this Callimachean account of Zeus' origins. Jupiter's return of the world to a watery chaos becomes more readily parsed through remembrance of his Callimachean birth, lending his actions a logic of literary pedigree. The Ovidian humor and irony is still present in the episode, but assumes a further depth with this awareness, as the Ovidian Jupiter discards the paradoxical remembrance (*reminiscitur*, 1.256) of a fiery future, in favor of a more diffuse remembrance in the (literary) past, of his own "chaotic," watery birth. Not only is this a watery, "chaotic" birth, it is also an Arcadian birth.

Peneus and Thessaly vs. Jupiter and Arcadia

The Ovidian flood is only one point of contact with the hymnic narrative of Zeus' birth in Callimachus' *Hymn to Zeus*. More prolonged subversion comes in the form of displacement: rather than relate the geomorphic transformation of the Arcadian landscape in a way that honors Jupiter, Ovid instead sketches out a poetic topography of a new region in honor of Apollo, in a fashion that borrows from the Callimachean narrative of praise. To understand this displacement, a brief rehearsal of the narrative progression of the first book is required.

Ovid's disjunctive play with geography is not as well remarked as his disjunctive play with narrative, although the two are difficult to disentangle. As previously recounted, Lycaon's lupine metamorphosis (the first of the epic, and one narrated by Jupiter from his seat on Heaven's Palatine) takes place in Arcadia, the Callimachean birthplace of the god. According to Jupiter's travelogue, the Arcadian landscape is not marked by water, but mountains and forests (*Maenala transieram latebris horrenda ferarum / et cum Cyllene gelidi pineta Lycaei*, "I had traversed Maenalus, shiversome with its lairs of beasts, and the pine-woods of cold Lycaeus, along with Cyllene," 1.216–17).[34] Lycaon's misdeeds provide the justification for the flood, which leads to the narrative of repopulation, culminating in the generation of earth-born creatures such as the Python, whose death at the hands of Apollo segues into the myth of Apollo and Daphne. Apollo and Daphne's tale transitions to the metamorphosis of Io (with the inset narrative of Syrinx); Io's tale leads into Phaethon's, which eventually gives way to the Arcadian narrative of Callisto's transformation—Callisto, the daughter of Lycaon. This brief overview of the narratives that entwine to form the first book and a half of the epic immediately reveals one important thing: Ovid is not relying on genealogy to forge epic continuity. But what of geography? Is geographical continuity a tool of narrative progression or transition? The concern that Jupiter expresses for Arcadia's well-being after Phaethon's destruction is almost ostentatious in its novelty, revealing for the first time any explicit special relationship between the region and god (2.401–8). Given the parallels between world destruction by flood and fire, and the opportunity for the reader to supply Phaethon's future conflagration as Jupiter's "remembrance" of a world aflame when he ponders how to punish humankind, Jupiter's seemingly belated concern for Arcadia invites curiosity or suspicion about

60 Divining Praise

the geographical contours of Book 1 after the flood, especially given the Callimachean context recently discussed.

With this narrative picture in mind, we can now look more specifically into the motivations and modality of Ovid's mythological settings. The geographical disruption from Arcadia that comes into light with the tale of Apollo and Daphne is, by all known accounts, specifically engineered by Ovid: he purposefully denies a geographical continuity to Book 1. Such a denial is crafted when he makes the nymph Daphne not a daughter of the Ladon (the river that begins the Callimachean catalog of Arcadian water sources, l.18), as commonly dictated by mythological tradition, but a daughter of the Thessalian river god Peneus.[35] Her new identity as a Thessalian nymph (a point of focus continued in the following chapter) is emphasized by persistent use of the patronymic (*Daphne Peneia*, 1.452; *nympha Peneide*, 1.472; *Penei*, 1.504; *Peneia*, 1.525). If Ovid's departure from geographical tradition causes readers to look for other sources of mythological continuity, it is soon made apparent that genealogy too will be an unreliable source, for Ovid's Daphne wishes to preserve her virginity:

> saepe pater dixit "generum mihi, filia, debes";
> saepe pater dixit "debes mihi, nata, nepotes."
> illa uelut crimen taedas exosa iugales
> pulchra uerecundo suffunditur ora rubore,
> inque patris blandis haerens ceruice lacertis
> "da mihi perpetua, genitor carissime," dixit
> "uirginitate frui; dedit hoc pater ante Dianae."
>
> (*Met.* 1.481–87)

> [Often her father said, "you owe me a son-in-law, daughter";
> often her father said, "you owe me offspring, child."
> But she, hating marriage torches, tantamount to crime,
> her pleasing face overpoured with a charming blush
> and clinging to her father's neck with coaxing arms,
> said "grant me the allowance of perpetual virginity, dearest father!
> Her father granted this previously to Diana."]

Peneus' repeated statements of Daphne's debt of descendants shows a humorous internal awareness of the Ovidian refusal to rely upon genealogy

Divining Praise 61

to forge epic continuity. However, it is not Peneus' wish but Daphne's plea that proves more revealing. Her first words in the epic are borrowed from the Callimachean Artemis, who prays to her father to remain a maiden for perpetuity (δός μοι παρθενίην αἰώνιον, ἄππα, φυλάσσειν, "grant me the preservation of eternal maidenhood, daddy," Callim. *Hymn* 3.6).[36] Daphne's own plea to the Peneus replicates the desires of the Callimachean Artemis (*"da mihi perpetua, genitor carissime" dixit / "uirginitate frui; dedit hoc pater ante Dianae,"* 1.486–87).[37] Daphne's reproduction of Artemis' prayer to Zeus unambiguously styles Peneus as a Zeus-type, and does so by using the framework of Callimachean quotation. The presence of a Zeus-like figure within the myth, and one who thwarts Apollo's desires, preserves a strain of the competitive tension between the two gods Ovid sets up by "locating" Jupiter in Apollo's most prominent place of worship. Peneus' identity as a Zeus-like figure shifts into greater focus simultaneous to the geographical anchoring of the tale within Thessaly:

> Est nemus Haemoniae, praerupta quod undique claudit
> silua; uocant Tempe. per quae Peneos ab imo
> effusus Pindo spumosis uoluitur undis
> deiectuque graui tenues agitantia fumos
> nubila conducit summisque aspergine siluis
> impluit et sonitu plus quam uicina fatigat.
> haec domus, haec sedes, haec sunt penetralia magni
> amnis; in his residens facto de cautibus antro
> undis iura dabat nymphisque colentibus undas.
> conueniunt illuc popularia flumina primum,
> nescia gratentur consolenturne parentem,
> populifer Sperchios et inrequietus Enipeus
> Apidanosque senex lenisque Amphrysos et Aeas,
> moxque amnes alii qui, qua tulit impetus illos,
> in mare deducunt fessas erroribus undas.

(*Met.* 1.568–82)

> [There is a grove of Thessaly, which on all sides
> steep forest hems in: they call it Tempe, through which
> the Peneus, wide-flowing, is unfurled with foaming waves,
> and casting out vapor tendrils in its steep drop,

62 Divining Praise

gathers cloud-cover and fills the treetops with spray
and wears out more than his surroundings with his roar.
Here are the home, the seats, the innermost sanctum of the great river,
presiding in a cave carved out from these rough crags,
where he customarily dispenses laws to his waters, to the nymphs dwelling
   there.
They gathered there, the ordinary, constituent rivers, first;
they are unsure whether to congratulate or console the father,
poplar-bearing Spercheus and restless Enipeus,
and ancient Apidanus and mild Amphrysus and Aeas,
and soon other rivers, who, where their force carries them,
in winding ways lead their weary waves down into the sea.]

This landscape description of Tempe is the first formal, prolonged land-
scape ecphrasis of the poem. Often, due to its narrative position, it is dis-
missed as a simple narrative bridge between the tales of Daphne and Io.[38]
Not much has been made of this passage beyond perfunctory statements
of its transitional purpose, and so, no real consequence has been identi-
fied from the rerooting of Daphne's tale within a specifically Thessalian
landscape, and the rerouting of the Ladon to make way for the Peneus. In
reading this passage as merely transitional, it is also easy to miss certain
similarities it holds to the Milky Way digression. These echoes are first cued
by the simple yet strong structural resemblance: the *est . . .* formula (*est
nemus Haemoniae; est uia sublimis*), followed by the specific place naming
(*uocant Tempe; Lactea nomen habet*). The spatial enumeration of constitu-
ent places also descriptively aligns the two passages (*haec domus, haec sedes,
haec sunt penetralia magni / amnis; hac iter est . . . hac parte . . . hic locus
est*), and the use of *penetralia* evokes the appearance of *Penates* among the
Olympian gods. Peneus' realm therefore appears as an earthbound version
of the Milky Way, and Peneus himself a counterpart to Jupiter. The river
god fulfils a role akin to Jupiter's convening of the gods in council, dispens-
ing laws to his constituents (*undis iura dabat nymphisque colentibus undas*);
the rivers all meet (*conueniunt*) as the gods gather in the house of Jupiter.[39]
The phrase *nubila conducit* also glosses the Homeric designator "Cloud-
Gatherer" (νεφεληγερέτα Ζεύς), a metrically expedient formula applied to
Zeus, commonly before the god makes a speech. The hierarchy of heaven
briefly explored in the Milky Way passage is also mirrored here: in the Milky

Way's masquerade as the Roman *Via Sacra*, Ovid includes the detail *plebs habitat diuersa locis* ("lesser gods live elsewhere," 1.173), a phrase that stands as a small intertextual echo of Ovid's account of the creation of the rivers:[40]

> addidit et fontes et stagna immensa lacusque,
> fluminaque obliquis cinxit decliuia ripis;
> quae diuersa locis partim sorbentur ab ipsa,
> in mare perueniunt partim campoque recepta
> liberioris aquae pro ripis litora pulsant.
>
> <div align="right">(<i>Met.</i> 1.38–42)</div>

> [And he integrated both the springs and spreading pools and lakes,
> and shelved sloping rivers with sloping banks,
> some of which, distributed widely, are drunk in by the earth
> and some of which make their way into the sea,
> and welcomed by the open expanse of water, make their rhythms
> against the shore, rather than banks.]

The admission of *plebs habitat diuersa locis*, with such an internal echo of the descriptive locating of rivers previous in the book, further links the two ecphrases. The designation of the rivers as *popularia* also reproduces the hierarchy seen in the heavens, and the difference drawn between Jupiter and the plebeian gods: Peneus appears to the "ordinary" rivers (cf. *OLD popularis*, s.v. 1c; for the political sense, s.v. 3) in his cave as Jupiter does to the lesser gods. Jupiter and the Peneus and the constituent gods and rivers can therefore be construed as reflective dualities. The parallel between the two passages is further seen with awareness of Jupiter's admission that there are rustic divinities not granted the honor of heaven; these are the beings who are being endangered by the impious events occurring on earth, of which Lycaon's transgression stands as the illustrative exemplar (1.192–95). Peneus' evocation of Jupiter not only looks back to the depiction of Heaven's domain and hierarchy, but the convening of rivers is also situationally reminiscent of the flood, recalling Neptune's summonses at the behest of Jupiter (*conuocat hic amnes*, "he summons the rivers," 1.276). Their eventual flow to the sea (*in mare deducunt fessas erroribus undas*) not only recalls their creation (see the passage above, *in mare perueniunt*) but repeats a critical, programmatic word of the proem (*deductum*; cf. *deducite*, 1.4). The

64 Divining Praise

compressed echoes of these previous narrative events and proemial language give this passage a more entrenched significance that is lost when its primary purpose is identified as transitional.[41]

The illustration of Tempe also includes a common epic feature that is curiously absent from the previous events of cosmogony and flood. This absence is more marked, given the ways the Tempe ecphrasis reflects scenes of the cosmogony and flood. Neither the creation of the rivers nor the flood, relying on their cumulative force, leads to a catalog of rivers. Ovid resists such a narrative opportunity until this very passage. The rivers are convened first as an audience to reflect on the recent event of Daphne's transformation: *conueniunt illuc popularia flumina primum, / nescia gratentur consolenturne parentem* ("they gathered there, the ordinary, constituent rivers, first; / they are unsure whether to congratulate or console the father, 1.577–78). In effect, this lends a second moment of closure to the myth of Apollo and Daphne. The rivers become the first to internally "read," or process, the event of Daphne's metamorphosis, which grants them a special status. The rivers are only named after this qualification of their visit to Peneus: they are the Sperchios, Enipeus, Apidanus, Amphrysus, and Aeas.[42] Why would Ovid be motivated to include a river catalog here, instead of either in the narratives of the cosmogony or flood? And why is it so localized? The answer lies with the Callimachean catalog of Arcadian rivers that leads into the birth of Zeus in the *Hymn to Zeus*. When Ovid moves the tale of Apollo and Daphne from Arcadia to Thessaly, disrupting the geographical continuity of his epic, he preserves the prominence of the landscape within the Callimachean *Hymn to Zeus*, by recreating it as Thessalian. The Thessalian river catalog, presided over by a figure resembling Zeus, replaces the enumeration of Arcadian water sources that arise with the birth of the god, as narrated in the *Hymn to Zeus*. Before we can explain the overarching interpretive significance and benefit of this relocation, some observations about the two catalogs will help illuminate the poetic intricacies at work and build to the cumulative effect. These observations rest on teasing out geographical and allusive complexities, and so, require quite a granular focus.

OVID'S THESSALIAN RIVER CATALOG AND THE CALLIMACHEAN *HYMN TO ZEUS*

There is much to be gained from assessing these two river catalogs jointly. Peneus himself as the *magnus amnis* ("great river," *Met.* 1.574–75) provides the analogue to Ladon as the Λάδων . . . μέγας ("great Ladon," *Hymn* 1.18). Both catalogs are arranged with attention to balance and juxtaposition. Within the *Hymn to Zeus*, Hopkinson points out two oppositional pairs: the color contrast between the Erymanthus, "whitest of rivers," and "black" Melas, and the bodily juxtaposition wrought by the image of a man crossing on foot rivers whose names indicate the head and brow.[43] These contrasts are both created etymologically. There is also a descriptive balance between the static, natural imagery of the oaks that grow above the Iaon and the snake-lairs found above the Carnion interwoven with the movement of man, in both wagon-courses across the future Melas and on foot, across the Crathis and Metope. Overall, Callimachus makes a contrast through opposition and polarity. He emphasizes the overarching juxtaposition between dry and wet, and the creation of the life-bringing waters simultaneous to the birth of the god.

Although similarly grounded in etymological play, the contrast in the Ovidian passage is more bound to rhythmic energy. As Stratis Kyriakidis stresses, catalogs traditionally follow a pattern of correlative increase between density of names and speed. However, Ovid's qualifying adjectives and use of etymological play flout this convention. In the line where only two rivers are named (Sperchios and Enipeus, 1.579) there is a dimension of speed and movement. This is first directly communicated by the adjective *inrequietus* ("restless"), and second, implicitly packaged into the etymologizing of the rivers' names: Enipeus from ἐνιπή (or ἡ ἀπειλή), "threat," and Sperchios from σπέρχω, "to make haste." In contrast, the following line contains three river names (Apidanus, Amphrysus, and Aeas, 1.580). Therefore, it (technically) contains greater rhythmic momentum—and yet, it is proportionally slowed by the specifications of *senex* and *lenis*, an attenuation of movement compounded by the further use of *fessas* to describe the motion of the rivers toward the sea.[44] Kyriakidis reads the resultant disconnect between form and content as a tension between tradition and innovation, with Ovid putting his own novel touch on the epic staple of the catalog. This may well be the case, but the conflict of rhythm that emerges also leads to a mood of natural confusion: a mood that illustrates the rivers' expressed uncertainty regarding the appropriate response to Daphne's transformation in the lines directly preceding the catalog: *flumina . . . nescia gratentur consolenturne parentem*, ("the rivers, unsure whether to congratulate or console the father," 1.577–78). The competing notions of speed and slowing in the motion of the catalogued streams paints a picture of hesitation in accordance with their status as unknowing (*nescia*). Their role as the internal "readers" of Daphne's metamorphosis is subtly reinforced.

Returning to Arcadia, we can observe that Callimachus' river catalog is qualified by geographically descriptive nuance in a way that reveals the complexity of its construction.[45] At first glance, the catalog shows an extreme regionality and reconditeness; only upon a full reading does it become clear how geography informs the progression of the hymn. However, a rigor of regional specificity becomes mediated by the prismatic quality of the adjective ἄβροχος (*Hymn* 1.19). Meaning "rainless, moistureless," and describing the overall Arcadian landscape, it prepares for the following play on Ἀζηνίς and ἀ-Ζήν in the following line. Furthermore, it can remind readers of Zeus' celestial guise as a rain-giver, a guise that gives rivers the epithet of διιπετής ("fallen from Zeus"). However, ἄβροχος has a more narrowly focused regional meaning. Within Egyptian sources, it is used to refer to land that has remained untouched by the Nile inundation.[46] Arcadia, therefore, becomes imaginatively assimilated to Egypt, anticipating the eventual Alexandrian swerve of the hymn. The Egyptian resonance of this term is further underscored by awareness of Μέλας (one of the featured rivers) as an early name for the Nile (cf. Ps-Plut. *Fluv.* 16).[47] And although the technical meaning points to Egypt, the geographical reality of dryness points not to Peloponnesian Arcadia, but Cretan Arcadia. Scholars have identified Callimachus' play with a geographical overlap between Arcadia and Crete by his citation of Thenae (*Hymn* 1.42) at a transitional moment in the hymn; Thenae is a town name common to both regions. There was also a Cretan town called Arcadia, and this Cretan Arcadia was also characterized by a lack of water.[48] Along the lines of these overlapping data points, Elwira Kaczyńska hypothesizes that Callimachus' relocation of Zeus' birth from Crete to Arcadia is not an arbitrary transition to the mainland, but reveals a poetic debt to Epimenides. She suggests that Epimenides located the birth of the god in the cave of Arkalochori, in Cretan Arcadia. This decision consequentially shaped Callimachus' decision to preserve the location's name, but shift its geography, combining tradition and innovation.[49] This suggestion is appealing for several reasons, not least in the way it allows a bookending of the hymn's Arcadian episode with localities common to both Arcadia and Crete. Furthermore, it lends a dimension of practical logic to the poet's emphasis on the subterranean nature of the Arcadian rivers, as Callimachus illustrates

Peloponnesian Arcadia's lack of water in knowing solidarity with this feature of Cretan Arcadia. Callimachus' use of ἄβροχος therefore prismatically reflects, indicates, and anticipates each geographical region of importance to the hymn, as it fluidly moves from Arcadia to Crete to Alexandria.

Ovid's Thessalian river catalog displays similar multidirectional characteristics. As we have seen, the catalog looks back to the creation of the rivers, the flood, and the Milky Way ecphrasis. It also looks forward to the more comprehensive river catalog enfolded within the narrative of Phaethon (2.239–59). In particular, the adjective *populifer* ("poplar-bearing," in all likelihood an Ovidian coinage), which describes the Spercheus, also looks forward to the transformation of Phaethon's grieving sisters into poplars by the banks of the Eridanus, where Phaethon falls (2.340–66).[50] This anticipation is assisted by Ovid's use of *populifer* to describe the Eridanus at *Amores* 2.17.32, in its only other extant appearance.[51]

The Apidanus is the one river in the Ovidian catalog that makes a directly textual overture toward the Callimachean list. The river name recalls Callimachus' use of Apidaneans (Ἀπιδανῆες, *Hymn* 1.14) to denote the Arcadians, a name used for the earliest, pre-lunar Arcadians. The Ovidian Apidanus is *senex*, a designator in knowing accord with the Apidaneans' sense of antiquity.[52] The Amphrysus, following the Apidanus, returns the narrative briefly yet powerfully to an Apolline context. The Amphrysus was the mythological locale of Apollo's pasturing duties when he was in service to Admetus.[53] The Amphrysus' accompanying adjective, *lenis*, carries an air of elegiac softness appropriate for the version of the myth Callimachus features in his *Hymn to Apollo*, where the god's servitude is motivated not by punishment, but by love.[54] Aeas, the final river, is not strictly Thessalian (rather, it originates on a peak in the Pindus range, but flows in Epirus, on the other side). The Aeas alone stands unmodified by an adjective but provides further assonance in the line.

Streams of Praise: Honoring Arcadian Zeus

Now that we have closely read the catalogs together and observed their stylistic affiliations, we can turn to the greater contextual issues at hand that reinforce the significance of the Callimachean catalog and its symbolism to Ovid's narrative. Apart from the Apidanus, which can serve as a linguistic hinge between the two lists, the Callimachean and Ovidian river catalogs are united not by intertextuality, but by other types of poetic resonance and

68   Divining Praise

concern. The absence of overt intertextual affiliation makes connecting these two passages more difficult, but no less feasible, if the wider contextual aims of each passage are taken into appropriate consideration. The first task is to establish a wider literary purpose for Rhea's extended water-seeking narrative in the Callimachean hymn. The second task is to understand Ovid's repurposing of this hymnic material.

Within a hymn to Zeus, the prolonged emphasis on Rhea's search for water to bathe her newborn in the opening narrative commands some type of literary justification.[55] The focus on the god is elliptical at best, nonexistent at worst. It is not that the subject matter itself is out of place in a hymn; the narrative recalls the newborn Apollo's bath (*Hymn. Hom. Ap.* 119–20). However, while Apollo's bath is dedicated only two lines, the Callimachean passage dramatically expands the search for water to almost twenty, before Rhea's divining efforts come to a curt close with the unelaborated ἐκ δ' ἔχεεν μέγα χεῦμα ("a great stream flowed forth," *Hymn* 1.32).[56] If we avoid the easy (yet occasionally tempting) pitfall of attributing Callimachus' focus on Arcadian hydrology to a desire to flaunt knowledge and poetic preciousness, what good reasons are there to merit inclusion of this catalog? Brumbaugh has recently provided an extended reading of this passage that sheds light in clear, compelling ways on this very issue.[57] In his reading, this passage (*Hymn* 1.10–32) is not simply digressive, but integral to revealing the poet's purpose: it dramatizes metapoetically Callimachus' own search for appropriate praise poetry to honor the god.

To introduce his argument, Brumbaugh states, "Instead of praising the god—the stated topic of the hymn (ἀείδειν . . . θεὸν αὐτόν, 1.1–2)—the Rhea narrative reflects on the poet's encomiastic project by dramatizing the *aporia* asserted repeatedly in the hymn's opening . . . the account of Rhea's search for a stream provides a dramatic parallel for the search for excellent praise poetry in which the poet, like the goddess, is frustrated in his attempts."[58] The search for water as a metaphorical search for praise poetry is supported by the commonplace of water sources as symbolic for poetry and poetic inspiration within ancient sources. In particular, Brumbaugh situates Callimachus' Arcadia through oppositional reference to the *Theogony*, where Helicon's idyllic waterscape is a place identified by flowing water, and so, flowing song; a flowing song specifically envisioned as a song of praise.[59] Brumbaugh notes how Callimachus frames this metaphor of water as praise by using εὔυδρος ("well-watered," *Hymn* 1.20) to imaginatively summon the

Divining Praise   69

presence of εὔυμνος ("well-hymned"). This adjective features in the aporic opening(s) within the *Homeric Hymn to Apollo* (cf. 19, 207) that informs and inspires his own hymn's introduction (*Hymn* 1.1–7, esp. 4). Beyond the affiliated context of these passages in the *Homeric Hymn*, where the poet similarly assumes a pose of helplessness when faced with finding an appropriate way to praise a god who is already a recipient of much laudatory beneficence, Brumbaugh locates the appearance of εὔυμνος within the matrix of encomiastic language, especially seen in Pindar.

Pindar's own work persistently features thirst as a metaphorical sensation, a "thirst" for poetry, which additionally inflects the Callimachean use of διψαλέος (*Hymn* 1.27): the poet's "description of the man who went 'thirsty' across the dry future-river in a 'land without Zeus'" (Ἀζηνίς < ἀ-Ζήν) may suggest the paucity of poetic praise before Zeus' reign. After Zeus is born, Azenis will no longer be without Zeus, nor will it be without water or poetry. Reading the passage in the context of the poetological metaphor, we see that in the future Arkadia will be full of poets praising Zeus and the land itself will be the recipient of praise (e.g., Kallimachos' *Arkadia*)."[60] Callimachus' equivocation of water with praise poetry, given the borrowed Pindaric significance of poetic thirst, can also be used retrospectively to confirm a reading of the famed opening of *Olympian* 1, ἄριστον μὲν ὕδωρ ("water is best"), as metaphorical for song. Callimachus' further engagement with water's metapoetic status as song within his opening hymn would aptly acknowledge and confirm this programmatic meaning for Pindaric epinician.[61]

After knitting together the metaphorical equivalence of water and praise, symbolically expressed by the Arcadian landscape, Brumbaugh further notes how the carefully crafted, multifaceted juxtaposition between εὔυδρος and ἄβροχος strengthens this affiliation. He further suggests that if εὔυδρος can associatively assume the meaning of εὔυμνος, ἄβροχος would then indicate the contrary nature of "unsung." Brumbaugh therefore identifies the layers of metapoetic signification that amount to reading the stream Gaia produces, at Rhea's behest, as a poetic stream of praise. To a certain extent, this further collapses the boundaries between internal and external identity: the poet identifies with Rhea, in their joint *aporia*; Rhea produces the god to be praised, and Gaia produces the stream of praise, two figures further enmeshed by their joint identification. The overall result is a new, intensely literary dimensionality to the passage beyond its allegorical meaning: it simultaneously describes the project of the poet, "birthing" a song of praise

70 Divining Praise

for the god. Within this narrative, the god himself is created and an uncovering of means for his praise is simultaneously encoded.

WHO COMES FIRST, ZEUS OR APOLLO?

It is worth spending a little more time on the concept of praise experienced within the hymn, and its potential models within the hymnic tradition, as it will lead us into questions of hymnic primacy that are ultimately applied to the narrative situation of the *Metamorphoses*. The simultaneity of creation—of object of poetic praise, and means of poetic praise—embedded within this Callimachean passage appears pointed when considered alongside another example of the hymnic tradition: Pindar's first *Hymn*, a composition in honor of Thebes.[62] Although fragmentary, Choricius of Gaza records a summary of a portion of the Muses' song, putatively near its close (13.1; 175 Foerster-Richtsteig):

ἐποίησε Πίνδαρος καὶ θεοὺς ὀκνοῦντας ὑμνῆσαι τὰς τοῦ Διὸς εἰς ἀνθρώπους φιλοτιμίας. ἐδόκει γάρ, οἶμαι, τῷ ποιητῇ τοῦτο εἶναι μέγιστον ἐγκώμιον τοῦ Διός, εἰ μηδεὶς τῶν Ὀλυμπίων αὐτὸν ἐγκωμιάσαι τολμήσει. Τοιγαροῦν καθῆστο μὲν ὁ Ζεὺς τῷ Πινδάρῳ τὸ πᾶν ἄρτι κοσμήσας, παρῆσαν δὲ οἱ θεοὶ σιωπῇ τεθηπότες τὴν ἀγλαΐαν τῶν ὁρωμένων, ἐρομένου δὲ τοῦ Διός, εἴπερ ἄλλου του δέοιντο, ἓν ἔφασαν οἱ θεοὶ τοῖς ἐκείνου δημι-ουργήμασι λείπειν, ὅτι μηδένα προήγαγεν ἀναβαίνοντα ταῖς εὐφημίαις ἄχρι τοῦ μέτρου τῶν τελουμένων

[Pindar portrayed even the gods as reluctant to sing in praise of Zeus' benefactions towards humankind. I think it seemed to the poet that it would be the greatest praise of Zeus if none of the Olympians dared to praise him. So, for Pindar, Zeus sat, having just created the universe, and the gods stood before him in silence, amazed at the splendour of what was before their eyes. And when Zeus asked if they needed anything more, the gods said that one thing was lacking from his works of creation: he had not brought forth anybody who could step up to the measure of his accomplishments with words of devotion and praise. (trans. Prodi)[63]]

Self-evidently, Zeus' solution to the request of the gods is the creation of the Muses, who are the mouthpiece of this very hymn. The connections between this hymn and the *Theogony*, in recounting the necessary preconditions for

Divining Praise 71

song and praise, are unmistakable.[64] In Pindar's *Hymn*, Zeus and praise are intertwined, as the god's marvels of creation occasion the need for their reflected celebration. In other words, Pindar represents a time where Zeus existed, but praise did not, an absence that demanded redress. This interstice of time is collapsed by Callimachus, and the moment of anxious opportunity and possibility not suspended between two acts of creation (the universe and the Muses) but promoted, dramatized by Rhea's search for water in the time before both Zeus and praise are simultaneously created to answer her need. The conditions of the necessity for praise that arise and are resolved in Pindar's first (programmatic) *Hymn* also receive their own corresponding treatment in Callimachus' opening *Hymn*, using the powerful water-as-song metapoetic formulation that also drives the momentum of Pindar's opening epinician, *Olympian* 1.

Pindar's first *Hymn* has been integrated into the conversation here not just for its applicability to the Callimachean hymnic tradition, but for a further interpretive gain when considered alongside the beginning of the *Metamorphoses*. Initially considered a hymn dedicated to Zeus, arguments have also been advanced for its status as a hymn to Apollo, or as a composition jointly honoring both gods.[65] In either case, the hymn's dedicatee would share considerable space with the other god, whether it be a mythological prominence of Apollo developed to display ultimately the might and justness of Zeus, or a theogony unwinding to the eventual praise of the god of music and poetry.[66] This discrepancy of clear dedicatee is a reminder of the occasionally unstable or fraught relationship between father and son. Between Zeus and Apollo, there exists an inherited anxiety that stems from the succession myth. Such anxiety is exploited by the opening of the *Homeric Hymn to Apollo*, which sees the Olympians tremble with the approach of Apollo (1–12). Within the same hymn, Apollo's temperament is also of concern to Delos, who reports the god-to-be's overweening spirit and imposing dominance to Leto (*Hymn. Hom. Ap.* 67–69), additionally underscoring the threatening potential of Zeus' male heir.[67] These fears are assuaged at the hymn's opening, when Apollo is relieved of his bow and quiver and seated near his father, and reiterated by the speech he makes at birth, in which he states he will serve the will of Zeus (*Hymn. Hom. Ap.* 132). Although it is not made explicit in the *Homeric Hymn* what the precise seating arrangement of the gods is, within the Callimachean *Hymn to Apollo*, the god is present at the right hand of Zeus (δύναται γάρ, ἐπεὶ Διὶ δεξιὸς ἧσται, "he is able to do this, since he sits to Zeus' right," *Hymn* 2.29). This locating statement can be read in two ways. Literally, it indicates Apollo's power as derived from the powerful presence of Zeus, therefore also defusing any latent memories of the *Homeric Hymn's* opening tension. Literarily, as Marco Fantuzzi explains, the text itself of the second hymn, the *Hymn to Apollo*, "sits next to" the first hymn, the *Hymn to Zeus*, and would begin on a column placed to the right of the *Hymn to Zeus*. The line placement (29) could also mark the end of the hymn's first column.[68] In this reading, the text itself metapoetically proclaims and justifies the ordering of the hymnic collection. In Callimachus' collection, the primacy of Zeus is made explicit with the dedication of the first hymn.[69] However, the Homeric sense of unease about Apolline power is nevertheless contextually packaged into a reading of this hymn: the reader must supply or apply the appearance of εὔυμνος and its resonance from the *Homeric Hymn to Apollo* in order to parse Callimachus' metapoetic construction of Zeus' own praise. Consequentially, Zeus' own praise comes at the intertextual mercy of the Homeric Apollo. Granted, there is no narrative *Homeric Hymn to Zeus* to create a parallel understanding, but the interdependence forged between Zeus and Apollo in the creation, allocation, and understanding of praise (and praise poetry) within the *Hymn to Zeus* (and with knowledge of Pindar's first *Hymn*) still acknowledges the conditions ripe for a divine rivalry.

Close readers of the *Metamorphoses* can perceive how Ovid capitalizes on the opportunity to play more expansively with the notion of a divine rivalry between Jupiter and Apollo. This rivalry, one of both power and textual primacy, is suggestively built over the first two books of the epic, as explored by discussion of the paired ecphrases. The metapoetic reading of Callimachus' Arcadia accomplished our first task: establishing a wider literary purpose for Rhea's extended water-seeking narrative in the Callimachean hymn. Our second task is to understand Ovid's repurposing of this hymnic material. So, we now turn to how this metapoetic reading can help illuminate this divine rivalry, especially one specifically denoted in territorial or spatial terms.

Diverting the Praise of Jupiter

We can now apply the symbolism of the Callimachean Arcadian landscape to the *Metamorphoses*. In brief, the argument is simple: if Callimachus' Arcadian rivers are metaphorical for praise poetry of Zeus, created in celebration

Divining Praise 73

of his birth, Ovid's marked refusal to preserve the geographical continuity of his epic between the tales of Lycaon and Daphne—making the setting Thessalian instead, and only here including a river catalog—amount to a refusal to praise Jupiter. This refusal is grounded in learned literariness, and revelatory of Ovid's contrary wit. Although the ultimate point of interpretive significance is simple, its explanation requires some sustained focus, as Ovid's dynamic strategy is uncovered.

Ovid's avoidance of divine praise is made explicit by the inclusion of the catalog of Thessalian rivers, one even surrounding a figure designed to recall Jupiter, but only *after* a foray into exploring the birth of "praise" for his own epic has been made. As such, we need to examine the concept of praise as it is introduced in the epic. The first divinity expressly concerned with praise in the *Metamorphoses* is Apollo. Espying Cupid stretching a bow, Apollo, with an air of arrogance assumed by his recent conquest of the Python, scoffs at Cupid's suitability to wield these arms, and attempts to put Venus' son in his place: *tu face nescioquos esto contentus amores / inritare tua, nec laudes adsere nostras* ("you, be content with whatever loves you can rile up with your torch—no grubbing for *my* praises!," 1.461–62). Revising his own dictum of "know thyself" into a threat, the territorial Apollo warns Cupid against interfering with his rewards of praise. Cupid, rather, should be content with kindling love's fire. Apollo's dismissive description follows the narrative introduction to Cupid, where Apollo's love is attributed to Cupid's fierce anger (*saeua Cupidinis ira*, 1.453). Cupid's possession of the epic emotion par excellence (*ira*) contributes one aspect to the many ways the myth of Apollo and Daphne is presented as a second beginning to the *Metamorphoses*, a re-inaugurating of the epic under familiar terms, where the recognizably Ovidian theme of love will lend an expressive logic to the narrative ebb and flow.[70] If we endorse this reading, and treat *primus amor Phoebi* ("the first love of Phoebus," 1.452) as a new epic beginning, Cupid's anger exists in parallel with the anger of Jupiter that motivates the first consequential narrative events after the cosmogony: the first metamorphosis, in the transformation of Lycaon (*ingentes animo et dignas Ioue concipit iras*, "[from Lycaon's deed] he drew a massive anger in his spirit, an anger worthy of Jupiter," 1.166) and the subsequent flood (*ira deorum*, 1.378; cf. also 1.330). In short, when the reader encounters the tale of Daphne and Apollo, they are not only primed to think of it as a new beginning for the epic (*primus amor Phoebi*), but they are also directly told that Apollo's concern for *laus* (like κλέος, a signalling word for epic) is what incites Cupid's wrath (*tu face nescioquos esto contentus amores / inritare tua, nec <u>laudes</u> adsere nostras*, 1.461–62).

Praise runs as a theme throughout the encounter of god and nymph on levels both explicit (Apollo praises Daphne's form, *laudat* . . . 1.500–502) and implicit (he "hymns" himself, the subject of the following chapter, in an attempt to persuade the nymph to check her flight). After Daphne's transformation, Apollo's hymn of praise, prophesying the laurel as the perpetual emblem of Augustan power and triumph, serves to complete her metamorphosis by declaring its symbolic dimension. Additionally, he claims the laurel as a new attribute of his divine identity (*"arbor eris certe" dixit "mea; semper habebunt / te coma, te citharae, te nostrae, laure, pharetrae,"* "surely, you'll be my tree! Always you'll adorn my hair / you, my lyre—you, my quiver, laurel," 1.558–59).[71] His words end with *finierit Paean* ("Paean had finished"), before the laurel moves its canopy seemingly in assent. At this critical juncture, naming Apollo as Paean adds another explicit notion of divine praise, given the hymnic genre of the paean.[72] This not only reinforces his authorial position of the self-hymn, but attracts the hymn to the laurel that he has just performed into a further self-reflective context, additionally indicated by Daphne's nod (*adnuit*, 1.567): albeit ambiguous (is she making a powerful statement of assent, or merely acting as a tree does in a breeze?), it nevertheless performs one recognizable sign of Apolline epiphany.[73] Keeping in mind this current of praise that contextually frames and permeates the episode, and informs its interpretation, I want to widen the paradigmatic and programmatic readings of Daphne's transformation to include further aetiological significance. By doing so, we see an extension of Ovid's strategy toward praise policy: we have traced how Callimachus packages together an understanding of the birth of Zeus and the origins of praise poetry, grounded in the Arcadian landscape, a landscape subsequently avoided by Ovid in the opening of the *Metamorphoses*. Ovid diverts the geographical focus to Thessaly physically—metaphorically, he diverts praise away from Jupiter. Now, we can see how the concept of praise informs Ovid's Thessalian river catalog in a different way, by refocusing the myth of Apollo and Daphne as motivated by praise, rather than love.

THE *LAUS* OF THE LAUREL

Traditionally, the aetiological significance of the episode is read on two different levels. First, the aetiological level of physical creation, with Daphne's transformation from nymph into the first laurel tree, which provides its foliage for the Pythian crown.[74] This literal understanding is expanded to include a literary dimension when her transformation is read as the aetiology of elegy, as she becomes the *tenuis liber*, a "'thin bark/slender book,' the slim volume of the love elegist,"[75] a reading that has taken imaginative prevalence in studies of the Ovidian poetic agenda for the *Metamorphoses*. As such, Daphne's elegiac nature has somewhat eclipsed the idea that she can also be read as the arboreal embodiment of *laus*, a monument to praise in especially hymnic fashion. Apollo's mention of the triumph (1.560–61) within his hymn to the laurel already builds a conceptual relationship between *laurus* and *laus*, reinforced by the closeness of *honor* and *laurus* that both begin the narrative (*aesculeae capiebat frondis honorem. / nondum laurus erat*, "[the victor] was used to taking away the honor of an oaken frond. There was not yet the laurel," 1.449–50) and bring it toward closure (*tu quoque perpetuos semper gere frondis honores. / finierat Paean; factis modo laurea ramis*, "so you too will always bear the honors of being evergreen! / Apollo had finished: the laurel, with branches just now made . . . ," 1.565–66).[76]

Within Latin literature, the laurel and praise occupy a space of what could be considered a traditional juxtaposition. Their pairing is observable from Plautus (*parite laudem et lauream*, "bring forth the praise and the laurel!," *Cist.* 201) to Seneca (cf. *Herc. fur.* 828–29)—although Cicero arguably most significantly roots its juxtaposition in the national consciousness (*concedat laurea laudi*, "may laurels yield to praise," *Pis.* 74.4, *Off.* 1.77.3; cf. also *Fam.* 15.6.1).[77] Verbal parallelism also allowed an etymology to arise, explaining the name of the plant as derived from its symbolic use within the Roman triumph (Serv. Dan. ad *Ecl.* 8.12; Isid. *Orig.* 17.7.2). Within the *Metamorphoses*, Ovid hints at closing the gap between aetiology and etymology by allowing Daphne's creation to be read simultaneously as the embodiment of hymnic *laus*.

There are some additionally relevant hymnic works that similarly make use of or allude to this etymological play. In the beginning of his elegiac hymn to Apollo, Tibullus hints at the etymological connection between *laurus* and *laus* (*nunc precor ad laudes flectere uerba meas. / ipse triumphali deuinctus tempora lauro*, "now, I pray, for words that bend toward praise. / He himself, temples bound with triumphal laurel . . . ," 2.5.4–5).[78] This connection is echoed by the later appearance of triumphal laurel in the poem, within a descriptive passage containing numerous synonyms for praise

(Tib. 2.5.115–20).[79] Ovid reaffirms the significance of the link between *laus* and *laurus* made by the Tibullan hymn when he borrows Tibullus' final gesture of prayer. This gesture is made in the hymn's concluding couplet, after the celebratory appearance of triumphal laurel: *adnue: sic tibi sint intonsi, Phoebe, capilli* ("nod assent: and so may your hair remain unshorn," Tib. 2.5.121, cf. *intonsis . . . capillis, Met.* 1.564). The Tibullan prayer for divine acknowledgment (*adnue*) is "answered" by Daphne's nod (*adnuit*), as Ovid transforms the Tibullan covenant between Apollo and poet into one between Apollo and the laurel. Ovid's intertextual acknowledgment of the Tibullan hymn ratifies the folk etymologizing of *laurus-laus* that frames Tibullus' poem, by applying it to his own creation of the laurel. Ovid shows an advanced dependency on the Tibullan text through the divine symbol of the laurel, while its status as an elegiac hymn additionally colors Apollo's own "hymn" to the laurel.

Within the Ovidian passage, the laurel not only can be read as embodying a sense of hymnic praise, but it also gives way narratively to a different type of praise. The ecphrasis of Tempe that follows (*est nemus Haemoniae*) can be considered a type of *laus locorum* (cf. Quint. *Inst.* 3.7.27), the poetic "placing" of a grove (cf. Persius' *ponere lucum, Sat.* 1.70) in a way that celebrates the landscape. Tempe, simultaneously a real location and an idealized "everygrove," presents the perfect opportunity for a fusion of topographia and topothesia in creating the epic's first, true set-piece landscape description. Daphne's rootedness within the landscape disseminates the sense of praise. The dimension of her identity as a celebration of hymnic praise is then transmuted and transferred into a rhetorical praise of her natural surroundings, the most notable feature of which is the Peneus, her father's river. Given the similar presentation of Peneus and Jupiter, this is as dangerously close as Ovid gets to symbolic praise of Jupiter, but Jupiter's own words regarding the rustic gods prevent it from being taken seriously as transferred praise on his behalf: Peneus belongs to the category of gods not worthy of the heavens. Peneus as a Jupiter-figure, ultimately, is another index of strategic Ovidian coyness in building these associations between Arcadia and Thessaly, and thwarting the Callimachean hymnic agenda that so enduringly associates Arcadia with the praise of Zeus.

The focus on Peneus within the description, however, reminds us that although Daphne's transformation does yield to a *laus locorum* inclusive of a river catalog, this catalog is not used to communicate praise. Instead, as previously noted, the rivers are present as an internal audience. They are the first "readers" of Daphne's metamorphosis: *conueniunt illuc popularia flumina primum, / nescia gratentur consolenturne parentem* ("they gather there, the ordinary, constituent rivers, first; they are unaware whether to congratulate or console the father," 1.577–78). The uncertainty of the rivers as to how appropriately react to her metamorphosis seems to gesture toward the two different, available "generic" understandings Daphne's narrative pioneers: a rejoicing (*gratentur*) is consonant with understanding Daphne's new role as a symbol of hymnic praise, while lamenting (*consolentur*) is consonant with understanding lament as the root of the elegiac genre. The rivers, therefore, appear especially attuned to the aetiological dimensions of the episode. The hymnic context is suggestively encapsulated by the verb *grator*. *Grator* is an equivalent of the Greek χαίρω, the verb that often provides a beginning or ending to hymns (χαῖρε) and linguistically structures the reciprocal relationship of χάρις between god and worshipper, a relationship that informs the nature and purpose of hymns. Both possible understandings (of hymnic praise and/or elegy), furthermore, become crystallized within the new direction that the narrative takes: the tale of Io. ἰώ is a ritual cry associated with the paean, and therefore with a sense of triumphant joy, but it is also a cry of mourning. Io's name itself represents the indecision of the rivers' response to the Peneus, and narrative continuity is established in a subtly delicate fashion.[80]

In sum, Ovid's Thessalian rivers occupy a subtly important role within this narrative. However, their literary purpose is not in parallel with the Callimachean catalog of Arcadian rivers. While Callimachus' Arcadian rivers arise to celebrate Zeus, embodying praise and poetry for the new god, Ovid's Thessalian rivers functionally alert the reader to question the diverse interpretability of Daphne's metamorphosis, including her identity as an instantiation of hymnic praise. Ovid not only refuses to set the myth that serves to aetiologize praise in Arcadia, disrupting the geographical continuity of the epic, but he also refuses to share the literary purpose of the narrative feature he has conscientiously deployed as the myth's ending: a highly regionalized river catalog, for which he has clearly eschewed the more natural, generically suitable narrative opportunities (cosmogony and flood). Supplying the literary background of the Callimachean *Hymn to Zeus* to this suite of Ovidian decisions amounts to a programmatic statement of refusal to engage with praise of Jupiter, and a refusal to assign him a territory

78   Divining Praise

mythologically due. The resultant political ramifications of this literary mechanism hardly need belaboring. Filling in the blanks of the corresponding political analogy amounts, of course, to a reluctance to assign a specialized "territory" of praise to Augustus, after the council of the gods is depicted as a thinly guised senatorial meeting, with Jupiter at its helm.

ARCADIAN INTERLUDES

An overt epic agenda of diverting praise from Jupiter would, naturally, prove dangerous to the poet. This is one practical justification for Ovid's ingeniously allusive treatment of the Callimachean intertext. However, tactful pragmatism (not Ovid's strong suit) may not be cause enough to explain the delicacies of these textual interactions. If an avoidance of Jupiter's praise seems too symbolically or metaphorically abstract to explain the poet's geographical diversion of the significant myth of Apollo and Daphne from Arcadia to Thessaly, we can look to the eventual resurfacing of the narrative thread of Arcadian myth. Where the narrative "rejoins" the thread of continuity Ovid has disrupted proves telling, in confirming the relevance of this reading. As such, I provide here a coda of argumentative support.

Ovid's epic narrative resumes a sense of geographical continuity with the tale of Callisto in Book 2. Callisto is the daughter of the Arcadian king Lycaon; the seam of Arcadian myth is therefore first disrupted by the flood, and only resumes after Phaethon's conflagration. The appearance of Callisto also marks the end of the Arcadian portion of Callimachus' *Hymn to Zeus*:

> [τὸ χεῦμα] . . . τὸ μέν ποθι πουλὺ κατ' αὐτό
> Καυκώνων πτολίεθρον, ὃ Λέπρειον πεφάτισται,
> συμφέρεται Νηρῆϊ, <u>παλαιότατον δέ μιν ὕδωρ</u>
> <u>υἱωνοὶ πίνουσι Λυκαονίης ἄρκτοιο.</u>
>
> (Callim. Hymn 1.38–41)

> [This great stream somewhere by the very city of the Caucones (which is called Lepreion) mingles with Nereus, and this most ancient water, the descendants of the bear, the daughter of Lycaon, drink. (trans. Stephens)

"The bear, the daughter of Lycaon" is Callisto, whose descendants drink the ancient Arcadian water. The drinking of water cements the identity of the Arcadian landscape as a land now rich in water, and therefore, rich in Zeus'

Divining Praise 79

praise, forming a clear contrast with the early, thirsty regional travelers (διψαλέος, *Hymn* 1.27). Callisto's myth in Ovid begins as Jupiter's love for the Arcadian landscape, voiced for the first time, is transmuted into his love for the Arcadian nymph. The god's project to rehabilitate the scorched land leads him to be kindled with the flames of love:

Arcadiae tamen est impensior illi
cura suae; fontesque et nondum audentia labi
flumina restituit, dat terrae gramina, frondes
arboribus, laesasque iubet reuirescere silvas.
dum redit itque frequens, in uirgine Nonacrina
haesit et accepti caluere sub ossibus ignes.

(*Met.* 2.405–10)

[However to him, his own Arcadia was of more grave concern:
he brought back the springs and the rivers not yet daring to flow,
he gave grass back to the lands, leaves to the trees, he bade
the wounded forests to be green, vigorous anew.
While he made his frequent visits there, he was caught by the sight
of the maiden from Nonacrine, and the fires of love kindled,
admitted to his marrow.]

Jupiter's regeneration of the land includes restoring its water sources, both springs and rivers. Previously, they were "not yet daring to flow" (*nondum audentia labi / flumina*). This scenario, in which the rivers remain hidden under the earth, is reminiscent of the pre-Zeus Arcadia of Callimachus' hymn. Within the lengthy catalog of rivers affected by Phaethon's ride (2.239–59), the sole Arcadian river included is the Erymanthus. It appears only here as the name of a river in Latin poetry. Even in Greek, it is more commonly used to designate the mountain Erymanthus (e.g., in the case of the Erymanthian boar; cf. also *Met.* 5.608). However, it is one of the rivers featured in the Callimachean catalog of Arcadian rivers. There, it is paired with the Ladon (*Hymn* 1.18). Within the Ovidian catalog, the Arcadian Erymanthus is paired with the "swift Ismenus" (*et celer Ismenos cum Phegiaco Erymantho*, 2.244).[81] Returning to the passage of Jupiter's regenerating efforts, and cross-referencing it with the catalog of landscape features affected by Phaethon's fires, it is clear that Jupiter's reintroduction of water

80 Divining Praise

to Arcadia must include reintroducing the flow of the Erymanthus, which bears distinct, if trace, awareness of Callimachus' hymn. The adjective "Erymanthian" is also used twice in the exile poetry to describe Callisto as the constellation Bear (*Erymanthidos Ursae*, *Tr.* 1.4.1, 3.4b.1). This distinct connection is offered more distantly by the *Metamorphoses*, where she is catasterized after her son comes across her in the *siluae Erymanthidae* (2.499). The introduction of Callisto thus provides a notable textual hinge to Callimachus' *Hymn to Zeus*, bringing the texts into purposeful alignment. Callisto anchors the Arcadian portion of Callimachus' *Hymn*, and her narrative can also make clear to the Ovidian audience the complex play Callimachus has made with this hymn.[82]

When we turn to the Ovidian corpus, Callisto's identity is obsessively, yet variably, constructed as Arcadian, making clear her relevance to understanding Ovid's play upon Arcadian myth. She is Erymanthis, Maenalia/Maenalis, Lycaonia/Lycaonis, Tegaeae, and in the *Metamorphoses*, Nonacrina and Parrhasis.[83] In her role as an archetypal representative of Arcadia and its landscape, Callisto's myth confirms Ovid's subversion of the metaliterary purpose of Callimachus' river catalog. It gets the epic back on track, so to speak, after the disruptions of flood and fire, destruction and recreation: her myth picks up the thread of the Arcadian myth of Lycaon, and directly connects Jupiter with the mythological region of his birth, in contrast with the oblique hinting at the relationship found in Book 1. To look more closely, we can see the geographical connectors more clearly: Diana enters the scene coming from Maenalus (2.442), one of the mountains that sketches the Arcadian setting of Lycaon's myth (1.216), connected first to Callisto at the beginning of the myth (*nec Maenalon attigit ulla / gratior hac Triuiae*, "nor does any nymph more dear to Diana than her tread Maenalus," 2.415–16). A specific sense of geographical continuity is given to these tales of father and daughter. Jupiter seduces Callisto in the guise of Diana (*protinus induitur faciem cultumque Dianae*, "forthwith he puts on the countenance and accessories of Diana," 2.425; the repercussions of this act feature in the following chapter); this deception has lasting consequences for the nymph, who, upon being hailed by the goddess, still worries it may be Jupiter (*clamata refugit / et timuit primo ne Iuppiter esset in illa*, "although summoned she flees and fears first of all, that Jupiter may still be present in her form," 2.443–44). Diana eventually recognizes the consequences of Jupiter's

Divining Praise

action when she decides to bathe after the exertions of the hunt, and bids her nymphs to do the same:

> orbe resurgebant lunaria cornua nono
> cum dea uenatu et fraternis languida flammis
> nacta nemus gelidum, de quo cum murmure labens
> ibat et attritas uersabat riuus harenas.
> ut loca laudauit, summas pede contigit undas;
> his quoque laudatis "procul est" ait "arbiter omnis;
> nuda superfusis tingamus corpora lymphis."
> Parrhasis erubuit. cunctae uelamina ponunt,
> una moras quaerit; dubitanti uestis adempta est,
> qua posita nudo patuit cum corpore crimen.
> attonitae manibusque uterum celare uolenti
> "i procul hinc" dixit "nec sacros pollue fontes"
>
> (*Met.* 2.453–64)

[The horns of the moon were rising anew after nine circuits,
When the goddess, overcome by lassitude from hunting and the heat of
fraternal rays,
came upon a cool grove, from which slipping along with a murmur
a river flowed, swirling fine grains of sand.
As she praised the place, she touched the top of the water with her toes;
and after praising this too, she said, "any onlooker is far distant:
let us bathe, pouring water over our nude bodies."
The girl from Parrhasia blushed; they all set aside their filmy garments;
one contrived delaying tactics. The clothing was snatched from her, hesitating;
when she stood, nude, her body was bared along with her transgression.
To the thunderstruck maiden, frantically trying to cover her middle with her
hands,
the goddess pronounced, "be gone with you—don't sully the sacred waters!"]

Diana chooses to refresh herself in a cool grove, where a river flows gently over smoothed sand. Although Ovid does not specify where the grove is, there is no reason to suspect it is outside Arcadia. The swirling grains of sands (*attritas . . . harenas*) could indicate the river's identity as the Ladon,

82   Divining Praise

which appears as *harenosus* ("sandy") at 1.702. The first thing Diana does is praise the place (*ut loca laudauit*) and touch the water, which also receives her praise (*his quoque laudatis*). Within the description of this Arcadian landscape, Hinds calls attention to Ovid's playfulness as he stages a ceding of his own poetic control to the internal figure of the goddess: the scene is of "a *locus amoenus*; but the self-conscious twist is that, before immersing herself in it, Diana herself *praises* it, step by step. The goddess rhetoricizes the moment of her own entry into the landscape, and thus usurps the poet's expected function: the [explicit expression of praise] functions in a quasi-technical way to represent the set-piece *laudes* which are the poet's and rhetorician's stock-in-trade in such a context."[84] In Hinds' reading, Diana's self-consciousness of the text in which she is operating is the interpretive payoff.[85] However, this moment can also be used as the confirmation of Ovid's knowing act of geographic displacement, and its metaliterary repercussions: only now is the land of Arcadia allowed to engage with the concept of praise, when the Arcadian landscape itself (and particularly its river) become the object of praise in an unmistakably self-conscious way. Ovid now literalizes the Callimachean symbolic relationship between praise and Arcadian water, in active recognition of the metapoetic mechanism of the *Hymn to Zeus* as the poetic road not taken within his own *Metamorphoses*: the Arcadian land is not in the service of praising Jupiter. The timing of connecting praise to Arcadia only as the Arcadian seam of mythology is narratively resumed within the epic is calculated to belatedly confirm the Thessalian landscape as a narrative interloper, but a purposeful one, which sets up relationships of divine rivalry through the modality of geographic space. Arcadian praise, voiced only by Diana, is also separate from the praise of Jupiter. Ovid teases this fact with Jupiter's deceptive impersonation of Diana to seduce Callisto. He almost spells this out when Callisto greets "Diana" with the assessment that she is greater than Jove (2.427–29); in response Jupiter "laughs, delighted to be preferred to himself" (*ridet . . . / et sibi praeferri se gaudet*, 2.429–430).

There are additional contextual cues to connect this myth to Callimachus' hymn, further confirming the importance of the *Hymn to Zeus* for these initial allocations and explorations of the physical space within the *Metamorphoses*. Diana dismisses Callisto (who is "thunder-struck," *attonitae*, 2.463) to avoid polluting the river (*"i procul hinc" dixit "nec sacros pollue fontes,"* 2.464). It is a commonplace that childbirth is a source of pollution, but Diana's dismissal also cues remembrance of the holiness of the place

Divining Praise 83

where Rhea gave birth to Zeus. This holiness is protected by a decree against any pregnant creature from approaching:

ἐν δέ σε Παρρασίῃ Ῥείη τέκεν, ἧχι μάλιστα
ἔσκεν ὄρος θάμνοισι περισκεπές· ἔνθεν ὁ χῶρος
ἱερός, οὐδέ τί μιν κεχρημένον Εἰλειθυίης
ἑρπετὸν οὐδὲ γυνὴ ἐπιμίσγεται, ἀλλά ἑ Ῥείης
ὠγύγιον καλέουσι λεχώϊον Ἀπιδανῆες.

(Callim. *Hymn* 1.10–14)

[In Parrhasia Rhea bore you, where the mountain was especially dense with thickets. Afterwards the place was sacred; nothing in need of Eileithyia, neither crawling thing nor woman approaches it, but the Apidaneans call it the primeval childbed of Rhea. (trans. Stephens)]

Callisto is named as *Parrhasis* (2.460) just prior to her dismissal. This designation allows her expulsion to be read within the specific Arcadian holiness of the place described in the Callimachean hymn, named overall as Parrhasia. Cumulatively, the myth of Callisto brings to light all the ways Ovid has avoided promoting Arcadia as a region of divine importance.

Ovid's narrative reluctance as regards Arcadia is further evident when considering the one additional place Arcadia *does* appear within Book 1 after the flood, in the embedded narrative of Syrinx that Mercury tells Argus. Syrinx is a clear mythological doublet of both Daphne and Io (and therefore, anticipant of Callisto).[86] As a daughter of the Ladon, Syrinx appears as a figure calculated to further remind readers that Daphne, too, was a daughter of the Ladon in other mythological accounts. However, Syrinx's parentage, indicated by the plea to her "watery sisters" (*liquidas . . . sorores*, 1.704) after her flight to the Ladon exists in a narrative limbo: it forms part of the myth included in the epic itself, but not part of what Mercury narrates to Argus, as Argus has already fallen asleep (1.700–712). The Ladon, as an Arcadian river, is not given the full range of narrative privilege and possibility. Syrinx is not introduced as the daughter of the Ladon, instead relegated to only the narrative level outside of Mercury's tale. The displacement of Arcadia and the Ladon as the setting of the Apollo and Daphne tale is therefore reinforced not only by Syrinx's lineage and the mythological similarities, but also awareness of this narrative displacement. The exclusion of Jupiter's

84   Divining Praise

Arcadia is only allowed to receive an explicit recognition when the Arcadian narrative of Lycaon is "resumed" by the myth of Callisto (which also preserves genealogical continuity). This exclusion is made for the ultimate promotion of an Apolline-centric Thessaly.

All Is Fair in Love and War, But Who Is First?

Redistributing the region of divine praise from Jupiter's Arcadia to Apollo's Thessaly within the first book of the epic speaks to a struggle between Jupiter and Apollo for textual primacy that is waged with an acute sensitivity to space and territory, additionally in evidence from the corresponding pair of ecphrases. Two other scenarios that surround the issue of primacy rounds out this picture of competition. By putting the gods in conflict over two specific contexts of "firsts," Ovid asks if all is fair in war and love: first exploits are measured, as well as first loves. Jupiter's first epic exploit, which leads into the council of the gods, is his defeat of the Giants, represented here as a solo effort (1.151–62). The defeat of the Giants is an important act for the expression of Jupiter's power and authority and affirmation of his divine leadership. Along these lines, Callimachus' first specialized hailing of the god is as Πηλαγόνων ἐλατῆρα (*Hymn* 1.3), largely understood as a reference to the Giants ("router of the Giants"). Jupiter's defeat of the Giants also becomes the apparent internal textual model for Apollo's defeat of the Python (1.438–49), in a paired parallelism of the gods' first narratives of divine force. Once again, the flood and world recreation stand as the narrative barrier between these parallels. With the new beginning of the postdiluvian world, Apollo's slaying of the Python is a clearly staged reminiscence of Jupiter's defeat of the Giants.[87] The echo of Jupiter's might against the Giants in Apollo's actions paints Jupiter as a model of power, in acknowledgment of a traditional, authoritative hierarchy where the son's power in some ways is circumscribed by the father (as in Callimachus' *Hymn to Apollo*, where Apollo is seated by Zeus). The two moments achieve an even greater closeness if we can speculate about the access Ovid had to Callimachean texts and scholarship: Πηλαγόνων ἐλατῆρα is derived from ancient quotations, but the manuscript reads Πηλογόνων ("mud-born"). This distinction has been understood as mediating between "Earth-born" Giants (or Titans) versus "mud-born" human beings, leading to a variety of interpretations.[88] Ovid's Python is not only depicted as a textual double of the Giants, but is also a *nouum monstrum* ("new monstrosity") generated from mud left behind by the recent flood:

> ergo ubi diluuio tellus <u>lutulenta</u> recenti
> solibus aetheriis altoque recanduit aestu,
> edidit innumeras species partimque figuras
> rettulit antiquas, partim nova monstra creauit.
>
> (*Met.* 1.434–37)

> [And so when the earth, muddied from the recent flood,
> warmed anew with the deep heat from the sun's rays,
> it produced innumerable creatures and some of these were
> old forms returned, some were monsters created anew.]

If Ovid had access to this Callimachean textual variant, it brings the two moments of divine combat into even greater proximity, and further entrenches the *Hymn to Zeus* as a text of significance for the *Metamorphoses*. Apollo is endowed with further Zeus-like power, and "mud-born" is transformed into a conscious echo of the Giants' similar, earthy origin. Speculation of Ovidian knowledge aside, the neat parallel line of the two divine combats is unsettled by the intervening moment of Jupiter's enthroning in the seat of Apollo, which introduces an instability to this authoritative dynamic of the divine father modeling martial behavior for the son; as discussed at the opening of the chapter, this enthroning subsequently finds its sequel when Sol appears in Zeus' palace. The exchange of power continues.

However, just as the divine combats are consciously presented on one level as parallel events, establishing interconnected divine resumes and identities, there is also a narrative tension suggested between first loves. Apollo's love for Daphne, displacing an opportunity for Jovian praise, narratively privileges Apollo over Jupiter (*primus amor Phoebi* rather than *primus amor Iouis*). Ovid includes textual clues that hint at this privileging as a pointed authorial choice.

The introduction of Inachus, hiding underground, simulates the subterranean hiding of the Arcadian rivers presented within the Callimachean hymn. Inachus would, in fact, come into close contact with these streams, as the river rises on the borders of Arcadia (cf. Paus. 2.25.3, 8.6.6).[89] As

86 Divining Praise

previously noted, Callimachus (among others) names the Arcadians "Api-danians," a reference to their traditional antiquity. However, the Hellenistic poet Rhianus also recounts that Achaia (Argos) was called "Apia" after Apis, the son of Phoroneus and grandson of Inachus; the inhabitants of the region thus received the name "Apidanes" (*FGrHist* 265 F 1 = fr. 13 Powell).[90]

Ὑμετέρη τοι, τέκνα, Φορωνέος Ἰναχίδαο
ἀρχῆθεν γενεή· τοῦ δὲ κλυτὸς ἐκγένετ᾽ Ἆπις,
ὅς ῥ Ἀπίην ἐφάτιξε καὶ ἀνέρας Ἀπιδανῆας

[Your lineage, children, has its first origin from Phoroneus, Inachus' son, from him famed Apis was born, who named Apia and the Apidanian men.]

By many accounts, Phoroneus is the first human and the head of the Argive line. His daughter Niobe is conventionally the first (mortal) love of Zeus.[91] Ovid does not explicitly endorse this lineage within the *Metamorphoses*. Nevertheless, he twice identifies Io as *Phoronis* (1.668, 2.524). Ovid's use of this patronymic has been largely explained by the genealogy of Castor of Rhodes, who records that Io and Phoroneus are both the children of Inachus. In Thomas Cole's reading, the oddity of using a patronymic to mean "sister of Phoroneus" could express Ovid's desire to conflate the figures of Niobe (the daughter of Phoroneus) and Io, the daughters of the first man and first king, both beloved by Zeus.[92] If Cole is correct, and Ovid's ambiguous patronymic signals that Io should be read as a doublet of Niobe (the first mortal love of Jupiter), the story of Io that directly follows Daphne's myth becomes an even closer echo. Parallel experiences of first love are thus created for the gods Apollo and Jupiter. Only this time, unlike the myths of first combat, the Apolline myth is the textual model, rather than the imitator.[93] Recognizing Io as a doublet of Niobe is also predicated on awareness of the genealogical lineage that descends from Inachus to Phoroneus to Niobe, the sister of Apis. In this way, Ovid also hints at the assimilating potential of the regions of Arcadia and Argos under the shared name "Apidanians," creating a shadowy sense of continuity with the myth of Arcadian Syrinx enfolded within Io's narrative.[94]

CONCLUSION

This chapter has traced the tensions between Jupiter and Apollo in the opening of the epic and documented the instabilities Ovid creates over which god has a greater sense of command and control, of power, and primacy. One repercussion that arises from seeing Ovid's game of avoidance when it comes to directly trafficking in the poetic praise of Jupiter is the issue of conclusive interpretability. Is the diversion of praise from Jupiter, traceable through Ovid's treatment of the Arcadian landscape and its inheritance of hymnic importance from the Callimachean *Hymn to Zeus*, the same thing as praise of Apollo? And if so, what commentary would this form on Ovid's political reality, given the analogies that can be made between imperial and divine power? After all, the very concept of praise is pioneered in the epic as an identifying concern of Apollo. Ovid certainly narratively privileges Apollo over Jupiter, as he reinaugurates his epic with the myth of Apollo and Daphne—but this is not the same thing as praising Apollo. Ovidian readers must look to the laurel and its potential as an aetiology of praise. Ovid's overt nod to the creation of praise, embedded within an Apolline myth, and in a symbol reflective of both Apolline and Augustan authority, is a smoke screen for his encoded political commentary: a sly refusal to engage with the tradition of praise of Jupiter, the epic figure truly analogous to Augustus.

3

Rivaled Affection and Affectation

Diana, Apollo, and Delian Disguise

As the previous chapter showed, looking at the relationship between praise and the laurel (*laus*/*laurus*) sheds light on the competitive interactions between Apollo and Jupiter within the opening books of the *Metamorphoses*. Now, the focus turns to Apollo's identity, and how Ovid constructs it in relation to his sister Diana. While the laurel is a known attribute of Apollo, Daphne is first introduced through her connection to Diana. Throughout the myth of the laurel, the narrative moves between the poles of Daphne/Diana to the laurel/Apollo, a narrative significantly punctuated by two Apolline pronouncements, both addressed to Daphne: a self-hymn, and a prophecy that can also be read as a hymn in praise of the laurel.[1] In this chapter, the modalities of Apollo's hymnic self-construction are situated relative to Diana, and Daphne as a Diana-like figure. Although the narrative of Apollo and Daphne has received much critical interpretation and remains one of the most popular mythological narratives of the epic, the influence of hymns in creating the dynamic between Apollo and Daphne has repercussions for understanding the relationships between (and identities of) Apollo and Diana that have not been fully explored, particularly within the Augustan framing of the episode.

In this chapter, I argue that Ovid bypasses recent Augustan commitments to portraying the pair as harmonious, and instead looks back to the Greek hymnic tradition to portray his Delians as competitive rivals. Rather than continue building upon a depiction of harmony between Apollo and Diana, as receives an apex of expression in the Horatian hymn *Carmen Saeculare*, Ovid chooses instead to capitalize upon the rivalry that characterizes the

Callimachean hymnic interactions of the gods. Ovid brings this mode of competition to the forefront through Daphne: in the following, I show that Daphne herself is a poetic figure designed to dramatize the rivalry between the gods.[2] The poetic decisions that Ovid makes to individualize Daphne as a new iteration of Artemis/Diana cumulatively challenge the supremacy of Apollo in subtle and significant ways. One especial part of this argument, to show Daphne herself as a space created upon which and over which to stage this rivalry, is uncovering and analyzing her relationship with Cyrene, a figure common to two Callimachean hymns. Cyrene appears in both the Callimachean *Hymn to Artemis* and *Hymn to Apollo*, in ways designed to make the reader assess the versions of the gods each hymn showcases, and, in continuation, to confront the dueling veracities of the hymnic realities each presents. In short, Cyrene is a figure over whom the gods vie for competitive ownership: when Ovid makes his Daphne a neo-Cyrene, he can opportunely reprise and redramatize the Callimachean hymnic competition between Apollo and Artemis. Reading Daphne in this fashion, as an imaginative reception of the dynamics of the Callimachean hymn collection, additionally tells us about Ovid as a reader of Callimachus. This forms one important nexus of detailing Ovid's poetic use of the Callimachean hymns in the myth of Apollo and Daphne. The final part of the chapter, however, shifts to show Daphne's dependency on a different hymnic model from Callimachus: Asteria, from the *Hymn to Delos*. Taking this new aspect of Daphne's literary identity into account allows us to extend our critical perception of Ovid as a Callimachean reader. If we understand how Ovid deploys Daphne as this carefully crafted, narratively active agent of Callimachean hymnic reception, we can also begin to understand how Ovid experiences Callimachus' *Hymns*. In this light, I conclude the chapter with a new interpretation of the suite of Callimachean hymns, as gleaned through the receptive perspective of Ovidian epic. All told, this chapter uses the relationships between the Delians and Daphne to reevaluate Ovid's literary engagement with hymnic sources, and how these sources have influenced the shaping and interactions of his epic personalities.

An Arch Likeness: The Closeness of Diana and Apollo

As the relationship between the Delians must first be foregrounded in and for the context of the Ovidian myth of Apollo and Daphne, this section presents a necessary overview of their literary interactions and points of natural comparison (names, epithets, attributes, descriptors); indeed, names will be a defining thread of discussion for the entirety of the chapter. In one capacity, the Ovidian altercation between Apollo and Cupid that catalyzes the creation of the laurel is the literary legacy of a divine dysfunction that reaches back to Homer, who first lent the gods their existence as literary characters; competition is a familiar dynamic of family relationships, and the Olympians and their offspring pose no exception.[3] At heart, the myth is motivated by the need for praise: it also represents the first direct depiction of divine rivalry in the poem, between Cupid and Apollo.[4] This overt rivalry, however, masks the more subtle competitive tension that simmers between Apollo and his sister divinity. Although Apollo directly censures Cupid for his use of the bow, another divine figure is nevertheless contextually evoked by these Ovidian terms of engagement. Apollo's protectiveness of the bow as his personal attribute can be usefully construed in light of his relationship with the other archer-divinity: his sister Diana.[5] Apollo's slaying of the Python has purportedly given the god his recent pride in the bow, but the account of the narrator indicates that previously, the god (despite being named *deus arquitenens*, "the bow-toting god") had used only it for hunting red and roe-deer (1.441–42).[6] Hunting is not typically the use of the Apolline bow.[7] Hunting is, however, its primary use for the huntress Artemis, the goddess hailed as ἐλαφηβόλος ("deer-shooter") in a defining *Homeric Hymn to Artemis* (*Hymn. Hom.* 27.2).[8] Even before he accuses Cupid of appropriating "his" weapon, Apollo already seems to be dangerously trespassing on the divine sphere of Diana.[9]

The siblings have a history of clashing over Apollo's use of the bow. In the *Iliad*'s theomachy, Artemis attempts to provoke Apollo into fighting after he refuses to engage in combat with Poseidon:

τὸν δὲ κασιγνήτη μάλα νείκεσε πότνια θηρῶν
Ἄρτεμις ἀγροτέρη, καὶ ὀνείδειον φάτο μῦθον·
φεύγεις δὴ ἑκάεργε, Ποσειδάωνι δὲ νίκην
πᾶσαν ἐπέτρεψας, μέλεον δέ οἱ εὖχος ἔδωκας·
νηπύτιε τί νυ τόξον ἔχεις ἀνεμώλιον αὔτως;
μή σευ νῦν ἔτι πατρὸς ἐνὶ μεγάροισιν ἀκούσω
εὐχομένου, ὡς τὸ πρὶν ἐν ἀθανάτοισι θεοῖσιν,
ἄντα Ποσειδάωνος ἐναντίβιον πολεμίζειν.

(Hom. *Il.* 21.470–77)

Rivaled Affection and Affectation

[His sister Artemis, the untamed mistress of beasts,
heckled him, and delivered a chiding speech:
You flee, far-archer, and so, surrender victory
fully to Poseidon, giving him unearned bragging rights:
why, foolish one, do you wield a bow, in this manner of empty vanity?
Don't let me overhear you exulting in our father's halls
as you previously boasted among the immortal gods.
that you bested Poseidon face-to-face.]

The question she poses is especially pointed: why does Apollo bear a bow, if he is so unwilling to use it? She calls his bow ἀνεμώλιος—literally, "windy," but used metaphorically to mean "in vain," or "empty." A pressure point indeed for Apollo, whose use of the bow in Homer is, in truth, more metaphorical.[10] Artemis' desire to shame her brother in this pointed fashion speaks to an undercurrent of rivalry involving this instrument that is only gestured at here, as opposed to fully explored. Her following reprimand, involving Apollo's idle threats, also implicates his words as being ἀνεμώλιος; her scorn extends to acting as a subtle commentary on his name, if Gregory Nagy is right to attach Apollo to the verb ἀπειλέω, "to make a promise, boastful promise, threat."[11] Artemis' attempt to take Apollo down a peg, however, soon comes at her own expense: Artemis' defining epithet ἰοχέαιρα ("scatterer of arrows") is then literalized in a humorously marginalizing fashion when Hera responds to her words, easily disarming the goddess and beating her with her own bow and quiver, causing her arrows to fall and scatter (*Il.* 21.489–92).[12] The siblings both become the target of a speech or action that questions their suitability to bear the bow, in a way that also addresses a crucial signifier of name or epithet.[13]

Naming is an especially important part of identity, especially hymnic identity. In one sense, hymns can be thought of as narrative explorations of names and epithets. Artemis and Hermes both stand as Homeric challengers to their brother Apollo's identity and attributes, a role that Ovid transfers to Cupid.[14] The role of Homeric challenger may be borrowed, but Cupid shares with Diana an Ovidian identifier that allies them in their use of the bow: the poetic adjective *pharetratus* ("sporting a quiver") is used only of Cupid and Diana, never Apollo.[15] Diana appears as the *pharetrata uirgo* in the opening poem of the *Amores* (*Am.* 1.1.10), and is called the *pharetrata dea* in the *Heroides* (*Her.* 20.204).[16] The poet dismisses Cupid at the opening of *Amores* 2.5 with *abeas, pharetrate Cupido* ("begone, quiver-bearing Cupid,"

Am. 2.5.1) and cites *pharetratos . . . Amores* ("quiver-bearing Loves") as the province of Elegia in the *Remedia* (*Rem.* 379). The *Metamorphoses* grants the descriptor once to each god: *pharetrata Diana* (3.252) and *pharetratus puer* (10.525).[17] Conceptually, Diana and Cupid meet in the triangulating space between the hunt as practice for war, love as a hunt (as is the sustained metaphor of *Ars amatoria* 1), and love as war itself (the elegiac *militia amoris*). In the *Metamorphoses*, Apollo's attack on Cupid seems to betray a sense of acute insecurity about not only Cupid's use of the bow, but Diana's ownership of it. Apollo's parting shot is for Cupid to busy himself with his torch, kindling loves (1.461).[18] The torch is also an attribute of Diana as "light-bringer" (Lucifera/Phosphoros).[19] Apollo subconsciously reinforces the lurking identity of Diana in this scenario by his dismissal of Cupid, which pushes him toward further identification with Diana via a different attribute. Apollo tries to control his own sense of identity by not only restricting Cupid's but suppressing Diana's.

Cupid's address to Apollo as he expresses his own sense of supremacy is additionally telling. He addresses Apollo as Phoebus (1.463), which echoes the narrator's naming of the god at 1.452 (*primus amor Phoebi*). One way the siblings become further drawn together is by the shared name of Phoebus/ Phoebe, a name that reinforces their similarities and relationship as the pair of solar and lunar brightness.[20] Another name-pair they share is Delius/ Delia, after their birthplace, the island Delos. Within the Ovidian corpus, Apollo is first named Delius at *Met.* 1.454, but Diana had received previous addresses as Delia at *Her.* 4.40 (and, if an exilic date is not accepted for the double *Heroides*, at 20.95). Apollo is only Delius in the *Metamorphoses*. Even more specific is their ability to share the name Cynthius/Cynthia, after the Delian mountain.[21] Apollo is never Cynthius in the epic *Metamorphoses*, only in the erotodidactic *Ars amatoria* (2.239) and elegiac *Fasti* (3.346, 3.353). Diana is Cynthia across the genresphere (*Her.* 18.74; *Fast.* 2.91, 2.159; *Met.* 2.465, 7.755, 15.537). Within the *pompa circensis* depicted at *Amores* 3.2, Ovid presents the siblings in a neat juxtaposition: *auguribus Phoebus, Phoebe uenantibus adsit* ("may Phoebus be present for seers, Phoebe for hunters," *Am.* 3.2.51).[22] In this lapidary fashion, he simultaneously assimilates and differentiates the paired divinities by means of a shared name and mirrored syntactical structure, but different, crystallizing spheres of power. *Augur Apollo* is representative of a new and true Augustan litero-cultural identity of the god (cf. Hor. *Carm.* 1.2.32, *CS* 61–62; Virg. *Aen.* 4.376), while Diana's affiliation

Rivaled Affection and Affectation

with hunters is more reaffirming of purely literary roots. The close contact in this hexameter presents them as a paired, equal unit, without a hint of competition. Although it comes in a poetic description, this image of Apollo and Diana represents a scene of visual reality, reminding us that the children of Leto are presented as a harmonious and balanced unit within the Roman cultural world—a harmony that comes to especial fruition under Augustus.

Apollo and Diana's shared names provide one aspect of visual assimilation based on the experience of reading the text; this is especially evocative with the use of the vocative *Phoebe*. The divine identities of Apollo and Diana are also tied up in their accessories and how these accessories are used as visual indices of their identification. Already, we have seen how the quiver can be applied to visualize the identity of Diana, Apollo, or Cupid.[23] Ovid's Sappho provides a handy shortcut to assuming Apolline identity: *sume fidem et pharetram—fies manifestus Apollo* ("take up a lyre and a quiver—you become Apollo in the flesh," *Her.* 15.23). Her guidance, as discussed in the previous chapter, points to Delian Apollo specifically, and his Delian utterance of "let the bow and lyre be mine" (*Hymn. Hom. Ap.* 131). Similarly, Syrinx is said to be indistinguishable from Diana, apart from the material of her bow:[24]

> Ortygiam studiis ipsaque colebat
> uirginitate deam; ritu quoque cincta Dianae
> falleret et posset credi Latonia, si non
> corneus huic arcus, si non foret aureus illi.
> sic quoque fallebat.

(Met. 1.694–98)

[She was worshiping the Ortygian goddess in the cultivation of her rites and
  virginity;
kitted out in the manner of Diana, she could fool the eye, and be taken for
  Leto's daughter,
if there was not to this one a bow made of horn, to that one not a bow made
  of gold.
Even so, she was able to deceive.]

In both of these cases, divine markers exist as readily assumed or discarded as a costume, a very superficial "metamorphosis." Ovid elsewhere remarks on other cosmetically superficial ways to resemble Apollo and Diana:

94 Rivaled Affection and Affectation

alterius crines umero iactentur utroque:
    talis es assumpta, Phoebe canore, lyra.
altera succinctae religetur more Dianae,
    ut solet, attonitas cum petit illa feras.

(*Ars am.* 3.141–44)

Let the hair of another flow from either shoulder:
You become just like tuneful Phoebus, lyre in hand.
Another has garments tied out of the way, in the manner of Diana,
as she customarily appears when she attacks unreactive beasts.

A girl can emulate the style of Apollo Citharoedus or of the *uenatrix* Diana, with tresses either loosened or bound.[25] It is telling that Apollo can provide a model for feminine hairstyles. Apollo Citharodus is the appearance of the cult statue of the god, however, which contrasts with the "moving" image of the hunting Diana. Within these lines, there is a calibrated balance between a framework of similarity (*alterius . . . altera*) and descriptive difference.

APOLLO AND DAPHNE: DISGUISED DIANAS, COMPETITION, AND HARMONY

With these shared resemblances, epithets, and related points of contact in mind, we can begin to address the Ovidian narrative of Apollo and Daphne, and what it means to construct the identity of Leto's children: what it means to be or appear like them within the world of the *Metamorphoses*. Apollo and Diana present a case of mutually informed identity—literally, of relative identity.

Much of the poet's art is about choice. As a poet invested in not only creating a world history, but a world literary history, and an epic cycle of one continuous song, Ovid has a wealth of texts to choose from: what to highlight or suppress, expand, or compress; what versions to follow or adapt. When it comes to this myth, there is a set of choices that Ovid can make about how to represent Apollo and Diana that have not necessarily been recognized as such. On one hand, there is a strong thematic motif of competitive rivalry that shapes the Homeric and post-Homeric hymnic profile of each god: this is the especial purview of the Callimachean hymns, particularly the *Hymn to Artemis*.[26] On the other hand, there is a defining Augustan presentation of the pair that works especially hard to not only mediate Greek and Roman elements, but show the two gods as balanced, harmonious forces, working together in concert to look over the Roman state: Horace's *Carmen Saeculare*. The *Carmen Saeculare* is a hymn that also weaves its poetic representation of Apollo and Diana from previous iterations of Latin hymnic material such as Catullus 34, Tibullus 2.5, Propertius 4.6, and Horace's own *Ode* 1.21. Ovid's choice, therefore, can be bluntly framed as one between (Callimachean) competition and (Horatian) harmony. This chapter unpicks how Ovid tackles this polarity of interaction in setting out the personalities of these gods within his epic universe.

One overarching difference lies in how the divinities are introduced to the world of the epic, and, concomitantly, how much control they are narratively granted over their presentation. While Apollo is allowed to define his own attributes, beginning with the voicing of his "self-hymn" in pursuit of Daphne (1.512–24), Diana is instead first introduced obliquely through a series of figures that resemble her: Daphne, Syrinx, and Callisto. Diana's first appearance in the epic is, in fact, not even Diana herself, but the disguised Jupiter, who has assumed Diana's appearance in order to seduce Callisto (*protinus induitur faciem cultumque Dianae*, "at once he assumes the appearance and accessories of Diana," 2.425).[27] This line brings up a few things that deserve highlighting here. Most overt is the two-part nature of the "Diana" disguise (*facies* and *cultus*).[28] *Cultus* first looks back to the passage of the *Ars amatoria* that offers the advice of the "Diana" hairstyle, as well as to the material of Diana's bow as an identifier.[29] More importantly, with the alternate meaning of *cultus* borne in mind, it warps the previous conception lent by Diana-like figures in the *Metamorphoses* that imitation is not only the sincerest form of flattery but also the sincerest form of worship. Jupiter, who imitates Diana not to emulate but to undermine, by thwarting Callisto's commitment to virginity after the sacred model of Diana, uses her own identity against her.[30] To a certain extent, his ability to assume and take ownership of her form can be parsed by the relationship between father and daughter that opens her Callimachean hymn: Zeus grants Artemis her defining characteristics, so who better than to fraudulently make use of them?

Ovid seems to have borrowed the detail of this disguise from New Comedy (Amphis, fr. 46 K-A). This comedic borrowing is in accordance with the image of Apollo Ovid builds throughout the epic: generally, the god is not the dignified figure of Augustan reverence, but a hapless youth. Ovid largely bypasses the recent poetic upgrades to Apolline standing afforded by Virgil and Horace. Instead, he reroutes the expressive tone of the god's identity back to comedy and his appearances as a "figure of fun" in early Republican poetry.[31] Diana becomes initially complicit in this comedic framing when Jupiter first assumes her appearance for the undignified purpose of seducing an unwitting virginal huntress. Apollodorus, however, records a different disguise taken by Zeus (*Bibl.* 3.8.2). In this version, Zeus appears as Apollo. Although no other extant sources locate Apollo within Callisto's myth, it is easy to see how this disguise would have made an appealing (still comedic) variation. If this is part of an earlier complex of comedic myth, and not an innovation of Apollodorus, this would also be material understandably ripe for satirical purposes. One of Apollo's appearances as a "figure of fun" occurs within Lucilian satire, where he complains about being labeled *pulcher*. He speaks of comparing his looks to Leda and Dia, riffing off an Iliadic line (fr. 28–29 Warmington; cf. Hom. *Il.* 14.317). Apollo's "feminine" beauty is a subject of contention here, and his comparison to the mortal loves of Zeus provides an interesting point of comparison for Zeus' assumption of his form to seduce a mortal woman. Apollo's objection also points to his "prettiness" as an especially identifying characteristic, one easily drawn into comparison with Diana.

However, there is also a hymnic lesson hidden here about the Diana disguise, which is telling for the way the goddess is introduced in the *Metamorphoses*. The interaction between Artemis and Aphrodite in the *Homeric Hymn to Aphrodite* can provide a brief window of understanding how to approach the text. Beyond the two short *Homeric Hymns* to Artemis (9, 27), there is a detailed, even hymnic, image given of the goddess within the *Homeric Hymn to Aphrodite* as one of the goddesses untamed by love (*Hymn. Hom. Ven.* 16–20): in this miniature hymn, Artemis delights in archery, the slaying of beasts on mountainsides, the lyre, choral dances and ritual cries, shady forests, and the cities of just men. As has been noted, Aphrodite gradually absorbs all these spheres of activity in her false narrative to Anchises, to whom she appears in the guise of the virginal Artemis. So successful is her disguise, in fact, that Anchises first guesses that the goddess before him is Artemis (*Hymn. Hom. Ven.* 93).[32] Aphrodite's appropriation of Artemis' attributes to create her false identity is not to impersonate Artemis herself, however, but to impersonate a virgin; adopting the trappings of Artemis is the easiest way to communicate this.[33] The goddess of love pretending to be a virgin is almost as humorous as Jupiter pretending

Rivaled Affection and Affectation

to be Diana. However, Aphrodite's seduction of Anchises, accomplished by the borrowing of Artemis' virgin costume, is in fact set into motion by Zeus as comeuppance for her meddling in the love-affairs of the gods. Zeus, in other words, has seen that one way to successfully seduce a mortal is to assume such a costume: to become not just *a* virgin but *the* virgin is the collapsing of the distance between mortal and immortal that Aphrodite needed to use to her advantage, which catapults Jupiter's assumption of this costume into the realm of comedy. The *Homeric Hymn to Aphrodite* provides a model of seduction that Amphis' Zeus and Ovid's Jupiter have read humorously literally and humorously limitedly. Furthermore, the *Homeric Hymn to Aphrodite* teaches that "Artemis" can be visual code for "virgin," a blurring of boundaries be-tween immortal and mortal, worship and being. This blurring informs the parade of Diana lookalikes in the *Metamorphoses*, who appear in a series of narratives that ultimately end by showing the triumph of love and desire over virginity. Artemis may not ever be able to be tamed by love, but "artemis," in the Ovidian landscape, can be tamed by metamorphosis or assault. Just as Artemis' characteristics are most fully explored not in her own short *Homeric Hymns*, but throughout the narrative *Homeric Hymn to Aphrodite*, as Aphrodite progressively assumes them and assimilates herself to their contours, Ovid uses doubles to frame the identity of Diana. He embeds the hymnic experience of how Diana's identity is explored in preparation for the moment when the goddess herself enters the space of the epic, which also exploits the way hymns can be narratively used to introduce epics.[34]

The complicated relationship set up between Aphrodite and Artemis in the *Homeric Hymn to Aphrodite* is most fully explored in the myth of Callisto, who is introduced by the unusual description of *miles erat Phoebes* ("she was a soldier of Diana," 2.415).[35] Jupiter assumes the guise of the virginal goddess in order to make an assault on her virginity, and thus, her tie to Diana. Functionally, he weaponises the virginal costume, as he uses Diana's virginity against Callisto's own emulated virginity of Diana. In this light, we can see the idea of *miles Phoebes* as militated against the idea of *miles amoris*, redressing the appropriative work elegy had already done by borrowing the term *miles* to describe the metaphorical battles and hunts of love. The work of Phoebe's soldiers is to protect virginity and to engage in the literal hunt as an expression of purity, in landscapes that evoke this physical purity.[36] Being a *miles Phoebes* means being a soldier *against* love's

98 Rivaled Affection and Affectation

army, an anti-Venus, evoking the polarity between Artemis and Aphrodite explored and manipulated in the *Homeric Hymn to Aphrodite*. Ovid's introduction of Diana through figures of emulation that are subjected to the force of desire draws upon the hymnic background of the *Homeric Hymn to Aphrodite*, and the work done there to establish the identity of Artemis as an exploitable visual medium that derives meaning from a purposeful contrast with Aphrodite's own identity and motivations.

From Artemis to Diana

With one hymnic background established for framing Diana's characterization and appearances in the *Metamorphoses*, we now turn in this portion to the literary progression of Artemis to Diana via hymnic texts, and the hymnic tropes that are carried forward from the Greek into the Roman world to represent the goddess and her identifying traits. The passages in this section are where we see the literary context for choices made between Callimachean rivalry and Horatian harmony. As the *Homeric Hymn to Aphrodite* tells us, the point of departure is her virginity. The dynamic between the goddesses within the *Homeric Hymn to Aphrodite* relies on Artemis' virginity as her primary identifying characteristic. Artemis' virginity becomes a defining characteristic of the goddess, so giving Callimachus the opportunity to present its aetiology: he begins his hymn with the young goddess in the act of asking her father for this attribute:

> ἄρχμενοι ὡς ὅτε πατρὸς ἐφεζομένη γονάτεσσι
> παῖς ἔτι κουρίζουσα τάδε προσέειπε γονῆα·
> "δός μοι παρθενίην αἰώνιον, ἄππα, φυλάσσειν"
>
> (Callim. *Hymn* 3.4–6)

> [beginning from the time when still a little girl, sitting upon her father's knees, she spoke in this childish way to her father: "gimme virginity, Daddy, to preserve forever" (trans. Stephens)]

Callimachus gives the goddess the power to choose and cultivate her virginity as an act of self-expression: the young goddess sitting on the lap of her indulgent father is a scene of Homeric fan fiction, but not from the *Homeric Hymns*. It literalizes the image of the "childish" Artemis being consoled by her father after Hera's beating in the Iliadic theomachy (*Il.* 21.505–10).[37] In Homer, Artemis acts like a child; in Callimachus, she is one. In examining

Rivaled Affection and Affectation

early literary depictions of Artemis, Ivana Petrovic shows how her divine persona is prevailingly Homeric, which negates attentiveness to local cultic or ritual identities; she notes, "it seems that the depiction of gods in poetry demanded a careful negotiation of their identity with respect to their Homeric personae."[38] She locates Callimachus' hymnic innovation in his attention to the goddess' *cultic* aspect: instead of neglecting this essence, Callimachus re-defines Artemis as a goddess who reflects Homeric heritage *and* cultic reality, therefore redefining her hymnic authority (and his own, in the process). Callimachus' negotiation of her Homeric persona is evident from the hymn's beginning, and his redrawing of the Homeric vignette "child-like Artemis consoled" to "infant goddess demands favors from father."

In creating Daphne, Ovid closely reprises the Callimachean scene: it is less Callimachean fan fiction than Callimachean adaptation.

> illa uelut crimen taedas exosa iugales
> pulchra uerecundo suffunditur ora rubore,
> inque patris blandis haerens ceruice lacertis
> "da mihi perpetua, genitor carissime," dixit
> "uirginitate frui; dedit hoc pater ante Dianae."
>
> (*Met.* 1.483–87)

> [But she, hating marriage torches, tantamount to crime,
> her pleasing face overpoured with a charming blush
> and clinging to her father's neck with coaxing arms,
> said "grant me the allowance of perpetual virginity, dearest father;
> Her father granted this previously to Diana."]

Ovid's change is not to the image, but to its application. It is not Diana who begs her father for virginity, but Daphne. And Daphne does so with studied awareness of how the goddess came to this defining aspect in Callimachus.[39] Daphne's recent description as a "rival of unmarried Phoebe" cements this affiliation between nymph and goddess:

> Protinus alter amat, fugit altera nomen amantis,
> siluarum latebris captiuarumque ferarum
> exuuiis gaudens innuptaeque aemula Phoebes.
> [uitta coercebat positos sine lege capillos.]
>
> (*Met.* 1.474–77)

[At once one loves, the other flees the very label of a lover,
rejoicing in the shadows of the forests and the spoils of
captured beasts, a double of unwed Phoebe.
a ribbon kept her hair back, its only check for unruliness.]

Philip Hardie contextualizes Daphne's rivalry of Diana in act and appearance with Ovid's own literary *aemulatio* of Callimachus,[40] but Callimachus is already in rivalry with Homer; as a rival of Diana, Daphne is also a metaliterary gloss on the Callimachean Artemis' rivalry with the Homeric Artemis. And this Homeric Artemis is one who needs consoling after Hera's attack on her identity as ἰοχέαιρα, which she brings on herself by attacking Apollo's use of the bow.

Callimachus' awareness of this Homeric episode as humorously alluding to the internal rivalry of the archer gods is made clear by the very next demand he places in Artemis' mouth: καὶ πολυωνυμίην, ἵνα μή μοι Φοῖβος ἐρίζῃ ("and [give me] to be called by many names, so that Phoebus may not rival me," *Hymn* 3.7). The poet acknowledges his source for the portrait of the goddess at the very same time he alludes to a point in time when Apollo refuses to engage with Artemis despite her insults about their shared attribute, hinting at a reason for this refusal. Her desire for "many-namedness" responds to both her own Homeric presentation and the praises of the Callimachean Apollo.[41] Artemis has four Homeric expressions that describe her in strictly Apolline terms: κασιγνήτην Ἑκάτοιο (*Hymn. Hom.* 9.1); ὁμότροφος Ἀπόλλωνι (*Hymn. Hom. Ap.* 199); ὁμότροφον Ἀπόλλωνος (*Hymn. Hom.* 9.2); αὐτοκασιγνήτην χρυσαόρου Ἀπόλλωνος (*Hymn. Hom.* 27.3).[42] Notably, these all occur within the *Homeric Hymns*. By her Callimachean request for an individualizing "manynamedness," Artemis resists a Homeric mode of hymning that sees her identity dependent on Apollo. Her request to their father is motivated by a desire to detach herself from this Homeric dependency. It also responds competitively to the Callimachean Apollo. Within Apollo's hymn, the poet addresses Apollo with a variety of cult names:

ὤπολλον, πολλοί σε Βοηδρόμιον καλέουσι,
πολλοὶ δὲ Κλάριον, πάντη δέ τοι οὔνομα πουλύ·
αὐτὰρ ἐγὼ Καρνεῖον· ἐμοὶ πατρώϊον οὕτω.

(Callim. *Hymn* 2.69–71)

Rivaled Affection and Affectation

[O Apollo, many call you Boedromios, many Clarius, and indeed everywhere many a name is yours. But I call you Carneius, for thus is my ancestral custom. (trans. Stephens)]

Apollo's name here is also punned upon by the repetition of πολλοί . . . πολλοί, hinting at a link between Apollo and πολύς, further emphasizing the fittingness of "many names" for the god whose primary name indicates "many."[43]

Callimachus' choice to promote this aspect of Artemis—it comes even before her desire for a bow, her third request—also provides a useful way to conceptualize the Roman Diana as well, as evidenced in hymnic texts. Catullus' hymn to the goddess moves through praising her as Juno Lucina, Trivia, and Luna (Catull. 34.13–16), before ending with the following prayer:[44]

> sis quocumque tibi placet
> sancta nomine, Romulique,
> antique ut solita es, bona
> sospites ope gentem.
>
> (Catull. 34.21–24)

[May you be made holy
by whatever name is pleasing to you
and, as you have done before,
may you keep Romulus' descendants
safe, with your good help and grace.]

The entreaty to the goddess to be venerated by "whatever name pleases you" looks back to the earlier sequence of her name-attributes, but the reference to a time previous (*antique*) could also be a gentle reminiscence of the demand the Callimachean Artemis makes, hinting at an array of further names that may please the goddess.[45] Artemis as a "helper" is also contained within the goddess' Callimachean expression of her identity:

> οὔρεσιν οἰκήσω, πόλεσιν δ᾽ ἐπιμείξομαι ἀνδρῶν
> μοῦνον ὅτ᾽ ὀξείῃσιν ὑπ᾽ ὠδίνεσσι γυναῖκες
> τειρόμεναι καλέωσι βοηθόον . . .
>
> (Callim. *Hymn* 3.20–22)[46]

[I'll dwell in the mountains, but mingle with the cities of men only when women who are worn down under the sharp pangs of childbirth call for my aid. (trans. Stephens)]

Artemis says that she will dwell in the mountains, only coming to cities when women in labor call upon her, responding to their calls for help.[47] The movement from mountain to city occasioned by her role as "helper" is also suggested by the movement of the Catullan hymn, contextualizing the allusion to the significance of her naming system. Catullus initially hails Diana as the "mistress of mountains" (*montium domina*, 34.9) before referring to her role as watching over women in childbirth (34.13–16), while the final prayer entreats her as the protectress (*bona/sospites ope*) of the Roman people. *Romuli . . . gentem* summons the implicit presence of the city of Rome alongside the explicit idea of protected generations of Roman people. As she proclaims it, Artemis' role as protecting women in childbirth provides the initial conduit for her movement from the wilds to cities; Catullus uses this as a model trajectory for his hymn, ending with a prayer that subtly reinforces her as a "city" goddess.

In the *Carmen Saeculare*, Horace also preserves this Callimachean-Catullan arc of mountain goddess to childbirth protectress.[48] After initially addressing her as *silvarumque potens Diana* ("Diana, powerful goddess of the forests"), the goddess' names are expanded upon in her next address, as a goddess of childbirth:[49]

> rite maturos aperire partus
> lenis, Ilithyia, tuere matres,
> siue tu Lucina probas uocari
>   seu Genitalis:

(Hor. CS 13–16)

[At the right time, bring to light timely births, gently
Ilithyia, protecting mothers, whether you prefer to be called
Lucina, or Genitalis.]

While Catullus uses three names to cover three attributes, Horace expands one category of attribute to three names: Ilithyia, Lucina, and Genitalis.[50] Horace's phrasing of the goddess' favor regarding the names she receives (*siue tu ... probas ... seu*) echoes the final courtesy of the Catullan prayer (*sis quocumque tibi placet / sancta nomine*). Horace, too, touches on the Callimachean "manynamedness" of Diana. The second person addresses in each poem (*sis, probas*) both respond to and fulfil the demand made by the young Callimachean Artemis.

In Horace's case, this responds in a way that is especially adapted for the Roman world. Horace's integration of Catullus 34, a hymn addressed only to Diana, in a way that preserves this defining moment for the goddess from her Callimachean hymn, represents a moment where we can conceivably see Horace yield allusive space to the existence of a rivalry between Apollo and Diana, despite his clear concern to present the gods as an equal pair. One other moment of potential acknowledgment comes in the preceding stanza, when Apollo is addressed as *alme Sol* ("nourishing Sun," CS 9). Coming on the heels of their (ostensibly) paired salutation as *lucidum caeli decus* ("bright ornamentation of the heavens," CS 2), the masculine use of *almus* is surprising, given its persistent feminine affiliation.[51] The label of *alme Sol*, therefore, seems designed as a clear "borrowing," and so, as a subtle expression of rivalry. However, this label can also be seen as a poetic response to Catullus 34, where the moon is described with an "illegitimate light" (*et notho es / dicta lumine Luna*, "and you are named Luna by your illegitimate light," 34.15–16). The light is "illegitimate" because it is borrowed from the light of the sun, Diana's brother Apollo.[52] Catullus' defining image of Luna, dependent on Sol, is balanced by Horace's dependence on Luna to depict the nature of Sol. What appears in isolation as an expression of competition becomes an expression of harmonious balance when the Catullan reference is supplied. Horace plays with the boundary between assimilation and appropriation, with knowing awareness of competition as the usual motivating dynamic between the two gods. Any hint that rivalry will become a prevailing dynamic within his hymn is first forestalled by learned allusion, but delicately reintroduced by lingering on Diana's "manynamedness" in the following stanza, introducing a subtle skein of tension to the progressively alternating hymnic invocations.

Horace's paired glorification of the twins represented the Roman culmination of their affiliation to date, as his song unites the textual, ritual, and physical dimensionalities of their power. The *Carmen Saeculare* doesn't just juxtapose the two divinities, as the coins struck by P. Clodius M. f. Turrinus in 42 BC, which depict a wreathed Apollo with a lyre on one side, Diana with quiver and torches on the obverse.[53] Nor does it simply evoke their familial connection, as communicated persistently by the numerous visual vignettes of Latona, Apollo, and Diana on display throughout the Greco-Roman world. Rather, it mutually invests the welfare of Rome in their joint hands. Part of this mutual investment is the way Horace brings together their physical centers of Roman power: the Palatine and Aventine. On this point, it is opportune to remember the ways the construction of Apollo's grand, new Palatine temple eclipsed the concomitant rebuilding of Diana's Aventine temple, under the sponsorship of Lucius Cornificius.[54] Extant artistic commentary favors the new temple, privileging its position in the historical record, but the ostensible domination of Roman attentions suggested by works like Propertius 2.31 should be tempered by awareness of the renovations made at the same time to Diana's Roman home. The network of their centers of Roman power, on the Palatine and Aventine, were further united by these shared attentions, which Horace's song could hardly fail to bring out.

Diana's rebuilt temple is also important as a locus for thinking about her Augustan prominence and appeal. It is in the context of her rebuilt temple that the goddess first receives the epithet Augusta, in acknowledgment of the celebration of the temple's dedication (shared with her important Arician shrine) in the month newly known as August.[55] Diana Augusta is a truly Roman instantiation of the goddess, whose importance spreads throughout Italy and into the provinces over the first century AD Horace's *Carmen Saeculare* is therefore also to be read with an understanding of how the divine twins are further united under their joint mission to communicate what it means to be "Augustan."[56]

DAPHNE, A DELIAN MIRROR

The previous section established a background for treatments of Diana's identity within the hymnic tradition, and as it moves from the Greek to the Roman world. Now, we can begin to see where Ovid arrives on the scene and start to delineate the nature of both his indebtedness and innovations. When Ovid introduces Daphne as *innuptae aemula Phoebes* (1.476), he anticipates the quotation of the Callimachean hymn by fusing the ideas of virginity and rivalry. By making Daphne a rival of Diana, and one who initiates the pattern of hymnically influenced Diana-lookalikes that populate the *Metamorphoses*, Ovid also expands the Callimachean remit of "manynamedness," beginning

Rivaled Affection and Affectation

to signal his commitment not to Horatian harmony, but to the complexities of Callimachean rivalry. Daphne, Syrinx, and Callisto all become "named" Dianas, an expansion of meaning that runs alongside Ovid's straightforward commitment to Callimachean polyonomasia: within the myth of Callisto, which stands parallel to Daphne's myth as the first narrative after destruction, the goddess is Phoebe (2.415), Trivia (2.416), Diana (2.425, 451), Dictynna (2.441), and Cynthia (2.465).[57] By contrast, within the Apollo and Daphne myth, Apollo is Phoebus (1.451, 452, 463, 490, 553), Delius (1.454), and Paean (1.566); the adjective *Apollineas* also appears at 1.473.[58] The equivalent structural standing of these myths is encouraged by the parallel use of *superbus* to introduce each god into the space of the myth: *Delius hunc, nuper uicta serpente superbus, / uiderat* ("the Delian god, proud because of his recent vanquishing of the serpent, had espied him," 1.454–55); *ecce suo comitata choro Dictynna per altum / Maenalon ingrediens et caede superba ferarum* ("behold Dictynna, surrounded by her chorus, as she proceeds along high Maenalus, proud in the slaughter of beasts," 2.441–42). Overall, Ovid honors the wishes of the Callimachean Artemis: Diana receives a notably greater multitude of names.

In the following sections, we begin to see the relationship Ovid builds between Diana and Daphne, and the influence it exerts upon Apollo and understanding his identity. Daphne, an emulator of Diana, is the modality for Ovid to signal rivalry between the Delians: she becomes a surrogate symbol of their competition. Daphne's rivalry of Diana begins with her hunting prowess (*siluarum latebris captiuarum ferarum / exuuiis gaudens*, "rejoicing in the shadows of the forests and in the spoils of captured beasts," 1.475–76) and extends to her appearance (*uitta coercebat positos sine lege capillos*, "a ribbon kept her hair back, its only check for unruliness," 1.477). The catalog of possible hairstyles for women Ovid has detailed previously in *Ars amatoria* 3 begins with the injunction of *non sint sine lege capilli* ("let your hair not be unruly," 3.133), an instruction that subsequently introduces "the Apollo" (flowing hair) and "the Diana" (tied up, for hunting convenience). Daphne's hair, *sine lege*, speaks to a lack of *cultus*, and so, belongs to neither "style" (but in fact, would greater resemble "the Diana"). When Apollo sees her hair (*spectat inornatos collo pendere capillos*, "he sees her unadorned hair lying upon her neck," 1.497), the first physical attribute he remarks upon, he asks, *quid si comantur?* ("and what would it look like, if it were arranged?," 1.498).[59] At the moment he sees Daphne's hair, it more resembles "the Apollo," loose upon her neck; his question, however, is one of *cultus*. With knowledge of the *Ars amatoria* and the terminology of cultivation, Apollo is asking what her hair would look like with applied *cultus*. However, the competing descriptions of Daphne's hair (1.477 and 1.497) and their loose analogues to the choices of hairstyle within the *Ars amatoria* then begs the question: is Apollo envisioning what her hair would look like in his style, or in Diana's? Diana's hairstyle is designed to be practical for motion, while his is designed for the aesthetic of static posturing; given the chase that ensues between god and nymph, one might suspect that Apollo is envisioning Daphne looking not like Diana, but like himself. Daphne's status as a rival of Diana is the mechanism for Ovid to explore the rivalry between Apollo and Diana, and he seemingly does so to the point of collapse: Apollo's desire for Daphne (a stand-in for his own twin sister) sets into motion a transformation that has been read as an obliteration of her own self, an effacing of identity that would consequentially leave only Apollo.[60] As tends to be the case with Ovid, however, it is not quite so simple.

The obliteration of Daphne's identity is conceptualized by her transformation into the laurel, a tree whose evergreen nature ratifies Apollo's own youthful appearance:

"utque meum intonsis caput est iuuenale capillis,
tu quoque perpetuos semper gere frondis honores."
finierat Paean; factis modo laurea ramis
adnuit utque caput uisa est agitasse cacumen.

(Met. 1.564–67)

["and as my head is youthful with locks unshorn,
so you too will always bear the honors of being evergreen!"
Apollo had finished: the laurel, with branches just now made
nodded and seemed to assent with her leafy canopy.]

As Hardie has pointed out, the end of Apollo's prophecy reconfigures Daphne's request for virginity by the shared designator *perpetuus* (cf. *perpetua*, 1.486). In the ending prayer of Tibullus 2.5, an elegiac hymn to Apollo, the laurel's leaves are made complicit in the perpetuity of both: *adnue: sic tibi sint intonsi, Phoebe, capilli / sic tua perpetuo sit tibi casta soror* ("nod assent: and so may your hair remain unshorn, so may your sister remain unendingly chaste," Tib. 2.5.121–22). The Tibullan Apollo's nod becomes the

Ovidian laurel's nod; the laurel simultaneously reflects Diana's virginity and Apollo's youthfulness. The ambiguity of the laurel's gesture affords a moment to reflect upon what this means. On one hand, the movement of the laurel is one sign of Apolline epiphany, recalling the epiphany that opens the Callimachean *Hymn to Apollo*: Οἷον ὁ τὠπόλλωνος ἐσείσατο δάφνινος ὄρπηξ ("how Apollo's branch of bay shakes in awe," *Hymn* 2.1).[61] On the other, the seeming gesture also recalls an epiphany of Diana from the *Heroides*, when the goddess marks the words of Cydippe's oath to Acontius: *adfuit et, praesens ut erat, tua uerba notauit / et uisa est mota dicta tulisse coma* ("she was present, and, as marking her presence, she acknowledged your words, and she seemed to move her hair, in response to the words," *Her.* 20.19–20). The connection between hair and foliage that leads to the ending image of the laurel further makes this ease of equivalence between Diana's hair and the laurel's leaves, reinforcing the relevance of the Tibullan intertext.[62] If allusion to the *Heroides* is accepted, the laurel is not wholly assimilated to communicating Apolline identity, but retains some essence of Diana.[63] If the laurel's gesture is understood not simply as the triumph of an Apolline desire so warped as to self-reflect, but a shared marker of epiphany, the competitive presence of Diana is still an active conceit. Therefore, Diana retains an ownership in the creation of Apollo's defining attribute, an attribute introduced by Daphne's description as a double of the goddess.

APOLLINE IDENTITIES

After briefly detailing how Daphne's introduction works to frame questions of identity between the Delians—questions raised by hymnic awareness—we now take a closer look at how the Ovidian Apollo frames his own identity vis-à-vis his previous literary appearances. The Ovidian narrator frames Daphne's identity as a Diana-double, an identity emphasized when Daphne herself is allowed to voice the request of the Callimachean Artemis. While Ovid introduces Daphne in a visibly Callimachean manner, Apollo, via the poet's construction, is made to strenuously resist this framework. When Apollo is given the opportunity to introduce himself, instead of aligning himself with his Callimachean precedent, he chooses to distance himself:

> cui placeas inquire tamen; non incola montis,
> non ego sum pastor, non hic armenta gregesque
> horridus obseruo.
>
> (*Met.* 1.512–14)

[Moreover, ask whom you please: I am no mountain-dweller,
I am no shepherd, nor do I, uncultivated, watch over herds or flocks here.]

Apollo's triple negation denies any connection to the wilds or a pastoral existence. Superficially, this denial presents the Ovidian Apollo's concern for civilized sophistication, an adherence to an ironic admixture of the primordial and Augustan Golden Ages, both free of agricultural labor and dedicated to *cultus*. In keeping with the pretext of Daphne as his *primus amor*, Apollo's disavowal of belonging to the pastoral world attempts to erase his Callimachean experience as the lover of Admetus, the Thessalian king for whom he played herdsman:

Φοῖβον καὶ Νόμιον κικλήσκομεν ἐξέτι κείνου,
ἐξότ᾽ ἐπ᾽ Ἀμφρυσσῷ ζευγίτιδας ἔτρεφεν ἵππους
ἠιθέου ὑπ᾽ ἔρωτι κεκαυμένος Ἀδμήτοιο.

(Callim. *Hymn* 2.47–49)

[Phoebus we also call *Nomios* from the time when, by the Amphryssus, he tended the yoked mares, burning with passion for the youth Admetus. (trans. Stephens)]

Specifically, Apollo denies his epithet Νόμιος. This epithet encompasses not only his guise as a herdsman, but his assistance with ensuring the fertility of the flock (*Hymn* 2.50–54), a role that brings him closer to the realm of his sister Artemis. Callimachus appends this role to his description of the four canonical Apolline powers (archery, prophecy, song, healing). Ovid's excision, or denial, is reactive to this Callimachean presentation.[64] The pointed use of *horridus* reveals that Apollo is not just seeking to negate this portion of his Callimachean hymnic identity, but the version it inspired for Roman elegy: in Tibullus 2.3, Apollo's mother laments at the state of the lovelorn Apollo's hair, as he neglects the upkeep of his identifying powers to play shepherd to his beloved Admetus: *saepe horrere sacros doluit Latona capillos* ("often Latona lamented, seeing his sacred locks in disarray," Tib. 2.3.23). Apollo's denial covers both original and imitation. The Ovidian Apollo is motivated to present an identity as "epic" as possible. As we have discussed, the poetic identity of the gods is in constant negotiation with their Homeric selves, a process innovatively and deftly managed by Callimachus' *Hymns* as he recreates their identities for his own poetic world. Ovid plays with this Callimachean "bringing up to date" by having his Apollo instead insist on a visible departure from his Callimachean self, and a negation of his Hellenistic advancement in identity; the Ovidian Apollo wants to exhibit the traditional weight of the Homeric hexameter tradition.

This desire is evident from the beginning, expressed by Apollo's verbal attack upon Cupid for bearing a bow. His eagerness to preserve his connection with the bow can be framed as a desired monopoly upon his Homeric adjective κλυτότοξος ("famed for the bow"), which further contextualizes Artemis' taunt about his bow being used "in vain."[65] The Homeric references move from the contextually implicit to the textually explicit when Apollo departs from his anti-Callimachean hymnic stance:

> "nescis, temeraria, nescis,
> quem fugias, ideoque fugis. mihi Delphica tellus
> et Claros et Tenedos Patareaque regia seruit;
> Iuppiter est genitor; per me quod eritque fuitque
> estque patet; per me concordant carmina neruis.
> certa quidem nostra est, nostra tamen una sagitta
> certior, in uacuo quae uulnera pectore fecit.
> inuentum medicina meum est opiferque per orbem
> dicor et herbarum subiecta potentia nobis.
> ei mihi, quod nullis amor est sanabilis herbis,
> nec prosunt domino quae prosunt omnibus artes!"
>
> (*Met.* 1.514–22)

> ["You don't know, impetuous girl, you don't know
> whom you flee, and yet, you still flee! Me, the
> Delphic land, and Claros and Tenedos and the Patarean court serve;
> Jupiter is my father; through me, what will be, what was, and what is
> lies open; through me, strings find their harmony.
> My aim is true, but there is nevertheless one bolt
> of truer aim, which has now made a wound in my empty heart!
> The invention of medicine is owed to me, and I am called
> healer throughout the world, he who possesses the power of herbs.

110

Rivaled Affection and Affectation

But alas, as love is not curable by any herb, nor do these skills,
which profit everyone, profit their master at all!"]

The inclusion of Tenedos in his list of cult-sites is notably Homeric. Although minor in comparison to the other major Apolline cult centers, it signals reminiscence of Chryses' prayer to Apollo as the god who "rules over Tenedos" in *Iliad* 1 (Hom. *Il.* 1.38). Likewise, the following statement of his prophetic powers looks back to the Homeric description of Calchas' sight (ὅς ἤδη τά τ᾽ ἐόντα τά τ᾽ ἐσσόμενα πρό τ᾽ ἐόντα, "who had known the things being, the things that would be, and the things that had been before," *Hom. Il.* 1.70). Apollo strives for the authentic epic *grauitas* only Homeric authority can impart.[66] Apollo's prophetic art is the first in his list of four traditional attributes, his spheres of (usual) competency: prophecy, song, archery, and healing.[67] This is a list familiar from the Callimachean hymn:

τέχνη δ᾽ ἀμφιλαφὴς οὔτις τόσον ὅσσον Ἀπόλλων·
κεῖνος ὀϊστευτὴν ἔλαχ᾽ ἀνέρα, κεῖνος ἀοιδόν
(Φοίβῳ γὰρ καὶ τόξον ἐπιτρέπεται καὶ ἀοιδή),
κείνου δὲ θριαὶ καὶ μάντιες· ἐκ δέ νυ Φοίβου
ἰητροὶ δεδάασιν ἀνάβλησιν θανάτοιο.

(Callim. *Hymn* 2.42–46)

[No one has as many skills as Apollo. That one has received the archer as his lot, and the singer (for to Apollo is entrusted the bow and song), and his are diviners and prophets. And from Phoebus doctors have learned the postponement of death. (trans. Stephens)]

The four spheres of power are the same, albeit in slightly different order; the hymn then goes on to hail Apollo as Nomios, the portion of praise excised by the Ovidian Apollo.[68] For his part, Callimachus has taken inspiration from Pindar:[69]

ὃ καὶ βαρειᾶν νόσων
ἀκέσματ᾽ ἄνδρεσσι καὶ γυναιξὶ νέμει,
πόρεν τε κίθαριν, δίδωσί τε Μοῖσαν οἷς ἂν ἐθέλῃ,
ἀπόλεμον ἀγαγών

ἐς πραπίδας εὐνομίαν,
μυχόν τ᾽ ἀμφέπει
μαντήϊον·

(Pind. Pyth. 5.63–69)

[He also bestows remedies for grievous illnesses
upon men and women; he has provided
the cithara and confers the Muse on whomever he pleases,
after putting peaceful good governance
into their minds;
and he rules over
his oracular shrine (trans. Race)]

Pindar lists the attributes of the god as he transitions narratively from Apollo's healing of Battus to the founding of Cyrene. The one traditional Apolline attribute he passes over is the bow, as he emphasizes peace, unity, and order, especially as presided over by the oracular god.[70] By beginning with healing and omitting reference to his punitive weaponry, Pindar, in a sense, presents all Apolline powers as remedies for human conditions. Callimachus, rather, packages together Apollo's bow and lyre as ἔντεα (Hymn 2.19; cf. also 44), mutually investing the polarities of Apolline undertaking. He does not reproduce a Homeric alteration between the two instruments, as represented by Iliad 1's trajectory, where Apollo first dispatches the ranks of Greeks with his arrows (Il. 1.44–52) before he harmonizes on his lyre in song with the Muses (Il. 1.601–4).[71]

APOLLO/OPIFER

The list of Apolline powers as found in Pindar and Callimachus functionally creates a poetically canonical list, one the Ovidian Apollo responds to: this enumeration of power is significant for how Ovid's Apollo presents himself to Daphne. The emphases Apollo insists upon also have repercussions for both understanding the Ovidian text and its sociopolitical context; here, we will address one such emphasis made, upon the art of healing. Looking at what happens to this list of powers within the world of Roman poetry, we can see that within the Latin tradition, the only poem that enumerates Apolline powers comprehensively for the god himself is the Carmen

Saeculare. Near the hymn's close, his four traditional activities are neatly packaged within the four-line Sapphic stanza:[72]

> augur et fulgente decorus arcu
> Phoebus acceptusque nouem Camenis,
> qui salutari leuat arte fessos
>   corporis artus,

(Hor. CS 61–64)

> [Phoebus, the seer adorned with gleaming bow,
> dear to the nine Camenae
> who with salving art, lifts up
> the beleaguered limbs of the body.]

Although Horace's list, inclusive of his bow, seems at first more Callimachean than Pindaric, Apollo appears with the bow in a fashion that recalls the decorative program of statuary, as opposed to an active or threatening use.[73] In line with Pindar, both the Ovidian and Horatian text lend a similar proportion of sustained emphasis to the *ars* of healing.[74] When we turn to Ovid, the Ovidian Apollo's bald statement of *inuentum medicina meum est* moves away from the weight of Greek literary tradition to Roman cultural rootedness: he summons the identity of Apollo Medicus, the first instantiation of the god to receive cult worship in Rome. Before Apollo's Palatine quarters were even dreamt of, the first and only temple in Rome dedicated to the god was the temple of Apollo Medicus, vowed upon the guidance of the Sibylline books in 433 BC.[75]

Negotiating the boundary between Greek and Roman is a crucial agenda of the *Carmen Saeculare*, a concern already visible within Ovid's myth of Apollo and Daphne, as the prophecy of Apollo already looks forward to Augustan Rome: the very Rome that Horace conceptualizes his hymn for. Much of the Augustan cultural agenda can be briefly summarized as a repackaging of innovation as renovation, and as a literary exercise designed for a specific Augustan cultural moment, the *Carmen Saeculare* is no exception. Horace lends a veneer of tradition to the hymn's opening: as Barchiesi illustrates, "the poem is being quietly daring and witty in its address to Apollo and Diana as *colendi semper et culti: semper . . . culti* is the avowal of a Greek tradition which has never become Roman before, and it is up to this song to make the tradition happen."[76] Whereas Horace might have felt some discomfort about being pressed into service as an Augustan brand ambassador—Horatian anxiety about imperial praise permeates his later poems, and *Odes* 4 begins to stand as a perhaps unwitting (or unwilling) barometer for the necessity of acknowledging the age as "Augustan"[77]—Ovid openly brings a sense of comic relief to this role. After summoning Apollo "the Healer," the first Roman Apollo, the god elaborates, *opiferque per orbem / dicor* (*Met.* 1.521–22). This is the first appearance of *opifer* in extant Latin.[78] Apollo also seems to be inventing tradition—positioning himself as a "neotraditional" Apollo, mirroring the spirit of Augustan policy boldly embodied by Horace in the *Carmen Saeculare.* Apollo as *opifer* is sandwiched between two other aspects of his role as a healer, which he frankly acknowledges are of no current use:[79]

> inuentum medicina meum est opiferque per orbem
> dicor et herbarum subiecta potentia nobis.
> ei mihi, quod nullis amor est sanabilis herbis,
> nec prosunt domino quae prosunt omnibus artes!
>
> (*Met.* 1.521–24)

> [The invention of medicine is owed to me, and I am called
> healer throughout the world, who possesses the power of herbs.
> But alas, as love is not curable by any herb, nor do these skills,
> which profit everyone, profit their master at all![80]]

The emphasis that Horace and Apollo both place upon Apollo within these hymns as a healer introduces the question of an especial Augustan resonance to this role: did Augustus actively position himself in alignment with Apollo as a "healer" of the state?[81] According to Pliny, Valgius Rufus dedicated his (unfinished) treatise on medicinal herbs to Augustus as a healer (*HN* 25.4.2). Another intriguing piece of evidence is Dio's record of Augustus' speeches on marriage legislation.[82] Although later than can directly inform the *Metamorphoses,* Dio's version of the speech presents Augustus comparing himself to a physician taking necessary curative steps for the health and longevity of the Roman state (Cass Dio. 56.6). This marriage legislation features prominently in the *Carmen Saeculare* (17–20). Apollo's desire to marry Daphne (*Phoebus amat uisaeque cupit conubia Daphnes,* "Phoebus falls in love, and upon seeing Daphne conceives the desire for marriage," 1.490; *at quoniam coniunx mea non potes esse*, "but since you are not able to be my wife," 1.557) also reflects the priorities of this Augustan legislation.[83] The demands Daphne's father Peneus makes for a son-in-law and grandchildren (1.481–82) additionally paint him as a vocal promotor of the Augustan focus on the family, a focus soon echoed by Inachus, the father of Io: *spesque fuit generi mihi prima, secunda nepotum* ("first and foremost, I had the hope of a son-in-law; secondly, for descendants," 1.659). Inachus laments the hope he had for his continuing line, a lament that reflects the increasing attraction of *spes* into a realm of meaning especially tied to family and dynastic concerns. An especially familial sense of hope is already perceivable in the *Aeneid*, which features the phrase *spes . . . Iuli* four times (Virg. *Aen.* 1.556, 4.274, 6.364, 10.524). Horace ends his hymn with the image of hope being brought home (*spem bonam certamque domum reporto*, "we bear homewards a sure and good hope," *CS* 74); when "hope" also entails "the hope of future generations," "bring hope home" is a ready-made Augustan slogan. When Horace hails Diana to oversee the success of the marriage law (*CS* 17–20), he also uses the verb *prosperes*; *prosperus* is popularly (falsely) etymologized from *pro + spes*, further integrating the ideas of hope and continuity.[84] The myth of Apollo and Daphne is also permeated by hope (*sperat*, 1.491; *sperando*, 496; *sperat*, 536; *spe*, 539). Apollo's love is nourished and motivated by hope. However, Apollo's inability to cure his love is also an inability to cure his childlessness, as far as Daphne is concerned; once again, we return to Apollo's self-identification as *opifer*.

When the Ovidian Apollo tries to capitalize upon this identification as an *opifer*, it brings him back into competitive contact with his sister Diana, mediated by the ways Daphne attempts to evade his affections. While *opifer* appears nowhere else in extant Latin, an inscription to Diana Opifera appears at her cult site of Aricia, where there is evidence of Diana as a healing goddess.[85] Apollo's "neotraditionalism" is perhaps inspired by rivalry, an attempt to gain ownership of one of Diana's many names. After all, the sole positive presentation of Artemis in the *Iliad* occurs when she heals Aeneas with the assistance of Leto (Hom. *Il.* 5.447–48). Although Artemis likely appears here as a surrogate figure for Apollo, given that the space of healing is the temple to Apollo, the scene can nevertheless be drawn upon to set up a rivalry over the healing arts.[86] The question of *opifer/opifera* as title of the Delian twins and its hymnic potential can be addressed in light of the prayer that Daphne makes for transformation to her father, a prayer laden with significant Apolline language: "*fer, pater*," inquit, "*opem, si flumina numen habetis; /*

qua nimium placui, mutando perde figuram" ("'bear, father,' she said, 'help! if your streams hold divine power, lose this form in change, with which I was too much pleasing,'" 1.546–47). The plea of *fer . . . opem* plainly reconfigures *opifer*. Daphne's prayer attempts to use Apollo's power and self-constructed sense of divinity against him, which gains a different currency if Apollo has appropriated the title of *opifer* from Diana.[87]

The way Daphne's prayer attempts to ward off the god in language that recalls his self-identification is further underscored by the imperative of *perde*. John Miller interpreted the use of this verb to describe the Python's slaying (*perdidit*, 1.444) as hinting at a linguistic awareness of Apollo's name as derived from ἀπόλλυμι. Within her prayer, Daphne's language is once again loaded as she attempts to change the identity of the form that so pleased Apollo in a way that nevertheless implicates him by a veiled onomastic reference. Daphne's change itself is additionally described in a manner that unsettles Apollo's reliance on healing to construct his hymnic self-image: *uix prece finita torpor grauis occupat artus* ("scarcely was her prayer complete when a heavy numbness stole over her limbs," 1.548). The words of her prayer elide into her metamorphosis, a process described as a paralysis, replicating symptoms of disease.[88]

The medicalization of Daphne's metamorphosis provides a pendant to the portion of Apollo's self-hymn that laments the incurability of love, even for the healer-god: love is an "illness" Apollo cannot cure himself of, but Daphne's escape from his love is only wrought by the "disease" of metamorphosis. Most specifically, Daphne's metamorphic paralysis unravels the illustration of Apolline healing in the *Carmen Saeculare*, where Apollo "lifts up" (or "makes light") "the body's wearied limbs with his healing art" (*qui salutari levat arte fessos / corporis artus, CS* 63–64).[89] Daphne's prayer and transformation therefore provide their own commentary on Apollo's identity, particularly as it relates to his own expression of identity. In one aspect, this is entirely consonant with the final portion of her metamorphosis into not just the laurel tree, but the laurel into the symbol of Apollo. The circumstances of the prayer, however, make this reading more problematic. No matter how you read it, Daphne wants to escape Apollo, not become a visual indicator of his divinity.

APOLLO PAEAN

The constellation of issues Daphne's prayer raises when read conscientiously with both versions of sibling relationships in mind (Callimachean rivalry vs. Horatian equitability) gain new currency when Apollo is named Paean at the close of his prophecy about the newly created laurel (1.566). This name, and the genre of the same name, are worth dwelling on, and will provide new focus. The Sibylline oracle that prescribed the order of ceremonies at the Augustan *Ludi Saeculares* in 17 BC demanded "Latin paeans" to be sung: καὶ ἀειδόμενοί τε Λατῖνοι / παιᾶνες κούροισι κόρῃσί τε νηὸν ἔχοιεν / ἀθανάτων ("and let Latin paeans sung by youths and maidens fill the temple of the immortals," 149–51).[90] This ritual advice was actualized by Horace's *Carmen Saeculare*, allowing the label "paean" to be affixed to this song (as twice ritually encountered) and text (as received). In Barchiesi's reading, it is not simply or only a paean, but a "neo-Pindaric paean": a meditation on the literary genre that mediates between Greek and Roman literary texts, ritual, and cultural mentality in deliberate and self-conscious ways.[91] The dictate of the oracle elevated the paean to the level of national consciousness by making it a part of the *Ludi*'s proceedings, rendering it a promotional vehicle for the Augustan agenda—the same agenda the oracle itself was fabricated to promote, in ensuring creative control over this new manifestation of the Augustan age.[92]

As the label of paean does a lot of work to identify the nature of the Horatian song (and carries a lot of interpretive baggage), there has been some attention to how this song choice is integrated within the wider Augustan litero-cultural landscape. Notably, Miller has suggested that the *Carmen Saeculare* is anticipated by a moment within the *Aeneid*, showing up against part of the Virgilian underworld's pageantry: paeans are sung by the Trojan heroes in a laurel grove (*laetumque choro paeana canentis / inter odoratum lauris nemus*, "and singing a blessed paean in a chorus, amid the grove of fragrant laurel," Virg. *Aen.* 6.657–58).[93] On Virgil's use of *paean*, Servius comments, "Paean is properly praise of Apollo, which is here appropriate because of the 'grove of laurel.'" To Servius, the presence of the god is communicated by the physical space of the grove, and the songs work in harmony with their surroundings to cumulatively praise the god. Lauren Curtis picks up Miller's brief suggestion more expansively, identifying Horace's interest in "recreating the paeanic voice of Virgil's heroes" to mark its lyric status, lifting the hymn from its embedded epic context to forge a new voice of specifically lyric authority.[94] However, Horace doesn't just "recreate" the communal, celebratory paeanic voice of the Trojan heroes; he expands this lyric voice to include praise of Diana, generating a more inclusive understanding of paean. Although this expansion in some ways is necessitated to accommodate and reflect the ritual reality of the hymn's performance, sung by a chorus of boys and girls, it also accommodates a literary reality of the genre's sacredness to both Apollo and Artemis, as detailed in a fragment of Pindar (*Thren.* 3, fr. 128c S-M).[95] Horace restores one aspect of the genre by directing his praise toward the pair of deities, honoring metaphorically their especial Pindaric nature as twins.[96]

Although the definition of paean as a genre is especially difficult to pin down, Apollo's title as Paean is typically understood as "Healer."[97] Calling Apollo Paean restates his role as a healer, reaffirming the continuous importance of healing as a thematic thread within this myth.[98] It can also suggest a moment of ring composition to the episode that begins with his slaying of the Python, the occasion that provided the *aition* for the paean-cry (Callim. *Hymn* 2.97–104; cf. also 21).[99] If Callimachus' hymn was conceptualized as a paean by its use of the paean-cry, Ovid incorporates the genre by the one indicator not used in Callimachus, as a title of the god. The verb *finierat* (and the fact that capitalization is a modern textual convention) indicates some slippage between Paean and paean: "Paean had finished," or, "the paean had finished." How detachable is the title from the genre?[100] Ostensibly, Apollo's address to the laurel can also be read as a self-hymn, as it cements and celebrates the laurel's new status symbolic of his divinity. However, as not only a self-hymn but a paean, it could continue to reflect Daphne's initial reflection of not Apollo, but Diana, a tension also apparent in the prayer that initiates her metamorphosis. Horace's return to the expansion of paean to include praise of Diana in the *Carmen Saeculare*, a literary product of the Augustan Rome that Apollo's prophecy looks forward to, and a hymn that sets an agenda for the identity of Augustan Apollo, lingers suggestively in this pointed label.[101] Ovid continues to raise the question of a subtle retention of Diana's identity in the laurel that speaks to the competitive stakes of the hymnically defined identity the episode enacts.

Cyrene and Daphne

We have begun to see how the figure of Daphne performs a commentary on the constructed identity of the pair of gods: again, the aim of this chapter is overall to demonstrate that the constructed, textual role of Daphne herself is to focalize the competing identities of these Olympian siblings. Previously, we have focused on Daphne's connection to the gods themselves, but at this stage, we delve into the rich and complex litero-mythological background Daphne boasts, in her role as the *innuptae aemula Phoebes*. In other words, we now look at the other figures Daphne is textually connected to that further deepens her role as a commentary upon Apollo and Diana. In this effort, we begin with Cyrene: Daphne's textual inheritance from Cyrene forms one significant node of this rich and complex litero-mythological background.

As previously discussed, Daphne borrows the voice of the Callimachean Artemis to define herself by a devotion to purity. An adherence to purity represents one strand of identity whose models will be discussed. However, Apollo's desire to marry Daphne, and her identity as a Thessalian huntress also clearly aligns her with Cyrene, the fearless maiden Apollo spirits away from Thessaly as his bride to become the queenly guardian of the Libyan land.[102] Pindar's ninth *Pythian* relates this myth most extensively, a myth the scholia record is Hesiodic in origin (fr. 215 M-W).[103] While the Hesiodic Cyrene is only distinguished via her physical beauty (cf. fr. 215 M-W), the Pindaric Cyrene stands out because of her strength and daring, not her appearance. Espying her wrestling a lion unarmed, Apollo marvels and calls Chiron to witness her strength, fearlessness, and stalwart heart (Pind. *Pyth.* 9.26–37). Her heroic demeanor, not her appearance, makes her worthy of spectacle. Although the Pindaric Cyrene is not characterized with specific reference to Artemis, her lifestyle (spurning feminine pursuits, hunting and killing wild beasts, sleep as her [only] "sweet bedfellow"; cf. *Pyth.* 9.17–25) shows her in alignment with the goddess.[104] Daphne, as a neo-Cyrene, is more explicitly a rival.

The Ovidian Apollo does not spectate and praise Daphne for her hunting prowess (information relayed only by the narrator, 1.475–76), but for her beauty and physical form:

spectat inornatos collo pendere capillos,
et "quid si comantur?" ait; uidet igne micantes
sideribus similes oculos; uidet oscula, quae non
est uidisse satis; laudat digitosque manusque
bracchiaque et nudos media plus parte lacertos;
si qua latent, meliora putat.

(*Met.* 1.497–502)

[He sees her unadorned hair lying on her neck
and says, "what would it look like, if it were arranged?"
He looks at her eyes, similar to the stars' fires in their sparkling;
he looks at her lips, which are not enough merely to have looked at;
he praises her fingers and hands and arms, as much of them as are bare;
and if anything lies hidden, he deems it even more praiseworthy.]

Apollo praises Daphne according to the priorities of Hesiodic genealogical poetry; that is to say, he praises her appearance.[105] Furthermore, the god's compromised oracular sight is highlighted by his exertion of a relentlessly literal sight.[106] Apollo's narrative priorities additionally clash with the Ovidian narrator, who is more concerned with an aetiological (Pindaric) privileging of information. They do, however, meld with the narrative priorities of Peneus, who is named as the paternal grandfather of Cyrene in Pindar (*Pyth.* 9.14–17) and her father in Virgil (*Georg.* 4.355).[107] A crucial part of casting Daphne as a neo-Cyrene is making her the daughter of Peneus, an ostensibly Ovidian mythological innovation that receives emphasis with continual use of the patronymic (*Peneia* 1.452; *nympha Peneide*, 472; *Penei*, 504; *Peneia*, 525). Although Cyrene was similarly pursued by Apollo with intention of marriage, a crucial aspect of Cyrene's identity is her mothering of Aristaeus, emphasized by Pindar, Apollonius, and Virgil alike.[108] This renders Daphne's evocation of Cyrene partial, further highlighting her strict adherence to purity. Peneus' demand for descendants is in conversation with Ovid's choices regarding his mythological portrait of Daphne, as it can be read against the fate of Cyrene.[109] On a metaliterary level, Peneus' self-conscious call for descendants expresses concern for the integrity and continuity of the epic narrative: his request attempts to steer the epic into a known literary territory, by desiring the narrative to take the form of genealogical epic.

Ovid's poetic decision to use both Cyrene and the Callimachean Artemis as recognizable literary templates for Daphne sets their defining identities on a collision course. Now that a foundational connection between Cyrene and Daphne has been established, we can investigate the appearance of Cyrene in the Callimachean hymns, and how her Callimachean hymnic self informs Daphne's characterization. Crucially, Callimachus includes Cyrene in both hymns dedicated to the Delians: she can be found in both his *Hymn to Apollo* and *Hymn to Artemis*, making her a shared feature that highlights

120   Rivaled Affection and Affectation

further the drama of sibling rivalry that forms an especially prevailing aesthetic feature of Artemis' hymn.[110]

In the *Hymn to Apollo*, Cyrene appears in the sequence detailing the history of Cyrene's colonization (*Hymn* 2.65–96), as the poet turns to praise of Apollo Carneius and the Spartan festival *Carneia* that was brought to Libya. Although she gives her name to the city,[111] she only appears at the end of this narrative section:

τοὺς μὲν ἄναξ ἴδεν αὐτός, ἑῇ δ' ἐπεδείξατο νύμφῃ
στὰς ἐπὶ Μυρτούσσης κερατώδεος, ἧχι λέοντα
Ὑψηὶς κατέπεφνε βοῶν σίνιν Εὐρυπύλοιο.
οὐ κείνου χορὸν εἶδε θεώτερον ἄλλον Ἀπόλλων,
οὐδὲ πόλει τόσσ' ἔνειμεν ὀφέλσιμα, τόσσα Κυρήνῃ,
μνωόμενος προτέρης ἁρπακτύος.

(Callim. *Hymn* 2.90–95)

[These did the god himself see, and he showed his bride, standing upon horned Myrtussa, where the daughter of Hypseus killed the lion that was the plunderer of Eurypylus' cattle. Apollo has seen no other dance more divine, nor to a city has he allotted so much good fortune as he allotted Cyrene, mindful of his earlier carrying off of the nymph. (trans. Stephens)]

When it comes to the mythological treatment of Apollo and Cyrene, Callimachus ends (ἁρπακτύος) where Pindar begins (ἅρπασ', *Pyth.* 9.6). Common to both authors is Cyrene's distinguishing act of killing a lion, although Callimachus sets this deed in Libya: after Cyrene slays the lion, the king Eurypylus grants her the land.[112] He preserves her Thessalian lineage as a daughter of Hypseus, however, and her status as a bride (νύμφη) of the god. She is never named, although her eponymous city is.

Within the *Hymn to Artemis*, Cyrene is listed as part of the section on Artemis' favorite nymphs, as a favored companion of the goddess. Gifted with two hunting dogs, she distinguishes herself in the hunt:

καὶ μὴν Κυρήνην ἐταρίσσαο, τῇ ποτ' ἔδωκας
αὐτὴ θηρητῆρε δύω κύνε, τοῖς ἔνι κούρη
Ὑψηὶς παρὰ τύμβον Ἰώλκιον ἔμμορ' ἀέθλου.

(Callim. *Hymn* 3.206–208)

[And furthermore, you made Cyrene your companion and gave her two hunting hounds, with which the daughter of Hypseus won a prize alongside the Iolcian tomb. (trans. Stephens)]

Interpretation of Cyrene's ἄεθλον ("prize") is split between referring to the lion she defeats, or a reference to an event at the funeral games of Pelias (the "Iolcian tomb" is identified in the scholia as Pelias' tomb).[113] Of all Artemis' nymphs enumerated (Britomartis, Procris, Anticlea, Cyrene, and Atalanta), only Cyrene's narrative is mythologically and aetiologically unembellished.[114] This gap, and her direct naming, implies that it is designed as a cross-reference to the *Hymn to Apollo*. Cyrene receives two hunting dogs from Artemis, which looks back to the moment in the hymn where Artemis herself goes to collect her hounds: in Arcadia, Pan gifts her with six hounds of various colors (*Hymn* 3.90–91), which are said to take down lions (*Hymn* 3.91–93). Artemis doesn't use her hounds in her first hunt, and so Cyrene is the first depicted as hunting with hounds in the hymn; in this way, Callimachus hints at the "prize" being a lion. The Thessalian location (Pelias' tomb), by aligning with Pindar, chronologically supplants the version given in Apollo's hymn, and gives Artemis a prior claim to Cyrene.[115] Callimachus possibly also alludes to the Libyan account of Cyrene's lion-slaying by transferring the language of the Libyan land as a prize (ἄθλον, cf. Acesandros *FGrHist* F4) to the lion itself.[116]

Although Callimachus separates the treatment of Cyrene between the hymns, the poet nevertheless designs the two passages to be read in concert. Such a reading highlights Cyrene's emulation of Artemis, and thereby puts tension on the literary authenticity of her Libyan appearance, where her prowess as a huntress leads to the foundations of a city. The passage that leads into Cyrene's appearance in Artemis' hymn explains the exclusion of myrtle in Cretan ritual (*Hymn* 3.200–203), which additionally forms a contrast with her appearance on Myrtussa (cf. μυρτόεσσα, "covered in myrtle") in the *Hymn to Apollo* (*Hymn* 2.91). The adjective modifying Myrtussa, "horned," also recalls the collaborative work of Artemis and Apollo on Delos in constructing the altar of horns (*Hymn* 2.58–63).[117] Resonances of Artemis' appearance within the textual picture of Cyrene would also be recognizable as belonging to the physical landscape of Cyrene: Myrtussa, the natural terrace that comprises the sanctuary of Apollo in Cyrene's acropolis, holds the temples to Apollo and Artemis on its northern slope,

122   Rivaled Affection and Affectation

and the springs of Cyre and Apollo on its southern.[118] Callimachus' readers in this regard would understand the game Callimachus is playing with competitively summoning, but not fulfilling, Artemis' presence in the Cyrenean portion of Apollo's hymn. Across the pair of hymns, Cyrene's purity and allegiance to Artemis as a huntress in Artemis' hymn is set against her civilizing role as the bride of Apollo within the hymn to Apollo; the hymns present her in mutually exclusive roles that require a choice to be made about her Callimachean identity and her loyalty, but at the same time competitively vie for her Pindaric glory.

The Ovidian equation between Daphne and Cyrene is also perceptible in Cyrene itself, in an inscription that accompanied either the painted image of a laurel or an actual planting near the Propylaea (GVCyro28). Again, we can think of Cyrene potentially as the setting for the epiphany that opens *Hymn 2*. Although the inscription is later (ca. 2nd c. AD), it nevertheless brings together Daphne and Cyrene in an unambiguous way, and even suggests a marriage between Daphne and Apollo (γαμέτιν, 6).[119] According to the inscription, the laurel "fled" (φυγὰς, 4) from Delphi to Libya, merging Daphne's flight with Apollo's transport of Cyrene from Thessaly to Libya. Her origin in Delphi is also implicated with Thessaly, as Apollo carried the laurel for his purification from Tempe to Delphi, rendering the Delphic laurel originally Tempean.

HYMNING DAPHNE: CLOSURAL NOTES

Before we look at a different Callimachean hymnic model for Daphne's Ovidian characterization, we can pause to examine some additional ways her myth raises structural signs of poetic indebtedness to the hymnic tradition. Some points within the narrative progression can be discussed in light of the competitive dynamic of closural praise exhibited between Homeric and Callimachean hymns and can also be used to illuminate further Daphne's resistance to being fully absorbed into a purely Apolline attribute. As just discussed, Thessalian Daphne reconciles the nymph's split Callimachean presences to act as an embodiment of sibling rivalry, both physically and symbolically. Her myth kaleidoscopically reflects aspects of the divine personalities of both Diana and Apollo as experienced in hymnic texts, automatically entrenching her being within the context of Delian praise. And as described at the beginning of this chapter, praise motivates her myth. Apollo's

Rivaled Affection and Affectation

praise of himself is preceded by his praise of Daphne (*laudat*, 1.500). When she flees his praise (in both senses), the god still dwells on the loveliness of her form (1.527–30). When the nymph is said to flee him "prepared to say more" (*plura locuturum*, 1.525), leaving him with "words unsaid" (*uerba imperfecta*, 1.526), Ovid invites speculation about what would comprise the rest of this Apolline song: more praise of himself, or praise of Daphne? The information that he could not waste time upon further compliments (*sed enim non sustinet ultra / perdere blanditias iuuenis deus*, "but the youthful god could not abide losing further time to idle flatteries," 1.530–31) suggests the latter. However, the narratorial voice has just painted a picture of her especial loveliness in flight, possibly blurring the boundaries between the authorial voice and Apolline opinion.[120] The dual expression of Apollo's capacity to carry on with his song brings up the idea of hymnic length. At this juncture, this detail can be read as a humorous Ovidian gloss on the argument over proper hymnic length that Envy initiates in the Callimachean *Hymn to Apollo* (*Hymn* 2.105–6), censoring the hymn for not going to the same "oceanic" (Homeric) length as the *Homeric Hymn*.[121] Daphne's flight forces a narrative rupture that can be read as dramatizing this interpretive issue within the tradition of praising Apollo, a Homeric potential that is cut off to conform to a Callimachean reality. However, if Daphne's praises occupy the truncated version of the song, the reader would be returned to the praise of Daphne that led into Apollo's own (self-)praise: the interdependence of praise filters the literary legacy of the competitive allocation of praise to Apollo and Artemis within Callimachus' hymns.

The question of hymnic length and the sense of hymnic endings is also brought up by the episode's concluding mechanisms. The transformation of Daphne into the laurel provides one ending, but the reaction to her transformation provides another. From this ending, we are led into Io's tale. This suspension of closure is an aesthetic at work not in the Callimachean *Hymn to Apollo*, but the *Hymn to Artemis*, which frustrates expectations about narrative length and progression built by structural allusion to the *Homeric Hymn to Apollo*.[122] The *Hymn to Artemis* first appears to be ending at line 141, as the poet discusses his care for singing of Artemis. The hymn then carries on, as the metaphorical material of the poet's song becomes actualized.[123] Similarly, the use of χαῖρε at 225 seems to indicate closure, only for another episode to begin.[124] Even at 141 lines, the first half of Artemis' hymn is longer

Rivaled Affection and Affectation

than the 113-line *Hymn to Apollo*; Daphne's story itself would fit in perfectly with the section of Artemis' hymn where the singer lists the goddess' favorite nymphs, with an emphasis on the protection of virginity (*Hymn* 3.189–224).

After Daphne's metamorphosis, the Ovidian narrative proceeds to a description of Tempe. The description then segues to the convening of the river gods who respond to Daphne's new arboreal form. Assigning this response—in one sense, an interpretation of genre—to the rivers recalls the earlier narratological role of Daphne's father, the river Peneus. Peneus is positioned to reflect metapoetically on the generic identity of the narrative by attempting to steer it into securely epic territory and continuity. Here, the response of the rivers is not a matter of continuity, but one of active reflection, poised between the acts of congratulation or consolation. If we remember the hymnic understanding of rejoicing that can be mapped onto *gratentur* (cf. 1.578), it can now be read against the context of rivers rejoicing in Callimachus' *Hymn to Artemis*. The young goddess initially requests sixty Oceanids to form her chorus and twenty Amnisian nymphs, from the Cretan river Amnisus, as her hunting attendants (*Hymn* 3.13–17).[125] When Artemis travels to Crete to select her companions, her first stop after receiving Zeus' approval of her requests and his granting of additional honors to this small ambitious goddess, there is both repetition and divagation from her request. Line 43 repeats line 14, reaching in the direction of Homeric formulae, but subsequently, there is the information that the nymphs are selected from the river Caeratus, not Amnisus: χαῖρε δὲ Καίρατος ποταμὸς μέγα, χαῖρε δὲ Τηθύς, / οὕνεκα θυγατέρας Λητωίδι πέμπον ἀμορβούς ("the Caeratus river rejoiced muchly, Tethys rejoiced, on account of sending their daughters to be the attendants of Leto's daughter," *Hymn* 3.44–45). Regarding the poetic modification from the larger Amnisus to the smaller, parallel-flowing Caeratus, Susan Stephens notes the pun on χαῖρε and Caeratus: the poet literalizes the flow of hymnic rejoicing in the form of the river itself.[126]

The meeting of the two water sources in Callimachus—the small Caeratus and large Ocean—also relates to the image of the rivers making their uncertain way down to mingle with the sea in Ovid. Reproducing for the first time the critical proemial verb *deduco*, Ovid uses the rivers joining with the sea to depict metapoetically his paradoxically Callimachean epic, adopting and adapting for his own agenda the Apolline system of metapoetic waters. If Ovid's rivers operate with an awareness of how the *Hymn to Artemis* first "receives" and hints at this system of polemic, using it to depict an image of

Rivaled Affection and Affectation

bodies of water rejoicing about nymphs becoming the attendants of Artemis, we can see a further resistance to interpreting the laurel's existence as a total effacing of Daphne's imitation of and loyalty to Diana, and a suspended ending more at home in the Callimachean *Hymn to Artemis*. Apollo's hymnic self-definition needs not come at the full expense and erasure of the laurel's original identity.

ASTERIA AND DAPHNE:
THE CALLIMACHEAN *HYMN TO DELOS*

Up until now, the Callimachean texts of focus have been the individual hymns to the Delians, and the appearance of Cyrene in both that establishes her as a textual precursor to Daphne's receptive mode of depicting divine rivalry. At this point, we turn to a new Callimachean text, and with it, a new model for Daphne, yet one that still retains a sense of Callimachean competition. In order to do so, we return once again to one of Daphne's defining characteristics: her purity. Daphne's original identity is predicated on the idea of purity, explored by her evocation of the Callimachean Artemis and challenged and thrown into further relief by her reflection of Cyrene. Daphne's adherence to purity is, however, not limited to one Callimachean hymnic model. The second Callimachean model further entrenches the issue of competition between Apollo and Diana, as it is derived from the *Hymn to Delos*, which focuses on the island as the birthplace of Apollo. Daphne's Thessalian identity has first been reckoned with as the basis for her identity as a reimagined Cyrene, a nymph with dueling presences in the Callimachean hymns to Apollo and Artemis. Her status as a Thessalian nymph is also highly relevant when it comes to integrating the *Hymn to Delos* into understanding just how deeply entrenched Ovid's myth is in hymnic identities. As a daughter of Peneus, Daphne also maintains a silent presence within the *Hymn to Delos* that Ovid uses to forge a sense of connectivity between the two Thessalian episodes involving Apollo. Peneus, as both a physical river and its eponymous god, figures most prominently within the literary tradition in the *Hymn to Delos*.[127] The Peneus is one of the many places in which Leto seeks asylum—which could also be construed as the Peneus being one of the many figures from whom help is solicited in the face of Hera's overweening anger. Apart from the predestined Delian site of Apollo's birth, his stream is the closest that the goddess comes to finding a haven that will welcome the divine child. Like the other geographical entities she

126   Rivaled Affection and Affectation

approaches, the river initially flees the goddess. In her woe, Leto then entreats the river-god and his nymphs, an entreaty that goes unacknowledged. Only when Leto beseeches neighboring Pelion does Peneus show awareness of her plight, first to reject her plea, but then he surprisingly recapitulates.[128] Leto, however, spares him imminent punishment at the hand of Ares, who threatens from his defensive position above on Mt. Haemus, and she moves on. The interaction between Leto and the Peneus is a substantial portion of the hymn's narrative (almost fifty lines: *Hymn* 4.105–52). This is further notable given the fact that the interaction is unexampled in the *Hymn's* most overt literary source, the *Homeric Hymn to Apollo*. While it is a foregone mythological conclusion that within the Callimachean hymn, Leto must give birth to the god on Delos, Ovid returns to the site of this meeting between goddess and river and enterprisingly renegotiates the poetic space opened by the Callimachean encounter.[129]

Ovid's occupation of this poetic space creates a variety of repercussions. Significantly, Daphne as a daughter of the Peneus now has a literary background. As Jeffrey Wills notes in his important discussion of the *Hymn to Delos* as a source inspiration for Daphne's myth, "Ovid's reattribution of Daphne as a daughter of Peneus (rather than of Ladon) introduces an anachronistic irony into our reading of Callimachus. Leto's plea to the daughters of Peneus must now, for the Ovidian audience, include a plea to Daphne. Accordingly, we see a possible effect of Ovid's allusion to Callimachus: the *nympha* Daphne has fled from Apollo before. Ovid establishes his originality by telling a story that is new and simultaneously old, but only because his new genealogy has changed Callimachus' characters, allowing us to reread the *Hymn to Delos* with Daphne as one of the Νύμφαι Θεσσαλίδες."[130]

Ovid's use of the Callimachean hymn also reminds us that the tale of Delos is fundamentally a tale of metamorphosis. After the nymph Asteria flees from the advances of Zeus, she is transformed into a wandering island (cf. *Hymn* 4.37–41; 244–48). After the birth of Apollo, she is fixed in place and celebrated as the island Delos (cf. *Hymn* 4.251, 256, 268–69).[131] Ovid deploys hints of Delos' dual-stage metamorphosis in his description of the fleeing Daphne. Under Apollo's gaze, Daphne's eyes sparkle like stars (*uidet igne micantes / sideribus similes oculos*, "he looks at her eyes, similar to the stars' fires in their sparkling," 1.498–99), recalling the "starry" Asteria.[132] Just prior to the nymph's flight, after marveling at her eyes, lips, fingers, hands, and arms, Apollo also favorably assesses her hidden charms (*si qua latent, meliora putat*, "and if anything lies hidden, he deems it even more praiseworthy," 1.502). Once in flight—a flight "swifter than the breeze," *ocior aura*, 1.502[133]— the winds then lay bare Daphne's body (*nudabant corpora uenti*, 1.527). The lingering detail on what is not seen begins as a humorous literalization of Apollo's ability as a "seer," but when combined with the later detail of her further exposure, integrates subtle engagement with the metamorphosis of Asteria to Delos, as Ovid plays upon what Delos' name comes to signify: the visibility or "seenness" (δῆλος) of the once-wandering island. Daphne's eyes, likened to the stars that lend Asteria her name, initiates this set of visual cues that plot an allusive trajectory of the Asteria—Delos metamorphosis along the course of Daphne's flight. Both metamorphoses end the same way: fixity, an exchange with Apollo, and onomastic fulfillment. In the case of Delos, Callimachus makes this change explicit before the primary narrative of his hymn:

ἡνίκα δ' Ἀπόλλωνι γενέθλιον οὖδας ὑπέσχες,
τοῦτό τοι ἀντημοιβὸν ἁλίπλοοι οὔνομ' ἔθεντο,
οὕνεκεν οὐκέτ' ἄδηλος ἐπέπλεες, ἀλλ' ἐνὶ πόντου
κύμασιν Αἰγαίοιο ποδῶν ἐνεθήκαο ῥίζας.

(Callim. *Hymn* 4.51–54)

[But when you offered your soil for Apollo as a gift for his birth, sailors gave you this name in exchange, for you no longer sailed about inconspicuous but into the waves of the Aegean sea you put down the roots of your feet. (trans. Stephens)]

With her land offered to Apollo in safety for his birth, the island is no longer ἄδηλος; she becomes Δῆλος. The stability and permanence of her conspicuousness upon the waves requires her putting down the "roots" of her feet (ποδῶν . . . ῥίζας, *Hymn* 4.54). This description is equally applicable to Daphne's metamorphosis; she too, puts down roots in the moment she literalizes the meaning of her name (daphne/laurel) in becoming Apollo's most recognizable emblem (*pes modo tam uelox pigris radicibus haeret*, "her foot, recently so swift, stuck fast with stubborn roots," 1.551).[134]

Asteria's purity is what enables her to welcome Apollo into the world.[135] The god himself prophecies the importance of this trait from the womb (*Hymn* 4.98). When Delos welcomes Apollo, she proclaims that the god shall be called Delian after her, even though she is δυσήροτος ("difficult to plow," *Hymn* 4.268). The Homeric Leto capitalizes upon the poor quality of the Delian soil as a pressure point to coerce Delos into allowing her to give birth on her shores (*Hymn. Hom. Ap.* 53–55), with Delos herself admitting readily of her being κραναήπεδος "with hard, rocky soil" (72). The Callimachean Delos, however, needs no such persuasion, and offers her lands freely to Leto, contrarily upholding this quality as proof of her triumph (*Hymn* 4.268–70). With the birth of the god, Delos' immobility becomes her hallmark quality.[136] The island's immobility is connected to her poor soil quality by a scholion's explanation of ἄτροπος (*Hymn* 4.11) as ἀγεώργητος, "uncultivated."[137] The pride Delos takes in being δυσήροτος can also be construed as a concern for her purity.[138] Delos' self-conscious elevation of this characteristic could feasibly point to her existence as a nymph (plowing as sexual metaphor) or an island (its literal, physical sense).[139] A third possibility is found in Peter Bing's metapoetic reading: he identifies the poet's adoption of the guise of a rustic ploughman at *Hymn* 3. 175–82 as trading upon the conceit of poetic composition as "ploughing" and the poet-persona as a "ploughman"; he further argues that Callimachus' assumption of this guise makes a programmatic statement about privileging Hesiodic material over Homeric, heroic-epic material, and therefore demonstrating poetic, rather than agricultural, preferences.[140] Delos, in calling herself "difficult to plow," points to Callimachus' originality in his assumed theme and the poetic prowess necessary to tackle this innovative subject matter: the poet sets himself apart from both the *Homeric Hymn to Apollo* and Pindar's fifth *Paean*, both of which engage with the same body of mythological material.[141] In this metapoetic self-definition, Delos links herself not to the *Hymn to Apollo*, but the *Hymn to Artemis*, using Artemis as a figure to help define this originality. Delos' self-proclaimed purity, read across these three levels, cumulatively defines Callimachean innovation within this hymn.

Delos' use of a metapoetic image from the *Hymn to Artemis* to define herself naturally leads to the question of Artemis' presence within the hymn. The song ends with the poet addressing his favor to Delos, Apollo, and "she whom you, Leto, bore": ἱστίη ὦ νήσων εὐέστιε, χαῖρε μὲν αὐτή, / χαίροι δ' Ἀπόλλων τε καὶ ἣν ἐλοχεύσατο Λητώ ("O well-hearthed of the islands, hail, you, and hail also Apollo and her whom Leto bore," *Hymn* 4.325–26).[142] The reference to Artemis is surprising, as she is only elliptically mentioned throughout the hymn (*Hymn* 4.229, 292), which led to some scholars excising or emending this coda. Karina Ukleja uses this reference to Artemis to push further Bing's suggestion that the hymns to Artemis and Delos initially formed a pair of companion hymns.[143] In her elaboration of parallels between *Hymns* 3 and 4, she discusses how Callimachus takes especial pains to keep Artemis as an "absent presence" (to borrow the phrase Hardie applies to Ovid[144]) throughout the poem. The actual birth of Apollo is rife with contextual clues and hymnic allusions that Artemis plays the role of midwife—Eileithyia for her mother Leto, designed for the learned reader to supply. This imaginative exercise is then gratified and ratified by the direct mention of Artemis at the poem's end, as the other child born of Leto.[145] The overly careful absenting of Artemis as Apollo's twin is underscored by Callimachus' active suppression of an additional familial relationship: the sisterhood of Leto and Asteria. Hera's anger is mitigated by Asteria's flight from Zeus (*Hymn* 4.240–48), which can be read against the statement of Zeus in the beginning of Artemis' hymn about Hera's jealousy regarding his children (*Hymn* 2.29–31), further linking the figures of Asteria and Artemis. Delos' statement that no other land shall be more beloved to a god than Delos is to Apollo, not even Crete to Zeus (*Hymn* 4.268–73) can also be read against the suggestive matrix of clues about Artemis' presence and the mythology of the twins' birth. Ukleja connects the hymnic *aporia* about the location of Zeus' birth in the *Hymn to Zeus* with the absence of any reference to the (actually) contested version of Artemis' birth on Ortygia or Delos throughout the hymns; Delos' privileging of Crete over Arcadia not only reminds the reader of alternate divine birth locales, but the ways that Artemis promotes herself as a child of Zeus via association with Crete in her hymn. The status of both Apollo and Artemis as children of Zeus naturally provides a point of ready comparison and competition, and the *Hymn to Delos* overtly praises Apollo, but meanwhile builds an imaginative supplement that alludes to Artemis as the firstborn. In this way, the Delian hymn further engages with the theme of competition and rivalry that Callimachus explores to fashion the literary personalities of his divinities.

Ovid's Daphne, therefore, has a complex set of hymnic models, both directly invoked and textually veiled. As the Callimachean Artemis and Delos (*Hymns* 3 and 4), she staunchly chooses and defends her virginity. As Cyrene (*Hymns* 2 and 3), she dramatizes the Callimachean tension between a role as civilizing bride and virgin huntress, and the loyalties split between Apollo and Artemis.[146] This tension is further complicated with the integrated

130   Rivaled Affection and Affectation

awareness of Cyrene's roles in Hesiod and Pindar. In one respect, Daphne is crafted to enact the legacy of hymnic tension between Apollo and Artemis that was recently set aside in Augustan poetry in favor of a more harmonious, balanced image of the divinities, as in the *Carmen Saeculare*. Addressing these models of textual inspiration for Daphne allows the conversation to be redirected toward the issue of praise, instead of love, which comprises its canonical readings. In some ways, love acts as a smokescreen for the myth's true motivation and the political implications of its messaging, which center on praise. Apollo's chase of Daphne is not just readable as a hunt made literal by love, but as the original footrace for the Pythian crown.[147]

OVID AS A READER OF THE CALLIMACHEAN HYMNIC COLLECTION: REWRITING THE *HYMN TO DELOS* IN THE APOLLO AND DAPHNE MYTH

The final portion of this chapter broadens its purview to make a wider case for Ovid as a certain type of reader of the Callimachean hymns. With Daphne's hymnic models carefully uncovered, we can now see a wider interpretive gain to be made from considering the ways that Ovid makes use of the Callimachean hymns. This interpretive gain goes beyond the formative issue and repercussions of competition in paired hymns. To do so, we return anew to Daphne's Ovidian genealogy and geographical rootedness. If we recall the role of the Peneus within the *Hymn to Delos*, and the poetic means Ovid uses to receptively reroute this hymn onto Thessalian ground, we can see how the literal birth of Apollo, a central feature of Apolline hymns, takes a metaphorical, symbolic turn in Ovid. His divine image is completed by the creation of the laurel, as Apollo becomes the recognizable poet-prophet of the Augustan age. By superimposing over Thessaly the Callimachean landscape of Delos, a land created for the god of poetry,[148] Ovid forces a reckoning of what the meeting of these two landscapes means. The primacy of the Peneus in this defining myth of the *Metamorphoses* could be interpreted as Ovid stepping in to supply the "reward" Leto mentions in the hymn for offering his stream as haven (χάριτος δέ τοι ἔσσετ' ἀμοιβή, "there will be compensation for your favor," *Hymn* 4.152), but there is a larger strategy at work that also reveals how Ovid read the book of Callimachean hymns.

When Ovid rewrites the *Hymn to Delos* in the Thessalian portion of Book 1, where he cumulatively engages with *Hymns* 1–3 to define his epic

Rivaled Affection and Affectation

divinities and their relationship to praise, the poet is suggesting that the *Hymn to Delos* acts as a metapoetic encapsulation and recapitulation of *Hymns* 1–3. As recently discussed, the hymn ends with the poet's farewell to his divine subjects, including Artemis (*Hymn* 4.325–26). As Fantuzzi notes, "line 326 . . . could easily be understood as a sort of *sphragis* to the sequence of *Hymns* 2–4 or more generally to the small portrait gallery of the family of Zeus and Leto depicted in the first four hymns."[149] Ovid's use of *Hymn* 4 as an overarching framework to engage with textual specifics from *Hymns* 1–3 support this interpretation, and can indicate that *Hymns* 1–4 were considered together as a special or discrete set within the poetry book of *Hymns*.[150] Peneus' initial hesitation to assist Leto is due to his fear of being destroyed by Ares (*Hymn* 4.124–27), but when he changes tack, he resigns himself to a subsequent existence as a "thirsty" stream, bereft of honor:

τλήσομαι εἵνεκα σεῖο, καὶ εἰ μέλλοιμι ῥοάων
<u>διψαλέην</u> ἄμπωτιν ἔχων αἰώνιον ἔρρειν
καὶ μόνος ἐν ποταμοῖσιν <u>ἀτιμότατος</u> καλέεσθαι.

(Callim. Hymn 4.129–131)

[I shall risk it for your sake, even if I should wander for eternity, ebbing and thirsty, and alone among the rivers should be called the least honorable. (trans. Stephens)]

Peneus invokes the dry, honorless existence of the pre-Zeus Arcadia (cf. διψαλέος, *Hymn* 1.27), reinforcing the metaphor of water as praise poetry. The close appearances of ῥεῖα and ἔρρειν (*Hymn* 4.126, 130) likewise signal reminiscence of the birth of the flowing rivers as akin to Zeus' birth from Rhea, and the nexus of semantic and symbolic play of the verb in the *Hymn to Zeus*.[151] Ovid shows his understanding of the Callimachean metaphor by ensuring the praise of Peneus, making him the central feature of the landscape where he roots his allusive replay of *Hymns* 1–4, and reinforcing his character as akin to Jupiter's. The Callimachean metaphor of water as praise and praise poetry is also confirmed by Ovid's ending of the Apollo and Daphne myth, with the assessment of the rivers: the image of the rivers meeting the sea and their conceptual rejoicing evokes the catalog of *Hymn* 1, the watery polemic that ends *Hymn* 2, and Tethys and Caeratus rejoicing in *Hymn* 3. How Ovid uses the Thessalian setting is critical for recognizing this packaging together of the Callimachean hymns into one familial unit: Tempe is both a real and imaginary place, an idealized landscape. As the previous chapter discussed, Callimachus layered the landscapes of Crete and Egypt onto Arcadia, imbuing Arcadia with hybrid geographical and cultic significance. Callimachus does this by employing a different tactic from the geographical sweep of the *Hymn to Apollo*, where he took space away from the Homeric locales of Delos and Delphi, allocating it instead to the lengthy middle portion dedicated to Cyrene, home to cults of Apollo, Artemis, and Zeus. By eschewing Arcadia for Thessaly, lending it the significance of the Callimachean Delos, and embedding a neo-Cyrene within this landscape, Ovid universalizes Tempe as τέμπη, an "everygrove" given shape by hymnic reference that encompasses the landscapes of significance featured in this set of hymns.[152] In the context of the laurel, we recall that overall, the bonds between Delphi and Thessaly are both ancient and strong: Pausanias records that the first offering at Delphi was made by a Thessalian (10.16.8).[153] More critical is the iconographic presence of Apollo Citharoedus accompanied by Leto and Artemis that appears on a number of fourth-century Thessalian reliefs, found in multiple cities. The frequency of this representation, not tied to one location, has been read as a reaction to a new cult statue of the god housed in a Thessalian sanctuary, perhaps Tempe.[154] If Tempe did feature a cult statue of Apollo, Artemis, and Leto, this location is further apt to recall the *Hymn to Delos*, and to connect with the statue group within Apollo's Palatine home. The collective and mutual reliance of the Apollo and Daphne myth upon hymnic references from *Hymns* 1–4 to create and illuminate divine identity bring to light the original interdependencies of the hymns in establishing the literary and cultic personalities of the gods for the Hellenistic age. These coherencies argue for the hymns' order and arrangement as purposeful and meaningful. Ovid's combination of these hymns in introducing the concept of praise into his epic is intimately tied to the idea of rivalry, but one that nevertheless acknowledges a harmony derived from this set of allusive source material, the unity of *Hymns* 1–4.

CONCLUSION

This chapter is about relationships: the relationships between Apollo and Diana, between Apollo and Daphne, and between Daphne and Diana. Naturally, from the Ovidian vantage point, these relationships also entail additional ties to reckon with: the relationships that Apollo and Diana each hold with their previous literary selves, as well as those Daphne holds to her own literary models. What I have argued, in detailing this network of relationships, is for a new understanding of Daphne's role within the Ovidian myth. Rather than read Daphne as emblematic of elegy, and/or as a figure whose individual identity becomes effaced by her transformation into an Apolline symbol of power, I treat Daphne as a literary device, constructed to comment on the competing identities of Apollo and Diana. She does this by both evoking and reflecting the Delians themselves, and by becoming a new literary instantiation of figures who occupy competing interests to them. Ovid designs her textual identity via studied reference to both Apollo and Diana themselves, but also writes her as a new Cyrene, a figure who appears in both the Callimachean hymns to Apollo and Artemis, providing a skein of connective tissue aptly read as an example of the Callimachean aesthetic of competition that motivates his hymnic depictions of divinities. When Daphne inherits this legacy of embodied rivalry from the role the Callimachean Cyrene plays, she reveals Ovid's commitment to the Callimachean hymnic portrait of the Delians, striving with each other for power and notoriety, as he eschews the literary portraits of harmony that had come to emblematize the pair in the early Augustan period, as especially crystallized by Horace. The way the figure of Daphne borrows Callimachean models from across *Hymns* 1–3, along with the argument set forth in the second chapter, also allows a further contribution of interpretation on Ovid as a reader of Callimachus. Not only is he seeking to preserve the prevailing divine dynamic of competition from the hymnic collection, he is also showing us that he reads the *Hymn to Delos* as a metapoetic recapitulation of *Hymns* 1–3, thus illuminating this series of Callimachean hymns as the key to interpreting the mythological, geographical, and narrative decisions he makes within this programmatic myth.

4

Ovid's *Lavacrum Dianae*

The Huntress Muse of the Metamorphoses

The previous chapter explored the figure of Diana through the shifting images of her imitators or surrogates, and how her identity is constructed harmoniously or agonistically in relation to her brother Apollo. This chapter looks at the Ovidian Diana from a different perspective. Overall, I use the myth of Actaeon to examine Diana's independent characterization and create the space necessary for a more expansive awareness of Ovid's source texts. Instead of primarily focusing on the transformation of Actaeon, which tends to overshadow the narrative other elements of this myth, the goddess herself and the relationship between Diana and Actaeon becomes the primary node of textual interest. A large part of this reexamination rests on renegotiating the Ovidian relationship of influence with the Callimachean hymns. Cumulatively, I consider how the traditional singular focus on Callimachus' fifth *Hymn*, the *Bath of Pallas* (which presents this version of Actaeon's fate as an embedded mythological *exemplum*, participating in the hymn's generic interactions with tragedy) occludes the importance of the Callimachean *Hymn to Artemis* to understanding Ovid's myth. The present discussion instead outlines how Ovid constructs this myth as a sequel to the Callimachean *Hymn to Artemis*. By aligning this episode with the *Hymn to Artemis*, Ovid repositions its original place within the Callimachean corpus. As such, Ovid defers the presence of Minerva in his epic, bringing the two goddesses into a space of competitive interaction. Part of this discussion also entails tracing Diana's role as a Muse, further anticipating the later appearance of Minerva when Ovid does broach an epic redesign of the *Bath of Pallas.* To reinvigorate the importance of hymnic texts to understanding Ovid's divine identities, I suggest that Grattius' *Cynegetica,* structured as a hymn to Diana, mediates between the Ovidian myth of Diana and Actaeon and the Callimachean *Hymn to Artemis.*[1] Ovid therefore takes care to position his divine personality at the intersections of Greek and Roman texts, revealing the cumulative character accrued through the absorption of hymnic influence. Ovid presents his reader with a Diana not only Callimachean but enriched by Grattian allusion.

APPENDING CALLIMACHUS' *HYMN TO ARTEMIS*: ACTAEON AS CAUTIONARY TALE

We begin by looking jointly at how Callimachus and Ovid represent the goddess and her divine status. Callimachus' hymn opens with the expression that "for singers, passing over (or forgetting) Artemis is no light matter" (οὐ γὰρ ἐλαφρὸν ἀειδόντεσσι λαθέσθαι, *Hymn* 3.1). With this statement, the poet indicates his intention to remedy Artemis' lack of a long, narrative *Homeric Hymn.* Additionally, he issues a warning about slighting the goddess—a warning that will provide thematic momentum for the hymn's end.[2] Artemis is first identified by her involvement with the bow and the shooting of hares (τῇ τόξα λαγωβολίαι τε μέλονται, "the bow and shootings of hares represent concerns to you," *Hymn* 3.2). The appearance of "hare-shooting" already introduces Callimachus' playfulness and contrariness: hares as hunting targets are indeed "light," but the designation ἐλαφρός conjures momentarily the appearance of the ἔλαφος ("deer") and her epithet ἐλαφηβόλος, prey more suited to a goddess.[3] Artemis will eventually grow into this prey (cf. *Hymn* 3.17, 100–106), but Callimachus plays on his reader's expectations from the outset, emphasizing simultaneously the infancy of both the goddess and her extended hymnic tradition.

Ovid, too, teases the sentiment that to pass over Artemis is no light matter: as previously discussed, he only introduces the goddess herself after an array of imitators or impostors of huntress-nymphs, all of whom have their own identities circumscribed to varying degrees by their relation to the bow (especially the Arcadian nymphs Syrinx and Callisto). Although Ovid seems to playfully riff on this hymnic opening to stage a sequence of epic narrative that emphasizes the novelty of his epic's landscape, he does ultimately take it to heart: within the myth of Actaeon, he restores Diana to

136   Ovid's *Lavacrum Dianae*

a main poetic space and primary level of narrative, and it is a Diana not to
be trifled with.

Ovid borrows one view of this dangerous Diana from the simile that de-
scribes Nausicaa in *Odyssey* 6, already once utilized in his myth of Callisto.
The crowning visual image of the goddess surrounded by, and towering
over, her nymph companions, focalized through the adoring gaze of her
mother, is the view Actaeon sees of the goddess:

> γέγηθε δέ τε φρένα Λητώ
> πασάων δ' ὑπὲρ ἥ γε κάρη ἔχει ἠδὲ μέτωπα,
> ῥεῖά τ' ἀριγνώτη πέλεται, καλαὶ δέ τε πᾶσαι
> ὣς ἥ γ' ἀμφιπόλοισι μετέπρεπε παρθένος ἀδμής.

(Hom. *Od.* 6.106–9)

[and the heart of Leto is gladdened,
for the head and the brows of Artemis are above all the others,
and she is easily marked among them, though all are lovely,
so this one shone among her handmaidens, a virgin unwedded.
   (trans. Lattimore)

qui simul intrauit rorantia fontibus antra,
sicut erant nudae uiso sua pectora nymphae
percussere uiro subitisque ululatibus omne
inpleuere nemus circumfusaeque Dianam
corporibus texere suis; tamen altior illis
ipsa dea est colloque tenus supereminet omnes.
qui color infectis aduersi solis ab ictu
nubibus esse solet aut purpureae Aurorae,
is fuit in uultu uisae sine ueste Dianae.

(*Met.* 3.177–85)

[As soon as he entered the cave, dripping from water fountains,
just as they were, the nymphs, bare, beat their breasts
because a man saw them, and filled the grove's entirety with
their sudden shrieking and poured themselves around Diana,
protectively interweaving with their bodies; however, the goddess herself
was taller than they were, and towered over all; they only reached her neck.

Ovid's *Lavacrum Dianae*

And just as the color that clouds characteristically carry, when they are stained
by the opposing strikes of the sun, or the color of purple-bright Aurora—
so it was the color in the face of Diana, seen without her clothing.]

In other words, the myth of Callisto presents the image from the first half of the simile (the goddess hunting along the mountain ridges with her nymphs), while Actaeon sees the goddess as Leto does in the simile's second half. Diana, like Artemis, not only towers above her handmaiden nymphs, but "shines" through the additional description given by the simile of her blush. Ovid takes Artemis out of the embedded narrative level of descriptive comparison (the simile-world) and promotes her to being the primary image of visual and descriptive concern. On an even more substantial level, Ovid also does this with his version of the myth of Actaeon itself: the poet removes it from its position as an embedded mythological *exemplum* within Callimachus' fifth *Hymn* (*Hymn* 5.57–131).[4] The hymn narrates Tiresias's blinding as the consequence of seeing Athena bathing on Helicon. While Callimachus puts Actaeon's fate into Athena's voice as a comparative consolation for Chariclo, Tiresias' mother, Ovid makes Actaeon's story his narrative focus, even before Tiresias is introduced.[5] Instead, Tiresias' myth feeds into the myth of Narcissus, which displays thematic concerns and imagery found not in Callimachus' fifth *Hymn*, but in the sixth, the *Hymn to Demeter*. Ovid's narrative reprioritization of the goddess ultimately aligns with the statement that opens her Callimachean hymn, establishing the goddess as worthy of individual focus.

The note of caution issued by the hymn's opening also shapes the relationship of this Ovidian myth to the vignettes detailed within Callimachus' song of Artemis. Callimachus prolongs his hymn by signing off with a series of warnings against dishonoring the goddess:

πότνια Μουνιχίη λιμενοσκόπε, χαῖρε, Φεραίη.
μή τις ἀτιμήσῃ τὴν Ἄρτεμιν (οὐδὲ γὰρ Οἰνεῖ
βωμὸν ἀτιμάσσαντι καλοὶ πόλιν ἦλθον ἀγῶνες),
μηδ' ἐλαφηβολίην μηδ' εὐστοχίην ἐριδαίνειν
(οὐδὲ γὰρ Ἀτρεΐδης ὀλίγῳ ἐπὶ κόμπασε μισθῷ),
μηδέ τινα μνᾶσθαι τὴν παρθένον (οὐδὲ γὰρ Ὦτος,
οὐδὲ μὲν Ὠαρίων ἀγαθὸν γάμον ἐμνήστευσαν),

138   Ovid's *Lavacrum Dianae*

μηδὲ χορὸν φεύγειν ἐνιαύσιον (οὐδὲ γὰρ Ἱππώ
ἀκλαυτεὶ περὶ βωμὸν ἀπείπατο κυκλώσασθαι)·
χαῖρε μέγα, κρείουσα, καὶ εὐάντησον ἀοιδῇ.

(Callim. *Hymn* 3.259–68)

[Mistress of Munychia, guardian of harbors, hail Lady of Pheraea. Let no one dishonor Artemis. (For no fair contests came to the city when Oeneus dishonored her altar.) Do not contend with her in the shooting of deer or in marksmanship. (For the son of Atreus boasted at no small price.) Let no one court the maiden. (For neither Otus nor Orion courted her for a happy marriage.) Do not flee her yearly dance. (For not without tears did Hippo refuse to dance around her altar.) Hail greatly, queen, and graciously encounter my song. (trans. Stephens)]

He briefly enumerates a sequence of negative *exempla*, a list of figures who disrespected Artemis: Oeneus, Agamemnon, Otus and Orion, and Hippo. The first and last are figures who fail to properly act in honor of the goddess (failure to make sacrifice, to dance), whereas the middle two figures commit hubristic acts, active trespasses against core identities of the goddess (boasting about hunting prowess, attempting to compromise Artemis' virginity). Four of these figures appear earlier in the hymn (Oeneus, Agamemnon, Otus, and Hippo). The last-minute inclusion of Orion, and the earlier, unelaborated reference to a tale of Hippo indicates that the poet has not run out of appropriate material for hymning the goddess.[6]

In particular, this list begs the question of what Callimachus might have said about Orion. The mythology surrounding Orion is rich and varied, but of perpetual emphasis is his status as a hunter. Occasionally, his huntsmanship is said to be a point of boasting, which earns him divine punishment. A different variant tells of his attempted sexual pursuit of Artemis. An old strain of myth also details his blinding as punishment.[7] Cumulatively, Orion can join the figures of Tiresias and Actaeon featured in the *Bath of Pallas*, all hunters who receive divine punishment. More specifically, the mythological tradition regarding Actaeon is such that the two active transgressions can be combined into one figure: in some versions he is punished for vaunting about his superior hunting skill, and in others for pursuing Semele (which angered Zeus, who instigates Artemis' punishment of the hunter), a pursuit

Ovid's *Lavacrum Dianae*

that is occasionally transferred to Artemis herself.[8] Altogether, the tale and fate of Actaeon fit the criteria of inclusion for the cautionary coda that closes the Callimachean hymn, again, a restatement of the fact that it is "no light matter" to forget or pass over the goddess: Actaeon's tale can not only be positioned as suitable for the hymn's *envoi*, but also as additional filler for the narrative gap suggested by Callimachus' naming of Orion. Ovid's tale of Actaeon subtly promotes itself as a continuation of or supplement to the Callimachean hymn, giving full narrative rein to exploring the goddess' divinity, and her protection of this divine identity.

DIANA AND MINERVA

From this point, we can shift into discussing the relationship between the Ovidian myth and Callimachus' fifth *Hymn*, the *Bath of Pallas*. Framing Actaeon's tale as an Ovidian appendix to Callimachus' *Hymn to Artemis*, as well as an expansion of the *Bath of Pallas*, also encourages a sense of rivalry between Diana and Minerva. Ovid plays with the proportions of Callimachean hymnic space and praise by presenting the mythological *exemplum* embedded within Athena's hymn as the continuation of Artemis'. As has been briefly noted of the *Bath of Pallas*, Athena has taken on a role arguably more suited to Artemis, which forges a sense of greater continuity between the framing myth of Tiresias and inset tale of Actaeon. Ovid seems to take this (contextually forced) resemblance of Athena to Artemis to one full logical conclusion by his overt focus only on the figure of Artemis, rerouting the narrative emphasis of Callimachus' fifth *Hymn*. In part, this puts a narrative strategy of misdirection into play that lays groundwork for the subsequent appearance of Minerva on Helicon in Book 5 (the subject of chapter 5). Callimachus himself hints at a similarity between the goddesses when he describes the "war-dance" performed in honor of Artemis:

> αὐταὶ δ᾽, Οὖπι ἄνασσα, περὶ πρύλιν ὠρχήσαντο
> πρῶτα μὲν ἐν σακέεσσιν ἐνόπλιον, αὖθι δὲ κύκλῳ
> στησάμεναι χορὸν εὐρύν· ὑπήεισαν δὲ λίγειαι
> λεπταλέον σύριγγες, ἵνα ῥήσσωσιν ὁμαρτῆ
> (οὐ γάρ πω νέβρεια δι᾽ ὀστέα τετρήναντο,
> ἔργον Ἀθηναίης ἐλάφῳ κακόν)·

(Callim. *Hymn* 3.240–45)

140   Ovid's *Lavacrum Dianae*

[They themselves, Oupis, Queen, danced the war dance, first armed with shields, then arranging the broad chorus in a circle. Pipes provided delicate accompaniment with a clear sound, so that their feet might beat in time. (For they did not yet drill holes in the bones of the fawn, a work of Athena, an evil for the deer.) (trans. Stephens)]

The *pyrriche* is also linked to Athena. Although not its inventor, the goddess (especially as Pallas) is closely linked to its practice.[9] The poet's explicit mention of Athena alongside the invention of the deer-bone *aulos* also provides a subtle cross-reference, and seam of continuity, to the deer bones that appear within the *Bath of Pallas*: the bones of Actaeon that his mother will gather amid the forest copses (τὰ δ' υἱέος ὀστέα μάτηρ /λεξεῖται δρυμὼς πάντας ἐπερχομένα, "the mother will gather the bones of her son, traversing all the forest copses," *Hymn* 5.115–16). Stephens notes the irony of Callimachus' aside about the production of musical instruments from their bones being an "evil" for the deer, given their status already as prey of Artemis, but this statement becomes more loaded in light of the Actaeon myth. Athena's connection with music and dance also begins to gently condition her appearance as a Muse-like figure in *Hymn* 5, where she engages in the Muse-like pursuit of bathing with her nymph companion in the Heliconian springs. Within the *Hymn to Artemis*, Hippo is said to be the first to perform this rite for the goddess (*Hymn* 3.239); as previously mentioned, Hippo also appears at the hymn's end, where Callimachus hints at a time where the goddess does not participate in the dance. Within the fifth *Hymn*, it is said that the dances of Athena and her nymphs were not sweet without Chariclo leading them (*Hymn* 5.66–67); after her son's blinding, Chariclo also expresses that she will no longer traverse Helicon, which also hints at an absenting from the (choral) dance (*Hymn* 5.90). Chariclo is presented in danger of being or becoming like Hippo, a further thread of continuity between the hymns that could have inspired Ovid's assumption of the literary opportunity to fill in the narrative gap left by Orion.

Just as Callimachus' Athena assumes some characteristics more suited to Artemis, Ovid is sure to repay the favor to his source text by gifting Diana with some Athena-like characteristics, closing the textual loop. One hint is the status of one of her nymphs as an *armigera* (3.166), a designator more automatically appropriate for Minerva. Although *arma Dianae* is a Virgilian periphrasis for arrows (cf. *Aen.* 11.652), arrows have their own accessory for

Ovid's *Lavacrum Dianae*

conveyance (the quiver); the concept is less "arms-bearer" than "armor-bearer," and so less applicable to Diana, summoning as it does the idea of a shield (cf. the Greek equivalent ὑπασπιστής).[10] Diana's Ovidian "costume" is also notable. In preparation for her bath, after she hands off her hunting equipment, another nymph companion takes off her garment, a *palla* (*altera depositae subiecit bracchia pallae*, "another positions her arms for the taking off of her robe," 3.167). The *palla*, a long outer garment, is equivalent to the Greek πέπλος.[11] Within the *Bath of Pallas*, Athena and Chariclo "loosen the pins to their *peploi*" in order to bathe (πέπλων λυσαμένα περόνας, *Hymn* 5.70). The long robe is not the usual wardrobe of Diana, whose active lifestyle requires instead a knee-length garment, typically a chiton (cf. Callim. *Hymn* 3. 11–12). Why would Ovid specify this difference in garb? While it suggests the chaste attire of the *matrona*, therefore highlighting Diana's *pudicitia*, I would suggest it also acts a veiled hint at Pallas (Παλλάς), a divine name of Athena, as Ovid alludes to his source text in a way that reveals the complex interplay of the goddesses exchanging costumes and roles.[12]

MOTHERHOOD, METAMORPHOSIS, AND LAMENT

There are other subtleties to Ovid's blending of the two myths, as he further acknowledges his Callimachean source material. One of the features of the Callimachean hymn is its emphasis on motherhood and grief, embodied in the figure of Chariclo.[13] Chariclo's lament for her son occasions Athena's rather tone-deaf rhetoric of "cheer up, it could be worse," the *consolatio* featuring Actaeon's fate. Within the *Metamorphoses*, Actaeon is first identified as the *iuuenis . . . Hyantius* ("the Boeotian youth," 3.146–47). The geographical epithet *Hyantius* anticipates its later use to describe the Heliconian spring Aganippe (5.312), where the setting of the Callimachean hymn returns to focus. Immediately after his transformation into a stag, Actaeon is called *Autonoeius heros* (3.198). This is a rare use of the matronymic ("son of Autonoe"), which defines him via maternal presence.[14] Chariclo's presence is recalled in another way in the Ovidian myth that also reveals Ovid's adept hand with his chosen theme of metamorphosis, and the metamorphosis of his sources that underpin his chosen theme. After the poet records Chariclo's lament, he ends her speech with the detail that Chariclo mourns like a nightingale, and weeps (μάτηρ μὲν γοερᾶν οἶτον ἀηδονίδων/ἆγε βαρὺ κλαίοισα, "the mother, weighed down in weeping, gave forth the mournful fate of the nightingales," *Hymn* 5.94–95). Philomela (or Procne), as the metamorphosed

142 Ovid's *Lavacrum Dianae*

nightingale, is the mythological model par excellence for maternal mourning. Regarding this moment of comparison, Richard Hunter argues that the nightingale's song of lament is specifically poised to recall elegy, and therefore provide a self-conscious comment on the chosen meter of the hymn, the elegiac couplet.[15] The Callimachean allusion to a metamorphosis is, of course, ripe for Ovidian comment and manipulation. In outlining the various dependencies and divagations Ovid makes from Callimachus in this myth, Heather Van Tress notes how Ovid combines the physical and emotional responses of Tiresias and Chariclo within the figure of Actaeon, who expresses in tandem the silenced bewilderment of the son and the psychologically laden grief of the mother.[16] Her discussion of the Ovidian conflation of Tiresias and Chariclo can be supplemented further. Before the moment of his death, Actaeon issues his own lament:

> gemit ille sonumque,
> etsi non hominis, quem non tamen edere possit
> ceruus, habet maestisque replet iuga nota querelis
> et genibus pronis supplex similisque roganti
> circumfert tacitos tamquam sua bracchia uultus.
>
> (*Met.* 3.237–41)

[He groaned forth and it had a sound,
that although wasn't of human making,
was nevertheless not something a stag was able to utter,
and he filled afresh the familiar mountain ridges with mournful plaint
and as a suppliant, on bended knees, similar to a pose of pleading,
he swings his silent head around, as if compensating for his lost arms.]

Actaeon acts, and sounds, not quite like a stag, but also not quite human.[17] However, his utterance is akin to a different register of natural sound: the mourning song of the nightingale. There are a few notable passages from the Latin tradition that highlight this mourning song. Catullus will sing "mournful songs" (*maesta . . . carmina*, Catull. 65.12; cf. also *gemens*, 14) in the manner of the mourning nightingale; in the famous Virgilian simile of Orpheus, the mourning nightingale (*maerens, Georg.* 4.511) "fills the landscape far and wide with her sad lamentation" (*et maestis late loca questibus implet, Georg.* 4.515). This passage stands as clear inspiration for the Ovidian description of the mourning Demeter in the *Fasti* (*miseris loca cuncta querelis / implet,* "she fills all the landscape with wretched lamentation," *Fast.* 4.481–82; cf. also *gemit,* 4.482). *Maestisque replet iuga nota querelis* bears clear textual resemblance to these depictions of the nightingale's song. Ovid signals his use of Virgil by the substitution of *replet* ("fill *again*") for *implet* ("fill"), as the now-Ovidian landscape is "filled again" with the nightingale's lament. Ovid preserves the Callimachean descriptor of the nightingale, but transfers it to Actaeon, accruing allusions from the Latin poetic tradition along the way.

However, Ovid may have found additional literary motivation from the Greek tradition to transfer the motif of the mourning nightingale to Actaeon. Pausanius records how Stesichorus phrased Actaeon's transformation (Στησίχορος δὲ ὁ Ἱμεραῖος ἔγραψεν ἐλάφου περιβαλεῖν δέρμα Ἀκταίωνι τὴν θεόν, "Stesichorus of Himera recorded that the goddess threw a stag's hide around Actaeon," Paus. 9.2.3). This fragment garnered some linguistic interest regarding the potential usage of περιβαλεῖν to mean "transform." Herbert Rose identifies a parallel usage in Aeschylus that describes the transformation of Philomele into a nightingale (περέβαλον γάρ οἱ πτεροφόρον δέμας, "for they have thrown around her a feather-bearing hide," Aesch. *Ag.* 1147). Nagy discusses these two usages together to rehabilitate reading Stesichorus' phrasing as indicative of a full transformation, and not simply a "clothing."[18] In Ovid's phrasing, the goddess "hides his body with a spotted hide" (*uelat maculoso uellere corpus,* 3.197), where *uelo* is in accordance with the more standard meaning of περιβάλλω and does not indicate "transform." In fact, the idea of "clothing" is assisted by Diana's mention of her *uelamen* only five lines previously. However, nobody can doubt that within Ovid, Actaeon is undergoing a transformation. If Stesichorus' usage was indeed poetically remarkable for its ability to simultaneously indicate a full transformation or a mere physical cloaking, Ovid may have viewed this as further fodder to showcase his learnedness, and to embed further the presence of Philomela in Actaeon's tale.

POETIC CAMOUFLAGE AND THE QUARRY OF ARTEMIS

Ovid's visual description of Actaeon becoming a deer holds further points of interpretive significance, and tracing their poetological import will lead us back to the Callimachean *Hymn to Artemis*. Actaeon's transformation into a stag, specifically, is made clear from the beginning, when Ovid cites the *aliena cornua* ("foreign horns", 3.139) he will sport. The horns become the visual index of his new cervine identity (*ut uero uultus et cornua uidit in unda,* / *"me miserum!" dicturus erat,* "when, in truth, he saw his face and horns in the water, he was about to say, 'woe is me!,'" 3.200–1; cf. also 3.194).[19] However, the detail of Actaeon's *uellus maculosum* is a complicating factor, as it hints instead at the spotted hide of fawns. The jolt of fear the goddess adds as part of his transformation (*additus et pauor est,* 3.198), right before the use of the matronymic, likewise hints at the fearful reputation of fawns and their frequent poetic depiction in association with their mothers.[20] As an adjective, *maculosus* carries both physical and metaphorical/moral meanings: "spotted," as in "speckled" or "variegated" (e.g., of animals, cf. *OLD* s.v. 2a), or "spotted," as in "stained" or "defiled" (*OLD* s.v. 3; cf. also 1). Similarly, *infectus* (*inficio*) exhibits a similar range of meaning: it can mean "dyed," "colored," or "tinged with," or "tainted," "infected," or "spoiled." This adjective sets the scene for the myth: *Mons erat infectus uariarum caede ferarum* (3.143). Is the landscape tinted or tainted with blood? The adjective *uarius* adds a further dimension of significance. It can serve as a synonym for *maculosus,* so, "t(a)inted with the blood of variegated beasts."[21] It can also indicate a difference or diversity, so, "t(a)inted with the blood of various beasts." The deliberate use and prominence of the adjectival network of *maculosus, infectus,* and *uarius* suggests there is a wider poetological significance at work.[22]

We can look to Callimachus for help with this interpretive question and begin to build a context for the Ovidian web of descriptors. When the young goddess Artemis demands her followers from indulgent father Zeus, she asks for two different cadres of companions. The first is sixty Oceanids to form her chorus (*Hymn* 3.13). The second is for twenty Amnisian nymphs:

δός δέ μοι ἀμφιπόλους Ἀμνισίδας εἴκοσι νύμφας,
αἵ τε μοι ἐνδρομίδας τε καὶ ὁππότε μηκέτι λύγκας
μήτ᾽ ἐλάφους βάλλοιμι θοοὺς κύνας εὖ κομέοιεν.

(Callim. *Hymn* 3.15–17)

[Gimme twenty Amnisian nymphs as attendants, who would take care of my high hunting boots and, whenever I am no longer shooting at lynxes and deer, my swift hounds. (trans. Stephens)]

Ovid's *Lavacrum Dianae* 145

These followers will look after Artemis' hunting boots and her hounds, when she is not engaged with hunting lynxes or deer. Immediately after, the goddess also asks for "all mountains" (δὸς δέ μοι οὔρεα πάντα, *Hymn* 3.18), establishing her territory. In the *Metamorphoses*, two of Diana's nymphs attend to her footwear (*uincla duae pedibus demunt*, "two remove her laced footwear from her feet," 3.168). Despite the fact the goddess has clearly been hunting (perhaps aligned with the impracticality of the *palla* as hunting garb) *uincla* is conventionally translated here as "sandals."[23] However, the word is just a substantive for "laces," meaning that it could also indicate the laced-up *cothurni*, the high hunting boot that is the equivalent of the Callimachean ἐνδρομίς, the Cretan "running boot" (*Hymn* 3.16).[24] Ovid's transfer of this Callimachean task for the goddess' nymphs further builds an association between the texts, and, significantly, calls attention to the conspicuous absence of hunting hounds in attendance of the goddess within the *Metamorphoses*.

Artemis' envisioned quarry comes back into focus when she goes to collect these very hunting dogs from Pan. Once in Arcadia, she espies the god cutting up a Maenalian lynx to feed to his dogs (*Hymn* 3.88–89). Oliver Thomas has outlined a clever allusion here, explaining this moment as the source of the lynx pelt Pan wears in his *Homeric Hymn* (*Hymn. Hom.* 19.24); Andrew Faulkner further reads the allusion as a "powerful metaphor for intertextuality . . . in which Artemis' hounds are literally nourished with the meat of the intertextual fulcrum, the lynx."[25] As Stephens notes, lynxes are not common poetic animals, which seems to indicate a purpose to cross-reference these appearances within the hymn. While Artemis does not go on to hunt lynx, she is granted her hunting dogs with three references to deer: fawns (νεβρούς, *Hymn* 3.95); full-grown deer, whether harts or stags (ἐλάφοιο, *Hymn* 3.96) and roe-deer (ζορκὸς, *Hymn* 3.97). Her first hunt is also the pursuit of Arcadian deer (*Hymn* 3.98–106). These four deer, who are captured without the help of her hounds, become the mode of conveyance for her chariot. Later, these deer are depicted under the care of the Amnisian nymphs (*Hymn* 3.162–67), a different responsibility than what the reader may have been led to believe about their duties of care.

As previously discussed, when Diana first appears in the *Metamorphoses*, she is hunting on Maenalus: *Dictynna per altum / Maenalon ingrediens et caede superba ferarum* ("Dictynna, proceeding along high Maenalus, proud with the slaughter of beasts," 2.441–42). This is her first hunt in the epic,

146 Ovid's *Lavacrum Dianae*

mirroring the locale of her first hunt in her Callimachean hymn. Her pride in the kill (*caede superba ferarum*) is echoed in the opening of Actaeon's myth, where the mountain itself now bears the mark of successful hunting (*Mons erat infectus uariarum <u>caede ferarum</u>*, 3.143). If we now supply one specific meaning to *uarius*, we can see the allusion made here to the Callimachean Artemis' envisioned "first quarry" of lynx and deer as she hunts with her hounds. Instances within the Latin verse tradition connect these adjectives with the lynx. Within the *Georgics*, lynxes are *uariae* (*Georg.* 3.264). Turning to the *Aeneid*, we see Venus (who is impersonating a virgin huntress in a well-known echo of the *Homeric Hymn to Aphrodite*) looking for her "sister," who is costumed with a quiver and a lynx pelt that is *maculosa* (*succinctam pharetra et maculosae tegmina lyncis, Aen.* 1.323).[26] Although as a virgin huntress Venus herself is costumed similarly enough to be mistaken for Diana (Aeneas asks, *an Phoebi soror?*, 1.329), a descriptive choice that echoes the active conceit of the Homeric hymn, Virgil could additionally be playing a different version of the Callimachean game of intertextuality: in other words, he hints that Venus' huntress "sister" is sporting the lynx pelt that she alludes to killing within the *Hymn to Artemis*. Regardless of the depth of the lynx's intertextual fate, the point here is the shared designation of *varius* and *maculosus*. For Actaeon, as a stag, is also *maculosus*.[27] The Callimachean pieces of Artemis' first expressions of the hunt, the Maenalian lynx Pan is butchering, and the focus on deer within the description of her hunting dogs can be combined with the Ovidian introduction of Diana, the opening of Actaeon's myth, and the adjectival sharing of *uarius* and *maculosus* between lynx and deer: combining these elements can suggest that the *uariarum . . . ferarum* Actaeon has hunted are lynxes and deer, the focus of Artemis' "first" (in the sense of hymnic mention) hunt with her dogs.

The Huntress Muse: Grattius' "Hymn to Diana"

What might be the purpose of suggesting that the Ovidian Actaeon shares hunting quarry with the Callimachean Artemis? It brings the two figures closer together, in a manner that shows awareness of their closeness within the *Bath of Pallas*. Athena describes Actaeon as the close companion of Artemis in the hunt, a sort of protégé of the goddess (καὶ τῆνος μεγάλας σύνδρομος Ἀρτέμιδος / ἔσσεται, "and he will be the companion of great Artemis," *Hymn* 5.110–11).[28] Literally, he "runs together" with the goddess, which lends σύνδρομος the meaning of "companion." Ovid hints at this closeness in the opening of the myth, underscored by the intratextuality of *caede ferarum*, reminding readers of the mythological version where Actaeon was a close affiliate of the goddess.

The subtle, enmeshed closeness between hunter, goddess, and landscape that Ovid builds in this myth is one especial poetic triumph that further illuminates Diana's literary identity. In exploring the nuances of this closeness, we can now also begin to productively integrate Grattius' didactic text on hunting into our literary awareness. Actaeon's first words are *lina madent, comites* ("the lines are sodden, comrades," 3.148). In an example of especially brief ring composition, his speech also ends with reference to the hunting nets, encircling his speech in the manner of the net itself: *sistite opus praesens nodosaque tollite lina* (3.153). Actaeon's focus on the net can be read alongside the priorities of the Grattian text. After Grattius' opening hymn to Diana (1–23), the first "art" of hunting he turns to is the construction of nets: *armorum casses, plagiique exordia restis / prima* ("purse nets are the beginning of our equipment, and cordage is the first beginning of net work," *Cyn.* 24–25).[29] Varro says that "Diana gave" (*dedit Diana*; cf. *Sat. Men.* 385.2) the skill and craft of making nets; Grattius takes this up as the beginning to the body of his didactic work. In this opening Grattian statement, *exordium* pulls a lot of interpretive weight. It simultaneously indicates the warp on a loom beginning a net, a general beginning, and the specific undertaking of beginning of a work of literature: Grattius weaves together form and content in suitably poetic manner.[30]

As for the materiality of the nets, Grattius proclaims that the best raw material comes from Cinyps, a small Libyan river: *optuma Cinyphiae, ne quid cunctere, paludes / lina dabunt* ("the best material is from Cinyps—don't doubt me on that, their marshes will provide the threads," *Cyn.* 34–35).[31] *Lina dabunt* echoes the *arma dabo* that closes Grattius' proem (*Cyn.* 23) and the poem's opening *dona cano diuom*, slightly raising the poetic profile of this seemingly straightforward piece of information. As already indicated by the multivalent use of *exordium*, Grattius is concerned with the learned aesthetic of his didactic; for the Augustan poets, engaging in Callimacheanisms was a secure way to show this concern. Callimachean aesthetics were not only in the water, so to speak, for the literary culture that Grattius was operating in, but specifically, the *Hymn to Artemis* is relevant for the hymnic portions of his own didactic, which are addressed to the goddess of the hunt herself. The threads that make up the hunting nets also stand

148   Ovid's *Lavacrum Dianae*

as the material with which he weaves his verses, implicating this information in the weaving metaphor he uses to introduce his didactic. Regarding Cinyps, Herodotus tells us that the region surrounding the river that bears the same name is the only part of Libya that can compete with the fertile excellence of Asia or Europe, as the soil is exceptionally well-watered and rich (Hdt. 4.198). The historian likewise cites that the Cinyps flows initially from a hill called the "Hill of the Graces" (Hdt. 4.175), a name that also appears in a fragment of Callimachus (fr. 673 Pf.). Although the "Hill of the Graces" is not a feature of Cyrene, but of the wider Cyrenaica,[32] there is nevertheless reason to read the "Cinyphian thread" as a subtly Callimachean literary *materia* for Grattius' poem, as well as being the physical *materia* for the nets invented and gifted by Diana.[33]

The combination of the river with a hill of the Graces is not just relevant to Grattius, but to Ovid. The poet sets the myth of Actaeon in a Boeotian valley called Gargaphie (3.156). Gargaphie is less commonly the name of a valley or region than a spring (often spelled Argaphia), which was said to be sacred to the Graces.[34] A note on the variation in spelling preserves a fragment of Parthenius that describes the Graces bathing in the spring (νιψάμεναι κρήνης ἔδραμον Ἀργαφίης, fr. 56 Lightfoot; cf. Herodian, Περὶ παθῶν p. 187.24 Lentz). The Graces are supplied as the subject via the evidence of Alciphron, who has echoed this fragment in depicting the Graces leaving Orchomenos and bathing in the Argaphian spring (*Letters* 1.11.3). Diana's bath therefore not only evokes the *Bath of Pallas*, where Athena is functionally playing nymph, or Muse, but also the bathing of the Graces, and the metapoetic locality evoked by Grattius.[35]

Within the Ovidian myth, the threads (*lina*) of Actaeon's nets soon reappear, recontextualized in a way that speaks to Diana's familiarity with the accessories of the *ars uenandi*. The Theban nymph Crocale dresses the goddess' hair in preparation for her bath: *nam doctior illis / Ismenis Crocale sparsos per colla capillos / colligit in nodum* ("for more skillful than others, Ismenian Crocale gathers the flyaway hairs strewn across her neck into a knot," 3.168–70). Crocale gathers Diana's hair into a knot (*in nodum*) that suggests the knotted form of the hunting nets (*nodosa . . . lina*, 3.153).[36] The similarity between threads (of a net) and strands of hair is made further by the etymological significance of Crocale's name. A κρόκη is a "thread which is passed between the threads of the warp" (*LSJ* s.v. κρόκη 1), indicating the suitability of Crocale ("Thread") to perform her duty of collecting hair into a tidy knot.[37] Crocale's name also evokes hair-dressing as a type of weaving, a well-established activity for metapoetic reflection. The relationship between Actaeon and Diana is once again hinted at by the way Actaeon's nets are imagistically transformed into the agents of the goddess' *cultus*, reminding of her power over the sphere of hunting.[38]

There is also an intermediary stage where nets are evoked as part of Diana's hunting arsenal. The cave in Gargaphie where Diana bathes is marked by a "natural arch" (*natiuum . . . arcum*, 3.160), a shape that quite naturally recalls a bow (*arcus*). The affiliation is marked when Diana hands over her hunting accoutrement to a nymph in a list that ends with *arcusque retentos* (3.166). The literal level of interpreting *retentos* is that her bow is "relaxed" (i.e., unstretched), with the use of the poetic plural. Its plurality is underscored by the earlier appearance of *arcum*, an obvious singular. In this light, we can see the possibility of a translingual pun: in Greek, an ἄρκυς is a hunting net (cf. again Varr. *Sat. Men.* 385.2). *Retendo* is a rare verb, and its use creates two reasons for reading *arcus retendos* as a reference not to an unstretched bow but to unstrung nets. First, the opening of the verb glosses the pun (*rete*, " net"). Secondly, *tendo* is commonly used for stretching nets; Ovid uses this verb in combination with *rete* with frequency (*Am.* 1.8.69; *Her.* 21.206; *Ars am.* 1.45, *Rem.* 202; *Met.* 4.513, 7.701, 8.331).[39] With this reading in mind, Diana's taking a break from hunting with nets brings her closer to Actaeon and makes the absence of hunting hounds yet more marked.

DIANA'S BODY OF WORK

Keeping Grattius in mind, and Diana as the Grattian Muse, reinforces the goddess' power over hunting and its expressive literary potential. However, she naturally also exhibits ownership over the territory of the hunt itself (*mons*/ὄρος; cf. again *Hymn* 3.18, δὸς δέ μοι οὔρεα πάντα, "give me the remit of all mountains [as my territory]"). In this light, we should also consider the landscape of the hunt and her appearance as an expression of her divine power. Ovid takes especial care to describe the landscape in a way that makes it evocative of the goddess herself. Largely, scholars focus on the landscape as symbolic of Diana's virginity, noting this natural symbolism as a narrative pattern within the first few books of the epic; these symbolic readings point further to interpreting Actaeon's trespass as a sexual transgression.[40] What is missing from these readings is closer attention to Actaeon's status as a hunter, and Diana's similarity to a Muse or one of the Graces.

150   Ovid's *Lavacrum Dianae*

Before we look at Actaeon's characterization as a hunter, we can first see how the landscape of Gargaphie reinforces Diana's resemblance to a Muse, and how this further integrates awareness of the *Bath of Pallas*. The myth starts afresh with a new landscape ecphrasis:

> Vallis erat piceis et acuta densa cupressu,
> nomine Gargaphie, succinctae sacra Dianae,
> cuius in extremo est antrum nemorale recessu
> arte laboratum nulla; simulauerat artem
> ingenio natura suo, nam pumice uiuo
> et leuibus tofis natiuum duxerat arcum.
> fons sonat a dextra tenui perlucidus unda,
> margine gramineo patulos incinctus hiatus;
> hic dea siluarum uenatu fessa solebat
> uirgineos artus liquido perfundere rore.

(*Met.* 3.155–64)

> [There was a valley thickly wooded with pine and severe cypress,
> Gargaphie, by name, sacred to readily belted Diana,
> in the innermost hollow of which is a sylvan grotto
> worked due to no art; nature had imitated art
> with its own inborn nature; for it had coaxed out
> from living pumice and brittle tufa a natural arch;
> a fountain burbled to its right, transparent, with delicate wavelets,
> enclosed round its spreading pool with a grassy bank.]

The "enclosed" (*incinctus*) fountain echoes the "girdled" Diana (*succincta Diana*). Similarly, as previously noted, the arch of pumice monumentalizes the bow (*arcus*) of the goddess, reinforced by the subsequent *arcus*, in its literal meaning (3.166). The image of the mountainside tinged (*infectus,* 3.143) with blood reappears, this time on the canvas of the goddess' face as she blushes:

> qui color <u>infectis</u> aduersi solis ab ictu
> nubibus esse solet aut <u>purpureae</u> Aurorae,
> is fuit in uultu uisae sine ueste Dianae.

(*Met.* 3.183–85)

Ovid's *Lavacrum Dianae*

[And just as the color that clouds characteristically carry, when they are stained
by the opposing strikes of the sun, or the color of purple-bright Aurora—
so it was the color in the face of Diana, seen without her clothing.]

The overtly poetic nature of this passage, and the way the landscape directly evokes the goddess herself, lends further weight to the idea of Diana as a Muse. The sanctity of this location to Diana is reinforced by other descriptive details. *Nemorale* (3.157) evokes her cult site of Aricia: Grattius describes a ritual of Diana at Aricia, where her shrine is denoted as *sacrum ad nemorale Dianae* (*Cyn.* 484). Elsewhere within the Ovidian corpus, three of the four other appearances of the adjective *nemoralis* appear in descriptions of Aricia (*Ars am.* 1.259, *Met.* 14.331, *Fast.* 6.59).[41] The lake at Aricia was known as the *speculum Dianae*, typically because of the way one could see the moon reflected on the water, but Ovid plays upon this idea in making the area "mirror" the physicality of the goddess in a broader sense.

The idea of water as a mirror is also evoked within Callimachus' *Bath of Pallas*. To build a sense of the goddess' natural beauty, Callimachus describes how Athena does not require a mirror; to illustrate this fact, he cites the goddess' lack of vanity prior to the famous beauty contest judged by Paris:

οὐδ' ὅκα τὰν Ἴδᾳ Φρὺξ ἐδίκαζεν ἔριν,
οὔτ' ἐς ὀρείχαλκον μεγάλα θεὸς οὔτε Σιμοῦντος
ἔβλεψεν δίναν ἐς διαφαινομέναν·

(Callim. *Hymn* 5.18–20)

[Not even when on Ida the Phrygian was judging the contest did the great goddess glance into the orichalc or into the transparent eddies of the Simois. (trans. Stephens)]

Athena neither consults a mirror nor looks at herself in the water of the Simois, the natural equivalent of a mirror, with its translucent waves (δίναν . . . διαφαινομέναν). In Ovid's Gargaphian *locus amoenus*, the water of the fountain is *perlucidus* ("transparent," 3.161). *Perlucidus* comes from the verb *perluceo*, which functionally translates the Greek διαφαίνω. The ability for the fountain to be used as a mirror (never explicitly stated, but hinted at by the emphasis on *cultus* in the nymphs' attendance of the goddess) further

152   Ovid's *Lavacrum Dianae*

integrates the *Bath of Pallas* as a source text for Ovid. Along with the use of *nemoralis*, it also suggests that this site evokes Diana's sanctuary at Nemi, fusing together Greek and Roman landscapes and reality and text in a way that suggests that within the chronology of the epic, Diana's Arician sanctuary is the "nature" that will simulate the present Ovidian "art."

ACTAEON AS A GRATTIAN HUNTER

The Muse-like Diana is therefore presented as simultaneously being defined by and defining this sacred landscape. Ovid's myth consciously triangulates the relationships between land, hunter, and goddess. As a hunter, Actaeon bears a certain relationship to the land. As the son of Aristaeus, he has hunting in his blood, so to speak: Aristeus receives the epithet "Hunter" (Ἀγρεύς).[42] Critically, Actaeon is also the first mortal hunter in the epic. This status, of Actaeon's emphatic primacy as the first mortal hunter, allows him to be read productively alongside Grattius' two (otherwise unattested) pioneers of the hunting art: Dercylus and Hagnon.

When we turn to the Grattian text, we can see that Grattius relies on familiarity with a tradition of didactic allusivity to introduce the otherwise unknown Dercylus, lending him a literary authority:[43]

> o felix, tantis quem primum industria rebus
> prodidit auctorem! deus ille an proxuma divos
> mens fuit, in caecas aciem quae magna tenebras
> egit et ignarum perfudit lumine volgus?
> dic age Pierio (fas est) Diana, ministro.
> Arcadium stat fama senem, quem Maenalus auctor
> et Lacedaemoniae primum vidistis Amyclae
> per non adsuetas metantem retia valles
> Dercylon. haut illo quisquam se iustior egit,
> hau fuit in terris divom observantior alter:
> ergo illum primis nemorum dea finxit in arvis
> auctoremque operi dignata inscribere magno
> iussit adire suas et pandere gentibus artes.
>
> (Gratt. Cyn. 95–107)

[O how blessed was that man whom determined effort first brought to recognition as the instigator for such great matters!

Was he a god, or did he have a mind very close to the gods
which in its magnificence drove its clear gaze into the blind darkness
and bathed the ignorant crowd with light? Come speak, Diana—
for it is lawful—to a servant of the Muses. The story holds that
there was an old Arcadian man, whom Maenalus, his progenitor,
and you, Spartan Amyclae, first saw measuring out long nets across
unfamiliar valleys—and his name was Dercylos. By no means
did anyone conduct himself more justly than that man, nor by any means
was there another man on earth more respectful of the gods:
for this reason the goddess of groves fashioned him in the first fields
and, having deigned to inscribe him as the author for the great work,
she bid him to come close to her arts and open them up to the nations.
    (trans. S. Green)]

With Diana acting as his Muse, the poet extols the skills of the Arcadian
Dercylus. Dercylus was chosen by the goddess to receive from her the arts
of hunting; the first skill granted is hunting with nets (*Cyn.* 102), but he is
also responsible for creating hunting spears (*Cyn.* 108–9). Dercylus' knowl-
edge of the hunting *techne* is first metaphorically described as a "gaze" (*acies*)
that illuminates the "ignorant crowd" (*ignarum . . . uolgus*) with its light.
Such an image glosses one interpretation of his name, etymologized from
δέρκομαι ("to see clearly," "see").[44] Actaeon's name, too, can be etymologized
in a way that involves sight: ἀκτίς, "sunbeam, ray," but also "gaze." Ovid
shows sensitivity to this origin through the simile of Diana's blush upon
being seen by Actaeon (*qui color infectis aduersi solis ab ictu* / *nubibus esse
solet aut purpureae Aurorae*, "and just as the color that clouds characteris-
tically carry, when they are stained by the opposing strikes of the sun, or the
color of purple-bright Aurora," 3.183–84).[45] The Latin *acies*, as a sharpness
of gaze or point/edge of a weapon (a literal or metaphorical keenness),
combines the Greek root present in ἀκτίς and ἀκοντίζω (cf. ἄκων, "javelin"),
bringing together into one word the ideas of hunting and looking that pro-
vide the core activities of Actaeon's myth.[46] While Ovid does not use *acies* to
hint at Actaeon's name, its use to introduce Dercylus, the Arcadian hunting
"visionary" opens a space of suggestive influence between the two figures.
There are a few observations that can be placed within this space, to further
illuminate the ways Grattius stands as a productive intermediary between
Callimachus and Ovid in thinking about the construction of Actaeon's myth.

Ovid's *Lavacrum Dianae*

Actaeon's first words cite both of Dercylus' innovations, the net and spear: <u>lina</u> *madent, comites,* <u>ferrum</u>*que cruore ferarum,* "the lines are sodden, comrades, and the spear-points, from the slaughter of beasts," 3.148). Actaeon's Callimachean tutelage under the hunter goddess can be matched with Diana's sponsorship of Dercylus. Dercylus' Arcadian heritage and his literary purpose within Grattius' didactic also align him with Aristaeus, the *Arcadius magister* of the *Georgics*.[47] If we read Dercylus as a textual double of Aristaeus, he is additionally able to provide a literary lineage for Actaeon, the son of Aristaeus. In this light, we can further recall that Palaephatus' rationalizing tale of Actaeon makes him Arcadian, not Boeotian.[48]

The implications of sight in the names of both Dercylus and Actaeon are also connected by Callimachus' narrative in the *Bath of Pallas*. As is thematically appropriate, the hymn is threaded with the vocabulary of sight and seeing.[49] Critically, this includes a range of words affiliated with δέρκομαι. Athena herself was also known as Ὀξυδερκής ("keen-sighted") in one of her two Argive temples.[50] Tiresias' prey is the δορκάς ("roe-deer," "gazelle," *Hymn* 5.91), so named from its large eyes (and so, from δέρκομαι).[51] The irony of Tiresias losing his sight while hunting an animal named for his eyes has not escaped commentators. However, awareness of δέρκομαι's thematic relevance to the myth has not been extended to reading it as an internal signaling of one of Callimachus' literary sources for the hymn: Dercylus' *Argolika*.[52] If Callimachus is integrating a subtle flagging of his source, then Ovid has an opportunity to use Grattius' Dercylus as a window-reference back to his own source, Callimachus' *Bath of Pallas*, in a way that shows his perception of Callimachean cleverness. Grattius' Arcadian culture-hero mediates between the Callimachean and Ovidian texts, allowing Ovid to deepen the contexts of hymnic significance for Diana as the Roman goddess of the hunt.

The Ovidian Actaeon also bears allusive traces of Grattius' other pioneer of the hunt, Hagnon (*Cyn.* 213–52). Hagnon, a Boeotian, was the first to hunt with dogs. Grattius describes the process of the tracking dog, ending with how the dog shares in the recognition of success, which leads into the finale of praise for Hagnon:

> ergo ubi plena suo rediit victoria fine,
> in partem praedae veniat comes et sua norit
> praemia: sic operi iuvet inservisse benigne.

Ovid's *Lavacrum Dianae* 155

hoc ingens meritum, haec ultima palma tropaei,
Hagnon magne, tibi divom concessa favore:
ergo semper eris, dum carmina dumque manebunt
silvarum dotes atque arma Diania terris.

(Gratt. *Cyn.* 246–52)

[Therefore, when victory has made a full return with proper end,
let him come as companion to share the plunder
and let him recognize his own prize: in this way,
let it please him to have acted as a willing servant for the work.
This was the mighty service, this was the ultimate palm of victory
granted to you, o great Hagnon, by the favor of the gods:
so will you be eternal, as long as my songs shall remain, and as long as
the endowments of the woods and the arms of Diana shall endure on earth.
 (trans. S. Green)]

With victory assured, the hunting dog is invited as a companion (*comes*) in its share of the prey (*praedum*) and reward (*praemium*) as recompense for its service (*inservisse*).[53] The relationship here depicted between hunter and dog serves as a descriptive touchstone for the perversion of order that occurs in Actaeon's death, as he is transformed from hunter into hunted:

ea turba cupidine praedae
per rupes scopulosque adituque carentia saxa
quaque est difficilis quaque est uia nulla sequuntur.
ille fugit per quae fuerat loca saepe secutus,
(heu!) famulos fugit ipse suos. clamare libebat,
["Actaeon ego sum, dominum cognoscite uestrum!"]
uerba animo desunt; resonat latratibus aether.

at comites rapidum solitis hortatibus agmen
ignari instigant oculisque Actaeona quaerunt
et uelut absentem certatim Actaeona clamant
(ad nomen caput ille refert) et abesse queruntur
nec capere oblatae segnem spectacula praedae.

(*Met.* 3.225–31, 242–46)

156   Ovid's *Lavacrum Dianae*

[That crowd, with the greedy desire for prey
follow [Actaeon] along the crags and cliffs and rocks lacking access,
by whichever way there is no purchase and whichever way is no way at all.
He flees through the places he so often followed prey
alas—he flees his own slaves. It was to his liking to shout,
"I am Actaeon: recognize your master!"
the words are nowhere but in his head; the very heavens echoed with
    barking.

But his comrades, unaware, urged on the swift-ordered pack
with customary shouts and sought out Actaeon in their lines of sight
and they compete in their shouting for the missing Actaeon
(who turns his head toward his name), and complain he is missing out,
and complain the laggard won't capture the magnificence of their bestowed
    prize]

Actaeon's dogs are *famuli* ("slaves") that cannot recognize their prey as
their master; Actaeon's companions share in this failure. Denoting the dogs
as *famuli* further underscores the relationship described by *inservisse* in
Grattius.[54] The hounds who initially bring down Actaeon are the dogs who
made up for lost time by finding a shortcut across the mountain (*tardius
exierant, sed per compendia montis / anticipata uia est*, "they had set out
later, but they got a lead by means of a shortcut along the mountain," 3.234–
35). Ovid literalizes the Grattian spatial metaphor, as this echoes ironically
the description of Hagnon's innovation as "finding a more direct path" (*pro-
prior . . . via, Cyn.* 218).

    The notion of a "more direct path" is critical to Grattius' poetic agenda,
as it forms the language of the proem: men initially living astray (i.e., with-
out the guidance of hunting) are then led by reason onto a different, more
direct path:

dona cano divom, laetas venantibus artis,
auspicio, Diana, tuo; prius omnis in armis
spes fuit et nuda silvas virtute movebant
inconsulti homines vitaque erat <u>error</u> in omni.
post alia, <u>propiore, via</u> meliusque profecti
te sociam, Ratio, rebus sumpsere gerendis;

hinc omne auxilium vitae rectusque reluxit
ordo et contiguas didicere ex artibus artis
proserere, hinc demens cecidit violentia retro.

(Gratt. *Cyn.* 1–9)

[I sing of the gifts of the gods, the arts delightful to hunters,
under your auspices, Diana. In former times all hope lay in
arms, and uneducated men stirred the woods with brute courage,
and there was aimlessness in all (areas of) life. After this,
having made a better start on another, more direct path,
they took you, Reason, as companion in performing their tasks.
From here came every aid in life, and righteous order shone out its light,
and from (existing) arts men learned to produce connected arts;
from here, mindless ferocity fell behind. (trans. S. Green)]

With the repetition of this concept within the *Cynegetica*, Hagnon becomes
a surrogate for the author, but the implications for the *Metamorphoses* are
more cynical: Actaeon's fate is the result of *error* (3.142). From the begin-
ning, Actaeon's hunt is marked by pathlessness and wandering (*iuuenis . . .
per deuia lustra uagantes / participes operum*, "the youth, wandering through
the pathless wilds, a partaker of the hunt," 3.146–47). In contrast, Hagnon
hunts in known areas (*lustrat per nota ferarum*, "he traverses known beast
haunts," *Cyn.* 221). The pack of dogs pursues Actaeon along pathless ways
(3.227), but the successful hounds find the shortcut: the reversal of hunter
and hunted is complete, as Ovid has the hounds follow a known "path," the
first to do so over the course of the myth.

Hagnon's episode can also be read in a way that further illuminates in-
fluence upon not just Actaeon, but the Ovidian Diana. To endow Hagnon
with the immortality of poetic praise, Grattius packages together his songs
with the "dowries" of the woods and the arms of Diana (*ergo semper eris,
dum carmina dumque manebunt / silvarum dotes atque arma Diania terris*,
"so will you be eternal, as long as my songs shall remain, and as long as
the endowments of the woods and the arms of Diana shall endure on earth,"
Cyn. 251–52). Lisa Whitlatch, noting the unusual formulation of *silvarum
dotes*, explains it not just as an equivalent to the *ars uenandi*, but as an
endowment of land with responsibility due to the hunter. Like a dowry, "the
hunter should be preserving nature not only for his own sake, so that the

woods, like the poem, will last forever, but also for the sake of his bride, be that nature (*silvarum*) or the goddess of nature (Diana). The dowry imagery underlines the role of the hunter in a sustainable environment."[55] Whitlatch's interpretation provides a different nuance when mapped upon the close relationship Ovid forges between the landscape of Gargaphie and Diana previously discussed, and Actaeon's role within that landscape. With this concept loosely in mind, the closeness of the relationship between Actaeon and Artemis that is a feature of the *Bath of Pallas* and the mythological variant that has Actaeon desire marriage with Artemis also becomes embedded in the Ovidian landscape via Grattian awareness. This lends a potentially erotic aspect to the contract between hunter and environment, additionally reinforcing Diana's presentation as a Roman matron and the subdued eroticization of that landscape that she presides over, made descriptively contiguous with her body.

However, Whitlatch omits one aspect of the unusual formulation of this phrase, coming as it does at the close of the Hagnon excursus. *Silvarum dotes* is a phrase further striking given the connotations of his name (ἁγνός, "pure"). Hagnon's name and status as a favorite of Diana places him in contact with Hippolytus, who hunts with his swift dogs alongside the goddess and enjoys a companionship more than is usual for a mortal (Eur. *Hipp.* 17–19). Hippolytus' nature is emblematized within the Euripidean play when he declares his purity when confronted with the statue of Aphrodite: πρόσωθεν αὐτὴν <u>ἁγνὸς</u> ὢν ἀσπάζομαι ("I greet her at remove, being pure," Eur. *Hipp.* 102). Hagnon's custodianship of nature and the *ars uenandi* can therefore be read as a devotion to Diana that stands as a symbolic marriage, a reading that becomes less paradoxical if understood as a parallel to Grattius' own relationship with Diana as his Muse. If we then read Hagnon as a textual influence upon Ovid's Actaeon, there arises a corresponding parallel to reading Dercylus as a textual influence. Just as Actaeon's evocation of Dercylus can be read back into the Callimachean sources of the *Bath of Pallas* (Ovid's own overt source for the myth), Actaeon's evocation of Hagnon likewise can be read back into the hymn as evidence for its use of the *Hippolytus*.[56] Once again, Grattius provides a medial layer of allusivity that Ovid uses to signal Callimachus' sources, using Grattius himself like a hunting dog to track down literary clues.

Before we move on to talking about the hunting dogs themselves, there is one more supporting example of the way Actaeon and his myth coheres

Ovid's *Lavacrum Dianae*

with the presentation of the goddess within the Callimachean hymns that will appropriately lead into our focus upon the hounds. Like Hippolytus, Actaeon appears within the *Bath of Pallas* as an intimate of the goddess. Athena says that Actaeon's status as a favorite of the goddess can do nothing to spare him:

> ἀλλ᾿ οὐκ αὐτὸν ὅ τε δρόμος αἵ τ᾿ ἐν ὄρεσσι
> ῥυσεῦνται ξυναὶ τᾶμος ἑκαβολίαι,
> ὁππόκα κ᾿ οὐκ ἐθέλων περ ἴδῃ χαρίεντα λοετρά
> δαίμονος· ἀλλ᾿ αὐταὶ τὸν πρὶν ἄνακτα κύνες
> τουτάκι δειπνησεῦντι·

(*Hymn* 5.111–15)

[But neither the hunting course nor their common skill in archery in the mountains shall save him, when, even though inadvertently, he sees the fair bath of the goddess. But his own bitches shall dine upon their former master. (trans. Stephens)]

Within the *Hymn to Artemis*, the goddess' favors are never shown to male followers, only female, and largely within the context of the hunt. Cyrene, as a companion, is gifted with two hunting hounds (*Hymn* 3.206–8); Procris is also named as her companion in the hunt (*Hymn* 3.209–10). Artemis teaches Atalanta how to hunt with hounds and how to shoot (*Hymn* 3.215–17). The mythological variant of Artemis giving Procris a hunting hound of incredible ability is suggested by her inclusion in the catalog alongside the gifting of hounds to Cyrene and Atalanta's tutelage in hunting with dogs.[57] Regarding the vignette of Atalanta, Stephens (ad 223) says that Callimachus is the first to use τοξότις, "archeress," but it seems that this designation would rather recall the play of Aeschylus called Τοξότιδες, "Archeresses," a drama about none other than Actaeon. The easy mythological contamination or conflation of the Arcadian huntress Atalanta with the Boeotian runner Atalanta is interesting to note alongside a potential Arcadian lineage for Actaeon, who is designated as a σύνδρομος of Artemis, a role emphasized by the repetition of δρόμος in the following line. The Arcadian location of Atalanta's hunting and her instruction in κυνηλασία ("hunting with dogs," *Hymn* 3.217, appearing only here[58]) looks back to the moment in Artemis' hymn where she obtains her own hunting dogs from Pan in

160   Ovid's *Lavacrum Dianae*

Arcadia. Artemis' gifting of hunting dogs to her especial companions in the hunt is an especially ironic background for Actaeon's tale, and one that Ovid enjoys exploiting—where we will again see him placing Grattius in the middle.

ALLUSION HUNTING WITH HOUNDS

At last, we turn to one of the notable features of Ovid's Actaeon myth: the dogs themselves. Ovid's catalog of Actaeon's hounds has been largely read as a witty take on the epic catalog.[59] The catalog is not purely a product of Ovidian irreverence, but seems to be a traditional mythological feature of Actaeon's tale: a fragment of Aeschylus records the names of four dogs, while the catalog elsewhere is listed at fifty strong.[60] Mining this catalog for additional influences has not been a priority of readers and interpreters; however, we will do just that in order to continue our discussion of Callimachean and Grattian influence.

Ovid's list begins with Melampus ("Blackfoot," 3.206) and Ichnobates ("Tracker," 3.207), and repeats these names along with their origins (*Cnosius Ichnobates, Spartana gente Melampus*, 3.208). The famed kind of dog that Grattius says Hagnon first hunts with, the otherwise unknown *metagon*, hails from Sparta and Crete: *Sparta quos et Creta suos promittit alumnos* ("Sparta and Crete pledge you as their own local proteges," Gratt. *Cyn.* 212).[61] The Ovidian catalog gains momentum with a new flurry of names:

> inde ruunt alii rapida uelocius aura,
> Pamphagos et Dorceus et Oribasos, Arcades omnes,
> Nebrophonosque ualens et trux cum Laelape Theron
>
>   (*Met.* 3.209–11)

> [Thence others rush forth, faster than the fast wind,
> Pamphagos and Dorceus and Oribasos, all Arcadians,
> and strong Nebronos and snarlsome Theron, with Laelaps.]

The qualification "faster than the fast wind" anticipates the proliferation of "windy" names (*Laelaps*, "hurricane," 3.211; *Aello*, "stormwind," 3.219; *Labros*, a Homeric designation of the wind, "furious," 3.224), but it is most closely descriptive of the Arcadian dogs. Within the Callimachean hymn, the set of seven dogs that Pan gives Artemis are also "faster than the wind" (ἑπτὰ δ' ἔδωκε / θάσσονας αὐράων Κυνοσουρίδας, "he gave her seven Cynosurian bitches, faster than the wind," Callim. *Hymn* 3.93–94). However, the sole "speckled" dog (ἕνα δ' αἰόλον, *Hymn* 3.91) Artemis is given also has a "windy" name that anticipates this description (cf. Αἴολος, lord of the winds). These Cynosourians are also the dogs that hunt down fawns (*Hymn* 3.95) and roe-deer (*Hymn* 3.97). Ovid seems to absorb these Arcadian dogs into Actaeon's catalog, merging the enumeration of gifts that honor and define Artemis' burgeoning divinity with the traditional catalog of Actaeon's myth.[62] This splicing of tradition lends a further ironic slant to the myth: via the Callimachean allusions, the dogs intrinsically honor the power of the goddess.

Beyond the shared origin and descriptor of swiftness, further connections can be made between Artemis' dogs and the Ovidian list. The name Dorceus comes from the Greek δορκάς (Callimachus uses the variant ζόρξ at *Hymn* 3.97);[63] as previously discussed, the roe-deer (or gazelles) were given this name by their large eyes, connecting it to δέρκομαι. Dorceus, therefore, is "Roe-deer," or "Big-eyes," a name that recalls the prey of both Artemis' Arcadian hunting dogs and Tiresias in the *Bath of Pallas*. Grattius also mentions the *dorcas* when enumerating breeds of hunting dog:

> at te leve si qua
> tangit opus pavidosque iuvat conpellere dorcas
> aut versuta sequi leporis vestigia parvi,
> Petronios (haec fama) canes volucresque Sycambros
> et pictam macula Vertraham delige falsa:
> ocior adfectu mentis pennaque cucurrit
>
> (Gratt. *Cyn.* 199–204)

> [But if a light sort of hunting interests you,
> and if it is your pleasure to drive together terrified gazelles
> or to pursue the shrewdly made tracks of the small hare,
> choose Petronian dogs—this is their reputation—
> and winged Sycambrians and the Vertraha adorned with deceiving spots:
> more swiftly than a state of mind or winged flight does it run
>   (trans. S. Green)]

Grattius names the breeds suitable for "light" hunting, the pursuit of roe-deer and hares. This "light work" (*leue . . . opus*) recalls the opening of Artemis'

162   Ovid's *Lavacrum Dianae*

hymn, and the latent potential of seeing ἔλαφος in ἐλαφρός before the pivot to hares as her hunting quarry (λαγωβολίαι, *Hymn* 3.2). Grattius seems to suggest that rather than Arcadian dogs, Petronian, Sycambrian, and Vertrahan hounds would be suitable companions for the goddess if she wants to hunt roe-deer and hares, which are two of the four designated targets of her Cynosourian bitches (*Hymn* 3.95–97). The singular Vertrahan amid the plural Petronian and Sycambrian dogs, marked with camouflaging spots (*pictam macula . . . falsa*) also recalls the singular "speckled" dog Artemis receives from Pan. Their speed, demonstrated by a mix of metaphorical and physical swiftness—"quicker than a state of mind or a wing"—further reminds of the hymnic immediacy of action that brackets Artemis' journey to Arcadia: ἄφαρ δ᾽ ὡπλίσσαο, δαῖμον. / αἶψα δ᾽ ἐπὶ σκύλακας πάλιν ἦιες ("forthwith you were readied with equipment, goddess; with speed you sallied forth for your puppies," *Hymn* 3.86–87); ἔνθεν ἀπερχομένη (μετὰ καὶ κύνες ἐσσεύοντο), "departing from there [and the dogs made hunting haste with you]," *Hymn* 3.98). *Adfectu mentis* also thematically picks up the aside of (*haec fama*), while *penna* looks back to the *uolucres Sycambros*,[64] emphasizing the singularity and even textual camouflage of the Vertrahan.

The spottedness of this dog is also notable given the absence elsewhere of color descriptions in Grattius' text. On the Callimachean use of αἰόλος, Stephens refers to Xenophon's advice that dogs should not be a single color (*Cyn.* 4.7).[65] In this light, she also supports reading παρουαίους at 3.91, a variant of παρώας ("chestnut"), instead of the transmitted παρουατίους ("with hanging ears"), arguing that context dictates a color term: Pan gives Artemis two half-white hounds, three chestnut, and one speckled. There is also further dispute over the color terminology of πηγός, which can indicate white or black; Callimachus splits the difference by making this color only "half" of the dog, embracing the ambiguity.[66] In looking at the Ovidian catalog, there are a number of color descriptors, but only with overt reference to black or white: Melampus ("Blackfoot," 3.206); *et niueis Leucon et uillis Asbolos atris* ("and Leucon with a snow-white coat, Asbolos with black," 3.218); *et nigram medio frontem distinctus ab albo / Harpalos et Melaneus* ("Harpalos, distinctly marked by a black splotch on his otherwise white brow, and 'Blackie,'" 3.221–22); Melanchaetes ("Blackhair," 3.232).[67] Harpalos, a black dog with a white mark on his forehead, fits the mold of Xenophon, who says that red or black dogs should have white foreheadhairs (Xen. *Cyn.* 4.7–8). Red is not a color feature of the Ovidian catalog,

Ovid's *Lavacrum Dianae* 163

nor of the Callimachean list, without the emendation of παρουαίους to evoke Xenophon's third color choice (πυρρός). When discussing the physical appearance of the best dogs, Grattius does not mention color, but he does mention a different feature of interest. His list begins *sint celsi voltus, sint hirtae frontibus aures* ("let their faces be lofty, their shaggy ears down by their brows," *Cyn.* 269).[68] Although not a translation of the hapax παρουατίους, Grattius' description nevertheless evokes the word, introducing the possibility that this Callimachean textual question was already open to scholarly comment and interpretability in the Augustan age. The absence of the color red from the Ovidian and Grattian descriptions of dogs further suggests this possibility.

Returning anew to the Ovidian catalog, we can observe other connections with both Callimachus and Grattius. The dog Ladon also sports a Grattian feature: *et substricta gerens Sicyonius ilia Ladon* ("and Sicyonian Ladon, girt with narrow flanks," 3.216) evokes the Grattian description *adstricti succingant ilia ventres* ("may close-set flanks gird their stomachs," *Cyn.* 271). Ladon's name, which he shares with an Arcadian river, additionally puts him in dialogue with the Arcadian trio; his thinness also contrasts actively with the image Pamphagos' name summons ("All-Eater," "Greedy"). Pamphagos' name can also remind us that Pan was preparing food (the Maenalian lynx) for his dogs when Artemis arrived in Arcadia.[69] Oribasos ("Mountain-Roamer," 3.210) is also a name suitable for an Arcadian dog, as the region's most defining literary features are its mountains (Maenalus, Cyllene, Parthenius).

The significance of Artemis' Arcadian hunting dogs to the Ovidian catalog bleeds beyond the strict boundaries of line 210, where the Arcadian hounds Pamphagos, Dorceus, and Oribasos are named. The dog that follows in the catalog, Nebrophonos ("Fawn-killer"), evokes the embedded list of prey for Artemis' dogs (νεβρούς, Callim. *Hymn* 3.95) as well as the goddess' own designation of Ἐλαφοκτόνος / Ἐλαφηβόλος. Other names similarly cue remembrances of the portion of Artemis' hymn that deal with her female companions in the hunt. Laelaps is the name of the dog Procris gives to her husband Cephalus as a dowry, which in one version she receives as a gift from Artemis herself; Ovid himself preserves this version in the *Metamorphoses* (7.753–55; cf. 771 for the name). Hylaeus is one of the names Xenophon suggests for a dog (*Cyn.* 7.5), but it is also the name of one of the centaurs "boar-slaying" Atalanta kills in Arcadia (Callim. *Hymn* 3.221).[70]

164 Ovid's *Lavacrum Dianae*

Ovid specifies that the dog Hylaeus was recently gored by a boar (3.213), uniting Atalanta's prey and victim in one image. Altogether, there is cumulatively evidence to suggest that the catalog of Artemis' hunting dogs was inspirational to both Grattius and Ovid in ways both manifold and manifest.

NYMPHS AND HOUNDS: CATALOGED FOLLOWERS

The significance of the catalog form itself within the mythological episode also needs recognition. The dog-catalog is actually the second catalog appearing within Actaeon's tale. The first is the catalog of Diana's nymphs: the three unnamed nymphs who assist with her physical accoutrement, followed by the named coterie of Crocale, Nephele, Hyale, Rhanis, Psecas, and Phiale (3.165–72). When Actaeon enters the grove, the nymphs protectively surround Diana, beating their breasts and wailing:

> per nemus ignotum non certis passibus errans
> peruenit in lucum; sic illum fata ferebant.
> qui simul intrauit rorantia fontibus antra,
> sicut erant nudae uiso sua pectora nymphae
> percussere uiro subitisque ululatibus omne
> inpleuere nemus circumfusaeque Dianam
> corporibus texere suis; tamen altior illis
> ipsa dea est colloque tenus supereminet omnes.

(Met. 3.175–82)

> [Through the unknown grove, wandering with no fixed direction,
> he came into the grove: thus the fates were bearing him along.
> As soon as he entered the cave, dripping from water fountains,
> just as they were, the nymphs, bare, beat their breasts
> because a man saw them, and filled the grove's entirety with
> their sudden shrieking and poured themselves around Diana,
> protectively interweaving with their bodies; however, the goddess herself
> was taller than they were, and towered over all; they only reached her neck.]

Although the similarity in catalogs may initially appear only superficially formal, there are an array of thematic and textual threads drawn between the company of nymphs and Actaeon's hunting dogs. This similarity also draws out the anthropomorphism of Ovid's canine catalog.[71] The sound the nymphs make in alarm (*ululare*) is also the sound of dogs barking (*OLD* s.v. 1). Within the *Homeric Hymn to Aphrodite*, Artemis is said to love the ὀλολυγή ("loud [hunting] cry," *Hymn. Hom. Ven.* 19), from the verb that gives Latin *ululare*. The immediate flooding of the nymphs around Diana's body is echoed by the dogs' encircling of Actaeon as they close in for the kill (*undique circumstant*, "from all sides they press around," 3.249). Both groups of nymphs and dogs are also denoted by *turba* (3.186; 3.225; 3.236). The nymphs bear thematically appropriate names, just as the dogs display monikers of etymological significance.[72]

Readers familiar with the Ovidian corpus will also recognize that Nape (3.214) is also the name of Corinna's hairdresser (cf. *Am.* 1.11, 1.12). Nape is also a name appropriate for a nymph: in the *epyllion* that ends *Georgics* 4, the nymph Cyrene advises Aristaeus to supplicate the Napaeae, nymphs who take their name from the "vales" (νάπαι; cf. *Georg.* 4.535).[73] Looking at the overlap elsewhere between the names of nymphs and hunting hounds, Claudian names Nebrophone as one of the "chief" nymphs of Diana (*Cons. Stil.* 3.250, 314–15; cf. Nebrophonos, *Met.* 3.211).[74] The nymph Nebrophone is Arcadian, from Mt. Lycaeus; in the Ovidian catalog, the dog Nebrophonos follows the Arcadian dogs, as noted above. The phraseology of *Arcades omnes* to describe the hounds also looks back to Virgil in a noteworthy way. It simultaneously evokes the famous *Arcades ambo* of *Eclogue* 7 (7.4), descriptive of Thyrsus and Corydon and also part of the nymph catalog of *Georgics* 4: *Clioque et Beroe soror, Oceanitides ambae, / ambae auro, pictis incinctae pellibus ambae* ("Clio and her sister Beroe, both Oceanids, both gilded, both surrounded with decorated pelts," *Georg.* 4.341–42). As Richard Thomas notes, this couplet is adapted from Callimachus' *Hymn to Artemis* (*Hymn* 3.42–43), evoking the goddess' choice of attendants.[75] Virgil mixes Oceanids with other nymph groups, like Callimachus does before him and Ovid after him. Ovid's use of *Arcades omnes* stages Actaeon's dogs as akin to a catalog of nymphs, via the Virgilian reference that is itself adapted from Callimachus' hymn. Evoking a company of nymphs loyal to Diana here also complicates the irony of the myth, and the question of Actaeon's wrongdoing. Again, it may seem strange that catalogs of nymphs and hunting dogs can work in parallel to create a literary and interpretive significance, but this strangeness is first mitigated by the catalog of dogs occurring in Callimachus' hymn

166   Ovid's *Lavacrum Dianae*

after the goddess chooses her followers. And as we have seen previously, we can look to Grattius to provide a bridge between the Callimachean hymn and the Ovidian narrative.

Within the *Cynegetica*, Grattius provides a glimpse into the world of Diana's sanctuary at Nemi, as he records a performance for civic health and benefit that bears traces of old initiation rituals.

> idcirco aeriis molimur compita lucis
> spicatasque faces sacrum ad nemorale Dianae
> sistimus et solito catuli velantur honore,
> ipsaque per flores medio in discrimine luci
> stravere arma sacris et pace vacantia festa.
> tum cadus et viridi fumantia liba feretro
> praeveniunt teneraque extrudens cornua fronte
> haedus et ad ramos etiamnum haerentia poma,
> lustralis de more sacri, quo tota iuventus
> lustraturque deae proque anno reddit honorem.
> ergo inpetrato respondet multa favore
> ad partis, qua poscis opem; seu vincere silvas
> seu tibi fatorum labes exire minasque
> cura prior, tua magna fides tutelaque virgo.

(Gratt. *Cyn.* 483–96)

[For this reason we raise altars at the crossroads in the soaring groves
and place spiked torches at the woodland shrine of Diana,
and puppies are dressed in customary adornments, and the men
spread out their very weapons amid the flowers
in the middle of the grove's crossroads, weapons which lie idle
at the sacred rites and festal peace.
Then the jar and cakes steaming hot on a greenwood litter
are brought along first, and a young goat thrusting out horns
from its tender forehead, and fruits which are even now clinging
to their branches, following the custom of a purification rite,
by which the entire youthful band is purified and gives back honour
to the goddess in return for the year's produce.
Thereupon, having obtained her favour, she offers many responses

Ovid's *Lavacrum Dianae* 167

directed towards the areas for which you ask assistance;
whether it is your primary concern that you conquer the woods
or that the menacing destructive forces of the fates
be banished from you, your great guardianship lie with the maiden.
   (trans. S. Green)]

Describing this ritual procession, C. M. C Green narrows in on *velantur* to raise the question of identification. The logical subject is *catuli* ("dogs"), and yet in the process of reading, it seems more natural to take the subject of *stravere* as the same as *velantur*, rather than supply one for *stravere*; a supplied subject is also unusual here, as it entails the poet neglects to give the initiates themselves an identifying, collective noun. Supplying the parallel example of Artemis' "little bears" performing at Brauron, Green suggests that these initiates at Nemi were "in some way identified as young hunting hounds."[76] With this understanding in mind, the dogs of Ovid's catalog, evoking "initiates" of the goddess, come into greater alignment with the catalog of nymphs.

The ending prayers offered to Diana in the Grattian text take on new resonance when read alongside Actaeon's tale: *seu vincere siluas / seu tibi fatorum labes exire minasque* (*Cyn.* 494–95). Hunting and warfare often share a register of meaning, which makes the second item more interesting: the avoidance of fate's threats. When Actaeon enters the grove, Ovid relates that he was carried by the fates: *per nemus ignotum non certis passibus errans / peruenit in lucum; sic illum fata ferebant* ("through the unknown grove, wandering with no fixed direction, he came into the grove; thus the fates were bearing him along," 3.175–76). This fatal action was previously categorized as an *error* (3.142), echoed again by *errans*. In his proem, Grattius characterizes life in the woods without the gifts of Diana as one of *error* (*vitaque erat error in omni*, "and there was aimlessness in all (areas of) life," *Cyn.* 4). Although the idea of an *error* marks Actaeon's hapless innocence in Ovid, when it is read with Grattius in mind, Actaeon consequentially exists outside of those blessed by Diana, potentially alluding to versions of the myth where his treatment of the goddess earns him punishment. Ovid's assignment of fate to Actaeon's decision lends a different, specific valence to the prayers made to Diana at Nemi to safeguard from the dangers of fate, embedding a retrospective mythological element within Grattius' didactic.

168 Ovid's *Lavacrum Dianae*

Seeing similarities between Diana's coterie of nymphs and Actaeon's dogs begins to suggest Diana's power over hunting dogs. Ovid therefore uses this myth not only to showcase the goddess' anger (*ira*, 3.252), giving her a star turn wielding the epic emotion par excellence, but to address this constituent part of her divine identity, as explored in Callimachus and Grattius. Unlike other versions of the myth, where the goddess is said to have given the dogs a madness as well as transforming Actaeon, there is no specific mention of Diana encountering or altering the behavior of the dogs at all.[77] Ovid's account relies on the rational behavior of hunting dogs (as is in their nature, and honed by training, dogs will take down a stag), but the similarities forged between her nymph followers and the hunting dogs also bear subtle implications that the dogs respond to Diana and her will, given her status as the huntress deity.

Ovid's final glimpse of Diana is a goddess out for bloodthirsty vengeance:

> undique circumstant mersisque in corpore rostris
> dilacerant falsi dominum sub imagine cerui,
> nec nisi finita per plurima uulnera uita
> ira pharetratae fertur satiata Dianae.
>
> (*Met.* 3.249–52)

> [From all sides they press around, and shred to pieces
> their master, trapped under the false appearance of the deer,
> burying their muzzles in the body.
> Nor until his life was drained out through the most possible wounds
> was the anger of quiver-bearing Diana said to be sufficiently slaked.]

As the narrator, Ovid distances himself from Diana's reaction by his use of *fertur*; he does not commit himself to be the sole authority for her punitive satisfaction, signaling awareness of the myth's variations.[78] Like the responses of the convening rivers to Daphne's transformation, the audience to Diana's reaction is split:

> Rumor in ambiguo est; aliis uiolentior aequo
> uisa dea est, alii laudant dignamque seuera
> uirginitate uocant; pars inuenit utraque causas.
>
> (*Met.* 3.253–55)

Ovid's *Lavacrum Dianae* 169

[Rumor is in a wavering state; to some, the goddess seems more
more violent than just, others praise her, calling it
meritorious because of her strict vow of virginity;
each part finds plausible explanation.]

While to some, the goddess seems more violent than is just, others praise her
action as worthy due to the strictness of her chastity. Similarly, we can read
gestures toward different genres within these responses. First, the vocabulary
of praise (*laudant*) cues the context of hymns: the virginity of the goddess is a
point of emphasis within the *Homeric Hymn to Aphrodite* (16–20), an identi-
fying detail within Artemis' own *Homeric Hymns* (9.2; 27.2), and a continual
motif of importance within Callimachus' hymn, not to mention her appear-
ances in Horatian hymns. Less overt perhaps is the way that her violence, the
product of her anger, recalls her appearances within Homeric epic and trag-
edy, where she is enduringly depicted as exacting punishment (usually against
women) for slights or offenses committed. This image of the goddess, as a
cruel destroyer, is what Callimachus reminds his readers of at his hymn's
end: Artemis takes retribution against Agamemnon, Otus and Orion, and
Hippo for their array of misdeeds, but without any narrative elaboration.

ACTAEON AS A HYMNIC, CALLIMACHEAN MYTH

The nature of the Callimachean hymnic coda, with its numerous expres-
sions of latent narrative potential, takes us back to an interpretation I have
suggested for Ovid's Actaeon myth: as the continuation to the Callimachean
Hymn to Artemis. The opportunity offered by Callimachus at the end of
Artemis' hymn is appealing to Ovid on a grand scale, who demonstrates the
goddess' fearsomeness by projecting Actaeon retrospectively into the ranks
of the Callimachean list as a combination of Agamemnon, Otus, and Orion.
However, there is also a disputed passage of Grattius that can be additionally
explained by a desire to chase this Callimachean opportunity. Not long after
the conclusion of the proem, Grattius introduces a warning to his readers,
illustrated by a set of mythological *exempla*. The textual issues presented
have vexed editors and readers, who tend to interpret the passage as a
Gigantomachy:

magnum opus et tangi, nisi cura vincitur, inpar.
nonne vides veterum quos prodit fabula rerum

semideos—illi aggeribus temptare superbis
ire freta et matres ausi attrectare deorum—
quam magna mercede meo sine munere silvas
impulerint?

(Gratt. *Cyn.* 61–66)

[Great is the task and incapable of being grasped unless it is conquered by
  care.
Those whom the story of old times sets forth, the demi-gods—
they it was who had the audacity to attempt to cross the waves
by means of arrogant amassing (of mountains) and to assault
the mothers of the gods—do you not see at what great cost
they struck against the woods without my service? (trans. S. Green)]

These readers of Gigantomachic context favor the printing of *freti iram* over
the emendation *ire freta*. This preference stems from an eagerness to preserve
the hubristic nature of the Giants with the imagery of stacking mountains,
and factoring in the contextual awareness of Grattius' era: the Augustan poets
favored this imagery, but more typically as a motif of the *recusatio*. Dunstan
Lowe has argued instead for reading this *exemplum* as being primarily
about Orion, who is a more suitable figure to deploy when issuing cautions
to hunters.[79] In Lowe's reading, the additional figures that could be evoked
alongside Orion (the plural *semideos*) would be the Aloads, who similarly
fit the bill for an appropriate cautionary tale within a didactic about hunt-
ing. In one version, the Aloads died when Artemis, appearing in deer form,
tricked the brothers into killing each other with mutual spear-throws in-
tended for the doe (Apollod. *Bibl.* 1.7.4). Artemis was especially motivated
to dispatch Otus, who attempted to carry her off from Olympus. This is the
context in which he appears in the *envoi* of the Callimachean hymn: Otus
and Orion are mentioned together as those who attempted to "court" the
goddess (*Hymn* 3.264–65). As mentioned previously, Orion is the sole fig-
ure from this catalog that cannot be cross-referenced elsewhere within the
hymn. If we are looking for precedent for a mythological *exemplum* that
packages together a Giant and Orion, it is this small portion of Callimachus'
hymn. I suggest that Grattius too recognized that Orion had not received
his narrative due within the Callimachean hymn, and was inspired to make
him the focus of his own warning message about the gift of the hunt—the

Ovid's *Lavacrum Dianae*　　　　171

gift sponsored and nurtured by Diana. Grattius shifts the focus of Orion's myth to hunting, rather than assault, which can also apply to Otus. In this way, Lowe's reading can be refined: Grattius' *semideos* encompasses not the Aloads and Orion, but Orion and Otus, in an homage to Callimachus. Grattius preserves the figures of the *exemplum*, but shows his learnedness by shifting its focus to meet his poetic needs: Grattius marks out the poetic purpose of his own work by transferring their appearance jointly to an *exemplum* that relies on the hunt to construct its message and meaning, from a work that explores Artemis as a goddess of the hunt in multifaceted ways.

Grattius' use of this *exemplum* to cohere strategically the hymnic presence of Diana and his didactic purpose would appeal to Ovid's sense of competitive innovation. In transforming Actaeon into his role as the continuation of the Callimachean hymn, Ovid shows an awareness of Grattius' homage to the ending of the Callimachean hymn and the promotion of both his own poetic gifts and Diana as a hunting goddess. However, Grattius' promotion of Orion to receive narrative emphasis is subtle. Although he is more properly the central focus of the *exemplum*, the narrative and message evoked is also one still shared with Otus. When we consider Ovid's Actaeon, he combines the figures of Agamemnon, Otus, and Orion. Orion is a figure that is seamlessly absorbable into the salient details of the myth. Not only does he bear a known similarity to Actaeon as a protégé of the hunting goddess, he is also blinded (a punishment for raping Merope on Chios).[80] Orion therefore also links Tiresias and Actaeon. Drawing further mythological connective tissue between Tiresias and Actaeon, Orion becomes a narrative touchstone for Ovid's transformation of the *Bath of Pallas* via reference to the *Hymn to Artemis*. Ovid lifts the mythological *exemplum* of Actaeon from the *Bath of Pallas* to act as the narrative supplement hinted at by the mention of Orion in the *Hymn to Artemis*.

CONCLUSION

This chapter has reassessed the modality of Callimachean hymnic influence within Ovid's myth of Actaeon, and how it shaped the identity of the goddess. Rather than simply promote an inset myth from the *Bath of Pallas*, Ovid's reconfigures the mythological *exemplum* from the *Bath of Pallas* to form a creative supplement to the *Hymn to Artemis*. This repurposing of hymnic material places Diana and Minerva into a space of rivalry that initially promotes Diana, but also prefigures Minerva's appearance on Helicon in Book 5, when Ovid will broach the material of the *Bath of Pallas*. Reading Ovid's myth of Actaeon as a sequel, creative supplement, or appendix to Callimachus' *Hymn to Artemis* allows for further subtleties of interpretation and structural understanding to shine through. It also brings the goddess back to the forefront of the myth, focusing on how the relationship between Actaeon and the goddess can instead provide a different seam of investigative interest. However, the integration of Callimachus' *Hymn to Artemis* into the conversation surrounding Actaeon's myth is not the only interpretive benefit here: additional insight is gained with the application of Grattius to stitch together the layers of Callimachean inspiration and Ovidian creative impulse.

The influence of the *Hymn to Artemis* is significantly enriched by reading Ovid's use of a contemporary hymnic portrait of Diana as an intermediary for his myth and the Callimachean corpus of hymns: the goddess of Grattian didactic, hymnically addressed at strategic points throughout the poem. Ultimately, Ovid uses Grattius like a hunting dog, to uncover the traces and sources of the Callimachean hymn that inspired his own version of the goddess.

5

The Hymnic Battle for Helicon

Reflections over Contested Grounds

One persistent feature of characterization within the body of Callimachean hymns is the prominence of virgin goddesses acting in roles typically occupied by Muses. In each of their respective hymns, both Artemis and Athena become assimilated to Muses, yet with differing dynamics and poetic emphases. Artemis acts as an inspirational force to the poet in a way that reveals the goddess as responsible for the narrative progression of the poem; as such, she emblematizes the special relationship between Muse and poet first immortalized by Hesiod and Homer. Athena resembles a Muse due to her hymn's internal setting and activity (bathing on Helicon), and the way she presides over Tiresias' poetic initiation, brokering his absorption into the epic and tragic spheres. Her identity as a Muse is more constructed for the internal world of the poem. In both cases the identification is not made as explicit, for example, as the title of Muse granted via the laudatory label of "tenth Muse" to regents (Berenice) or poetesses (Sappho, Corinna). Ovid further endows the name Corinna with the powers of a Muse when he weaves his elegiac corpus around this *puella*, disrupting the nomenclatural pattern of Apolline affiliation displayed by Gallus, Varro, Propertius, and Tibullus. Corinna is a name also connected with the home of the Muses, Mt. Helicon: one of the extant fragments of the Boeotian poetess (*PMG* 634. Col I. 1–34; P. Berol. 264) records a contest between Helicon and Cithaeron.[1]

The contest between Helicon and Cithaeron is just one example of the tradition of singing contests, a tradition that includes the singing contest featured in *Metamorphoses* 5 between the Muses and Pierides.[2] Finally, at the end of the epic's first pentad, the Muses are introduced and explored in

174 The Hymnic Battle for Helicon

their collective role.[3] The contest between the Muses and the Pierides is the focus of both this chapter and the next. This chapter focuses first on the setting and audience of the contest, the relationship between the participants, and the song of the Pierides; the next chapter turns specifically to Calliope's song. In the present discussion, I first consider the implications of the setting alongside the audience for the contest narration: the goddess Minerva. The purpose of this joint consideration is to show how Ovid relies upon hymnic material to resolve the narrative challenge he has set for himself in terms of both the generic and character development of the contest episode. This resolution comes in the form of a Callimachean interpretive key: the poet borrows the staging of Callimachus' *Bath of Pallas* to condition internal listeners and external readers, framing the contest with this narratively postponed hymnic intertext. As the home of the Muses, the environment of the contest, and the hymnic setting of the embedded myth within the *Bath of Pallas*, Helicon itself demands special attention here for the role it plays.

The physical setting of the myth also poses a point of significance for understanding the ways territory shapes the identity and aims of the contest participants: not just for the Heliconian Muses, but also for the Emathian Pierides. Tracing the characterization of the participants as representative of their homelands brings to light how Ovid differentiates this contest from a prototypical pastoral singing contest. Ovid sets up the Muses and the Pierides as reflective entities to style their interaction as not just a competition or territorial dispute, but a hymnic battle representative of civil war. Part of this matched conflict is created by the way each party invests themselves in the poetic territory of Callimachean hymns. In the case of the Pierides, this means a competitive look toward the Callimachean *Hymn to Demeter*, which comes into contact with the use of the *Bath of Pallas* to frame the contest; this contact additionally demands appraising how this pair of hymns interact with each other in their original positioning, at the end of the Callimachean collection.[4] As such, one of the new contributions of this chapter is reading how the *Hymn to Demeter*, especially its imagery of literary polemic, has influenced the identity and song of the Pierides, further entrenching this episode in a matrix of Callimachean hymnic indebtedness.

A Visit to Helicon:
Audiences, Inhabitants, Challengers

Callimachus' hymns once again provide valuable intertexts for this portion of Ovidian epic. These textual relationships form a range of applicability from points of contextual reference to complementary mythological appendices and alternate paths of narrative opportunity. The first point of Callimachean importance discussed will be the *Bath of Pallas*, and what happens when the setting (Helicon) and goddess (Athena) of the hymn come into alignment within Ovid's epic. The competitive slippage in presentation between Athena/Minerva and Artemis/Diana has already been discussed in chapter 3. Now, the literary repercussions of Athena acting as a Muse can be directly interrogated.

A summary of the episode can recall some of the narrative complexities that come into play here. The major narrative event is the singing contest between two poetic rivals, the Pierides and the Muses. The contest does not unfold in real time—instead, it is told retrospectively to a curious (and patient) Minerva, who, after coming to Perseus' aid, has now come to Helicon to see the newly created Hippocrene for herself. Minerva's bemusement at the humanlike voices of the recently transformed *picae* prompts the retrospective narration of the contest: the challengers offer an impious song of Gigantomachy that Calliope, as the representative of the Muses, counters with a song of the rape of Proserpina. The fact that the contest is narrated retrospectively deserves emphasis: the original contest was judged by the Heliconian nymphs (*dirimant certamina nymphae*, "let the nymphs settle the contest outcome," 5.314), but the audience at the time of telling is now the Olympian goddess Minerva. The importance of this fact tends to be easily lost in interpretations of this episode. The nymphs as the body responsible for selecting the victors has led scholars to attribute the heavy prominence of nymph tales in Calliope's song to a narrative strategy of pandering to the judging panel.[5] However, this recognition comes at the expense of full audience contextualization. While it is inescapably true that the nymphs were the *original* audience (judges) of the contest, there is a new audience at the time the reader encounters this Ovidian presentation of the myth: the Olympian goddess Minerva. Having Minerva as an audience necessitates a reshaping of narrative expectations, as there is a considerable gulf of status and experience between nymphs and an Olympian goddess. In other words, the narrative framework that Ovid has imposed upon himself is a challenge designed to showcase none other than his own poetic virtuosity. Ovid's written version of the contest is the third level of presentation (the original contest, the relaying of the original contest to Minerva, and now, its presentation to the reader), and trumps the previous two in glorying in the skill necessary to negotiate such complex layers of narrative.[6] The importance of Minerva as a fundamentally "epic" audience (aligning her with the ultimate level of the reader, as they make their way through the epic text) must be tempered alongside the original level of narration, when each party presented their song to the nymphs. Unlike the song of the Pierides (which seems to be given shorter shrift in receiving a compressed, edited overview), we are given to believe that the full version of Calliope's song is being communicated to Minerva. When Ovid frames the narrative by means of a retrospective audience (and an audience with necessarily different generic expectations) he demands from the careful reader a constant duality of reference: the reader is imaginatively tasked with keeping both audiences in mind and accordingly, attributing narrative factors to these two vastly different parties. The poetic challenge Ovid has posed to himself thus stands as follows: to create a narrative that can be read on two simultaneous levels to satisfy two different audiences, but one that nevertheless presents itself as a cohesive, integrated whole.

To bridge this narrative gap, there must be a shift in perspective. Instead of focusing on the nymphs as the determining factor behind the promotion of certain narratives, the Heliconian landscape itself should stand as the inspiration. The strategic starting point for this shift in perspective is the acknowledgment of the Heliconian setting, with its prized fonts of poetry, as the factor that bridges the two audiences. Minerva comes to see the Hippocrene, and the contest is waged over the Heliconian territory, specified by its springs. This fact allows for a refocusing of what scholars have considered the prominence of "nymph" narratives. I suggest that the importance of the Heliconian springs as the identifying features of Helicon motivate the prominence of not nymph narratives, but *spring* narratives within Calliope's hymn, especially the tales of Cyane and Arethusa. However, we must first explore the effect that Minerva has upon these songs as an audience, and how these effects are determined by her connections to the Heliconian landscape. Overall, we can see the adaptive effort of the Muses at work, as they adjust to the new generic expectations represented by the figure of Minerva. The Muses identify themselves with the nymphs in currying favor for their contest win, and consequently, as part of this sliding scale of representation, try to identify Minerva as a Muse-figure, in order to condition her to react positively toward a tale that may not automatically prove conducive to her divine favor.

Helicon is introduced in Book 5 as the destination of a sight-seeing Minerva. The goddess has traveled to the mountain to see for herself the new fountain made by Pegasus:[7]

The Hymnic Battle for Helicon   177

uirgineumque Helicona petit. quo monte potita
constitit et doctas sic est adfata sorores:
"fama noui fontis nostras pervenit ad aures,
dura medusaei quem praepetis ungula rupit.
Is mihi causa uiae. uolui mirabile factum
cernere; uidi ipsum materno sanguine nasci."

(*Met.* 5.254–59)

[and she seeks virginal Helicon. With this mountain destination attained,
she establishes a position and so, addresses the learned sisters:
"the rumour of a new spring has reached my ears,
which burst forth from the toughened hoof of the winged Medusaen horse.
This spring is the reason for my journey. I wish to see this remarkable
    creation;
I myself witnessed the horse's birth from the blood of its . . . mother."]

Minerva outlines clearly the reason for her visit: having heard of this new
fountain, she is curious to see it for herself, as she also witnessed the birth
of Perseus from the head of Medusa (an event narrated by Perseus at 4.785–
86). The Muse Urania answers and welcomes her:

excipit Vranie: "quaecumque est causa uidendi
has tibi, diua, domos, animo gratissima nostro es.
uera tamen fama est; est Pegasus huius origo
fontis" et ad latices deduxit Pallada sacros.

(*Met.* 5.260–63)

[Urania received her, saying: "whatever your reason is for visiting
these locales—our home—goddess, yours is a presence most welcome to our
    spirit.
The rumor is indeed true; Pegasus is the source of this spring here,"
and she led Pallas down to the sacred water.]

The Muse corroborates the goddess' version of the tale as *fama* had reported
to her with the echoing *uera tamen fama est* (5.262). Any hint of aetiology is
simultaneously activated and dismissed with the summary *est Pegasus huius
origo / fontis* (5.262–63). In fact, the Muse reports even less than *fama* origi-
nally did; it is Minerva who relates that the spring was caused by Pegasus'

dura . . . ungula (5.257).[8] The Muse does not attach any descriptor to the act. In this introduction to the landscape, Minerva's communication of *fama's* report shapes the reader's perception of the fountain.[9] As the spring itself is not explicitly named, Minerva is also responsible for glossing the spring's name with her description. It is not until the reader hears of the challenge made to the Muses that the Hippocrene is named, and paired with a second spring, the Aganippe. Minerva's desire to tour the hydrographic wonders of Helicon seem limited to the "epic" Hippocrene; omitting any mention of a second spring, she sets the tone by indicating its status as a font of inspiration for epic through the descriptor *dura . . . ungula*.[10] The narrative juxtaposition of Minerva coming to Perseus' aid with a (relaxing?) sightseeing trip to Helicon seems itself incongruous, if not simply unexpected and humorous. Overall, she initially seems a surprising figure to introduce the Heliconian mount and its famed spring.[11]

HELICON AND THE *BATH OF PALLAS*: MINERVA AS MUSE

Knowledge of Callimachus mitigates this surprise factor: the *Bath of Pallas* provides useful precedent for Minerva's uncharacteristic appearance on Helicon. The ritual that occasions the hymnic celebration is Athena's bath, but the aspects of Athena's divinity that the hymn chooses to highlight depart from typical depictions of the goddess. Diverging from praise of Athena's usual spheres of bellicosity and revenge, or even artisan skills or heroic patronage, it is the femininity and beauty of the goddess that are of especial concern (*Hymn* 5.17–28).[12] Contextually, the feminine aspects of the goddess must not only be established, but highlighted, so the cautionary nature of Tiresias' tale can take full effect. The hymn's embedded myth of Tiresias ties Athena to the landscape of Helicon, and places Athena in an atypical role that, by virtue of the setting, necessarily forms a background to the Ovidian scene featuring the Muses and Minerva. The myth (*Hymn* 5.57–131) relates the blinding of Tiresias, who, in searching for water to slake his thirst, accidentally strays upon Athena bathing in the Hippocrene with his mother, the nymph Chariclo. To console Chariclo, distressed for her son over the severity of his punishment, Athena compares his fate to the future held in store for Actaeon, destined to be torn apart by his very own dogs after catching sight of Artemis bathing. The goddess cushions this blow of fate for Tiresias by giving him gifts, including the power of prophecy.

The presence of Artemis in Athena's "consolatory" tale can hardly fail to summon the thought that within the fifth *Hymn*, the role played by Athena is much more suited to Artemis. The Athena of the *Hymn* sports with beloved companions (Chariclo above all), and takes noontime baths, as is more customary of the huntress Artemis, or the Muses.[13] The chosen locale of the bath has presented a persistent puzzle, given the fact that neither Tiresias nor Actaeon have traditional ties to Helicon. Additionally, there is no ready answer to why an Argive ritual should incorporate the narration of a Theban myth.[14] Ultimately, a bath in the Hippocrene unerringly recalls the opening of the *Theogony*, where the Muses bathe in the spring (Hes. *Theog.* 5–6). The careful framing of the event[15] indicates its laden significance: Athena and Chariclo are not only behaviorally echoing the well-known mythological scene of Artemis and favored nymph-companion, but playacting as Muses, too.[16]

The noontime occurrence of the event is also a conspicuous detail. The hour of noon is a time primed for the related phenomena of divine epiphany and poetic initiation; Helicon, of course, is an inescapably resonant locale for the aspiring poet-initiate, including Callimachus himself.[17] In recompense for his punitive blinding, Athena grants Tiresias the power of prophecy (*Hymn* 5.119–26). Prophecy is not a power typically associated with the goddess. However, Athena not only gifts Tiresias with this superhuman awareness, but she herself prophecies the role that he will play as a seer. She speaks of the mythical context he will become part of, and in extension, the literary context into which he will be incorporated. Through this reparative gift, Athena "writes" Tiresias into the Theban cycle, known most notably and thoroughly through the "high" genres of tragedy and epic.[18] The power of prophecy Athena assumes is as foreign to her as the activities of bathing and frolicking. Callimachus makes his hymnic image of Athena even more elastic by attributing a power to her that is typically the exclusive property of the Muses or Apollo.[19] On one hand, the goddess who prophesies Tiresias' absorption into the world of epic is the goddess of war (cf. the attributes of *Hymn* 5.5–12), naturally associating her with heroic epic. On the other hand, she appears in a role atypical for her status, as a Muse.

A reminiscence of Athena's atypical role in Callimachus' *Hymn* is activated in Ovid via the commentary of a Muse herself:

180 The Hymnic Battle for Helicon

> quam sic adfata est una sororum:
> "o, nisi te uirtus opera ad maiora tulisset,
> in partem uentura chori Tritonia nostri,"
>
> (*Met.* 5.268–70)

> [One of the sisters thus addressed her:
> "O Tritonia, if your excellence had not borne you off to greater
>   achievements,
> you could have come into the company of our chorus."]

The Muse's editorializing remark about Minerva's visit is made more sensible by the assistance of the Callimachean background Ovid imaginatively restages for his own epic design.[20] Once the mytho-literary background of *Hymn* 5 has been supplied, a poem in which Minerva behaves like a Muse in their home territory of Helicon (and usurps some of their powers) her remark seems less out of turn.[21] Textual echoes of Gallus' Heliconian poetic initiation in *Eclogue* 6 further add to the background borrowed from *Hymn* 5. The resonance of *quam sic adfata est una sororum* with *Aonas in montis ut duxerit una sororum* ("how one of the sisters led [him] into the Aonian mountains," Virg. *Ecl.* 6.65) is clearly seen, while the Muse's use of *chori* to describe the collective unit of sisters also evokes the first appearance made in Latin of *chorus* in the following line of the eclogue (*utque uiro Phoebi chorus adsurrexerit omnis*, "and how all the chorus of Phoebus rose to their feet for the man," *Ecl.* 6.66).[22] Ovid's integration of Gallus' poetic initiation into this scene recalls Tiresias' experience on Helicon within Callimachus' *Hymn*, where a framework of divine epiphany becomes transmuted instead into a punitive brokering into the world of "higher" genres by Athena. The Muse's comment to Minerva about her belonging to their choral number similarly lends the idea of a quasi-initiation of Minerva into the ranks of Muses—at least for the duration of her Heliconian visit, where part of her role is to affirm the poetic primacy of the Muses and uphold their claim to Helicon.

In this suggestive network of textual cues that serve to affiliate Minerva and the Muses, there is additional weight borne by the epithet the Muse lends the goddess (*Tritonia*, 5.270). Although fundamentally employed as an epic epithet,[23] it nonetheless has a musical resonance that brings Minerva into greater contact with the Muses. According to some mythological sources, it

The Hymnic Battle for Helicon   181

was in Lake Tritonis that Athena catches sight of her reflection while she is playing the newly invented flute, and discards it in horror, seeing her distended cheeks.[24] The flute is a very early attribute of the Muses,[25] emphasized strongly within the visual tradition. The Muse therefore shows awareness of both aspects of Minerva's divinity on display in the *Bath of Pallas*. She acknowledges Minerva's "epic" presence, while alluding to other possibilities as indicated in Minerva's previous literary appearances. Developing a connection between the goddess and the Muses is a strategy that opens a window for empathetic exchange between the Olympian goddess and the Muses, mentally conditioning the goddess to receive favorably the subject matter of Calliope's song.

The Muses' attempt to integrate Minerva into their company first recalls her imaginative role in Callimachus' *Hymn*. Additionally, it sets the stage for an identity of Minerva that Calliope will subsequently evoke in her song: Calliope's reimagined hymn to Ceres involves one of the rare instances where Minerva appears in a nymph-like role. The *Homeric Hymn to Demeter*, which provides a mythological foundation for all subsequent narratives of Persephone's rape, includes an image of Athena attending the maiden: when Persephone recounts her abduction to her mother, beyond the list of Oceanids she also numbers the virgin goddess, along with Artemis, as one of her attendants as they were playing in the delightful meadow (Παλλάς τ' ἐγρεμάχη καὶ Ἄρτεμις ἰοχέαιρα, "and fight-rousing Pallas and arrow-scatterer Artemis," *Hymn. Hom. Dem.* 424). Pallas' inclusion in Persephone's nymph catalog only appears in Persephone's retroactive narrative of her experience. When coupled with the incongruity of Athena appearing amid a frolicsome group of Oceanids, this narrative fact has led some to suspect its textual authenticity.[26] Pallas' appearance only within an embedded story creates an inverse narrative parallel with Ovid's own textual structure, where Minerva is not present for the original contest, but is both catalyst and audience for its renarration. As Calliope relates in her song, Pallas and Diana are the two goddesses that Venus singles out as traitorous, shunning her sphere of influence (*Pallada nonne uides iaculatricemque Dianam / abscessisse mihi?*, 5.375–76). Her formulation is gently reminiscent of the *Homeric Hymn's* pairing, with *Pallada* mirroring Παλλάς and the thematically resonant (if not wholly substitutive) epithets used of Diana, ἰοχέαιρα and *iaculatrix*. Venus' complaint seems at least partially inspired by remembrance of their joint appearance in Persephone's narrative recap.

The Hymnic Battle for Helicon

The Muses' efforts to evoke Minerva as a figure natural, if not native, to their own Heliconian setting, preparing her to receive favorably a series of nymph narratives, nevertheless should be contextualized with regard to Minerva's characterization elsewhere within the epic. In short, the goddess is not a sympathetic audience to female figures and their plights. Instead, she largely appears as a supporter of male endeavors.[27] Readers of the epic have also just encountered the tale of Medusa, a tale revelatory of Minerva's attitudes toward women.[28] The Muses, therefore, appear in need of countering Minerva's epic role as an unsympathetic champion of male heroes to make her receptive to both Calliope's song and the contest victory that clinched their continued ownership of Helicon. To do so, they use the boundaries of the physical setting as a strategic framework, enlisting its help to assimilate her to the level of a Muse by recalling her previous literary experiences on Helicon. Employing a sense of environmental conditioning, they rely upon the natural setting to guide her reception of the song.

THE MUSES: HELICONIAN NYMPHS

While the Muses are allowed to characterize Minerva through their greeting, it is Minerva who not only focalizes the description of the Hippocrene, but the landscape itself more generally. What the goddess sees is what is communicated to the reader. Her assessment of the space also enfolds the Muses:

> et ad latices deduxit Pallada sacros.
> quae mirata diu factas pedis ictibus undas
> siluarum lucos circumspicit antiquarum
> antraque et innumeris distinctas floribus herbas,
> felicesque uocat pariter studioque locoque
> Mnemonidas. quam sic adfata est una sororum:
> "o, nisi te uirtus opera ad maiora tulisset,
> in partem uentura chori Tritonia nostri,
> uera refers meritoque probas artesque locumque,
> et gratam sortem, tutae modo simus, habemus."
>
> (*Met.* 5.263–72)

> [and she led Pallas down to the sacred water,
> who marveled for a long time at the water created by the blow of the
> horse-hoof

and took in the groves of ancient trees
and the grottoes and the grasses adorned with flowers uncountable
and she deemed the daughters of Memory equally fortunate
in both place and pursuit. And thus, one of the sisters addressed her:
"O Tritonia, if your excellence had not borne you off to greater
    achievements,
you could have come into the company of our chorus.
You say true things, and deservedly commend our artistry and home,
and we do have a blessed lot in life—or would, if only we were safe."]

Minerva's twinning of *studioque locoque* underscores Helicon as the Muses'
home. This praise intertwines the activity of the Muses and the Heliconian
landscape in a phrase of mutual dependency. The Muse verifies her assessment in an echoing affirmation: *uera refers meritoque probas artesque locumque*. With *artesque locumque*, the entwined fate of the Muses' art and home
receives double reinforcement.[29] The interdependency of setting and poetic
activity is especially critical to note considering their home was staked as
the prize of the singing contest, and the living representations of that landscape (the nymphs) were the original judging parties. As the living landscape, the nymphs have a vested interest in which party prevails.

Nymphs and Muses are closely connected figures.[30] The inspiring powers
of the nymphs were conceived of as localized, intimately tied to and sourced
from their natural settings.[31] The contingency between place and power
hinted at by Minerva bears clear affinity to a special ability determined by
setting. In a certain sense, it may seem surprising that Helicon even has
spring nymphs available to act as judges, as the Muses themselves receive
poetic addresses that present them in this way: for example, Propertius calls
upon them as *Pegasides* (Prop. 3.1.19).[32] The associations of nymphs and
Muses are so enduring as to lead to the assumption that the Muses exist in
one respect as the nymphs of Helicon, particularly the nymphs of its inspiratory springs.[33] Minerva's treatment of the Muses as Heliconian nymphs
at the most facilitates and at the least accords with the Muse's treatment of
her as a potential Muse. It bears reinforcement that these corresponding
assignations are afforded by the physical landscape of Helicon, and allowed
by the literary space Callimachus created in his fifth *Hymn*. Therefore, the
window for empathetic exchange in view of the narratives offered extends
from Minerva all the way to the original contest audience, the nymphs. What

184 The Hymnic Battle for Helicon

the interaction between Muse and goddess establishes is a sliding continuum between Olympian, Muse, and nymph, which has important narratological ramifications: once established, it can accommodate appropriately the multiplicity of registers within Calliope's song. Helicon, as a setting, is also the true accommodating force. The original gulf between Olympian and nymph is determined by the allocation of territory: as the head of the Olympian order and ratifier of Olympian power, Jupiter first denies heaven to sylvan deities, finding them unworthy (*Met.* 1.192–95). To appeal to both nymphs and Olympians, Calliope's song must transcend this gulf. Understanding the landscape of Helicon as a literary palimpsest, where Athena has once played the role of Muse and nymph within a hymn, makes this possible.[34]

When the Muse talks about Minerva's potential to join their chorus (*chori . . . nostri*, 5.270), she is not only recalling Athena's bathing on Helicon in the *Bath of Pallas*, but the image of her inspiratory sisterhood that Athena there imitates: the Muses as a specifically Heliconian chorus, brought into being to hymn the gods, as they famously appear in the *Theogony*.[35] This purpose is echoed by the aetiology of the Muses' creation as sung by the Muses themselves in Pindar's first hymn, a hymn that is also a cosmogony. Sung at the wedding of Cadmus and Harmonia, Pindar's hymn further reminds us that the Muses were the musical celebrators of divine nuptials. They also appear at the wedding of Peleus and Thetis, and Epicharmus features them at the wedding of Hebe and Heracles in his mythological comedy the *Wedding of Hebe*, apparently popularly remade as a new comedy entitled *Muses*.[36] The ordained union of gods therefore gives occasion to the Muses to reinforce their role as hymning and upholding the divine order specifically as wedding-singers, an occasion denied to Persephone by the circumstances of her kidnapping. A parallel tradition of hymnic song is instead built around the event of Persephone's rape: one that also focuses on the issue of divine order. Ovid sets up the contest between the Muses and the Pierides to encourage the reader to acknowledge it as an exercise in rifting tradition itself, and to comment simultaneously on both literary history and Roman history.

MUSES, PIERIDES, AND CIVIL WAR

Now that we have established the Heliconian landscape as a determining factor in shaping the narrative conditions and expectations of the contest,

The Hymnic Battle for Helicon

we can turn our attention to the competing parties, and the wider contextual framework in which the contest belongs and should be read. The contest is not merely a singing contest but, essentially, a hymnic battle. The Pierides sing a warped and partial reimagining of the *Theogony* (itself a partial hymn to Zeus); Calliope sings a hymn to Ceres, looking back to the *Homeric Hymn to Demeter*. The fact that the songs are hymns deserves as much emphasis as the novelty of the staking of Helicon itself as a prize for this hymnic combat. I choose the martial tags of "battle" and "combat" for this interaction deliberately, for the contest between two reflective entities allows Ovid to frame this contest not only as a hymnic war, but a hymnic *civil* war.[37]

By shifting familiarly theogonic material from the Muses to the Pierides, Ovid calls attention to the similarities between the two competing bodies. In fact, the Muses themselves are commonly invoked under the collective name Pierides.[38] In one tradition, the worship of nine Muses was established by a Macedonian named Pierus (Paus. 9.29.3). As the daughters of Zeus and Mnemosyne, they were born in Pieria, and so are known by this regional epithet. Cicero delineates that the third set of Muses were the nine daughters born to Pierus and Antiope, and that they were called by the same name as the preceding set of nine (*Nat. D.* 3.54). Notably, the Muses are most invoked as Pierides within pastoral, the genre that also exhibits the most sustained use of the singing contest as a generic feature. The Muses, as Pierides, appear four times in the *Eclogues* (6.13, 8.63, 9.33, 10.72, perhaps in the wake of Theocritean appearances at *Id.* 10.24 and 11.3), but not once in the pages of the *Aeneid*.

The ability to refer to both parties as Pierides provides the starting point for establishing a context to read the contest as a civil war. To flesh out this framework, we can look at the information given about the Pierides, and the challenge they issue:

> Pieros has genuit Pellaeis diues in aruis,
> Paeonis Euippe mater fuit; illa potentem
> Lucinam nouiens, nouiens paritura, uocauit.
> intumuit numero stolidarum turba sororum
> perque tot Haemonias et per tot Achaidas urbes
> huc uenit et tali committit proelia uoce:
> "desinite indoctum uana dulcedine uulgus
> fallere; nobiscum, si qua est fiducia uobis,

186 The Hymnic Battle for Helicon

Thespiades, certate, deae. nec uoce nec arte
uincemur, totidemque sumus. uel cedite uictae
fonte Medusaeo et Hyantea Aganippe,
uel nos Emathiis ad Paeonas usque niuosos
cedemus campis. dirimant certamina nymphae."

(*Met.* 5.302–14)

[Pieros fathered them, rich from his Pellaean land holdings,
while Paeonian Euippe was their mother; she called upon
powerful Lucina nine times, nine times preparing to give birth.
Puffed up with pride at their number, the flock of foolish sisters
came here, through legions of Thessalian and Greek cities,
and with such a proclamation, they begin the war:
"Stop swindling the ignorant rabble with your treacly vanities;
if you've any faith in yourselves, goddesses of Thespiae,
then compete with us! We shall not be defeated in either song or skill,
and we happen to be equal in number: either yield to the victors
the Medusaean spring and Boeotian Aganippe
or we will yield the Emathian plans, as far as snowy Paonia.
Let the nymphs settle the contest outcome."]

Helicon is identified by its two mountainside springs, the Hippocrene
and Aganippe. This territory contrasts with the expanse of the Emathian
plains stretching to Paeonia offered in exchange by the nine daughters of
Pierus. The designation of the Hippocrene as the *fons Medusaeus* matches
Minerva's introduction to the landscape and her stated justification for want-
ing to see it. From Hesiod onward, these springs are known foremost as the
sites of poetic initiation and inspiration, therefore providing the loci of ulti-
mate desirability for this coterie of aspirational poetesses looking to usurp
the Muses. The Pierides rightly recognize these defining features of poetry's
home. In attempting to paint the Muses as unworthy of their custodianship of
the Heliconian fonts, they invoke a connection first to the lowly *indoctum . . .
uulgus*, loosely capitalizing upon the metapoetic conceit of common water
suiting a common crowd.[39] Similarly strategic is their designation of the
Muses as Thespiades. This naming downplays the Muses' dominion over
the Heliconian springs, instead identifying them with the town at the foot
of Helicon. In notable contrast, the Muses call themselves Aonides (5.333, a

The Hymnic Battle for Helicon 187

designation upheld by Minerva at 6.2), an older epithet that bears Callimachean pedigree.[40] The Pierides associate the Muses with the lowest part of Helicon, preemptively trying to rob the goddesses of their poetic heights. Location dictates imagination. Ultimately, when the Pierides are deemed the losers of the contest, they are called Emathides (5.669) instead of Pierides, reinforcing their belonging to the low-lying plains of their homeland.

The geographical epithet Emathides is critical for reading this contest as redolent of civil war. Emathia is not a common poetical usage for denoting Macedonia, occurring only a few times prior to its appearance here.[41] Its most notorious use comes in the *Georgics*, with reference to critical clashes:[42]

> ergo inter sese paribus concurrere telis
> Romanas acies iterum uidere Philippi;
> nec fuit indignum superis bis sanguine nostro
> Emathiam et latos Haemi pinguescere campos.
>
> (Virg. *Georg.* 1.489–92)

> [Thus Philippi again bears witness to the Roman battle formations
> charging against their own selves with equal weaponry;
> nor was it intolerable to the gods to fatten twice
> Emathia and the broad plains of Haemus with blood.]

As the site of one of the most crucial battles of the civil war, Philippi is a forceful reminder of civil strife. Virgil's choice of Emathia to communicate the boundaries of this regionality is highly evocative.[43] Scholars have detected etymological and translingual wordplay within this Virgilian passage that gives further descriptive weight to the pathos of bloodshed: if Haemus evokes the Greek αἷμα, this glosses *sanguine nostro*, and, with *pinguescere*, can be taken forcefully to mean "plains of blood." Similarly, Emathia can be connected to ἄμαθος or the Homeric ἠμαθόεις, combining with the image of blood to create a shorthand of gladiatorial combat: blood and sand.[44] Further puns are also found in Latin poetry with the use of Haemus or Haemonia to create images of red-white or purple-white color contrasts.[45] Ovid's Pierid challenge receptively deploys both forms of wordplay, in the contrast made between the Heliconian springs and Paeonia and the Emathian plains (5.311–14). Ovid has displaced Haemonia from direct poetic interaction with these lines: it occurs seven lines previously, outside of the direct speech of the Pierides (*perque tot Haemonias et per tot Achaidas urbes*, 5.306), where it nevertheless remains an active presence within the passage at large. Instead, he has supplied the metaphorical "blood" typically glossed in Haemus or Haemonia by calling the Hippocrene the *fons Medusaeus*, recalling Pegasus' birth from the blood of Medusa. The "blood" (*fonte Medusaeo*, 5.312) and "sand" (*Emathiis . . . campis*, 5.313–14) is then highlighted by the opposition of "snowy Paeonia" (*Paeonas . . . niuosas*, 5.313). Ovid's use of Emathia redeploys the layered subtleties represented in the Virgilian passage: he reads the Emathian plains as already imbued with the blood of civil war and capitalizes upon this literary history to stage his contest between the Muses and Pierides.

Within the Ovidian poetic universe, the Virgilian etymologizing of "plains of blood" should also recall the Gigantomachy in Book 1, when the new race of men arises from the blood of the slain giants (1.151–62).[46] The Gigantomachy is often poetically employed to provide a model or allegory for speaking about civil war, and so Emathia becomes a powerful locus for talking about not only civil war, but its symbolic literary counterpart.[47] Emathia is used variously to refer to Thessaly or Macedonia, and to encompass both the locations of Pharsalus and Philippi, the defining clashes of the civil war. For its own part, the Gigantomachy was associated with the Thessalian mountain ranges, as in the passage above, or described as waged on the Phlegraean plain. At some point, the tradition surrounding Phlegraea was transferred as an expedient explanation for the geographical qualities of a different region, resulting in the existence of Phlegraean plains in both Macedonia and in Italian Campania.[48] The doubling of locations is therefore present on both levels of the allegory: both Emathia and Phlegraea denote two disparate locations, particularly apt for framing a contest between the doubled parties of the Muses and the Pierides. On the most important level, the Macedonian locale that the Pierides represent (and stake as their own contest offering) serves to bind together the different levels of conflict evoked: the Gigantomachy and the civil war, the levels of allegory and history. The territory serves as a literal foundation for both the interpretation of their song and the evocative context of civil war.

The Emathian homeland therefore builds a core identity for the Pierid singers. This identity cannot resolve into a successful mastery over Helicon's heights, despite the vaunted symbolic trajectory of their song, which echoes their desired trajectory from plains to mountaintop: the Gigantomachy is also, at heart, the topic of the Pierides' hymn. The Pierides choose material stereotypically identified as not just epic, but hyper-epic. Their attraction to this register of poetry is also encoded into their biographical details, and the attendant focus on quantity. Proliferation is emphasized throughout the introductory passage: their mother calls upon Lucina nine times, in her nine-fold birth (*nouiens, nouiens*, 5.304) and the sisters travel through so many Thessalian, so many Achaean cities (*tot . . . tot*, 5.306). Most tellingly, the crowd (*turba*) of sisters are puffed up with pride in their number (*intumuit numero*, 5.305). The concept of swollenness (*tumidus*) has a notable place in the lexicon of literary critical vocabulary. Often, it carries the connotation of misguided bombast, and falling short of one's literary aspirations.[49] The inclusion of *tumidus* in such a critical vocabulary allowed its transformation into an epic tag (a shorthand like *arma*) in certain frameworks.[50] Combined with the potential metrical allusion of *numerus*, this description of the Pierides paints them as overly ambitious epic poets, concerned with quantity over quality. The martial framework of their challenge (*committit proelia*, 5.307) and their homeland of Emathia further underscores their poetic ambitions to claim the heights of Helicon.

THE PIERIDES: ANTI-CALLIMACHEAN "MUSES"

The Pierides' outsize pride and ambition is also encoded into their very name, which allows Ovid to add a further dimension of literary criticism to his contest. Their father is named as Pieros, whence their name Pierides (5.302). The Greek adjective πιερός is a byform of πιαρός ("fat," "rich").[51] In the *Wedding of Hebe* Epicharmus combines this suggestive patronymic with the matronymic Pimpleias, which indicates one home of the Muses (Pimpleia), but also enfolds the root πίμπλημι ("to be full, satisfied"). In a recent rendering, the Muses are thus born of "Mr. Fat" and "Mrs. Full."[52] Ovid's Pierides, therefore, also exist in one reading as "Fatties." By pitting the Pierides against the Muses, Ovid toys with the famous Callimachean advice of "feeding the flock fat, but keeping a slender Muse" (*Aet.* fr. 1, 23–24 Harder); the Pierides are literally anti-Callimachean here, in name, nature, and poetic ambition. The rivalry between the two groups therefore also becomes one of literary polemic, representing the proponents of Callimacheanism or embodying anti-Callimachean poetics.

The Pierides, as antitheses of the Callimachean "slender Muse," also choose a theme that embraces "largeness" in a physical and metaphorical fashion:

the Gigantomachy.[53] The Muse records their contest song as follows, in what is a synopsis rather than an embedded direct quotation:

> bella canit superum falsoque in honore Gigantas
> ponit et extenuat magnorum facta deorum;
> emissumque ima de sede Typhoea terrae
> caelitibus fecisse metum cunctosque dedisse
> terga fugae, donec fessos Aegyptia tellus
> ceperit et septem discretus in ostia Nilus.
> huc quoque terrigenam uenisse Typhoea narrat
> et se mentitis superos celasse figuris:
> "dux" que "gregis" dixit "fit Iuppiter, unde recuruis
> nunc quoque formatus Libys est cum cornibus Ammon;
> Delius in coruo, proles Semeleia capro,
> fele soror Phoebi, niuea Saturnia uacca,
> pisce Venus latuit, Cyllenius ibidis alis."

(*Met.* 5.319–31)

> [She sings the wars of the gods above and raises the Giants
> to false heights of honour, cutting down the deeds of the
> great gods: that Typhoeus, issuing forth from the very
> bowels of the earth, wrought such fear for heaven's dwellers,
> and that they all turned tail and ran, until, in their exhaustion,
> Egyptian land took them in, and the Nile, perceptive,
> into its seven-mouthed river. Here too, earthborn Typhoeus
> came, and the gods hid themselves under feigned forms:
> "Jupiter became" she said "the leader of the flock,
> and even now Ammon, his Libyan form, displays curved horns:
> The Delian god became a raven, Semele's son a goat,
> the sister of Phoebus a cat, Saturn's daughter a snow-white heifer,
> Venus hid herself in fish-scales, Cyllene's son, the wings of an ibis."]

The grandiosity of their theme is announced by the opening *bella canit*, announcing a song that is anti-Callimachean and anti-Olympian.[54] The Pierides not only try to usurp the physical territory of the Muses, but both usurp and warp their traditional poetic territory, the hymning of the Olympic order. It is the Hesiodic Muses that affirm the Olympian order by exalting their father Zeus and delighting him with their hymns, songs that include the Gigantomachy (*Theog.* 50–52). The Pierides sing an impious variation, in which the dominance of the Olympian order never comes to pass. Instead, the gods flee to Egypt, hiding there fearfully in theriomorphic disguise. While this vignette of transformation might be appropriate for the Ovidian epic, it nevertheless perverts the course of the traditional hymnic (i.e., Hesiodic) poetic material of the Muses they attempt to supplant. Their Gigantomachy first negates the creation of the Olympian order, but consequentially, also presents a world in which the Muses do not exist: the containment of Typhoeus was the prerequisite for the establishment of an order that allowed the Muses to come into the world and celebrate that very order.[55] In the *Theogony*, the distribution of τιμαί only occurs after the Typhonomachy, which cements the dominance of Zeus and upholding of the Olympian claim to power. The Pierides rewrite the archetypal hymn of the Muses, and do so in a fashion that erases the Muses completely: they excise the sequence of events that catalyzed the birth of the Muses, also eradicating their hymnic purpose.

As relayed by the Muse, the Pierid focus is not on the triumph of Typhoeus so much as the fearful retreat of the Olympians to Egypt, the land of the Nile. The seven-mouthed river that features in their Gigantomachy symbolizes a properly "Gigantic" spring of inspiration for the Pierides, who communicated their desire for dominion of Helicon by identifying the mountain with its springs of inspiration (5.312). This unusual variant of the myth draws attention to the very land that once existed as a potential new zone of power for the Romans during the turmoil of civil war, when Alexandria was under consideration for Antony's new capital.[56] The Pierides, as Macedonians, can view Egypt as part of their geographical purview, through the legacy of Alexander: Virgil names Egyptian Canopus "Pellaean" after the Macedonian capital in the *Georgics* (Virg. *Georg.* 4.287), reminding of Egypt's conquest. For Antony, Cleopatra provided both physical and symbolic access to the storied legacy of Alexander, whose own construction of identity and power is recalled in the Pierid hymn by Jupiter's appearance as Zeus Ammon, Alexander's especial deity. The song of the Pierides replaces the image of the beleaguered Cleopatra retreating to the Nile that enduringly appeared in Augustan verse with the Olympians themselves, reimagining the famed Virgilian scene of Olympian triumph against the theriomorphic divine forces on Cleopatra's side.[57] Altogether, the Pierid song (even in its partial narration)

192 The Hymnic Battle for Helicon

repositions the most traditional hymnic material of the Muses to dishonor the Olympian order, and does so in a way that calls attention, in remarkably compressed fashion, to the numerous allusions made to the civil war that are couched in allegorical and geographical ways within the Augustan verse tradition.

OVID CUTS DOWN TO SIZE: CALLIMACHUS' *HYMN TO DEMETER* AND THE PIERID HYMN

When it comes to poetic tropes and styles, it is also critical to keep in mind that the conflict and competition between the Muses and the Pierides also exists on a metaliterary level: each party is representative of antithetical styles. These issues of size, substance, and sustenance, however, are also rooted in Callimachean poetics in a more specific way. This brings us to the relevance of his *Hymn to Demeter* and its systematic imagery, which I will focus on as a background to understanding the Pierid song. Overall, however, Callimachus' *Hymn to Demeter* is already in the poetic background because of the way it represents making choices of how to hymn the goddess. Calliope's song is a hymn to Ceres that focuses on the rape of Proserpina, the very myth eschewed by Callimachus in his own sixth hymn, the *Hymn to Demeter*. Instead of relating a tale that will "bring a tear to the goddess" (μὴ μὴ ταῦτα λέγωμες ἃ δάκρυον ἄγαγε Δηοῖ, *Hymn* 6.17), the poet contemplates first hymning the goddess in her roles as a law-giver and teacher of agriculture, before presenting the cautionary tale of Erysichthon (*Hymn* 6.18–23). Erysichthon's tale is what provides a hinge to the Pierid hymn. As Callimachus relates, Erysichthon offends the goddess by cutting down her sacred poplar to construct a banqueting hall. As divine recompense for his impiety, he is afflicted with an uncontrollable hunger. Erysichthon is kept cloistered in the royal house to hide his condition, but his appetite nevertheless eventually leaves the household in financial ruin, and he is forced to beg in the street.

In order to understand the influence of the *Hymn to Demeter* upon the Ovidian narration, we must first spend some time looking at the symbolism and imagery of this inset myth. Erysichthon's ruinous consumption explores the paradox of destructive abundance. The theme of excess and question of satiety makes this hymn ripe for metapoetic expression, and the lurking issue of size (and plays upon literary polemic) within the *Hymn* become amplified first through the figure of Demeter. When Demeter appears in her true,

The Hymnic Battle for Helicon 193

divine form to Erysichthon, she is huge in her anger (Δαμάτηρ δ' ἄφατόν τι κοτέσσατο, γείνατο δ' ἀ θεύς. / ἴθματα μὲν χέρσῳ, κεφαλὰ δέ οἱ ἄψατ' Ὀλύμπῳ, "Demeter, unutterably wroth, begot her goddess form; while her steps were on the ground, her head overtook Olympus," *Hymn* 6.57–58).[58] Demeter's size, stretching across the two lines, echoes previous hymnic epiphanies of Demeter and Aphrodite, where the goddess in all her divinity fills a given expanse—but in each case this is the space of a domestic interior, from floor to ceiling (cf. *Hymn. Hom. Dem.* 188–89 and *Hymn. Hom. Ven.* 173–74).[59] Demeter's head reaching all the way to Olympus is specific in its height; it is an image reminiscent of the Iliadic Eris, who grows until her head reaches the heavens, with her feet yet still striding on the ground (Hom. *Il.* 4.442–43), but the height of Olympus is a more targeted detail than merely "the heavens." Bing notes that the verb Callimachus uses to describe the height of her sacred tree reaching the sky (κῦρον, *Hymn* 6.37) replicates the verb of the goddess' epiphany in the Homeric hymn (κῦρε, *Hymn. Hom. Dem.* 189); subsequently, the epiphany of the goddess "tops" the Homeric description, already lent to the tree as a surrogate for the goddess and her power.[60]

The description of the tree comes directly after Callimachus labels Erysichthon's men as "man-Giants" (ἀνδρογίγαντας, 6.34), strong enough to overturn a city. The Callimachean description seems to be drawn from Capaneus' shield device in the *Phoenissae*, upon which an "earthborn Giant bear[s] a whole city on his shoulders" (Eur. *Phoen.* 1131–32).[61] Capaneus has also been attributed as an inspiration for this unusual epiphany of Demeter: when he falls from the ladder his head is flung toward Olympus, while his blood soaks the ground (Eur. *Phoen.* 1182–86).[62] Although Kenneth McKay's view that Demeter's epiphanic size is a comedic, "realistic" detail to match the Gigantic status of Erysichthon and his men has been met with resistance, it is nevertheless notable that this image relies specifically upon the target of the Giants' assault (Olympus), and appears within a myth set in Thessaly, one geographical home of the Gigantomachy.[63] Rather than reading Demeter's height as necessitated by Erysichthon's own giant stature, it seems more satisfactory to understand it as part of a network of Callimachean intratextuality exploring his own system of literary polemic. Following the literary comparisons of the *Aetia* prologue that give form to a polemic of "slender" versus "large"/"long," a hymnic version of Demeter who appears as a "large/ tall lady" to counteract the Gigantic impiety of Erysichthon would feed nicely into the overt comedic overtones of the inset myth. In other words, it would humorously and momentarily literalize known Callimachean literary symbolism in a hymn preoccupied thematically, structurally, and ritually with food: both its restriction, and its excess.[64] Along these lines, scholars have linked the ritual fasting that opens the hymn and Demeter's fasting while she searches for her daughter to the "new" Callimachean school of poetics. In this reading of the hymn as compositional metaphor, fasting creates fashionably slender verse.[65] Although it is tempting to divide the hymnic figures along such neat polemical lines, Faulkner has reasonably objected to the rigorously oppositional schema of Erysichthon as "old" poetics versus Demeter as the "new," given that Erysichthon's myth is nevertheless chosen for its ostensible ability to best please the goddess, instead of the other suggested topics.[66]

A narrative inversion of this sort, where Demeter is momentarily given an outsized epiphanic form—and so, is not contrasted to but *becomes* a "large lady"—fits in with the hymn's other narrative surprises. Hesperus' identification as the one responsible for persuading Demeter to break her fast is a significant example.[67] First, within the mythological-hymnic tradition this male figure effaces Iambe, the woman who makes Demeter laugh in the *Homeric Hymn* (*Hymn. Hom. Dem.* 202–5). Secondly, he provides a tonal inversion. In the Callimachean hymn, the myth is cut off to prevent Demeter's tears at the very same Homeric moment where Demeter laughs.[68] This inversion of emotional reaction especially paves the way for identifying a current of metaliterary humor, as Callimachus briefly allows the goddess to visualize, in her anger, a breach of his own aesthetic: faced with the giant dishonor of the giant Erysichthon, the poet depicts the anger of the typically mild, nurturing goddess as so great that it fails to be contained by the boundaries of even his own poetic decorum. An additional touch of humor may be found in the irony of her head touching Olympus out of anger, given her refusal to *go* to Olympus in her *Homeric Hymn*, a boycott that is part of her angered protest about her daughter's absence (*Hymn. Hom. Dem.* 331).

Instead of seeing her epiphany realistically occasioned by Erysichthon's giant height, the Callimachean Demeter's initial gigantic epiphany also reciprocally corresponds to Erysichthon's eventual emaciation: each seemingly contradictory or paradoxical visual appearance is engineered as a part of

Callimachus' metaliterary commentary. The poet translates literary polemics into physical forms, deepening the hymn's thematic focus alongside comedy's bodily rootedness. Along these lines, we can look to the Iambe appearing in a different hymn to Demeter, Philicus' hymn. The speech of Philicus' Iambe is introduced as ὁ γελοῖος λόγος ("a humorous tale," *SH* 680.55), and she goes on to invoke the "starving" goddess' γαστήρ λεπτή ("attenuated stomach," *SH* 680.57): this seemingly paradoxical phrase could humorously allude to her own paradoxical blend of humble character and learned diction,[69] but it also crystallizes in a different physical way the literary symbolism Callimachus is toying with in his own hymn to Demeter. In a similar fashion, we can observe the careful metaliterary relationship constructed between two reciprocal verbs Ovid uses to describe the Pierides and their song: *intumuit* (5.305) and *extenuat* (5.320). The Pierides swell in pride at their own number, and then winnow down the honors of the gods in their anti-hymnic Gigantomachy, a topic that ironically perverts and renders paradoxical any Callimachean resonance to be found in *extenuare*.

Within Callimachus' *Hymn*, Erysichthon is not only alluded to as a giant, but affiliated with "gigantic" poetry. Jackie Murray discusses the κακὸν μέλος emitted by the tree as it is struck by Erysichthon's axe (*Hymn* 6.39), contextualizing it within the metaphor of ὕλη ("forest") as compositional material—a material sacred to the goddess that Erysichthon wants to turn into a banquet hall for continuous feasting and revelry.[70] In her reading, the combination of the poplar's "evil song," the gigantomachic context, and Erysichthon's plan for the grove cumulatively make an "antiphrastic allusion" to Xenophanes' counsel not to relate epic material at a symposium for the gods (fr. 1.19–24 West): material that includes the Titanomachy, Gigantomachy, or Centauromachy. Altogether, Callimachus hints that Erysichthon's banquet hall would have been home to bad epic (including the Gigantomachy) instead of the appropriate divine celebrations.[71] The poem's own hymnic praise of Demeter runs parallel to this suggestive internal line of poetic composition, also setting her hymn against the poetic material of the Gigantomachy.

This poetic material is also implicated within the physical material of appetite. Erysichthon experiences a voracious, specifically carnivorous hunger.[72] His carnivorous desire reinforces the idea that the kind of feasting Erysichthon has in mind for his banquet hall is the feasting familiar from epic, namely, of meat-eating. The detail of ἄδην ("to excess, satiety," *Hymn* 6.55) also summons the image of the suitors from the *Odyssey*, who abuse Ithacan hospitality with their never-ending consumption. The emphasis on carnivorous feasts coheres conceptually with the type of poetry that would accompany such "epic" feasts. However, there is another layer of generic context introduced by the catalog of meat Erysichthon consumes. Particularly, it recalls comedy's presentation of meat-eating Thessalians. The appetite of a Thessalian becomes proverbial in a fragment of Antiphanes: "A: he has this one illness: he is always sharply hungry. B: He means the guest is an utter Thessalian." ([A.] ἓν νόσημα τοῦτ᾽ ἔχει·ἀεὶ γὰρ ὀξύπεινός ἐστι; [B.] Θετταλὸνλέγει κομιδῇ τὸν ἄνδρα, fr. 249).[73] The gluttony of Thessalians is a product of the richness of their land, which gave rise to a specific comic trope about Thessalian portion sizes, denoted by their lavish cuts of meat.[74] Erysichthon's appetite makes him a hyper-Thessalian; it is not just cuts of meat but whole animals and whole flocks that are "sacrificed" to his cursed hunger. His earlier characterization as a Giant can also implicate the immensity of his appetite. Although his extreme consumption does not lead to corpulence, there is a comic fragment that details an age of humorously spontaneous bounty capped off with the statement that "People were fat back then and as big as the Giants" (οἱ δ᾽ ἄνθρωποι πίονες ἦσαν τότε καὶ μέγα χρῆμα γιγάντων, Teleclides fr. 1.15).[75] The Thessalians shared this cultural definition by meat-eating with the Macedonians, to whom the delicacy *mattye* was attributed—a meat course that also ostensibly served as a dessert course.[76] The *mattye* is also a persistent feature of the comic fragments dealing with gourmand behaviors. In this sense, Pieria as a "fat" land comes back into play, sharing its sense of bounty with the richness of the Thessalian land.[77]

With this network of literary polemic, symbolism, and generic affiliation in mind, we can now begin to apply this reading of the Erysichthon myth from the *Hymn to Demeter* to the *Metamorphoses*. Examining the editorial choices Callimachus makes in crafting his hymnic offering to the goddess also shapes our relationship of understanding to Ovid's choices. While Callimachus rejects the rape of Persephone as appropriate for his hymn to Demeter, choosing the myth of Erysichthon, he privileges a persistent engagement with Gigantomachic themes, if not precisely the Gigantomachy itself. Ovid reverses this poetic priority and commitment. He assigns an impious variant of the Gigantomachy to the anti-Callimachean Pierides, and the rape

The Hymnic Battle for Helicon

of Proserpina to the Muses, as the winning material of their (fully narrated) hymn. The relationship between the *Hymn to Demeter* and the singing contest of *Metamorphoses* 5 is therefore one of more complex acknowledgment than previously recognized: Ovid's Muses overtly take the poetic path eschewed by Callimachus, but the Pierid Gigantomachy, as its counter, is thematically parallel to Callimachus' sixth *Hymn*. Ovid exploits the metapoetic imagery of size that was a point of Callimachean experimentation within the hymn, consequentially creating a layer of aesthetic significance within his epic's opposition of Muses and Pierides. Recognizing how Callimachus mixes epic and comedy to explore Erysichthon's Thessalian identity, knitting together Gigantomachic hyper-epic with Thessalian comedic stereotype, also allows the Ovidian reader to recognize the hymnic contest's subtle comedic notes.

The relationship between the Pierid hymn to Callimachus' *Hymn to Demeter* has also gone unacknowledged because of the overt way Ovid later purposes this material. At the epic's midpoint, Ovid gives his own version of the Erysichthon myth (8.738–878).[78] Naturally, this is where most scholarly focus is directed when discussing Callimachus' hymn as a literary model for the *Metamorphoses*. However, the Callimacheanisms of the Erysichthon myth are anticipated by Ovid's more subtle deployment of the Gigantomachic themes of Callimachus' hymn within Book 5. The Pierides as anti-Callimachean "Muses" anticipate the anti-Callimachean Achelous, who narrates the myth.

Within the Callimachean hymn, the goddess searches for the "unknown traces" (ἄπυστα ... ἴχνια, *Hymn* 6.9) of her kidnapped daughter, a metapoetic statement that openly ignores the fact that the rape of Persephone is well-trodden poetic ground. As Demeter's search takes her to the ends of the earth, the poet marks her crossing of the Achelous three times, as well as her triple crossing of each river (τρὶς μὲν δὴ διέβας Ἀχελώϊον ἀργυροδίναν, / τοσσάκι δ' ἀενάων ποταμῶν ἐπέρασας ἕκαστον, "three times, truly, you went across the silver-eddying Achelous; so many times, you forded each of the perpetually flowing rivers," *Hymn* 6.13–14). The Callimachean emphasis on the Achelous is notable for a few reasons. First, the poet seems to identify Achelous with Oceanus, lending a "cosmic" dimension to the river that emphasizes the breadth of her travels.[79] The specification of Achelous also has a ritual dimension, as Achelous receives sacrifice before Demeter, as the source of all crop-nourishing water.[80] The identification made between

198 The Hymnic Battle for Helicon

Achelous and Oceanus highlights the contrast in the metapoetic water imagery of this opening, with the pattern of Demeter crossing the cosmic expanse of the waters before coming to rest by the well "of beautiful dances" (Καλλιχόρῳ, *Hymn* 6.15). Without awareness of Achelous standing in for Ocean, the extent of the symbolic and metapoetic divide between these water sources (one immense, one small) loses significance. Within the Ovidian epic, as a river in flood, Achelous also recalls the image of the Euphrates at the end of the Callimachean *Hymn to Apollo*, and the literary polemic there communicated.[81] The tension between anti-Callimachean narrator and Callimachean material is teased by the ways Ovid exploits awareness of the cosmic dimension of the Achelous in the *Hymn to Demeter's* opening, as he persistently uses the imagery of river waters melding with the sea (cf. 8.585– 89, 8.835–36).[82] Achelous talks about his flood in conjunction with the sea, rendering it one force (*fluctus nosterque marisque*, "our floods, and the sea's [flood]," 8.587). Even though his Achelous is a river in flood, he is not the ultimate cosmic entity of all waters; Ovid hints that even his most seemingly anti-Callimachean narrators could be rendered even more paradoxical, yet still using native Callimachean identities. In this way, Ovid builds toward his direct use of the sixth Callimachean *Hymn* and his innovative mixing of anti-Callimachean narrators with Callimachean material. The poetic relationship between the *Hymn to Demeter* and the Pierid identity and song reinforces the point that Callimachean material and mechanisms can still provide foundational inspiration for passages that are not intrinsically mythologically related, despite the fact that most identification of Callimachean influence in Ovid's epic rests on examining treatments of the same myth or bodies of myth.

THE PIERID HYMN AND OVIDIAN POETIC AGENDA

Acknowledging the Pierides as anti-Callimachean "Muses" based on the etymology of their patronymic—the patronymic exploited comedically by Epicharmus—is one Ovidian defusing of the fundamentally impious nature of their song. Epicharmus may also provide an answer to a possible strategic lacuna in the renarrated Pierid hymn, which records the animal transformations of the Olympians amid their fearful flight from Typhoeus. One Olympian transformation not recorded is Minerva's, the goddess now in attendance for the renarration of the singing contest. Traditionally, Minerva plays a mythologically important role in the Gigantomachy, marking this

The absence as significant. Her fight against the Giants is even referenced in one of the opening descriptive vignettes within Callimachus' *Bath of Pallas* (*Hymn* 5.7–8). The absence of Minerva in the catalog of theriomorphic disguises potentially marks two narrative strategies: a tactful omission (the Muse does not wish to offend the goddess with such impiousness) or a self-interested omission (if the goddess was an object of Pierid praise, the Muse does not wish to let Minerva know, lest this information compromise the goddess' opinion of the Muses' victory). The Muses' song opens formulaically with a hymnic address to Ceres, an opening that suggests that the original Pierid song likewise chose a goddess to invoke hymnically; the pattern of singing contests dictates that the second singer opens their own song in a responsive fashion.[83] The Heliconian episode opens with Minerva's naming as Tritonia (5.250), echoed by the direct address of the Muse (5.270); within the narrative frame, she is referred to as Pallas (*Pallada*, 5.263; *Pallas*, 5.336), and within the hymn, also Pallas (*Pallada*, 5.375). As previously mentioned, one of the names of the Epicharmian Muses is Tritone; Τρίτων also refers to the Nile in both Apollonius (*Argon.* 4.269) and Lycophron (*Alex.* 119, 576).[84] In an unplaced dramatic fragment (fr. 135 K-A = A 12 Olson), Epicharmus also relates the birth of Athena from Zeus' head alongside mention of the Titanomachy; he says that the goddess' name Pallas comes from a giant named Pallas, whose skin Athena had used to make herself a cloak. This version of Athena's name is corroborated by no other source, indicating that Epicharmus is either following a lost source (likely an epic, given the traditional home of the material, his tendency for epic parody, and the presence of a Titan named Pallas in Hesiod; cf. *Theog.* 376, 383) or creating his own etymological play.[85] Athena's assumption of Pallas' name, along with his skin, stands as a metamorphosis of sorts that provides a humorous parallel to the theriomorphic disguises of the Olympians in the Pierid song. Ovid's clash of Muses and Pierides would provide a tempting outlet for the poet to integrate awareness of Epicharmus' epic parody in a way that further speaks to the issues of identity posed by an epic about change, the very theme that the Pierid hymn places front and center. Furthermore, if theories about the interconnection of Demeter cult and the rise of comedy on Sicily are borne in mind, the allusive presence of the Sicilian Epicharmus is also relevant here, as Ovid adds a new layer of comedic and competitive resonance to setting up the Muses' hymn to Ceres.[86] Understanding a purposeful dimension of comedy within the Pierid song continues to acknowledge the threads of comedic significance in Callimachus' *Hymn to Demeter*, put to expansive and innovative use in Ovid's reimagining of the Callimachean hymnic universe.

CONCLUSION

A more thorough reckoning with the Callimachean hymnic influence and presence within this episode allows different inflections of interpretive significance to arise. First, Minerva's appearance on Helicon, her interaction with the Muses, and the role of Helicon itself is given a poetic logic from applying the precedent of the *Bath of Pallas*. Ovid's reliance upon this hymn to frame the contest itself also hints at the relevance of the Callimachean collection to the internal contest offerings. By viewing the contest as a hymnic battle in a civil war, we can see how Ovid sets up the Muses and Pierides as reflective entities, warring over territory in a way that has historical and allegorical dimensions. A new layer of resonance, however, can be added by seeing a metapoetic dimension to their rivalry, over their Callimachean allegiances. As anti-Callimachean "Muses," the Pierides receive a new, contrasting identity to the Muses. This metapoetic dimension is further underscored by the role the Callimachean *Hymn to Demeter* plays in setting out these differences. The Pierides sing a hymn that encodes similar experimental poetic messaging, a song that shares its thematic investment in Gigantomachic imagery and themes; by investing themselves in the imagery of literary polemic and size on display in this Callimachean hymn, they further place themselves into opposition with the Muses, who choose to sing the narrative of Proserpina eschewed as an option by Callimachus before he settles on the myth of Erysichthon. The hymnic battle, therefore, is directly waged on the "territory" of Callimachean hymns. When we see how both the *Bath of Pallas* and *Hymn to Demeter* participate in Ovid's construction of this hymnic battle and the identity of its participants, we can also understand how this final pair of hymns in the Callimachean collection demand to be read together in a competitive fashion, with their competing, internal generic allegiances to tragedy and comedy. Ovid imports a sense of this paired contrast to additionally underscore the nature of the rivalry at hand he is exploring between the Muses and Pierides.

6

Calliope's Hymn

Musing on the Nature of Love

Returning to the beginning of Ovid's poetic career, his opening elegy (*Am.* 1.1) introduces us to a possible world of confused identity. This is the world the poet imagines when he realizes that Cupid has seized control of his would-be epic verses, hijacking his poetic agenda. Ovid's reaction is indignant and dramatic as he envisions an upheaval of divine responsibility, beginning with the Olympian goddesses: Minerva and Venus trading places, Ceres and Diana swapping roles (*Am.* 1.1.5–10). As the previous chapters have explored, in some ways the *Metamorphoses* takes imaginative cues from this scenario, presenting a world shaped by rivalries over divine identifiers and responsibility and the exchanges of power—especially in the case of Cupid appropriating other divine powers. The reluctant elegist also turns to the notion of territory, asking Cupid, *tua sunt Heliconia tempe?* (*Am.* 1.1.15). The implication is that the home of the Muses—the home of poetry— now also falls under Cupid's sway. Ovid's question, which implies a relationship between Love and the Muses, can also be used for thinking about the moment Helicon comes into focus in the *Metamorphoses*.

As the last chapter examined the contest frame and Pierid hymn, this chapter now turns to the contents of Calliope's hymn.[1] Similarly, my aim here is to renew interpretations of the contest by a focus on hymnic intertexts, and by employing the twinned critical lenses of rivalry and territory. Given that Calliope's hymn is a known portion of the text that relies upon a primary hymnic source (the *Homeric Hymn to Demeter*), my discussion here builds on these established textual affiliations, and integrates more diffuse hymnic material and meaning. There are four parts to this analysis.

In the first, I dissect the tension between Venus and Ceres as objects of hymnic praise. The second reassesses conversation about Venus' relationship to the Muses, the judging nymphs, and the nymphs of Calliope's song by looking at the role of virginity within the narrative, and how it comes into conflict with the power of love. The third portion sets out Arethusa's role as a Muse within Calliope's hymn, showing how Arethusa's assumption of this role also contributes to the identity of this episode as a metapoetic recapitulation of the first four books of the epic. As part of discussing this assumed identity, I further detail the ways Arethusa's story forces a reckoning with definitions of love for the epic, which returns to the ideas set forth about love in the first chapter. The final section returns to the framing of the episode: I suggest an identity for the narrating Muse, whose identity solidifies these readings of Ovid's reliance upon the hymnic tradition to create his divine personalities.

Venus versus Ceres: Cultivating Love

In order to fully understand how Ovid stages hymnic competition between Venus and Ceres, we can first look to the literary background of the *Homeric Hymns*, which reveals a latent potential for their divine overlap and conflict for Ovid to build upon. Near the beginning of Calliope's hymn, Venus makes an address to her son about her plans for universal control:

> "arma manusque meae, mea, nate, potentia" dixit,
> "illa, quibus superas omnes, cape tela, Cupido,
> inque dei pectus celeres molire sagittas,
> cui triplicis cessit fortuna nouissima regni.
> tu superos ipsumque Iovem, tu numina ponti
> uicta domas ipsumque regit qui numina ponti.
> Tartara quid cessant? cur non matrisque tuumque
> imperium profers? agitur pars tertia mundi.
> et tamen in caelo (quae iam patientia nostra est!)
> spernimur ac mecum uires minuuntur Amoris.
> Pallada nonne uides iaculatricemque Dianam
> abscessisse mihi? Cereris quoque filia uirgo,
> si patiemur, erit; nam spes adfectat easdem.
> at tu pro socio, si qua est ea gratia, regno
> iunge deam patruo."

> (*Met.* 5.365–79)

Calliope's Hymn 203

["my arms and my hands, my son, my executive power," she said,
"take up those arrows, the ones with which you conquer all things, Cupid,
and launch those swift missiles into the chest of a god—you know,
the one to whom the newest lot of the triple kingdom fell.
You conquer the gods, and Jupiter himself; the powers of the sea
you subdue, and have subdued even the god who lords over them.
Why does Tartarus remain uncultivated? Why not advance our empire,
    yours
and mine? A third part of the world is at stake.
And still—we are spurned in the heavens, despite its sufferance of us,
and the forces of love dwindle alongside my own. Don't you see how
Pallas and archeress Diana have withdrawn from me? The daughter
of Ceres, too, would be a virgin, if permitted; she assays the same hopes.
But you—if you possess any pride in our joint kingdom—join
the goddess to her uncle."]

The implications of this address formed part of the discussion of the first
chapter, tracing Ovid's poetic sidestepping of Jupiter's honor and praise. Now,
we return to Calliope's hymn to look more closely at Venus herself. Within
this address, Venus not only refers to the narrative events of *Homeric Hymn
to Demeter* but to her own *Homeric Hymn*, which begins with embedded
hymns to the goddesses who exist beyond her boundaries of her power:
Athena, Artemis, and Hestia (*Hymn. Hom. Ven.* 7–35). On a specific textual
note, Venus' use of *domas* borrows the Homeric hymnist's opening verb
of Aphrodite's works (ἐδαμάσσατο, *Hymn. Hom. Ven.* 3), which introduces
a central motif to the hymn and is redeployed in key passages.[2] We can use
this overlap of hymnic influence as the starting point in tracing an addi-
tional rivalry between Venus' praises and the praise of Ceres, the ostensible
subject of Calliope's hymn. Calliope's opening praise of Ceres (5.341–45) leads
into Venus' plan for domination, which reuses as justification the exem-
plary resistance of Pallas and Artemis from her own *Homeric Hymn*. The
prominent use of Venus' hymn within this passage already leads the reader
to question both the nature of divine authority and hymnic authority on
display. The notion of ἔργα that defines the Homeric Aphrodite's praises
also becomes a complicating tension for perceiving the boundaries between
hymnic praises of Ceres and Venus. As outlined in the first chapter, the word
dominates the opening of the *Homeric Hymn to Aphrodite*, delineating the
powers of the goddess amid the different spheres of the Olympians. After its

204 Calliope's Hymn

proliferation in the hymn's opening, it appears once more within the body of the poem when the disguised Aphrodite spins her tale to Anchises, detailing her journey after she was stolen away by Hermes. Here, it carries the more specific meaning of "fields":

ἔνθεν μ᾽ ἥρπαξε χρυσόρραπις Ἀργειφόντης,
πολλὰ δ᾽ ἔπ᾽ ἤγαγεν ἔργα καταθνητῶν ἀνθρώπων,
πολλὴν δ᾽ ἄκληρόν τε καὶ ἄκτιτον, ἣν διὰ θῆρες
ὠμοφάγοι φοιτῶσι κατὰ σκιόεντας ἐναύλους,
οὐδὲ ποσὶ ψαύειν ἐδόκουν φυσιζόου αἴης·

(Hymn. Hom. Ven. 121–25)

[From there, Hermes of the golden wand snatched me:
he led me over many fields of mortal men,
much land untilled, undistributed, through which
flesh-eating beasts stalked, in the region of shadowy lairs:
I reckoned not my feet would ever again
touch the life-bestowing earth.]

Her remove from mankind is detailed by the landscape itself. She is taken from cultivated fields into lands uncultivated and unpossessed, home to only beasts. The adjectives ἄκληρος and ἄκτιτος, distinguished by the alpha-privative, further relate to Aphrodite's self-description a few lines later: ἀδμήτην . . . καὶ ἀπειρήτην φιλότητος ("[a maiden] untamed and unexperienced in love," Hymn. Hom. Ven. 133; cf. also ἀεικής, "unseemly," 136).[3] The disguised goddess professes to be as untamed and inexperienced as the lands she was carried over, unowned and untilled. The semantic overlap between the goddess' "virginal" state and the natural landscape, linked by the prevalence of the alpha privatives, also make an implicit connection between the ἔργα she leaves behind and the ἔργα πολυχρύσου Ἀφροδίτης ("works of richly gilded Aphrodite," 1). The analogy between cultivation (ploughing) and sexual practices is well-established from Hesiod's *Works and Days* onward.

The paradoxical tension between Aphrodite's real identity and the self-presentation of her deceit-speech, rhetorically characterized by this ostentatious lack, is also implicit in her use of the adjective φυσίζοος ("life-producing,"

125).[4] φυσίζοος derives the power of its Homeric usages from active contrasts with death: the earth is "life-giving," or "life-producing," but also needs death in order to propagate life.[5] Absence makes new presence. The interplay of life and death, danger and wildness that permeates her description of the landscape, and the fact that Hermes acts as her divine courier, make Aphrodite's tale suspiciously close to a katabasis. She goes on to say that Hermes told her she would be a wife and mother before his departure (*Hymn. Hom. Ven.* 126–30). The act of a kidnapping for the purposes of a marriage (ἥρπαξε, 121; cf. the programmatic ἥρπαξεν at *Hymn. Hom. Den.* 3) and the atmospheric hints of a katabasis make Aphrodite's tale similar to Persephone's. The *Hymn to Demeter* may well rely on the textual authority of the *Hymn to Aphrodite*, but circumstantially, there is already an echo of the Persephone myth in Aphrodite's speech of deception. By deriving its significance from the landscape, and relying on the multivalent meanings of ἔργα, this portion of the *Homeric Hymn* already brings together the powers of Demeter, as a goddess of agricultural plenty and fertility, with the powers of Aphrodite.

Within the *Homeric Hymn to Aphrodite*, the issues of fertility and ownership mutually projected by the landscape of the goddess' journey and her disguised identity create a zone where the concepts of love and cultivation become inextricable. The dissolution of firm boundaries between the erotic and the agricultural also informs the Ovidian Venus' concept of the territorial world in a subtle but significant manner. Venus identifies Hades as the god *cui triplicis cessit fortuna nouissima regni* ("the one to whom the newest lot of the triple kingdom fell," 5.368). *Cedo* denotes how his kingdom came into his possession: it "fell" to him, a specific meaning of the verb (*OLD* s.v. 15). *Cessit* is echoed a few lines later by the similarly sounding but distinct verb *cessant* (*Tartara quid cessant?*, 5.371). Like *cedo*, *cesso* has many meanings. One of them regards land: "to be fallow, remain uncultivated" (*OLD* s.v. 4c). Tartarus, as a physical region, can fall under the appropriateness of this usage.[6] Venus' question, I suggest, should be understood specifically as "why is Tartarus left uncultivated?"[7] This meaning endorses a reading of Tartarus as contested ground. By borrowing a metaphor from the agricultural sphere to conceptualize her territorially imperialist desires, Venus can also implicitly express her metaphorical imperialist desires: to take over the space of praise in Calliope's hymn to Ceres. Venus' question operates in canny recognition of the boundaries their divine powers share, as once acknowledged by the speech of the disguised Aphrodite within her *Homeric Hymn*, and the enterprising hymnist of the responsively crafted *Homeric Hymn to Demeter*. Venus' query is not just a rhetorical question, but a cry to redress a hymnic balance. She wants to recalibrate the allocation of praise that saw inspiration move from praise of Aphrodite to praise of Demeter. Her dissatisfaction can be additionally felt given the hymn's Sicilian setting, where worship of Venus is not as deeply embedded as worship of Ceres. Her fears of being literarily overshadowed by Ceres are uncomfortably mirrored by the Sicilian cultic reality.[8]

Within Ovid's Augustan context, the two goddesses also share a certain overlap in honor. Both goddesses have been argued for as the identity of the female figure on the Ara Pacis frieze, which encapsulates the difficulties in decoupling the specific iconography of fertility as it belongs to each goddess.[9] Their sharing of attributes is not only visual, but textual. For the present discussion two shared epithets are notable: *alma* ("nourishing") and *genetrix* ("mother," "creator"). While Ceres is called *alma* within Calliope's hymn (5.572; cf. the earlier appearance of *alma . . . Tellus*, 2.272), the adjective is subsequently applied most frequently to Venus for the remainder of the epic (cf. 10.230, 13.759, 15.844). Before Ovid, Lucretius opens his work with *alma Venus* (*DRN* 1.2). On the other hand, Virgil invokes *alma Ceres* as he broaches his own didactic (*Georg.* 1.7), and in his *Aeneid*, Venus is twice designated maternally as *alma* (1.618, 10.332). Later in *Metamorphoses* 5, Arethusa also names Ceres as *frugum genetrix* ("mother of fruits," 5.490). Although Ceres appears as the *alma genetrix* within Calliope's hymn, within Venus' own hymn that begins the narrative, she already recalls the opening of the *De rerum natura*, where Venus is both *genetrix* and *alma*. In short, while Ceres may receive the *label* of the honorifics within the hymn, the opening portrait of Venus with her son *embodies* them, setting the two goddesses in a further space of tension and contention.

Venus' need to reclaim both literary and physical space from Ceres can also be understood as an additional response to some of the tensions of poetic allocation within the *Fasti*. In Ovid's calendrical verse, her month of April is dominated by the narration of Proserpina's rape; in other words, a *Hymn to Ceres*. The *Fasti* poet notes that there are some who would begrudge Venus "her" month, and reassign its ownership based on different etymologizing:

Calliope's Hymn

quo non liuor abit? sunt qui tibi mensis honorem
 eripuisse uelint inuideantque, Venus.
nam quia uer aperit tunc omnia densaque cedit
 frigoris asperitas fetaque terra patet,
Aprilem memorant ab aperto tempore dictum,
 quem <u>Venus</u> iniecta uindicat <u>alma</u> manu.

(Fast. 4.85–90)

[Where does envy not go? There are those who would wish
to snatch away the honor of a month from you, and begrudge it,
Venus. For, because spring opens all things, and the concentrated
harshness of the chill yields, and the fertile earth lies exposed,
they name April so-called from this time of opening,
which nourishing Venus claims, with a laid hand.]

The poet goes on to reassure the goddess by a hymnic exploration of her powers as *alma Venus*. The beginning of this hymn bears similarities to Calliope's invocation of Ceres in *Metamorphoses* 5. Both goddesses are law-givers (*iuraque dat caelo, terrae, natalibus undis*, "and she [Venus] gives laws to the heaven, the lands, and the waves that bore her," *Fast.* 4.93; *prima dedit leges*, "she [Ceres] first gave laws," *Met.* 5.343); both goddesses are responsible for crops (*illa satis causas arboribusque dedit*, "she gave first origins to cultivated crops and trees," *Fast.* 4.96; *prima dedit fruges alimentaque mitia terris*, "first she gave fruits and ripening sustenance to the earth," *Met.* 5.342). Part of Ovid's care to legitimize Venus' etymological and symbolic hold over April, however, redistributes an etymology of Ceres: before Venus' aetiological authority over crops is mentioned (*illa satis causas . . . dedit*), the poet proclaims, *illa deos omnes (longum est numerare) <u>creauit</u>* ("she created all the gods—it would take too much time to rehearse them," *Fast.* 4.95). When Servius comments on the *alma Ceres* who opens the *Georgics*, he attributes her name to *creare*; yet within the *Fasti*, Venus is both *alma* (echoing afresh the first word of *Fasti* 4) and the goddess responsible for the act of creation.[10] Ceres only appears as *alma Ceres* later, at *Fast.* 4.547. *Alma*, too, has been read as a gloss on Ceres' name, coming from *ab alendo* ("from the act of nourishing," cf. *alimenta, Met.* 5.342).[11] Within the *Fasti*, Ovid links the rape of Proserpina to the Cerialia, rather than to the more thematically appropriate matronal cult festival, which occurred in August.[12] Although

208 Calliope's Hymn

the placement of the myth has been justified as a conflation of cult practices, the lack of strict necessity for inclusion here gives Venus reason to perceive "her" month as being gratuitously ceded to celebrating Ceres. The latent subtext of divine rivalry within this book of the *Fasti*, also played out through the medium of hymnic invocation and material, adds further edge and clarity to the portrait of Venus' territorial dissatisfaction in the *Metamorphoses*. Her competitive desire to wrest focus away from a *Hymn to Ceres* is further encoded within the tissues of connectivity between the Ovidian texts.

The Love of the Muses?

Prompted by Venus' hymnic address to Cupid, much scholarly focus on Calliope's song overall is concerned with how Venus weaponizes sexuality, and how this weaponization interacts with the different levels of audiences and narrators: the virgin goddess Athena, the nymphs, and the Muses themselves.[13] On the whole, these readings present Venus and the parties of nymphs, Muses, and Minerva in opposition. However, there is reason to interrogate these sets of relationships more closely, with attention to the nature of virginity as it operates within the hymnic sphere. Purity is one marker of feminine divine identity that can be poetically channeled to assimilate the goddess in question to a Muse. The Callimachean Artemis and Pallas both visibly participate in this channeling: Artemis, as an external Muse for the composition of the hymn at hand, and Pallas, assuming internally the role of a Muse within her hymn's mythological *exemplum*. However, virginity is not a prerequisite for goddesses being aligned with the Muses. To a certain extent, any divinity that is the subject of a hymn exists as its "muse." When scholars stringently separate the values of Venus from the audiences of Minerva and nymphs and the narrating Muses within this portion of the *Metamorphoses*, there is a denial of or failure to engage with the literary hints that paint Venus *herself* as a Muse, and that call into question the virginity of the Muses. The following portion of the chapter redresses this lack of conversation about the relationship between Venus and the Muses within Calliope's hymn.

In Calliope's hymn, like the *Homeric Hymn to Demeter* before it, Venus' rivalry with Pallas and Diana is concentrated upon the issue of their sworn virginity. Venus takes counteractive measures to prevent Proserpina from following the same path (*Cereris quoque filia uirgo, / si patiemur, erit; nam spes adfectat easdem*, "even the daughter of Ceres too, should we permit it, will remain a virgin; for she harbors this same hope," 5.376–77). Venus conceives of the decision to remain a *uirgo* akin to an act of war; her solution is a route to the underworld. Her directive to Cupid displays some syntactical features that further underscore her territorial aim: *at tu pro socio, si qua est ea gratia, regno / iunge deam patruo* ("but you—if you possess any pride in our joint kingdom—join the goddess to her uncle," 5.378–79). The pause between *socio* and *regno*, and the ability of *socio* and *patruo* to be both nouns and adjectives, opens a space of linguistic possibility where *regno* can apply to either word: precisely Venus' goal, that Dis' kingdom will become part of hers. The syntactical ambiguity is mimetic of her desire. If we read *socio* as a noun (even if only momentarily), this also has a set of interpretive implications.

Venus' self-presentation is knowingly steeped in literary tradition and lineages of inspiration. There are several interpretive implications given how she conceives of herself in relation to other goddesses, including the Muses. Venus' expression of the extent of her influence, over sky, sea, and land, is a commonplace for hymnic addresses to the goddess. One especially powerful example is the so-called hymn to Venus that opens Lucretius' *De rerum natura* (1.1–43), briefly mentioned above.[14] The poet calls upon *alma Venus* to act in the capacity of a Muse, and to supervise his creative endeavor as a *socia* (*DRN* 1.24). The equation between Venus and Muse is made more explicit in the final book, when the poet invokes Calliope with the same opening descriptor used of Venus (*hominum diuomque uoluptas*, "pleasure of men and gods," *DRN* 1.1; 6.94).[15] The identification between Venus and Calliope has been compellingly traced to Empedocles, who links his cosmic force of Love to both a "much-wooed, white-armed virgin Muse" (B 3.3 D-K) and Calliope, whom he summons to stand by him (B 131.3 D-K).[16] Monica Gale suggests this notion of "standing by" extends inspirationally from Empedocles to become embodied in Lucretius' *socia*. O'Hara extends this reading to the possible presence of a double allusion. He identifies a line of further influence that proceeds first from Simonides to Empedocles, and then from Empedocles to Lucretius.[17] Simonides calls upon the Muse as an ἐπίκουρος ("ally," "auxiliary," fr. 11.21 West), rendered as *socius* in Latin. Therefore, Simonides' Muse is gesturally echoed by Empedocles' Muse, before being linguistically translated to Lucretius' Venus-Muse: Lucretius' invocation stands as a testament to both earlier poets. Given the pervasive

Lucretian allusions in the opening invocation of Calliope's hymn,[18] and the repositioning of his Venus-muse, the Ovidian Calliope's placement of *socius* in the mouth of Venus to describe Cupid cannot be wholly removed from Lucretian significance. Cupid acts as a *socius* in two senses: a militarily real sense and a metaliterary inspirational sense, reproducing the simultaneously physical and metapoetic senses of the *regna* Venus pursues. The syntactical ambiguity of *socius* to convey mimetically her goal further underscores the presence of poetic inspiration, in a way that draws poetic inspiration and love ever closer together.

Along these lines, the conflation of Muse and Venus/Aphrodite in Empedocles deserves a closer look for what it can tell us about the relationship between the forces of love and inspiration. In the invocation just cited (B. 3.3 D-K), Empedocles' Muse is hailed as a virgin (παρθένε). Traditionally, Muses fell into two camps: they were either virgins (e.g., Catullus' *doctis . . . uirginibus*, 65.2), or they became mothers within the heroic age.[19] Within Book 5, Ovid's Muses seem to fall into the former category. Helicon is twice called *uirgineus* (2.219, 5.254), an adjective also given to the minds of the Muses, when they express a set of fears within their pure environment (*omnia terrent / uirgineas mentes*, "all things terrify our virginal minds," 5.273–74). The brief story of Pyreneus' attempted rape that explains their present state of fear further explores this aspect of their identity.[20] However, when Helicon is first deemed "virginal," it is coupled in a catalog line with *nondum Oeagrius Haemus* ("Haemus, not yet of Oeagrus," 2.219).[21] This detail cannot fail to remind the reader of Oeagrus' eventual fathering of Orpheus with the Muse Calliope. As the epic chronologically unfolds, the adjective becomes outdated in Book 10, when Orpheus hails Calliope as *Musa parens* (10.148). Therefore, throughout the course of the epic, Ovid's Muses (or at least, Calliope explicitly) fall into both categories; Calliope is a sort of Schrödinger's virgin.

Calliope's more individual prominence and identity amid the Muses as a collective could explain this further distinction.[22] Propertius separates Calliope from her sisters by referring to her experience of love with Oeagrus (Prop. 2.30.33–36), a poetic precedent that may stand behind Ovid's singling out of Calliope via the geographical pairing of Haemus and Helicon.[23] Although the tradition of Muses bearing children has been cursorily noted in discussions of virginity as a shared concern to the narrators, judges, and listeners of Calliope's hymn, it is only made with reference to Calliope's

Calliope's Hymn

211

parentage of Orpheus within the world of the *Metamorphoses*.[24] In other words, it is not a rate-limiting detail, but rather, a narrative expedient. As Patricia Johnson says, they are virgins "for the purposes of this episode."[25] In Ovid's epic, Calliope's singling out as a mother is paralleled by her other status differential: her role as the chief representative of the Muses (*dedimus summam certaminis uni*, "we dedicated the greatest one of us to the contest," 5.337). In other words, her exceptionality is also marked by the privilege of representing the collective group in the singing contest.

Like saying Ovid's Muses are virgins to suit the needs of the narrative context, the choice of Calliope to perform the contest hymn has an expedient justification in her special identity among the Muses. The hint toward Calliope's eventual motherhood, however, reprised by the echo of *uirgineus Helicon*, are not integrated into discussion of the presentation of Venus within the hymn. Considering her own fluid circumstances regarding virginity within the poem, Calliope's depiction of Venus is worth considering with this taken explicitly into account. Is her hymn influenced in any way by the fact that Calliope (like the reader) knows that she, too, will eventually be under the sway of Venus? If Calliope is aware that not even *uirgineus Helicon* is safe from Venus, this awareness is what knits together the senses of real and metapoetic in Venus' concerns for *regna*. And as the Muses are conventionally gifted with knowledge of past, present, and future, ascribing this awareness to Calliope is not misplaced.

If we turn to the hymn with this question in mind, there is one especial junction in the hymn where Calliope draws attention to this matter of traditional Muse omniscience that stands out.[26] After narrating the metamorphosis of Ascalaphus, she asks about the nature of the Sirens' transformation:

> uobis, Acheloides, unde
> pluma pedesque auium, cum uirginis ora geratis?
> an quia, cum legeret uernos Proserpina flores,
> in comitum numero, doctae Sirenes, eratis?

(Met. 5.552–55)

[But from where, daughters of Achelous, did the feathers and talons
of birds come, since you nevertheless bear maidenly faces?
Is it because you among the number of her companions,
learned Sirens, when Proserpina was picking spring blossoms?]

By making this a question, Calliope steps away from her governing sense of narrative authority. This distancing invites the learned reader to consult their own accumulated knowledge of the event, whether mythological or literary. When Calliope does broach the reason for their metamorphosis, she transforms their new wingedness from a punishment (cf. Hyg. *Fab.* 141.1) into a useful tool to aid the maidens in their search for Proserpina (5.556–60). The Sirens are not featured in the *Homeric Hymn to Demeter*, where Persephone's companions are Oceanids (*Hymn. Hom. Dem.* 5); in Persephone's renarration to Demeter, where she catalogs the names of her witnessing companions, she also includes Pallas and Artemis (*Hymn. Hom. Dem.* 424). In other words, Calliope is consciously adding this narrative information, in the same manner as she expands the remit of the Homeric myth in her focus on Cyane and Arethusa.[27] Although Homer doesn't list the Sirens as the companions of Persephone, Apollonius does:

> αἶψα δὲ νῆσον
> καλὴν Ἀνθεμόεσσαν ἐσέδρακον, ἔνθα λίγειαι
> Σειρῆνες σίνοντ' Ἀχελωίδες ἡδείῃσι
> θέλγουσαι μολπῇσιν ὅτις παρὰ πεῖσμα βάλοιτο.
> τὰς μὲν ἄρ' εὐειδὴς Ἀχελωίῳ εὐνηθεῖσα
> γείνατο Τερψιχόρη, Μουσέων μία, καί ποτε Δηοῦς
> θυγατέρ' ἰφθίμην, ἀδμῆτ' ἔτι, πορσαίνεσκον
> ἄμμιγα μελπόμεναι· τότε δ' ἄλλο μὲν οἰωνοῖσιν,
> ἄλλο δὲ παρθενικῆς ἐναλίγκιαι ἔσκον ἰδέσθαι,
>
> (Ap. Rhod. Argon. 4.891–99)[28]

> [Very soon they sighted
> lovely Anthemoéssa, the island where those clear-voiced
> Sirens, daughters of Acheloös, with their seductive
> songs of enchantment destroyed all travelers who put in there.
> Terpsíchoré, one of the Muses, a beautiful creature, bore them
> after bedding with Acheloös; a time came when they served
> Demeter's powerful daughter, then still unmarried,
> sharing her play: but now to look at they were
> formed partly like birds, and partly like young maidens. (trans. P. Green)]

Like the Ovidian account, the Sirens' father is Achelous (*Acheloides*, 5.552; Ἀχελωίδες, *Argon.* 4.893).[29] Apollonius also tells us the Muse Terpsichore is

Calliope's Hymn 213

the mother of the Sirens (*Argon.* 4.896). Their singing, however, is described by μέλπω (*Argon.* 4.898). Given the presence of the collective Muses in the identification of Terpsichore as Μουσέων μία, this verb choice simultaneously alludes to Melpomene: a learned reference to a different tradition in which Melpomene is the mother of the Sirens.[30] Apollonius goes on to describe their "lily-like voice" (*Argon.* 4.903), which aligns their singing with the Hesiodic Muses, also famously possessed of "lily-like voices" (*Theog.* 40–41). The Sirens in Calliope's hymn are also connected to the Muses through the adjective *doctae* (*doctas . . . sorores*, 5.255; *doctae Sirenes*, 5.555). Calliope's use of *doctae* works reflexively here, not just describing the Sirens, but also internally flagging the "learnedness" of her narrative treatment of these hybrid creatures.[31]

The second question Calliope poses (*an quia, cum* <u>*legeret uernos Proserpina flores*</u>, / *in comitum numero, doctae Sirenes, eratis?*) refers back to the moment of Proserpina's rape earlier in her hymn (5.390–95). Calliope asks about the time when the maiden is picking flowers (*flores*, 5.390), specified as violets and lilies (*ludit et aut uiolas aut candida lilia carpit*, "while she plays and plucks violets, or shining-white lilies," 5. 392; cf. also *uer*, 5.391 and *legendo*, 5.394).[32] Both of these flowers have associations with the Muses, who possess "lily-like voices" and are "violet-haired" (cf. Pind. *Pyth* 1.1–2; Simonides fr. 11.16 West). If Proserpina's rape is symbolized by the plucking of flowers, these flowers also encode identifying, physical attributes of the Muses that symbolically place them in similar or shared danger. There is an additional relevant detail from the *Homeric Hymn* that ties together the Muses, Sirens, and Persephone: in the catalog of Oceanids Persephone enumerates, she includes Ourania, a name shared with a Muse (*Hymn. Hom. Dem.* 423); in Ovid, Ourania is the Muse that welcomes Minerva to Helicon (5.260).[33] In essence, Calliope goes out of her way to introduce narrative material to the hymn that unsettles their identification as virgins. In doing so, she gives further credence to the extent of Venus' conquering powers. The reader approaches Calliope's hymn with the suspicion about Calliope's virginity, and therefore, about her relationship with Venus; the hymn then proceeds to invite further suspicion about the company of Muses at large.

The further suspicions introduced by Calliope's narrative elaborations can provide commentary on the nature of the Muses themselves. While Calliope's motherhood has yet to happen in the epic, chronologically speaking, the mothering of the Sirens has already occurred. On one hand, this speaks to the Muses' knowledge of past, present, and future, confirming a crucial aspect of their inspiratory abilities. On the other, given the paradox introduced by Helicon's descriptor as *uirgineus*, this speaks to their professed ability to traffic in "believable deceptions." Calliope's unexampled treatment of the Sirens' transformation as a positive change—as useful for their efforts in searching, and as an index of their loyalty to Proserpina—also accords with this ability.[34] Calliope's insistence on their dedication to Proserpina, including their accompanying of the maiden in a flowery meadow, also transforms their Homeric nature. The Homeric Sirens sing from their flowery meadow (cf. *Od.* 12.159) for the purpose of seduction, delighting and charming with their song in a way that blends overtones of aesthetic and sexual pleasure.[35] Ovid himself in the *Ars amatoria* uses the seductive powers of their voice exemplarily (*Ars am.* 3.311–12). Calliope's assimilating act reassigns their Homeric powers of seduction to Muse-like learnedness, highlighting the inconsistencies in her account. This inconsistency is crystallized by her description of their dual form: *uobis, Acheloides, unde / pluma pedesque auium, cum uirginis ora geratis*? ("but from where, daughters of Achelous, did the feathers and talons of birds come, since you nevertheless bear maidenly faces?," 5.552–53). Calliope's description of their female form quotes the disguise assumed by the Virgilian Venus when she first appears to her son in Libya (*uirginis os habitumque gerens*, "bearing the face and demeanor of a virgin," *Aen.* 1.315).[36] There is implicit humor in Venus appearing as a virgin to her own son, a disguise that hearkens back to the *Homeric Hymn to Aphrodite*. Calliope's descriptive rehabilitation of the Sirens' transformation, based on a shared concern for maidenhood, also has perverse humor considering the tradition that makes a Muse their mother. Calliope's quotation of Venus' disguise, which stems back to an originally hymnic portrait of virginity itself as a disguise, further complicates the role of Venus within the Muse's hymn. It indicates still further an inability to escape fully the influence of love, and delicately places even Helicon as a territory of Venus and Cupid.

Reading Arethusa as a Muse

Calliope's subtle messaging about the futility of denying love's power therefore needs to be recalled within a specific context: the poetic and philosophical tradition that identifies Venus/Aphrodite with Calliope. This is the very tradition evoked by the posturing of Venus' internal hymn to Cupid. Calliope's hymn employs strategies of equivocation and adumbration to

Calliope's Hymn

215

downplay and resist this potential overlap in divine identity. However, the overt and rivalrous opposition of implicit doubles or selves Ovid stages between Calliope and Venus further mirrors the structural conceit of the singing contest with the Pierides, who are the collective double of the Muses, as discussed in the previous chapter. The boundary between internal and external narrative circumstance becomes more permeably fraught with recognition of this mirroring. And yet, the narrative complexities of the contest episode yield a further network of allusivity surrounding divine identity and rivalry within the hymn's congestion of contested space. There is another structural overlap between the framing mechanism of the hymn's retelling and the hymn itself that introduces another thread of suggestiveness about Venus' dominance. This involves the nymph Arethusa.

When Minerva visits Helicon, she is asked mid-narrative stream by the unnamed Muse if she has the leisure to hear the rest of the tale (5.333–34). The Muse pauses between the synopsis of the Pierid song and the renarration of Calliope's hymn. There is a structural similarity subsequently found in Calliope's song. Within Calliope's hymn, the nymph Arethusa briefly references her own experience when she pleads with Ceres on behalf of the earth, when she informs the goddess of her daughter's whereabouts (5.487–508). She tells the goddess that the full narration of her own tale can wait until more favorable circumstances:

> mota loco cur sim tantique per aequoris undas
> aduehar Ortygiam, ueniet narratibus hora
> tempestiua meis, cum tu curaque leuata
> et uultus melioris eris.
>
> (*Met.* 5.498–501)

> [For what reason I was moved and traveled
> to Ortygia, through the waves of such a vast sea,
> there will come a more opportune time for these stories,
> when you, with cares lifted, will be of better disposition.]

With Proserpina restored, Ceres returns to listen to Arethusa's tale (*exigit alma Ceres, nata secura recepta, / quae tibi causa fugae, cur sis, Arethusa, sacer fons,* "motherly Ceres, reassured by her daughter's return, asks what the reason was for your flight, Arethusa, and how you became a sacred spring,"

5.572–73). Regarding Arethusa's narrative, Hinds notes that the splitting of her story mimics the narrative structure of Persephone's abduction in the *Homeric Hymn*. Other commentators on her story note Arethusa's elevated prominence and status, as she communicates the information relayed by the god Helios in the *Homeric Hymn*.[37] The splitting of her story also mirrors internally the splitting of the contest narration by the unnamed Muse, casting her as a Muse figure within Calliope's hymn. Her elevated narrative status is additionally marked by the wealth of intertextual voices donated or borrowed to frame her experiences.[38] Two notable examples are *conticuere undae* ("the waters fell silent," 5.574), an echo of the *conticuere omnes* that prefaces Aeneas' tale of woe in *Aeneid* 2 (Virg. *Aen.* 2.1) and *aestus erat* ("it was sweltering," 5.586), which brings the reader back to Ovid's introduction of Corinna in *Amores* 1.5 (*aestus erat, Am.* 1.5.1).[39]

Arethusa's artistic status is further marked by the descriptive echo of the ecphrasis of the doors of Sol's palace: *dea sustulit alto / fonte caput uiridesque manu siccata capillos* ("the goddess lifted her head from the deep water, drying her kelp-green hair with a hand," 5.574–75) reminds the reader of the Oceanids there depicted (*Doridaque et natas, quarum pars nare uidetur / pars in mole sedens uiridis siccare capillos*, "and Doris and her daughters, part of whom are seen to swim, part to dry out their kelp-green hair, sitting on a cliff," 2.11–12).[40] The connections between the images of Oceanids and Arethusa in the *Metamorphoses* are further brokered by Arethusa's appearance with Oceanids in the nymph catalog of *Georgics* 4 (Virg. *Georg.* 4.334–44; they are called her *sorores* at 4.351).[41] Arethusa appears last in the nymph catalog (*et tandem positis uelox Arethusa sagittis*, "and at last, swift Arethusa, who has set her arrows aside," *Georg.* 4.344), but she is the first to react to Aristaeus' grief: *sed ante alias Arethusa sorores / prospiciens summa flauum caput extulit unda* ("but before her other sisters, Arethusa, raised her blonde head, peering out over the wave peaks," *Georg.* 4.351–52). The Ovidian Arethusa originally appears to Ceres in a textually similar fashion: *tum caput Eleis Alpheias extulit undis / rorantesque comas a fronte remouit ad aures* ("then the Eleian one raised her head from the waters of the Alpheus, and tucked the dripping hair from her forehead behind her ears," *Met.* 5.487–88).

The nymph catalog of *Georgics* 4 is also a critical intertext for the audiences and narrators of Calliope's hymn due to certain identifying names and descriptors: Ligea is also the name of a Siren (*Georg.* 4.336); Clio is also the name of a Muse (*Georg.* 4.341); and the pair of Cydippe and Lycorias are

Calliope's Hymn

217

distinguished in juxtaposition by the former's status as a virgin, the latter's as a new mother (*Georg.* 4.339–40). Arethusa herself has already occupied the position of Muse within the Virgilian corpus, as she shepherded the *Eclogues* to a successful close, inspiring the poet to sing of Gallus' *amores* (cf. *Ecl.* 10.1). The aetiological thrust of Arethusa's tale in the *Metamorphoses*—how she became not just a spring, but a Sicilian spring—also connects her to the external circumstances of the narrative, and the Muses' tale of the Hippocrene's creation. The poet Moschus also shapes thinking about Arethusa as a Muse: as he compares Homer and Bion he connects these two springs, also comparing their respective sources of inspiration:

> ἀμφότεροι παγαῖς πεφιλημένοι, ὃς μὲν ἔπινε
> Παγασίδος κράνας, ὃ δ ἔχεν πόμα τᾶς Ἀρεθοίσας.
>
> (Mosch. *Ep. Bion.* 76–77)

[Both beloved by springs, one of whom drank
the waters of the Pegasaean font, the other
downing draughts of Arethusa.]

The suggestion of Arethusa's aetiological identity as a pastoral spring conforms, in some way, to the narrative framework of the singing contest, notably a feature of pastoral poetry. Pastoral as a genre that houses competitive poetic interactions is also suggested before Calliope's hymn is renarrated. The exchange between the Muse and Minerva, the same narrative pause as recalled above, bears distinct pastoral traces:

> "Hactenus ad citharam uocalia mouerat ora;
> poscimur Aonides—sed forsitan otia non sint,
> nec nostris praebere uacet tibi cantibus aures?"
> "ne dubita uestrumque mihi refer ordine carmen"
> Pallas ait nemorisque leui consedit in umbra.
> Musa refert . . .
>
> (*Met.* 5.332–37)

["Until that point she had sung, with tuneful voice, to her lyre,
and we Muses were compelled—but perhaps you don't have the leisure,
perhaps not the idle time to offer your ears to our songs."

"Don't hesitate—and regale me with the progress of your song"
Pallas said, and settled down in the gentle shade of the grove.
The Muse began . . .]

The Muse's query about the goddess' *otium* is reminiscent of pastoral leisure time. Her suggestion is affirmed by the goddess as she sits in the shade. *Umbra* is the poetically circumscribed space of pastoral leisure, and expressive symbolic shorthand for specifically Virgilian pastoral. By sitting in the shade, Minerva sanctions the pastoral framework momentarily exposed (or imposed).[42] In these ways, Arethusa is a figure designed to evoke the Muses and the Hippocrene within the space of Calliope's hymn, drawing together strands of literary traditions where she appears as a Muse. Although Virgil integrates her into his collection as a pastoral Muse, drawing upon her Sicilian identity, the subject matter of *Eclogue* 10 is nevertheless dominated by love. Similarly, in the *Metamorphoses*, Arethusa's tale brings the reader back through a prominent narrative thread in the first five books of the epic: the erotic pursuit of a virgin within a *locus amoenus*.

ARETHUSA AND THE NATURE OF LOVE

Arethusa's identity as a virgin huntress reintroduces the figure of the Diana look-alike that populates the epic's early tales.[43] As such, it is tempting to set up her narrative as a counterbalance to the power of Venus and Cupid: another example of a nymph consciously denying love as life's guiding principle, in emulation of Diana. However, like the Arethusa of *Eclogue* 10, the story that she tells is one of love: *fluminis Elei ueteres narrauit amores* ("she told of the old loves of the river of Elis," 5.576; cf. *amatas . . . aquas*, "beloved waters," 5.636–37).[44] Even before Arethusa relates her tale, it is framed as a triumph of love. This is not to say that Arethusa's narrative is devoid of Diana's praises. Rather, they are presented as ultimately subject to love's overarching force.

The use of *amor* to describe the relationship between Alpheus and Arethusa comes after a defining moment regarding what love is in the hymn. When Ceres makes her angry plea to Jupiter for their daughter's return, she regards Dis' actions as unsanctioned theft, calling him a robber (*praedo*, 5.521) and the act a rape (*rapta*, 5.520). Jupiter responds to her accusations with a speech that generally recalls the sentiments of Helios in the *Homeric Hymn to Demeter*.[45] However, he does include an interpretive nuance of phraseology:

Calliope's Hymn

sed si modo nomina rebus
addere uera placet, non hoc iniuria factum,
uerum amor est;

(*Met.* 5.524–26)

[But if in this way it is pleasing to reckon with
the true names of things—this deed is no injury,
but truly, it is love.]

What is rape to Ceres is merely a *factum* to Jupiter. Moreover, it is a deed that is not an *iniuria*.[46] Jupiter's interest in ascribing "true names" (*nomina . . . uera*) to things casts him as an etymologist; the root word he arrives at is *amor*, emphasized by the repetition of *uerum*.[47] By this formulation, Jupiter essentially names *amor* as the equivalent of any act of *rapio*, acts that are sanctioned (not *iniuria*, but *iura*).[48] This is in loose accordance with Cupid's first act in the Ovidian corpus (*risisse Cupido / dicitur atque unum surripuisse pedem*, "Cupid, as it's said, laughed and snatched a foot away," *Am.* 1.1.3–4; *surripio*, sub + rapio).[49] Jupiter's attitude here also accords with his views in the parallel narration of Proserpina's rape in the *Fasti*: his speech is introduced with *Iuppiter hanc lenit factumque excusat amore* ("Jupiter soothed her and excused the deed as love," *Fast.* 4.597). If Jupiter in the *Metamorphoses* is concerned with "true names," in the *Fasti* he is concerned with aetiology (*excusat*, ex + causa). Each road, however, leads back to Amor/*amor*.

Jupiter's definition of *amor* has a number of repercussions for the world of Ovid's epic. First, it relieves Jupiter of divine responsibility. If we return to the first use of *rapio* in the epic to mean "rape," it appears in the narrative of Io (*cum deus inducta latas caligine terras / occuluit tenuitque fugam rapuitque pudorem*, "the god hid the broad earth by introducing a shroud of fog, halted her flight, and snatched away her chastity," 1.599–600). As discussed in the second chapter, Jupiter's love of Io appears as competition for the myth of "first love" in the epic, also lending it a touch of the programmatic. Jupiter's equation of *amor* with *rapina* (*raptum*) retrospectively exonerates his act as also occurring under the governance of the god; in his thinking, *rapuit* is equivalent to *amauit*.[50] We are further reminded of how *uis* plays a role in the identity of Iouis, and now, the role of Io herself in also defining his sense of divine self and order (Io + *uis*).[51] This reading not only lends a further aspect to the ongoing competition between Jupiter and Amor, but reminds the reader of the circumstances of the *Homeric Hymn to*

Aphrodite, where Zeus feels compelled to check Aphrodite's power. Even so, Zeus does not play a significant role within either *Homeric Hymn*, making the fact that Jupiter is granted this speech within Calliope's hymn significant. Jupiter's role in etymologizing love—in giving it a true name—reminds the reader that Ovid's Olympian power structure is not the same as the world of the *Homeric Hymns*, and Calliope's hymn traffics more directly in a praise of Venus than has been comfortably recognized. He admits to and excuses the sway of Amor in a manner that forces the reader to assess the narratives of erotic pursuit in the first pentad.

When it comes to Arethusa's narrative, the etymological understanding Jupiter implies by his use of *uera nomina* also gives us cause to think literarily about other linguistic relationships, and in particular, the relationship forged between *umor* and *amor*, and *amor* and *amoenus*. Arethusa's label of her newly transformed state (*amatas . . . aquas*, 5.636–37) hints at the Lucretian affiliation between *umor* and *amor* that informs the poet's polemical diatribe against love and its explorations within love poetry. Part of this polemic is formed by Lucretius lending love an imagistic and symbolic form reliant upon water, as opposed to flames.[52] Alpheus' "mingling" with Arethusa (*misceat*, 5.638; cf. her introduction as *Alpheias*, 5.487) achieves the desire of the lovers Lucretius mocks: a full merging of bodies (Lucr. *DRN* 4.1105–14).[53] The merging of selves that actualizes this desire also allows Arethusa's narrative to echo and refract the desires of both Salmacis and Narcissus, who find water an artistic medium that fuels their loves. The Lucretian overtones of the Narcissus episode are especially prominent and form a well-discussed focus of scholarship.[54] The water that nourishes the surrounding grass of Narcissus' pool (*umor alebat*, 3.411[55]) is the first instance we can observe Ovid directly playing upon the Lucretian equivalence of *umor/amor* in a way that further complicates the imagery of desire within his epic world: the reader now confronts in a newly direct way the competing strains of visualizing love as flame *or* moisture. Narcissus is aflame with love for his reflection, a possibility formed by the materiality of Lucretian love. A thirsting becomes a burning. This, in turn, revisits the second version of the Ovidian cosmogony, where all life is generated by the mixture of water and fire:

> quippe ubi temperiem sumpsere umorque calorque,
> concipiunt et ab his oriuntur cuncta duobus;

Calliope's Hymn 221

cumque sit ignis aquae pugnax, uapor umidus omnes
res creat et discors concordia fetibus apta est.

(*Met.* 1.430–33)

[When, as it happens, both moisture and heat assume
a proper mixture, they become conceptive, and all things arise
from these two things, and although fire may fight water,
heat and moisture generate all things, and this inharmonious
harmony is ripe for reproduction.]

As discussed in chapter 1, in one way, this conflict is symbolically translated into the series of myths where a god burns with love for a river nymph.[56] However, looking back upon the cosmogony from the vantage point of Arethusa's tale, which thematically and linguistically reincorporates not only the myths of erotic pursuit between god and nymph, but the myths of Narcissus and Salmacis, the paradox of *discors concordia* is resolved by love's simultaneous figural existence as both *umor* and *calor*, *ignis* and *aqua*. Within the first five books, these myths cohere to continually re-aetiologize *amor*; what love is, means, and does is reborn again and again, within these embodied, symbolic configurations of water and fire.

One objection to reading Arethusa's tale as a mythological commentary on Ovid's continual unfolding of love's identity within the first pentad—especially regarding Lucretian identities of *amor*—is the fact that *umor* is not used as part of her transformation. Rather than see this as a disqualifier, I would rather suggest the extreme wealth of watery vocabulary Arethusa employs serves instead to highlight the absence of *umor*. Throughout her myth, we see *aqua* ("water," 5.587, 595, 637), *gurges* ("whirlpool," 5.597), *unda* ("wave," 5.599, 638), *sudor* ("sweat," 5.632), *caeruleae . . . guttae* ("deep-blue drops," 5.633), *ros* ("dew," 5.635) and *latex* ("running water," 5.636).[57] Lucretius first begins to build an equivalence between *umor* and *amor* using *gutta* (*DRN* 4.1060), before his watery imagery progresses throughout an extended descriptive passage (*DRN* 4.1058–1140).[58] Love is a process of liquefaction (*liquescunt*, *DRN* 4.1114), and one marked by *sudor* (*DRN* 4.1128). Arethusa's transformation into the Lucretian material of love revisits some of its core, constituent vocabulary but also expands it, painting Alpheus and Arethusa as successful, anti-Lucretian lovers: Ovid marshals Lucretius' own semantic and symbolic system of love against the rationalizing poet. Arethusa's voice is therefore in further dialogue with the Lucretian overtones that open Calliope's hymn, and the use narratively made of the Lucretian hymn to Venus. Arethusa's story remythologizes Lucretian *amor* by a process of metamorphic literalization: it makes clear the use of water as a conduit for love within the epic.[59]

Arethusa's assessment of her new form as *amata aqua* also stands beside the identification of Alpheus as an *amnis*. Alpheus' existence as a river is also introduced by etymological play:

> lustrat caligine tectam
> amnis et ignarus <u>circum</u> caua nubila quaerit
> bisque locum, quo me dea texerat, inscius <u>ambit</u>
>
> (*Met.* 5.622–24)

> [The river runs his eyes over me, clouded in mist,
> and unaware, searches round the hollow hiding-cloud
> and unknowing, twice walks round the very place
> where the goddess had protectively hidden me.]

A river is a water-source that circles, as Varro says: *amnis id flumen quod circuit aliquod: nam ab ambitu amnis* ("a river, that is, a stream which circles something; for *amnis* comes from the act of going around," Varr. *Ling.* 5. 28.1–2).[60] Alpheus' act of circling the cloud-enveloped Arethusa linguistically defines and determines his identity as a river, a definition she cites again:

> sed enim cognoscit amatas
> amnis aquas positoque uiri, quod sumpserat, ore
> uertitur in proprias, ut se mihi misceat, undas.
>
> (*Met.* 5.636–38)

> [For the river at last recognized his beloved waters,
> and, dispensing with the human form that he had assumed,
> changes himself into his own constituent water,
> so as to mingle himself with me.]

The position of *amnis* between *amatas* and *aquas* could also hint at a shared etymology between *amnis* and *amor*. According to Isidore, an *amnis* is a river surrounded by forests and abundance of greenery, and therefore is so-called from its *amoenitas* ("pleasantness," 13.21.3). Isidore also derives *amoenus* from *amor*, upon Varronian authority: *amoena loca Varro dicta ait eo quod solum amorem praestant et ad se amanda adliciant* ("Varro says that pleasant places are those which offer forth only love, and entice to themselves things that ought to be loved," *Etym.* 14.8.33).[61] Arethusa's narrative of transformation therefore also seems to encode an understanding of the deliberate, complex uncanniness of the Ovidian landscapes by reaching toward both etymologies of *amnis*. She introduces her tale with the framing of *amor*, before detailing the *locus amoenus* she swims in, and then finally, her meeting with the *amnis* itself, a meeting that returns to *amor*. The ring-composition of love encircles the passage, just as a river does.

Arethusa's transformed state therefore pays symbolic homage to Amor in a variety of ways, and in ways that recapitulate one of the major narrative threads of emphasis throughout the first pentad: erotic pursuit within a *locus amoenus*. Alpheus' pursuit of Arethusa can be read as a metapoetic pursuit back through the pages of the epic, back to the tale of Apollo and Daphne that it most self-consciously echoes. In this capacity, Arethusa's poetic voice is also made akin to the Ovidian narrator himself, and not just Calliope's (or, as mentioned previously, the Virgilian narrator or the poet of the *Amores*).[62] And yet, within the form of Calliope's hymn, it is notable just how deeply Arethusa re-entrenches herself in both the pages of the epic and of the hymnic tradition. This re-entrenching is accomplished by the prayer she makes to Diana. Fatigued from being chased by Alpheus, she utters a prayer to Diana:

fessa labore fugae "fer opem, deprendimur" inquam,
"armigerae, Diana, tuae, cui saepe dedisti
ferre tuos arcus inclusaque tela pharetra."

(Met. 5.618–20)

[Beleaguered by the effort of my flight, I said,
"I am caught—bring help, Diana, to your
armouress, to whom so often you gave
your bow to carry, and your quiver, with its arrows
enclosed within."]

The vocabulary of Arethusa's prayer first embeds her further within Ovid's own epic by its recognizable echoes of Daphne's prayer to Peneus (*uicta labore fugae*, "overcome by the effort of her flight," 1.544; *fer, pater . . . opem*,

224   Calliope's Hymn

"bring help, father," 1.546). However, Arethusa's identification of herself as Diana's *armigera* also places her in the myth of Actaeon in Book 3: *nympharum tradidit uni / armigerae iaculum pharetramque arcusque retentos* ("she handed over to the armouress of the nymphs her spear and quiver and unstretched bow," 3.165–66). Arethusa's prayer provides a specific, text-based backstory to her relationship with Diana. However, her prayer also gives a quite specific description of the goddess' equipage: her bow (*arcus*) and quiver, with its arrows securely enclosed (*inclusaque tela pharetra*). The enclosure of the arrows is a detail that looks back to the equipping scene of the young Artemis in Callimachus' *Hymn*:

> "Κύκλωπες, κἠμοί τι Κυδώνιον εἰ δ' ἄγε τόξον
> ἠδ' ἰοὺς κοίλην τε κατακληῖδα βελέμνων
> τεύξατε·"

> (Callim. *Hymn* 3.81–83)

> ["Cyclopes, come and make ready for me
> a Cydonian bow and arrows and a
> capped quiver for my arrows."]

The use of κατακληῖς has occasioned some discussion about what kind of equipage is meant. In one interpretation, Artemis demands a quiver "fitted with a cap." The specific nature of this request has been explained as a Callimachean response to her Homeric epithet of "arrow-scatterer," and the Homeric vignette of Artemis' humiliating beating at the hands of Hera, which does result in the scattering of her arrows.[63] The Callimachean goddess, rather, will safeguard herself from the embarrassment of any recurrence (and so, abandon her identifying Homeric epithet), by a capped quiver. Adorjáni rejects this interpretation, reading the quiver itself substantively as the vessel that keeps the arrows securely inside, therefore excluding the need for further interpretative work.[64] However, Ovid's own adaptive vocabulary in Arethusa's depiction of Diana reflects on the Callimachean description. κατακληῖς stems from the verb κατακλείω ("to shut in, enclose"); the Latin translation of the verb is *includo*. The Ovidian phrase *inclusaque tela pharetra* can therefore stand as a translation of the Callimachean detail κοίλην τε κατακληῖδα βελέμνων. And it is further important to note that *inclusa* would only accurately describe a quiver in which the

Calliope's Hymn 225

arrows were unable to escape; in other words, one with a cap. Arethusa's description therefore showcases a special knowledge that further reflects upon her self-identification as Diana's *armigera*: she displays knowledge of the moment Artemis is equipped in Callimachus' hymn. With this detail of the goddess' capped quiver, and her role of *armigera*, Ovid's Arethusa embeds herself within the hymnic tradition of praising Diana, as well as its reception within the Ovidian epic, in Actaeon's myth. As the final "embedded voice" within Calliope's hymn, this self-quotation of her prayer reiterates the importance of the hymnic voice, form, and content for comprehending the poetic mechanisms of this episode—an episode designed to touch anew on the narrative and thematic pressure points of the first five books.

POLYHYMNIA, THE NARRATING MUSE

The complexities of Arethusa's poetic voice suit her internal role as a Muse. However, it is exactly the proliferation of hymnic voices and hymnic indebtedness that start to crystallize around an absence of information: the *identity* of the narrating Muse. Arethusa's role as a Muse is reinforced by the *memini* that deliberately punctuates her account (5.585); the first-person use of the verb aligns her with the daughters of Memory (*Mnemonidas*, 5.268; *Mnemonides*, 5.280).[65] Of the company of Muses, there is one Muse who can be further etymologically tied to memory: Polyhymnia (or Polymnia), whose name can reflect πολυμνήμων ("remembering many things"), as well as the standard πολύυμνος (either "much sung of," or "with many hymns").[66] "Much remembering" is also one interpretation of the epithet μολυμνήστη, used by Empedocles to hymnically address his Muse: μολυμνήστη λευκώλενε παρθένε Μοῦσα ("much-remembering, white-armed, maiden Muse," B3.3).[67] Hardie argues that there "is general support for the blending of a named Muse, here Kalliopeia, with allusion to another Muse-name, here Polymnia, in the standard lyric practice of co-locating Muse-names and Muse-name allusions in order to create multifaceted musical effects and coloring."[68] Within the Ovidian narrative, the contest song can be inarguably labeled the "hymn of Calliope," but it is *renarrated* by an unnamed Muse. The other Muse named within the narrative is Urania, who describes the origins of the Hippocrene to Minerva (*excipit Vranie*, "Urania explains," 5.260). Ourania and Calliope also narrate different reasons for May's name in *Fasti* 5. In each case, the introduction of the Muse's song can be readily cross-referenced with their respective introductions in *Metamorphoses* 5. *excipit*

Vranie appears in both narratives (cf. *Fast.* 5.55), while both portraits of Calliope preserve the details of her ivy-garlanded hair and status as the premier singer: *tunc sic neglectos hedera redimita capillos / prima sui coepit Calliopea chori* ("then Calliope, preeminent in our choir, thus began, her carelessly dressed locks bound with ivy," *Fast.* 5.79–80); *dedimus summam certaminis uni. / surgit et immissos hedera collecta capillos / Calliope* ("we dedicated the greatest one of us to the contest, and Calliope rose, her flyaway hair bound with ivy," *Met.* 5.337–39).

To stay momentarily with this portion of the *Fasti*, we can see that the first account of May's name belongs to a third named Muse. After the dissent (!) of the Muses is registered (*dissensere deae*, "the goddesses disagreed," *Fast.* 5.9), Polyhymnia steps forth to explain the month's origins to the poet: *quarum Polyhymnia coepit / prima* ("the first of whom, Polyhymnia, thus began," *Fast.* 5.9–10). Her narrative includes both a cosmogony and a Gigantomachy (*Fast.* 5.11–52). As Barchiesi notes of Polyhymnia's strongly Hesiodic narrative, Polyhymnia does not just provide the puzzled poet with an answer about the month's name: she sings a hymn. Barchiesi attributes the rare Latinate appearance of Themis within this hymn to Polyhymnia's desire to recall one of the genre's archetypes: Pindar's *Hymn to Zeus*.[69] The overlap between the hymnic material of the Pierides and Polyhymnia in *Fasti* 5 should not be read as an embarrassment of Ovidian narrative consistency or Muse authority, but as a conscious interpretive strategy. Integrating the information from *Fasti* 5, where Polyhymnia appears in charge of "original" hymnic material, alongside Urania and Calliope, it seems that Ovid is signaling the identity of the unnamed Muse: these literary cues suggest that Polyhymnia renarrates Calliope's hymn to Minerva.

The etymological valences of her name and affiliated epithets are attuned to this interpretation.[70] Firstly, the one who is "much sung of" reinforces the collective role of the Muses as they appear in Hesiod's *Theogony* (ὑμνεῦσαι, 11; ὑμνεῦσαι, 37; ὑμνεῦσι, 48; ὑμνεῦσαι, 51); she is therefore fitting to introduce the Muses within the space of Ovid's own epic. As one "with many hymns," she performs Calliope's hymn with a greater attunement to its genre, and further validates the proliferation of hymnic voices and strands of the hymnic tradition that cohere within the song. When her name recalls "remembering many things," it is apt for her role here as a hymnic re-performer, speaking to both her genre of hymn and the prodigious memory relied upon to reperform its lengthy content. While Calliope and Polymnia are suggestively paired in Empedocles, Ourania and Polyhymnia are paired in the *Symposium* as the sources of heavenly versus earthly love (Pl. *Symp.* 187d–e). With a view to the permutations of these suggestive pairings within a suite of significant texts, there is a reason to fill in the identity of Ovid's unnamed Muse as Polyhymnia, alongside the named Urania and Calliope. If we supply this identity to the Muse who relates to Minerva the story of Pyreneus and the contest with the Pierides, there is a greater sense of coherence given to this episode: her relationship with the hymnic genre crystallizes Ovid's narrative strategy in using hymnic knowledge to contextualize the episode's frame, knitting together the external framing of Minerva's visit to Helicon and the internal material of the contest hymns. Polyhymnia's identity becomes a reading strategy not only for this discrete episode, but also for understanding Ovid's divine personalities as explored in the first pentad.

CONCLUSION

This reading of Calliope's hymn reevaluates the narrative dynamics that strategically underpin Ovid's presentation of Venus, Ceres, and the Muses. Instead of simply focusing on Venus' weaponization of sexuality as a narratively shaping force, I have first built a context for seeing how Ceres and Venus share competitive space within the hymnic tradition, from their treatment in the *Homeric Hymns* to the hymnic invocations and narratives of *Fasti* 4. A Venus hungry for her allocation of both literal territory and metaliterary hymnic praise informs our perspective on the relationship between Venus and the Muses, specifically Calliope: an overlooked element of Calliope's hymn is the traditional modality of expressive overlap between Venus and Calliope herself that brings to light the ways in which the hymn shows the Muses reacting to the power of Venus and Love. Venus' relationship with Calliope is additionally used to highlight a figure within the hymn who echoes the role of the Muse: Arethusa. Investigating Arethusa's narrative affords us an expansive window into the structural subtleties of Ovidian epic. First, it allows us to perceive additional complexities of narrative reflexivity and parallelism as detailed in the previous chapter, but it also reveals how Arethusa, in her role as a Muse, presides over a metapoetic review of the first pentad, partially achieved by the way she redetermines the definitions of love for the epic. Finally, after narrowing the focus to analyze Arethusa as an internal Muse within Calliope's hymn, the discussion widens once more to the narrative frame, as I make a case for reading Polyhymnia as the Muse who renarrates Calliope's hymn to Minerva. It is when we see Polyhymnia, the voice of many hymns, as the party responsible for communicating this metapoetic review of the first pentad, that the importance of the hymnic tradition is truly crystallized as a sustained poetic influence.

Conclusion

Amor's Winged Words

As a general overview, this work raises the profile of the hymnic tradition as a significant literary influence upon the first five books of the *Metamorphoses*. More specifically, it has shown how the Callimachean hymn collection provides a suite of sustained inspiration for Ovid's narrative dynamism, in terms of poetic voice, structure, and characterization. At heart, Ovid's epic reception of the Callimachean hymns has also provided an opportunity to construct new hymnic lineages of influence, as Ovid actively "receives" Roman hymnic material that relies on the Callimachean collection and subsequently layers it into his poetic matrix. This is most evident from chapters 3 and 4, where Augustan hymnic material (notably, Horace's *Carmen Saeculare* and Grattius' *Cynegetica*) is read as mediating between the Ovidian and Callimachean texts. The close readings performed in these chapters are meant to provide sufficient and compelling evidence of both the literary filiation between Ovidian epic and hymns and the artistic relationship between Ovid and Callimachus, in ways innovative and original. They do so for two purposes: First (and simply), by enlightening readers further about the poetic nature and nuance of Ovid's epic, and its derivation from a set of sources if not unsung, at least undersung. Second, to reinforce a dimension of purely Callimachean interpretive significance: namely, that the set of six Callimachean *Hymns* were a poetic collection of intentional design, ordered and edited to be experienced together. I have taken especial care that the Ovid of these pages emerges as both a writer and a reader—a reader especially sensitive to the learned cleverness of the mutually implicated divine identities explored by the Callimachean hymnic collection. Ovid's

229

learnedly subversive manipulation of this body of work confirms its existence as a poetic collection. Although this is a conceit that runs throughout this work, it is most clearly evident in the third chapter, which details Ovid's literary rejoinder to reading the *Hymn to Delos* as a metapoetic recapitulation of *Hymns* 1–3, and the fifth chapter, which draws upon Ovid's receptive acknowledgment of *Hymns* 5 and 6 as experimenting with the embedded genres of tragedy and comedy. Overall, when we bind more closely the enterprises of Ovidian epic and Callimachean hymning, as this book has done, we can see more clearly the mutual seams of poetic allegiance: Ovid becomes not only a conscientious and competitive reader of the Callimachean hymnic collection but a poetic collaborator and colluder in promoting the Callimachean aesthetic, yet for epic purposes.

When looked at as a whole, the internal set of chapters 2–5 are more narrowly trained upon not only reinvigorating Callimachus' *Hymns* as texts of interest to Ovid but also reassessing the span and modes of their influence. Largely, as regards the *Metamorphoses*, Callimachus has stood as a learned source of mythological material, as opposed to providing a more comprehensive set of structural, narratological, and allusive influence. The contribution of these chapters, on the most general level, is to reveal a richer and more complex relationship than seeing Callimachus as mere mythological handbook or necessary source of allusion to confirm (or flaunt) one's Alexandrian bona fides. The more specific scholarly contributions come in how these complexities are revealed. Like the hymn collection itself, these chapters work progressively through a set of divine relationships and identities. The second chapter focuses on Ovid's imaginative rewriting of the Arcadian landscape of the *Hymn to Zeus* within Book 1 and 2 as he reallocates its symbolic embodiment of praise to the Thessalian landscape, a shift that forms a commentary on both the nature of praise and the epic enterprise of praising Jupiter within the Augustan historical landscape. Callimachus' hymn is the interpretive key for the geographical displacement Ovid performs, which reveals how Ovid uses the idea of territory to stage competitive conflicts of divine identity. The work of this chapter is in locating the rivalrous relationship between Jupiter and Apollo, in a literal and metaliterary way, and tracing the meaning and repercussions of praise both within the epic and for Ovid himself. The third chapter shifts to the expressive rivalry between Apollo and Diana, which I argue is a behavioral dynamic inherited from the Callimachean gods, repurposed by Ovid in knowing contrast to the newly Augustan hymnic portraits of the Delians predicated on harmony and balance. Seeing how Callimachus has first created this rivalrous dynamic that Ovid exploits by closely readings of the pair of hymns dedicated to Apollo and Artemis builds the foundation for a new argument—that the nymph Daphne, in her textually hybrid iteration as a neo-Callimachean hymnic figure, is designed as a literary mechanism to explore this rivalry. The fourth chapter stays with Diana by investigating her divine identity as displayed in the myth of Actaeon, and challenges the scholarly tradition by rereading the emphatic Callimachean influence as not the *Bath of Pallas*, but the *Hymn to Artemis*. When we view Ovid's Actaeon myth as a supplement to the *Hymn*, this opens a new window for interpretive possibility, and one further enriched by placing Grattius as a textual intermediary. The pair of *Hymns* 5 and 6, the *Bath of Pallas* and *Hymn to Demeter*, become the focus of the fifth chapter, and the critical roles they play in staging the contest between the Muses and Pierides in Book 5 as a civil war. The *Bath of Pallas* is supplied as a reading strategy for the context and framing of the contest, while the *Hymn to Demeter* is read as an unacknowledged inspiration for the Pierides' song. Ultimately, the Callimachean aesthetic explored and experimented with in the sixth *Hymn* permits Ovid to cast his Pierides as anti-Callimachean Muses, in a fashion that further emphasizes the different interpretive strata to this contest match-up (allegorical, historical, polemical).

From this brief rehearsal of content, it is easy to see that this internal run of chapters covers the span of the Callimachean hymnic collection, from Zeus to Demeter. The opening and closing chapters are dedicated to more diffuse treatments of the hymnic tradition and the hymnic form, and to a more panoramic purpose of using these hymnic texts to illuminate the nature of Ovidian epic. Through examining the interconnected natures of praise, love, and love of praise, we can more fully parse what motivates and sets apart the hexameter work of this committed elegist. The first chapter looks to the relationship between Jupiter and Amor to tackle the question of narrative control in this epic, uncovering how Ovid presses into service the cyclical exchange of primacy and power between Zeus and Eros pioneered by the hymnic tradition as he begins to establish the world of his epic. Analyzing the connection between cosmogony or cosmogonical material and hymns lends a new perspective on this question, as Ovid's symbolic allegiances to traditional epic power or personal elegiac force are disentangled from their purposefully ambiguous presentations. The issue of cosmic control introduces the concepts of rivalry and territory that underpin the entirety of this work in their largest, most expansive instantiations. The final chapter returns to this origin point through its discussion of Venus in Calliope's hymn, and the ways we see love redefined at the moment the first five books are being metapoetically repackaged in narratologically complex ways. The hymn of Calliope models anew, and on a smaller scale, the issues of cosmic control introduced in the first chapter and there enlightened by the application of hymnic awareness. These strands of influence cohere with the ending suggestion that it is the Muse Polyhymnia who is responsible for narrating Calliope's hymn. As the voice of many hymns, Polyhymnia subtly emblematizes the significance of the hymnic tradition to Ovidian narrative and the position it occupies.

Rather than belabor each point of Ovidian indebtedness to the hymnic tradition, in the spirit of Ovidian resistance to closure, we can spend a brief time dedicated to broadening the scope to both think about the rest of Ovid's epic, and the epic tradition at large. This may seem antithetical to creating an endpoint, but it is entirely within the space of appropriate Ovidian homage, as the Ovidian corpus directly communicates. The *Remedia* unpicks the work of the *Ars*, the *Tristia* threatens to take away the finality of the *Metamorphoses*, and there are certain myths that become zones of obsessive reworking and repackaging throughout his poetic oeuvre: Daedalus, Medea, Ariadne.[1] However, the *Metamorphoses* retains one singular feature within Ovid's wider body of work: its hexametric form. As an epic, the *Metamorphoses* is traditionally positioned to traffic within the currents of praise, love, and love of praise, amid the seam of contact between *kleos* and *eros* that first signaled what a renovation of what epic can do, from Homer to Apollonius. These twinned forces motivated the beginning of the Latin epic tradition whose lineage Ovid is most immediately responding to: Lucretius' *De rerum natura*, and its successor, the *Aeneid*.

> Nunc age, quod superest cognosce et clarius audi.
> nec me animi fallit quam sint obscura, sed acri
> percussit thyrso laudis spes magna meum cor
> et simul incussit suauem mi in pectus amorem
> Musarum. quo nunc instinctus mente uigenti
> auia Pieridum peragro loca nullius ante
> trita solo.

> (Lucr. *DRN* 1.921–27)

Conclusion

233

[Now come—learn and hear more clearly what remains.
Nor does my mind deceive me how mysterious these things are,
but a great hope for praise has struck my heart with a goad keenly felt
and at the same time, breathed into my breast the Muses' sweet love,
so thusly guided with flourishing mind, I traverse the Pierides' pathless
haunts, ground never encountered before.]

Lucretius' epic is owed to a hope for praise, and a love for and of the Muses;
an epic that opens with the hymn to Venus and progresses under the joint
auspice of Venus and Calliope.[2] The Romans, the race of Venus, are subse-
quently emblematized by Brutus in Virgil's underworld as those whose "love
of country will conquer, and the boundless desire for praise" (*uincet amor
patriae laudumque immensa cupido, Aen.* 6.823). This characterization is
soon echoed by the motivations of Iulus himself, the apple of Venus' eye (cf.
Veneris iustissima cura, Aen. 10.132), as he unwittingly plunges Italy into war
(*eximiae laudis succensus amore, Aen.* 7.496). The contact points between
love and praise make configurations of epic motivation, both internal and
external, native to this Latin tradition. Ovid's epic plays with these conceits
in different proportion, turning his mind to bringing these hexameters into
line with the rest of his elegiac corpus: how can epic be in praise of love?
This question leads to tracing the competition between the powers of might
and love, as was explored here in the first pentad, but it runs throughout the
poem's entirety. The subtle channeling of praise continues to form a map of
poetic subversiveness beyond the first pentad.

Ovid gives his reader no time to rest from considering these questions
about the allocation of praise and power when he opens the second pentad
with the episode of Arachne and Minerva. The artistic themes pitted against
each other on the opposing tapestries are the rivalry of Minerva and Posei-
don over Athens and transformations wrought by love. Arachne, who weaves
in a fashion reminiscent of the divine maker (*magni speciem glomerauit in
orbis*, 1.35; *rudem primos lanam glomerabat in orbes*, 6.19), weaves the stories
of the gods shape-shifting under the sway of love (6.103–28).[3] Minerva weaves
the story of the *antiqua lis* (6.71) over Athens, a moment of divine rivalry
and nomenclatural importance that equally has thematic relevance for the
Metamorphoses, as the first five books showed. The use of *lis* to describe this
event, however, also ties Minerva to the divine creator, who settled the dis-
pute of the elements (*hanc deus et melior litem natura diremit*, 1.21). *Lis* is

used in only these two places in the epic. The programmatic verb *deducitur* (6.69) similarly brings us back to the proem, as the epic renews its aesthetic commitments upon the point of broaching a new unit of narrative territory.[4] Although more focus trends toward seeing the differences in the tapestries, there is also a way to read the tapestries, reminiscent of the proem and cosmogony, as reinaugurating the rivalry between the Olympian hierarchy headed by Jupiter and the sovereignty of Amor once again—and once again, at the outset, leaving the clear winner ambiguous. The cyclic exchange of primacy between Jupiter and Amor first structured within the hymnic tradition is adopted by Ovid as a clear thread of consequence to be yet untangled anew at strategic points within the epic narrative. Here is simply one instance of a pattern this study examined that can be fruitfully followed throughout the rest of the poem.

Similarly, Calliope's song as a metapoetic replay or encapsulation of the first pentad is a framework that can be applied to the song of Orpheus in Book 10. Calliope's son inherits the narrative reins from his Muse mother to further explore the tensions between Jupiter and Love with his own hymnic rendition, which similarly excises ambiguity to confirm the mastery of love's powers:

> "Ab Ioue, Musa parens, (cedunt Iovis omnia regno),
> carmina nostra moue. Iouis est mihi saepe potestas
> dicta prius; cecini plectro grauiore Gigantas
> sparsaque Phlegraeis uictricia fulmina campis.
> nunc opus est leuiore lyra; puerosque canamus
> dilectos superis inconcessisque puellas
> ignibus attonitas meruisse libidine poenam."

(Met. 10.148–54)

> ["From Jove, my mother Muse, move my song—
> all things bow to Jove's reign—
> Often before, it was my prerogative to sing of Jove:
> I have sung the Giants victoriously bolted down,
> across the Phlegraean fields, with heavy-handed strains;
> now, the work calls for lighter refrains, so let me sing
> the lads beloved by gods, the girls besotted
> with forbidden fires, with penalty-worthy lust."]

Conclusion 235

Orpheus' song feints briefly in the direction of a hymn to Jupiter, in the vein of Aratus (ἐκ Διὸς ἀρχώμεσθα, "let us begin from Zeus," *Phaen.* 1.1) before leaving behind Jupiter's Olympian-clinching victory and turning to love.[5] The first installment of his hymn, of Jupiter's love for Ganymede (10.155–61), looks back to an embedded narrative Aphrodite tells Anchises in the *Homeric Hymn to Aphrodite* (202–17), before it turns to Apollo's love for Hyacinthus (10.162–219). This narrative sequence of love also recalls the question of primacy between Jupiter and Apollo in the first pentad, staged over the "first loves" Daphne and Io. However, the myth of Venus and Adonis Orpheus sings also spells a resurfacing of Diana's hymnic disguise and the conflict between love and maidenhood, as Venus not only imitates the lifestyle and pursuits of the huntress (cf. 10.533–36), but tells her own myth of Atalanta, a figure intimately connected to Diana. Orpheus' hymn therefore also recapitulates a number of narrative patterns that bear interpretive significance for the first pentad, and that continue to signal and accrue meaning as the epic progresses. Just like everything in Ovid's epic, the sense of hymnic rivalry also metamorphoses throughout its unfolding.

When Ovid's epic finally comes to a close, he claims that "nevertheless, I will be borne, everlasting, the better part of me, above the high stars" (*parte tamen meliore mei super alta perennis / astra ferar*, 15.875–76). Ovid's enduring *melior pars* begs to be read in dialogue with his demiurge, the *deus et melior . . . natura*.[6] His last lines have also been read in response to Ennius' so-called epitaph, ending with *uolito uiuus per ora uirum* ("I fly about, living, on the mouths of men"). Ovid's lasting image is one of taking flight, as Ennius' *uolito* can be found in the *pennis* ("feathers") of *perennis*, alongside the well-known pun on Ennius/*perennis*. At the very end of his epic, then, Ovid takes flight with the wings of his ultimate creative demiurge: at the outset of Ovid's elegiac career, Cupid may have stolen a foot away, but at the close of his epic effort, he has granted his poet wings.

NOTES

INTRODUCTION

1. Called aptly by Barchiesi (1999, 113) "the shortest divine invocation in world literature." For a detailed reading of the proem, see Heath (2011–12, esp. 193–94 and 200–201) for the role of the divine and hymnic relevance. Klein (2022) is the newest treatment of the proem, updating its Callimachean indebtedness via the Latin tradition, and giving the phrase *fert animus* equal billing to *carmen perpetuum*. All Latin text is from Tarrant (2004); all translations of the *Metamorphoses* are my own.

2. On the *Homeric Hymns* as guides to understanding the Olympian world order, the work of Clay (1989) is foundational.

3. The specific definitions and uses of ὕμνος ("hymn") are myriad. I use "hymn" not to mean a song of any sort, but a song that honors a god, or occasionally more generally, as a song of praise. Although discussions of the ambiguity and finer distinctions of its meaning are correspondingly myriad, the introduction of Furley and Bremer (2001, esp. 1–8) and Bulloch (2010) provide useful points of entry, as well as Furley (1995) on the function and features of hymns. See also the introduction of Stephens (2015, 9–12).

4. Garth Tissol's 1997 chapter on the *Metamorphoses* and the *Hymn to Artemis*, "Disruptive Traditions: Indecorous Possibilities: Callimachus' *Hymn to Artemis* and Ovidian Style" (131–66), embraces and explores this notion of a poetic kindred spirit. Tissol presents *Hymn* 3 as a comparative case study on a stylistic basis: he details the mechanisms by which Callimachus enacts his fondness for narrative misdirection and thwarting the expectations of his audience, and how these mechanisms can inform our understanding of the Ovidian narrator of the *Metamorphoses*. However, it is not a reading based on intertextual affiliation, only stylistic affinities, leaving open the avenues of discussion provided by chapters 3 and 4.

5. Interest in the individual Callimachean hymns is reflected in a proportionately large bibliographical record; this is less true of the commentary tradition. Individual

238   Notes to Pages 6–7

commentaries include Zeus: McLennan (1977); Apollo: Williams (1978); Artemis: Bornmann (1968) and Adorjáni (2021); Delos: Mineur (1984) and Gigante Lanzara (1990); Bath of Pallas: McKay (1962b) and Bulloch (1985); Demeter: McKay (1962a) and Hopkinson (1984b). For a modern critical edition of all six hymns, see Stephens (2015). Cf. also the monographs of Giuseppetti (2013) and Ukleja (2005) devoted to *Delos*. In some of these singular treatments, space of varying degrees is dedicated to the organization of the collection: mostly, this discussion is for the purpose of situating the hymn under specific focus. Vamvouri Ruffy (2004) is one full-length treatment. Ukleja's (2005) monograph on the *Hymn to Delos* grants the most attention to the collection's wider structural concerns. Petrovic (2007, 114–81) includes a chapter contextualizing the *Hymns* overall before moving to a specific focus on the *Hymn to Artemis*. Ambühl (2005, 99–362) also contains a more concerted analysis of more than one hymn. With attention to the collection, see Haslam (1993, 111–25); Stephens (2015, 12–14); and Depew (2004, 117n8), who promises a forthcoming study on the organizational principles in evidence; Harder (1992) also provides one briefer synoptic discussion. Hunter and Fuhrer (2002, 164n54) also discuss the first four hymns together, although not necessarily as a collection; tellingly, they note "it is worth pondering how the *Hymns* to Athena and *Demeter* are different from the rest in many more ways than just dialect."

6. Harder (2012, 1:2–8) reviews the evidence.

7. Cf. Stephens (2003, 75n3) for others on this belief in a self-edited collection.

8. I rely here on his introductory material (Brumbaugh 2019, 11–14) for situating the *Hymns* within the evidence provided by manuscripts, papyri, and relevant scholarship on the Callimachean editorial enterprise.

9. Again, see Klein (2022).

10. For overviews on Ovid and Callimachus, see Acosta-Hughes (2009) and Acosta-Hughes and Stephens (2012, 257–69).

11. Heather Van Tress' 2004 monograph *Poetic Memory: Allusion in the Poetry of Callimachus and the Metamorphoses of Ovid* is presently the most substantial work fully dedicated to Callimachus and the *Metamorphoses*. Three of her four body chapters attend to individual hymns: her third chapter is devoted to Book 3, Actaeon, and the *Bath of Pallas*; her fourth, to the *Hymn to Delos* and *Metamorphoses* 6, and her fifth, to Erysichthon in Book 8 and the *Hymn to Demeter*. Her analysis is structured by emphasis on individual books of the *Metamorphoses* (3, 6, and 8) and the individual hymns that serve as their respective sources (*Hymns* 5, 4, and 6).

12. As in Otis (1966, 134 and 367–70); cf. also the commentaries of Bömer, Anderson, and Barchiesi and Rosati ad loc. Van Tress (2004, 72–110), is the most comprehensive treatment.

13. Beyond commentary notices, see most recently Van Tress (2004, 160–90) and Murray (2004).

14. Van Tress (2004, 111–59).

Notes to Pages 7–10

15. A valuable exception is Wills (1990), who uncovers combined allusions to *Hymns* 2, 3, and 4 (*Apollo, Artemis,* and *Delos*) within Ovid's programmatic elegiac myth; his discussion provides the foundation for chapter 3.

16. Scholarship on especially the *Metamorphoses* has burgeoned since 2000. These studies follow in due course from the platform built by Otis (1966); Due (1974); Galinsky (1975); Knox (1986); Solodow (1988); and Schmidt (1991). For an introduction to the *Metamorphoses,* see Fantham (2004); full-length studies on the *Metamorphoses* on a variety of themes include Myers (1994), Tissol (1997), Wheeler (1999; 2000), Hardie (2002b), Salzman-Mitchell (2005), Holzberg (2007), Johnson (2008), Pavlock (2009), Feldherr (2010), Von Glinski (2012), Curley (2013), Ziogas (2013a), and Boyd (2017). Barchiesi (2001) provides valuable overall insight into Ovidian poetics. Collected volumes on the *Metamorphoses* include Hardie, Barchiesi, and Hinds (1999) and Fulkerson and Stover (2016). Companion volumes include Boyd (2002), Hardie (2002a), and Knox (2006; 2009). Myers (1999) and Schmitzer (2002) summarize trends in Ovidian scholarship.

17. To this effect we can note the three chapters in a collected 2016 volume on the reception of the *Homeric Hymns* devoted to Ovid: John Miller's "Ovid's Bacchic Helmsman and *Homeric Hymn 7,*" Alison Keith's "The *Homeric Hymn to Aphrodite* in Ovid and Augustan Literature," and Jason Nethercut's "Hercules and Apollo in Ovid's *Metamorphoses.*" Further evidence of the trend is adduced by Micah Myers' (2019) chapter "Lascivus Puer: Cupid, Hermes, and Hymns in Ovid's *Metamorphoses.*" The "hymn" to Bacchus that opens Book 4 has also attracted the attention of commentators and scholars alike; see especially Danielewicz (1990) and Jouteur (2001, 173–77). This focus, coupled with the lack of a Callimachean hymn to Dionysus, was reason enough to omit Bacchus from my present discussion. See also Damen and Richards (2012) for a reading of the *Bacchae* itself as a dramatic hymn.

18. Barchiesi (1999). This also provides the starting point for Syed (2004), with an investigation into hymnic material that focuses primarily on *Metamorphoses* 1; although she builds on Barchiesi's work by supplementing Homeric material with Callimachean references, this still did little to make the hymnic tradition a point of prolonged interest for Ovidian scholars.

19. Barchiesi (2002b) identifies the *Carmen Saeculare* as precisely this sort of composition, further dubbing it a "neo-Pindaric paean."

20. See Miller (2014).

21. The "proem theory" pioneered by F. A. Wolf (1795); see the volume of Grafton, Most, and Zetzel (1985).

22. Faraone (2021, 51–79).

23. Papaioannou (2007) and Von Glinski (2018) focus specifically on Ovidian reworkings of the Epic Cycle.

24. On how this issue affects narrative voices, see most recently Fitzgerald (2018).

25. On these hymnic features, see Harden and Kelly (2013, 16–29).

26. On the potential threat Apollo poses to Zeus, see Felson (2011, 275–83).

240   Notes to Pages 10–16

27. As established by Race (1982).

28. A close model for this work as a focused, text-based study of the *Metamorpho-ses* is Alison Keith's (1992) monograph *The Play of Fictions: Studies in Ovid's "Meta-morphoses" Book 2*, which similarly restricts discussion to one portion of the epic and rests on detailed close readings.

29. I am here differentiating intertextuality and allusion in recognition of the work of Hinds (1998). More specifically, I might state an especial subscribing to the under-standing of Ovidian intertextuality as pioneered by the Pisa and Cambridge schools. On this note, I believe that poetic allusion as a category of literary interaction has a fundamental plasticity: this belief means that I am not articulating any distinct theo-retical or methodological schemas for allusion to shape (or limit) my readings. Turn-ing to narratology, my curiosity (along with many previous scholars) lies with Ovid's internal narrators and internally expressed voices; cf. especially Barchiesi (1989, 2002b).

30. I am also largely engaging with the body of hymns considered to be committed to more literary purposes, viz. the Homeric and Callimachean (and subsequent texts dependent on these works); these are the hymns omitted by Furley and Bremer (2001), because they are not "cult songs proper" (ix).

31. Similarly, political readings of the *Hymns* as evidence for the Ptolemaic court is beyond the scope of my study.

32. Parry (1964); Segal (1969); Hinds (2002).

33. Cf. esp. Richlin (1992) and Sharrock (2002).

34. Using the term "geopoetics" allows for more precision than "landscape," cf. Italiano (2008). Barchiesi first popularly introduced this conceptual thinking to clas-sical literature in his lectures on "Virgilian Geopoetics"; cf. Barchiesi (2017, 152) for print use and discussion. Asper (2011) uses geopoetics as a framework for interpreting Callimachus, also in a pointedly political way; geopolitics and geopoetics are related but ultimately separable concepts.

Chapter 1. Amorphous Control?

1. Although a difference between the Ovidian Amor and Cupid can be made (e.g., Park [2009]), throughout this chapter I will refer to them interchangeably as agents of love, and so allied and united in the purpose they serve.

2. Throughout, I have underlined the key words in the original that my analysis centers upon.

3. O'Hara (2004–5; 2007, 105–8). For the use of *adnue* and *incepta*, cf. Ov. *Am.* 3.2.56, a prayer to Venus. Heath (2011–12) provides a detailed examination of the proem. Unless otherwise stated, all translations are my own.

4. Virgil moves to an invocation of the collective *di* at *Georg.* 1.13; cf. also Hor. *CS* 45–46, where he twice invokes *di* after the beginning address to Apollo and Diana.

5. Heath (2011–12, 200) reads the unelaborated *di* of the proem as akin to the unnamed creator. Hanses (2020, 130–33), identifying the acrostic *deus* at *Met.* 1.29–32, suggests Apollo or Cupid as the demiurge's identity.

Notes to Pages 16–22

6. This rivalry continues the competition Ovid previously sets up within his love poetry, pitting the epic god of the thunderbolt against the elegiac, arrow-wielding Cupid.

7. McKim (1984–85) provides one reading of the tension between myth and philosophy in Ovid's cosmogony; cf. also Wheeler (1995) for reclaiming the poetics of Ovid's cosmogony from strictly philosophical influence.

8. On Stoic readings of this figure, see Robbins (1913); Bömer ad 1.9. Cleanthes' *Hymn to Zeus* is one literary testament of the god's Stoic representation. On Zeus' role and limitations within Stoicism, see, e.g., Bénatouïl (2009); cf. also Algra (2009) for the relationship between Stoicism and Greco-Roman religion. Meijer (2007) collects the Stoic proofs for the existence of the cosmic god.

9. Kelly (2021, 742; 2022, 209).

10. On Cicero's *Timaeus*, see Hoenig (2018, 38–101). On the differences between the terms, we might think of the distinctions between a carpenter and a joiner.

11. On this formulation, see Ferrari (2006; 2014).

12. See Pender (2007, 21–36; 2010). For other readings of the Hesiodic influence and significance for the *Timaeus*, see Sedley (2010) and Regali (2010).

13. On Plato's demiurge as Zeus, see O'Meara (2012).

14. Textual loci of interest include Pl. *Leg.* 715e–716a and the speech of Aristophanes in the *Symposium*; see Santamaría (2016).

15. Protogonos is a feature of the Hieronyman Theogony and the Orphic Rhapsodies. West (1983) theorizes that the Derveni papyrus is an abbreviated version of a longer poem that he terms the "Protogonos Theogony" (cf. 69); more recently on this theory, see Meisner (2018, 36–39, 92–93).

16. Cf. Boys-Stones (1998, 170n8) for bibliography.

17. See Calame (1999, 178–81). For an overview of the philosophical sources of Eros as unifying principle, see also Clarke (1974, 63–65). On Eros in Acusilaus, see the commentary of Andolfi (2019 ad fr. 6, pp. 45–52).

18. Santamaría (2016, 219–20).

19. *OF* 243B; cf. also the partial quotation in the Derveni papyrus, *OF* 14.2B= *DP* 17.12.

20. Meisner (2018).

21. The duality of ποιητής is further enhanced by the different meanings of κόσμος ("ornamentation," but also "cosmos/universe").

22. Cf. Scully (2015, 113–15).

23. Ford (2019, 26). On the sympotic framing of the hymn, see also Caneva (2010, 297–99).

24. All text of the Callimachean *Hymns* is Stephens (2015).

25. Trans. Stephens.

26. See Cuypers (2004, 97).

27. Cuypers (2004, 98); cf. also Brumbaugh (2019, 98–99).

28. Cuypers (2004, 100).

242   Notes to Pages 22–27

29. See Stephens (2003, 80–82) for the ways Eros' divinity can illuminate Zeus', in the context of the Callimachean hymn and its intertexts. On how this quotation affects the reader's sense of hymnic authority, see Lüddecke (1998, 14–15). Callimachus also aligns his Zeus with a different primordial principle, as will be discussed in chapter 2.

30. The idea of strife can also hardly fail to bring up Empedocles' Neikos; the Empedoclean notes of the Ovidian cosmogony, while relevant, are beyond the scope of this discussion.

31. On Ovidian *lis* and Hesiodic *eris*, see Ham (2018, 285–93).

32. *Mutatur* (1.409) describes part of the creation of humans, while Daphne's prayer includes the directive *mutando perde figuram* ("destroy my form by transforming," 1.547).

33. On the punning presence of Io's still-beautiful *os* within *bos*, see Ahl (1985, 146).

34. The prominence of mud in the generative process could also bear traces of Orphic influence, where mud is a primordial element; mud is also a feature of Phoenician cosmogony. See Meisner (2018, 91, 126–29, 132, 137–44).

35. Wheeler (2000, 36), cf. esp. the description of the inflamed Apollo (1.492–96) countered by the emphasis on her status as a daughter of Peneus, and therefore of an especially "watery" identity.

36. Calame (1999, 180).

37. Cf. also the punishment threatened to the Inachid race by Zeus at Aesch. *PV* 667–68.

38. See Wheeler (2000, 27–28). Cleanthes underscores the primacy of fire within Stoic cosmogony by emphasizing the relationship between Jupiter and his lightning-bolt (*Hymn to Zeus*, 7–14). Heraclitus echoes this with his formulation of Zeus as "the thunderbolt that guides all things" (fr. B64 D-K). "Zeus is the onset of untiring fire" also appears in the Derveni papyrus as part of the hymnic section in praise of Zeus (col. xiii–iv.5).

39. Cornutus, *Theol.* 48.5–9 [Lang]; cf. Boys-Stones (1998, 170–71). Despite a strong identification between Zeus and fire as a cosmic animating force, an identification codified by philosophical belief and mythologically cemented by the picture of Zeus with his powerful lightning-bolt, Eros' torch can also accomplish this identification. "Eros fulminant" is also a recorded visual motif; cf. Plut. *Alc.* 16.1–2 and Athen. 534e for the shield of Alcibiades, and *LIMC* iii "Eros" 928 no. 948. On Stoic Zeus as inspiration for the Lucretian Venus, see Asmis (1982). Vanhaegendoren (2005) reads Jupiter's decision through the lenses of both textual criticism and Stoic thought to conclude it is "another instance of anti-Augustan irony" (204).

40. Hejduk (2020, 222).

41. This is also contextually reminiscent of the opening of Lucretius, and Venus causing Mars to set his weapons aside (*DRN* 1.31–43); cf. also Petron. *Sat.* 126.18.1–3 for verses about Jupiter surrendering his weapons for love.

42. This maxim is underscored by the signifying depth of the close uses of *morantur* and *amor*, which emphasize *amor*'s anagrammatic potential to integrate *mora* and *Roma* here, further politicizing and polemicizing.

Notes to Pages 28–37

43. Cf. also the self-identification of *Met.* 1.595–96 and the description at *Met.* 2.847–49.

44. See Peraki-Kyriakidou (2002, 479) for *uis . . . uerbi* as an etymologizing marker.

45. Ziogas (2016, 2–3).

46. Hinds (1992, 96–97).

47. Both gods also receive qualifications about their weaponry: Cupid has different arrows for different purposes, as described in the Daphne myth (*duo tela . . . diuersorum operum*, "two weapons of different work," *Met.* 1.468–69), while Jupiter has a different, "lighter" set of lightning-bolts he uses on Semele (*est aliud leuius fulmen . . . tela secunda uocant superi*, "there is a different, less intense bolt . . . the gods call them 'secondary' weapons," *Met.* 3.305, 307).

48. See Hejduk (2020, 231–32).

49. Keith (2010, 209–11).

50. Romano (2009).

51. Trans. Lloyd-Jones. See also the text and commentary of Sider (2017).

52. See Bremmer (2009; 2013); on the inscription generally, see also Isager (1998); Lloyd-Jones (1999); and Gagné (2006).

53. See the commentary of Sider (2017) ad loc. for the connection between the infant Zeus and Hermaphroditus via this inscription.

54. See Bremmer (2009, 293) and Romano (2009, 559).

55. Brody (2001, 101–2). On this local rivalry of worship, see also Chaniotis (2010).

56. Specifically, Salmacis' picking of flowers (*saepe legit flores*, 4.315) might recall the local priestesses called *anthephoroi*; cf. Brody (2001, 103–4). Salmacis' identity as the only nymph not known to Diana (*solaque Naiadum celeri non nota Dianae*, 4.304) is also interesting to note considering some historical evidence: there is a missive Octavian sent to the people of Ephesus, regarding a golden Eros Julius Caesar had dedicated to Aphrodite, which was subsequently set up as an offering to Artemis; cf. Brody (2001, 106–7).

57. Barchiesi (1999, 114–16). In addition, by opening with *arma*, Venus looks back not only to the opening of the *Aeneid* but to the opening word of the *Amores*. Ovid reminds his reader that his elegy has already infiltrated and colonized epic; ironically, the Ovidian Venus' fears over the territory of love are as situationally unfounded as the Virgilian Venus' fears assuaged by Jupiter (cf. *Aen.* 1.257–96). Venus' address to Cupid as *potentia* additionally resonates with the poet's initial elegiac address to the winged god about his realm (*sunt tibi magna, puer, nimiumque potentia regna: / cur opus affectas ambitiose nouum?*, "you have too much power and territory already, boy, why do you usurp this new work, you grasper?," *Am.* 1.1.13–14). These similarities serve as further reminders that the Ovidian *regna* of Cupid are both literal and literary, and Cupid's agenda has always been one of territorial ownership. On the shared resonances of Cupid's *regna* in *Met.* 5 and *Amores* 1.1, see Johnson (1996, 128). On Claudian's adaptation of these passages in his *Magnet* (51–53), see Hardie (2022, 339–40).

58. Cf. also Hes. *Theog.* 912–14.

244   Notes to Pages 37–42

59. On this Ovidian representation of Venus, see especially Johnson (1996).

60. Cf. e.g., *Hymn. Hom. Ven.* 1–6; Lucr. *DRN* 1.1–49; Eur. *Hipp.* 447–48, 1268–82; Aesch. fr. 44 Radt; on her especial power and danger, cf. also Soph. fr. 941 Radt.

61. On the linked etymologies of *Venus/uincere*, see Hinds (2006).

62. Richardson (2008, 118–20). Cf. also Virg. *Aen.* 6.791–97, describing Augustus' expansion of the empire, esp. *super et Garamantas et Indos / proferet imperium* (6.794–95), echoed by Venus' speech at *Met.* 5.371–72. See also *Res Gestae* 30 for the expansion of the empire's *fines*. On the *Res Gestae*, see Cooley (2009, 27–28 and ad 13), she cites an earlier work of Richardson for the concept of *imperium* as "territorial empire."

63. This realm is considered off-limits for Octavian in the invocation to the *Georgics* (Virg. *Georg.* 1.36–39); for a reading of Venus' ambitions and their possible political implications, especially concerning kingship, see Ham (2022, 171–72).

64. Richardson (2008, 132–34). Only within the Ovidian exilic corpus does he finds instances of *imperium* related to "territorial expansion."

65. Text is T. Allen (1912).

66. The Homeric/Hesiodic tag μητίετα Ζεύς is often translated as "Zeus the Planner," also found in the Derveni papyrus (col. XV.6.11).

67. Stephens ad loc.

68. For echoes of the *Homeric Hymn to Aphrodite* in other Callimachean hymns, see Olson (2012, 24–25).

69. For this statement as emblematizing the strategic praise of the hymnist, see Floridi (2004). On its Pindaric modeling, see Fuhrer (1988, 56–60).

70. Most notably, what the Muses tell Hesiod at *Theog.* 27–28. The baldly stated ψευδοίμην could also initially be seen as a reflection of the ψευδόμενοι of the *Homeric Hymn to Dionysus* (5), making additional reference to the *Homeric Hymns* as source texts; cf. Depew (1993, 73); Stephens (2003, 82–84). However, the bee maidens of the *Homeric Hymn to Hermes* also both tell the truth and lie to humans (560–63).

71. Text is T. Allen, Halliday, and Sikes (1936).

72. This will be discussed in the final chapter, when the Muses' hymn to Ceres becomes the text of focus.

73. On the similarities of the clausulae, see Brumbaugh (2019, 69).

74. Trans. Stephens.

75. The bee, poetry, and deeds of Zeus are more closely intertwined by Zeus' naming as ἐσσῆνα in the same line (66). ἐσσῆνα is a rare term in all probability linked to ἐσμός, "swarm," a collective noun that Callimachus uses to denote the Muses at the opening of the *Aetia* (fr. 2,2 Harder). On the significance of ἐσσῆνα, see Brumbaugh (2019, 70–73). Zeus is also called a "lover of lies" by a Trojan at Hom. *Il.* 12.164, who goes on to use a bee-simile to describe the dynamic of the battle (12.167–72).

76. Olson ad loc. discusses this distinction within the hymnic tradition. In the context of praising Aphrodite, ἔργα are also appropriate objects of celebration given that ἔργον is also a euphemism for sex.

77. On the surprising absence of Jupiter, see Ham (2022, 174).

Notes to Pages 42–51

78. Similarly, *manus* could also be punning on the idea of an "armed force," "troop" (*OLD* s.v. 22).

79. See Pendergraft (1991).

80. Anagnostou-Laoutides (2017, 177–78) reads this scene as a cosmic Eros' replacement of a Stoic Zeus, also incorporating Orphic contexts; her reading lends further credence to Ovid's receptivity of this dynamic between the divinities.

81. Kelly (2021, 745); see Pendergraft (1991, 99) for the possibility of Apollonius evoking an armillary sphere as used by Archimedes.

82. In the later hymnic tradition, Marullus can be used as evidence for reading and interpreting Ovid this way. He first hymns Jupiter as an *opifex* (*Hymns to Nature* 1.100; cf. also the process of creation from 60–100) but also gives Amor this role in his hymn to Love: *quid, quod et nouas Chaos in figuras / digeris* ("and what about your division of Chaos into new forms," *Hymns to Nature* 3.21–22; cf. also 13–20 for his power over Jupiter). The responsibility of Love to organize Chaos into "new forms" hints at the opening of the *Metamorphoses*.

CHAPTER 2. DIVINING PRAISE

1. Miller (2009a, 336). For his significant analysis of the Apollo of the *Metamorphoses*, see 332–73.

2. See the discussion of Miller (2009a, 325).

3. See the commentaries of Bömer and Barchiesi ad loc.

4. All Virgilian text is that of Mynors (1969). On the temple of Apollo Palatinus as being symbolic of the new Augustan statehood, see Marton (2022, 160).

5. Cf. O'Hara (1996, 216).

6. The description of the sky as *serenus* also contributes to the jarring effect of Jupiter's appearance: thundering (Tonans) from a clear sky was a clear omen of either divine warning or encouragement; cf., e.g., Enn. *Ann.* fr. 81 Skutsch and Virg. *Aen.* 9.630–31. Seneca explains this phenomenon in the *Natural Questions* (2.18.1).

7. See Schachter (1981, 48–49); evidence for the Galaxion is found in Plutarch (Plut. *De Pyth. or.* 29 [409A] = fr. 97 *PMG*). On the Daphnephoria, see further Schachter (2016, 255–78).

8. Boyd (2012; 2017, 112–26).

9. Knox (1988, 542).

10. It also gives its name to one of the Cyclopes, responsible for forging the bolts of Zeus; cf. Hes. *Theog.* 140, Callim. *Hymn* 3.68; Virg. *Aen.* 8.425; Ov. *Fast.* 4.172, 4.288; Stat. *Silv.* 1.1.4, 3.1.131.

11. Even if Ovid considers Sol and Apollo separate divinities, the reference to each as Phoebus encourages a connection between their divine identities. For Apollo as Phoebus, cf., e.g., 1.451, 1.452, 1.463, 1.490, 1.553; for Sol, e.g., 1.752, 2.24, 2.36, 2.110, 2.399. The sun is also identified as Apollo when Diana is said to be sleepy from hunting in the sun's "fraternal rays" (*fraternis . . . flammis*, 2.454).

246   Notes to Pages 51–58

12. στεροπή can be used to mean any strong or dazzling light, including that of the sun, e.g., Soph. *Trach.* 99. Similarly, the metal *pyropus* takes its name from the Greek πυρωπός ("fiery-eyed"), which is also an epithet of Zeus' thunderbolt (Aesch. *PV* 667) or of the sun, as in a reconstruction of Aeschylus' *Memnon* (fr. 300.4 Radt). The two passages are also brought into further alignment by shared etymological play on *caelum* (cf. the continuation of the ecphrasis at *Met.* 2.5–7); for the particulars of this etymological play, which reaches toward *celare* or *caelatum* respectively, see Michalopoulos (2001, 44–45).

13. Papaioannou (2003); Casali (2020). However, the Virgilian ambiguity about Jupiter's role in Arcadia may exist as an imaginative antecedent to Ovid's construction of the relationship between the god and region; cf. *Aen.* 8.349–54.

14. Farrell (2013, 239–50).

15. See Hejduk (2020, 231–32).

16. This pronouncement of power is unparalleled in epic, on which see Barchiesi ad loc.

17. The episode as political allegory, with Augustus at the center, has been well discussed. See esp. Feeney (1991, 199–200) and Barchiesi (2009).

18. On resisting the paradigmatic nature of the Lycaon episode, see Anderson (1989).

19. Cf. also *Hymn. Hom.* 25. 4. Most recently on the Hesiodic quotation in Callimachus, see Brumbaugh (2019, 79–83).

20. Kirichenko (2012), who follows and expands the reading of Hunter and Fuhrer (2002, 167–69) of the *Theogony* in his reading of Callimachus' *Hymn to Zeus*. On the myth of Lycaon as combining aspects of the two Hesiodic epics, see Feldherr (2010, 132–33).

21. See Barchiesi (2005, 177–79) for sources and variations of the Lycaon myth.

22. Anderson (1989, 96–97).

23. As in Book 2, after Phaethon's disastrous flight, where Arcadia is the god's priority for restoration (2.405–6).

24. Cf. Ov. *Am.* 3.10.20; *Fast.* 5.111–28.

25. See Nielsen (1999) for the complexities in conceptually defining the Arcadian people and land.

26. Fifth-century coins from Mantinea display acorns; cf. Walker (2006, n1470–74). On the pre-lunarity of the Arcadians, see Dueck (2020).

27. The geographical question is reminiscent of the opening of the *Homeric Hymn to Dionysus* (1–9), on which see Depew (1993, 73) and Stephens (2003, 82–84).

28. Pl. *Cra.* 396a–b; *SVF* 2.1021= DL 7.147; cf. also Arist. [*Mund.*] 401a13–15; Cornutus *Theol.* 2.6–8 [Lang]; *Etymologicum Genuinum* ζ 31 (cf. Choer. *Epim. Ps.* 183.9). Hladký (2020) provides a good overview of the complexities in naming the god.

29. Hopkinson (1984a, 141–42; 1984c); Depew (1993, 75); Kirichenko (2012, 188–89); Stephens ad 1.10). See also Hilton (1992) specifically on Arcadia as Azania and

Nielsen and Roy (1998) on the Azanians. A scholiast (Dion. Per. 415) makes the specific connection between these names.

30. Hopkinson (1984a, 141–42; 1984a); Kirichenko (2012, 189–90); Brumbaugh (2019, 107).

31. Hopkinson (1984c). For the "collaboration" of Gaia and Rhea in the hymn, see Brumbaugh (2019, 116–17).

32. Kirichenko (2012, 190). For Pherecydes' linking of Rhea to ῥέω, and his derivation of Chaos from χεῖσθαι, as advocated by Achilles Tatius (*Isogages exerpta* 3 [b1a]); see Granger (2007, 147). Wheeler (2000, 28) notes this etymology and the applicability of conceptualizing a watery chaos within the flood in the *Metamorphoses*.

33. As Depew (1993, 76) summarizes, "The earth simulates a human birth, and suddenly we see the birth of Zeus and the birth of Arcadia's rivers as the doublets they were in the tradition. It is this conjunction, constructed out of a subtle conjoining of geographical, lexical and generic arcana, rather than Zeus' birth, that is the focus of the narrative."

34. On the atmosphere and description of Arcadia here, see Segal (1999); Ziogas (2013b, 325–28); Lenzi (2015, 66–72).

35. As a daughter of Ladon, cf. Serv. ad *Aen.* 3.91 (*Daphne Penei, uel, ut alii dicunt, Ladonis filia*); Arr. *FGrHist* 157 F 87 = Eustath. Dion. Per. 916; Cassianus Bassius *Geoponica* 11.2; [Palaeph.] 50; [Lib.] *Progymnasmata* 17; Apth. *Prog.* 5 and Tzetz. ad Lycoph. 6. The other river identified as her father is the Amyclas, pioneered apparently by Phylarchus (cf. Plut. *Agis.* 9.2) and Diodorus of Elea, although Phylarchus' choice is suspected by some (e.g., Robinson [1936, 513]) to be motivated more by personal regional and political allegiances than mythological accuracy. Cf. also Parth. *Amat. narr.* 15.1–3. For the issue of Daphne's parentage, see esp. Knox (1990, 189, 194–96). On the connections between Ovid's Daphne and Phylarchus, see Williams (1981). On Ovid's choice between an Arcadian and Thessalian version, see Otis (1966, 352–53).

36. As discussed in Knox (1990, 196) and noted by Bömer ad 1.486; Barchiesi (ad 1.486–87) calls it "una vera e propria citazione . . . dall' Inno a Diana di Callimaco," also citing *Hymn. Hom. Ven.* 26 and Tib. 2.5.64.

37. Hardie (2004, 15). The direct formulation of *dedit hoc pater ante Dianae* serves to indicate both a mythological past and a literary past; *ante* alerts the reader to the presence of the same request granted in the literary precedent of Callimachus' *Hymn*.

38. Even as a narrative bridge, however, it has been tied to learned poetic precedents. In creating the transition to the company of rivers that feed the waters of the Peneus, the passage becomes stylized as an exception-as-introduction narrative segue: the absence of the Inachus at the meeting of rivers allows for his presence in the text, as the narrative unfolds to tell the tale of his own daughter, Io. Knox (1990, 194–95) discusses this transition in relation to Callimachus' twelfth *Iamb* (fr. 202.35–39 Pf.), where all the gods celebrate Hebe except for Demeter, who is absent as she mourns for Persephone. Pfeiffer (1965) ad loc. cites the Ovidian passage as a parallel for the Callimachean design.

248 Notes to Pages 62–67

39. The phrase *dare iura* is formulaic of legislation, often in a foundational sense; Ovid uses it in relation to Romulus (cf. also *Aen.* 1.293, 1.507) and the founding of Rome, e.g., at *Met.* 14.806 and *Fast.* 2.492. In a different sense, Dido uses the phrase in calling upon Jupiter's knowledge of the laws of hospitality when she formally welcomes the Trojans (Virg. *Aen.* 1.731). Such a context further unites the figures of the Peneus and Jupiter as well as looks forward to *Metamorphoses* 8, where Achelous, another river god in a home similar to the Peneus', will welcome guests and exchange epic tales, as the Trojans do after this display of hospitality.

40. Cf. also Virg. *Georg.* 4.363–73 for the phrase *diuersa locis* (367) within the context of a river catalog, detailing Aristaeus' journey beneath the source of the Peneus, further deepening the sense of the Peneus as a site of mediating space in Ovid.

41. On the Tempe passage as recalling the flood and creation of the rivers, see Wheeler (2000, 58).

42. In comparison, the prose list compiled by Herodotus lists Peneus, Apidanus, Onochonos, Enipeus, and Pamisos as the noted rivers of Thessaly (Hdt. 7.129.2), a list largely replicated by Pliny, who identifies Apidanus, Phoenix, Enipeus, Onochonus, and Pamisus as the *flumina Thessaliae* (*HN* 4.30.6). The further unnamed company (*alii amnes*) contains faint reminiscence of the Hesiodic ἕτεροι ποταμοί ("the other rivers") that closes the river catalog of the *Theogony* (367).

43. Hopkinson (1984a, 142).

44. Kyriakidis (2007, 43).

45. One opening indication of the hymn's emphasis on geographical learnedness is Callimachus' omission of the major Arcadian river Alpheus, which is one of the first three named by Hesiod in his catalog (Τηθὺς δ᾽ Ὠκεανῷ Ποταμοὺς τέκε δινήεντας / Νεῖλόν τ᾽ Ἀλφειόν τε καὶ Ἠριδανὸν βαθυδίνην, "Tethys and Oceanus bore the eddying rivers, Nile and Alpheus and deep-eddying Eridanus," *Theog.* 337–38).

46. Stephens ad loc.; cf. also Stephens (2003, 98–99).

47. Melas is also unattested elsewhere as an Arcadian river. Dionysius Periegetes is likely indebted to Callimachus here, as he includes the Melas, Crathis, Iaon, and Ladon as the rivers of the "Apidanian Arcadians" (Dionys. Per. 415–17). On other connections between Arcadia and the Nile, see Stephens (2002, 258n68; 2003, 97–101). In his list of Thessalian rivers, Lucan adds a Melas (6.374), which was identified as a tributary of the Apidanus (Vibius Sequester *de Flum.*, s.v. "Apidanos").

48. For a detailed reading on the Callimachean geographical misdirection between Arcadia and Crete, see Depew (1993, 76–77); for shorter reference to Cretan and Arcadian Thenae, see Hopkinson (1984a, 143) and Stephens ad loc. For evidence of Cretan Arcadia's waterlessness, cf. Plin. *HN* 31.30.

49. Kaczyńska (2016, 162–63). Epimenides' influence on the *Hymn* is indubitable; the framing assertion that Cretans lie (*Hymn* 1.8) is a quotation of Epimenides (fr. 5 Kinkel). Cf. also Callim. fr. 202 Pf. on the stereotype of Cretan liars.

50. Cf. Virg. *Ecl.* 7.66 for poplars growing by riverbanks.

Notes to Pages 67–68

51. There identified by the Latin name Padus. Ovid does not specifically state which tree the sisters become, but, with knowing cross-reference to this adjective previously employed of the Eridanus, and wordplay on the base *popul-* (*populis*, 2.215; *populos*, 236; *populante*, 319; *populos*, 370), he sets up their known metamorphic identity as poplars; cf. Ahl (1982, 410; 1985, 144). Naturally, the key difference is in the metrical length, and so these words are automatically distinguishable by length of the vowels; however, this difference does not rule out the potential for word play upon the similar looking (if not sounding) stems. For play upon words spelt the same but of different quantities, as revealed through metrical seating, see Quint. *Inst.* 9.3.69–70. For identification of a similar pun on *populus*, see Robinson (2011) ad *Fast.* 2.465.

52. The only previous extant poetic appearance of the Apidanus in Latin is in an early Propertian elegy, where it is described as *herbosus* (Prop. 1.3.6). A "grassy" river is one whose streams have dried up, which contextually paints the Apidanus like the subterranean Arcadian rivers of Callimachus' hymn.

53. Cf. esp. Virg. *Georg.* 3.2, *pastor ab Amphryso*; Luc. 6.368. Virgil names the Sibyl as *Amphrysia uates* at *Aen.* 6.398. In this way it also makes a pair with the Apidanus, as Apollo's son Aristaeus (described with many similar qualities) pastured his flocks by the Apidanus (Ap. Rhod. *Argon.* 2.513–15).

54. Callim. *Hymn* 2.47–54; cf. also the extended mythological *exemplum* at Tib. 2.3.11–32. Ovid's Apollo may be trying to contradict this potentially embarrassing episode when he exclaims to Daphne *non ego sum pastor, non hic armenta gregesque / horridus observo* ("I am no shepherd, I, unkempt, watch over no herds or flocks," 1.513–14). Although *lenis* is not a watchword of elegy to the same degree of familiarity as *mollis* or *leuis*, cf., e.g., elegy as *lenia carmina* (Prop.1.9.12) and *lenia uerba* (Ov. *Am.* 2.1.22). *Lenis* is also used to describe the Anapus at *Fast.* 4.469; it receives no adjective in the corresponding narrative in *Metamorphoses* 5, which is a point that could reinforce the discussion of Hinds (1987, 82–83), given his wider argument on the different generic emphases of the accounts (i.e., the *Fasti* as elegiac, as opposed to the epic *Metamorphoses*; cf. chap. 5, n. 5).

55. Citing Callimachean interest in river aetiology, as demonstrated by the (likely later) Περὶ ἐν τῇ οικουμένῃ ποταμῶν seems a rote, inadequate defense for the length and detail of this opening hymnic narrative.

56. Brumbaugh (2019, 105).

57. My discussion and understanding of this passage are heavily indebted to Brumbaugh's chapter on the *Hymn to Zeus*, notably pp. 104–24.

58. Brumbaugh (2019, 105–7). He notes specifically Rhea's use of *amechania* (*Hymn* 1.28) at the end of her search, which Callimachus, in the footsteps of Pindar, always uses as a synonym of *aporia*.

59. See Brumbaugh (2019, "Arkadia as a Hesiodic Locus Amoenus," 112–16); cf. also 117 for further resonances of compounds of ῥέω. The *Hymn to Zeus* also engages with the Heliconian landscape by alluding to the moment the Hippocrene was created, as told in the *Phaenomena*; cf. Stephens ad 1.18). Callimachus' metapoetic use of

250   Notes to Pages 69–75

water is well documented, especially regarding the pronouncement of Apollo about the Assyrian river versus the pure fountain that provides bees with its choice and holy dew (*Hymn* 2.108–12).

60. Brumbaugh (2019, 110).

61. For an argument toward reading water as song in this Pindaric opening, based on the conceptual metaphor of "an ode as a liquid," see Eckerman (2017, 9–14). He further argues that Bacchylides' own metapoetic statement at 3.85–87 also confirms a metapoetic reading of Pindar, *Olympian* 1.1, and serves as a cap to Pindar's statement of poetic prominence (cf. 24–27). Callimachean acknowledgment of this equation would, in a certain way, pave the way for the Horatian image of Pindar as an overflowing mountain river (*Carm.* 4.2). Lather (2019) reads this Horatian image as receptively implicated in Pindar's self-presentation of his song via use of the verb κελαδεῖν ("to sound as running water"). Her examination of Pindaric usages of κελαδεῖν and its cognates lead to a conclusion that it is "practically synonymous with 'to celebrate'" (470), further entrenching the ideas of water and praise in a way that is complementary to Brumbaugh's reading of Callimachus' *Hymn to Zeus*.

62. Cf. Pind. fr. 29 S-M as another good example of hymnic *aporia*.

63. Prodi (2017, 563).

64. Cf. Prodi (2017, 562).

65. As reaffirming the traditional identification of a hymn to Zeus, Angeli Bernardini (2009); as a hymn to Apollo, D'Alessio (2009); as jointly for Apollo and Zeus, Bowra (1964). There is likewise a Hellenistic hymn (PChic col. VI, 13) that records Zeus' victory over the Titans that has been attributed to either Zeus or Apollo; cf. Powell (1925, 84).

66. Prodi (2017, 565–66).

67. On the tension between the two gods in this hymn, see Felson (2011).

68. Fantuzzi (2011, 450–51).

69. On which, see Fantuzzi (2011, 448–50).

70. See especially Miller (2009b) for how this represents a new beginning for the epic.

71. Apollo's expression of ownership, *te . . . habebunt*, chimes with the supreme assertion of Jupiter, *uos habeo* (1.197).

72. See most recently Lightfoot (2018) for Callimachus' *Hymn to Apollo* as a paean. Van Tress (2004, 127–36) also delineates the paeanic background of the *Hymn to Delos*. Cf. also *Met.* 14.719–20 for the only other appearance of Paean, also in a triumphal context.

73. Hardie (2002b, 47–48, 129).

74. The episode is framed aetiologically by Hollis (1996) and Francese (2004). See also Miller (2009a, 347–48).

75. Hardie (2002b, 130; cf. also 45–50), a view subsequently endorsed by many scholars; cf. recently Mayor (2017, 172).

Notes to Pages 75–82

76. Pandey (2018, 279) sees a further metamorphosis, as "the *laurus* symbolically transmuted violence into cultural capital, or *laus.*" See her n. 79 for further sources on the etymological connection between and authorial play on *laurus* and *laus*, albeit without reference to Cicero or Tibullus.

77. On this line of Cicero, see Volk and Zetzel (2015).

78. Text is Postgate (1924).

79. ut Messalinum <u>celebrem</u>, cum praemia belli
> ante suos currus oppida uicta feret,
> ipse gerens <u>laurus: lauro</u> deuinctus agresti
> miles "io" magna uoce "triumphe" canet.
> tunc Messalla meus pia det spectacula turbae
> et <u>plaudat</u> curru praetereunte pater.

On this etymological play, see Cairns (1996, 51). Ovid's knowledge of this passage and awareness of this etymological play can be ascertained by an embedded quotation and imitation in the *Tristia* (*tempora Phoebea lauro cingetur "io" que / miles "io" magna uoce "triumphe" canet*, 4.2.51–52); this couplet is prepared for with the use of *circumplaudere* in 4.2.49 (cf. *plaudat*, Tib. 2.5.120). Tibullus' appeal to Apollo to disarm Cupid (Tib. 2.5.105–6) also informs the beginning of the Ovidian episode and Cupid's quarrel with Apollo. As such, just as Tibullus frames his elegiac hymn with the folk etymology of *laus-laurus*, Ovid frames his narrative of laurel with intertextual and thematic reference to the Tibullan hymn.

80. For a different reading of the significance of ἰώ in bridging the tale of Daphne and Io, see Curtis (2017, 316–17).

81. Pausanias relates that the Ismenus was previously known as Ladon (Paus. 9.10.6), which brings it into further proximity to Callimachus' *Hymn to Zeus*. Like the use of Erymanthus to name a river, the modifying adjective *Phegiacus* similarly appears nowhere else in extant Latin. Looking to Pausanias again, we find his record that that the town of Erymanthus was called Phegia after the king Phegeus, before once again undergoing a name change to Psophis (Paus. 8.24.2). However, Phegia also means "oak-town" (φηγός, "oak"), giving the meaning of "of oak-town" to the adjective *Phegiacus*. In this reading, the river is identified with the oaks that gave the city its name, a city once also identified with the same name of Erymanthus. Ovid's coining of this adjective aligns with Callimachus' coinage of an "oaky" word to describe the land above the Iaon (σαρωνίς, *Hymn* 1.22), a hitherto unseen usage whose meaning is only made clear by a scholiast; see Stephens ad loc.

82. Cheshire (2016) compellingly argues for the significance of Callisto to Callimachus' *Hymn to Zeus*, which provides further support for this argument, albeit from a different perspective.

83. For the enumeration of these Arcadian epithets, see Wilkins (1988).

84. Hinds (2002, 129).

85. It can also be read in competition with Jupiter's restoration of the Arcadian landscape, which brings him into alignment with the figure of the *poeta creator*.

252   Notes to Pages 83–90

86. Fränkel (1945, 85); Otis (1966, 108, 356–57); Hardie (2002b, 128–32; 2004, 9–13).

87. For close analysis of the passages, see Miller (2009a, 339–40).

88. See Hunter and Fuhrer (2002, 170n67) and Barbantani (2011, 187). As Stephens notes ad loc., it seems Nonnus is aware of the MS reading, which leads to his imitation of this phrase (Γηγενέων ὀλετῆρα, *Dion.* 18.266). For a discussion of Nonnus' and Ovid's sources using the Phaethon episode as a test case, see Knox (1988). On the question of scholia availability and mythographical choice, see Cameron (2004, 164–83).

89. Argos is also a region called "very thirsty" by Homer (πολυδίψιον, *Il.* 4.171), testament to the drying of the rivers on the higher, eastern side.

90. See Spanakis (2018, 316–17) for discussion and interpretation of the joint designation between Argos and Arcadia. For Argos as "Apian land" cf. also Aesch. *Supp.* 260–70, who also uniquely designates this Apis as the son of Apollo. According to Hesiod (fr. 128 M-W) the Danaids (descendants of Io) were responsible for making Argos "well-watered": this lends further irony to the paradoxical Ovidian picture of Inachus both hiding underground and yet swelling his streams with tears (*Met.* 1.583–85).

91. Akusilaos von Argos (2) *FGrHist* F 23A; Clem. Al. *Strom.* 1.21.6.

92. Cole (2004, 383n79; 2008, 166n399). The assimilation between Niobe and Io previously occurs in a Platonic scholion (*Tim.* 22a) and is suggested by the chapter name of *Niobe siue Io* in Hyginus (*Fab.* 145.1, 3–4).

93. On the closeness between these myths, see esp. Wheeler (2000, 58–63). The emphasis on father figures and descendants in both myths also cues especial attention to genealogical descent, internally hinting at these connections.

94. Apis can also look to Egypt (and therefore, anticipate the conclusion of Io's tale, her restoration to her original form by the Nile), which creates a similar multilayering of geographical allusion as in the Callimachean *Hymn to Zeus*. On the identification of Argive Apis with the Egyptian bull god Apis, cf. Aristippos *FGrHist* 317 F1; Apollod. *Bibl.* 2.1.1; August. *De civ. D.* 18.5, and hinted at in Aesch. *Supp.* 117, 128, 260–70. On the persistent Egyptian resonances built by Apollonius in the passage that identifies the Arcadians as "Apidanians," see Stephens (2003, 190). Notably, she details that Thessaly and Egypt are both described as ἠερίη πολυλήιος (of Thessaly, *Argon.* 1.580; of Egypt, 4.267), which also contextually recalls Callimachus' polysemic use of ἄβροχος.

Chapter 3. Rivaled Affection and Affectation

1. On the hymnic conventions of Apollo's "self-hymn" (Selbst-Aretalogien), see Fuhrer (1999, 357–58); for its similarities to the following "self-hymn" of Jupiter, see 359–62.

2. The impetus and inspiration for this chapter come especially from Wills (1990), to which much of the foundational discussion is indebted.

3. Myers (2019).

4. Apollo's territorial defensiveness has also been read as a reactive replay of the fraternal strife humorously depicted in the *Homeric Hymn to Hermes*, with Cupid now playing the role of the mischievous baby brother; see Myers (2019).

Notes to Pages 90–92   253

5. On the issue of Apollo and Diana as siblings versus twins, see Rutherford (1988, 72).

6. For a literary reading of the significance of his quarry, cf. Campbell (2018).

7. As Graziosi (2016, 54) bluntly puts it, "Unlike his sister, he does not even hunt with [his bow]." Ovid's use of *cornua* to describe the contested bow's arch (1.455) also indicates the bow's use as a hunting weapon.

8. Cf. also Anacreon's *Hymn to Artemis* (fr. 348 *PMG*) for the address of ἐλαφηβόλε (cf. also Soph. *Trach.* 213). For lyric influence on Callimachus' Artemis, see Stephens (2015, 105–6); for lyric influence on Catullus' hymn to Diana, see Johnston (2021, 279–82). The Ἐλαφηβόλια is also a festival dedicated to Artemis Elaphebolos; cf. Plut. *De mul. vir.* 244e.

9. As is well known, the scene replays the conflict between the poet and Cupid in *Amores* 1.1; Ovid hints at Cupid's use of the bow as trespass against moon-Goddess Diana in the description *lunauitque genu sinuosum fortiter arcum* ("he boldly arched the flexible bow upon his knee," *Am.* 1.1.23; cf. also Prop. 4.6.25).

10. Of course, the action of the *Iliad* is, in some ways, catalyzed by his arrows raining down on the Achaeans, as Homer emphasizes their sinister rattling (e.g., *Il.* 1.24); his deadly shower of arrows does cast him as a menacing god of plague.

11. Nagy (2004, 138–43). On etymologizing Apollo, cf. Pl. *Crat.* 404e–406a with the discussion of Hunter and Laemmle (2020).

12. Graziosi (2016, 54). This is Artemis' most important Homeric epithet, used twenty times in exclusive reference to her; on her Homeric epithets, see Skafte Jensen (2009, 56). Hera's words to Artemis at Hom. *Il.* 21.485–88 also reverberate through Cupid's parting words to Apollo at *Met.* 1.463–65.

13. On divine names and epithets in the Greek world, see generally Usener (1948); Versnel (2011, 60–88); Wallensten (2008); and Parker (2017, 1–32). The 2006 volume of Belayche et al. takes a panoramic view of the concept and significance of divine names.

14. *Sagittifera . . . pharetra* (1.468) recalls the Homeric φαρέτρα ἰοδόκος; cf. Hom. *Il.* 15.443–444, *Od.* 21.59–60; Callim. *Hymn* 3.212–13.

15. Apollo is seen with a *pharetra* but never described with this adjective. Cicero knows of one version of Diana who gave birth to Cupid; cf. *Nat. D.* 3.58.2.

16. Prior to Ovid, the adjective is used by Virgil and Horace (*Georg.* 4.290; *Carm.* 3.4.35); Virgil also uses it to describe Camilla (*Aen.* 11.649). Camilla's connection with Diana is a strong one; her activity in the following line of *spargens hastilia* (*Aen.* 11.650) could also serve to gloss the Homeric epithet ἰοχέαιρα, while her ties to the Herotodean Artemisia also connect her to Artemis in a different nomenclatural way; see Boyd (1992).

17. Cupid and Diana also appear as collaborating forces in Acontius' narrative, jointly compelling him to write to Cydippe (Ov. *Her.* 20.229–32); Acontius identifies Diana's and Amor's arrows as sources of harm, and so, as a shared attribute; the metaphorical wounds of love from Cupid's arrow are invoked alongside the brutally physical

254 Notes to Pages 92–96

wounds caused by Diana's arrows. On the Ovidian myth of Acontius and Cydippe as providing the aetiology of elegy, see Barchiesi (1993, 362).

18. Cf. esp. Ov. *Ars Am.* 1.21–22 for the torch as a weapon of Amor.

19. There are Athenian inscriptions to Artemis as "light-bearer"; Mejer (2009, 62). Cf. also Callim. *Hymn* 3.11 and 205, with the notes of Stephens ad loc.

20. Using Phoebe as the sole designator for Diana is more common in a Roman context; cf. Virg. *Georg.* 1.431.

21. For Apollo as Cynthius, cf. Virg. *Ecl.* 6.3 (with Prop. 2.34.80) and *Georg.* 3.36. On shared names (trans-divine epithets), see Parker (2003, 174); on shared epithets, see Parker (2017, 15). For Apollo and Diana, most shared pairs of epithets are due to shared worship at a particular cult site.

22. However, in this poem, Cupid is identified with a bow (*Am.* 3.2.55)

23. Cf. also *Met.* 10.515–18 for the distinguishing *cultus* of Amor.

24. On their similarity, see Hardie (2004, 13).

25. Eumolpus' elegy on hair in Petronius' *Satyrica* also plays upon the similarity of the divinities and their hair(styles) (109.9–10). This scene also humorously indicates hair as the defining identifying feature: only when Giton is given a wig does Tryphaena recognize his true (*uerus*) self.

26. See especially Plantinga (2004, 258–66); Stephens (2015) selectively on the *Hymn to Artemis*; Fain (2004); Petrovic (2010, 223n54) provides additional bibliography. Hunter and Fuhrer (2002, 163) are more dismissive, stating, "The prominence of 'sibling rivalry' as a motif and narrative impulse . . . is in fact too obvious to require lengthy discussion."

27. Jupiter's disguise lends a pointed irony to his statement in Callimachus' *Hymn to Artemis* about dismissing the jealousy of Hera if goddesses give him children such as Artemis (*Hymn* 3.29–31), as the Callisto myth is one defining mythological showcase for Hera's punitive jealousy.

28. One might also compare the *cultus* described of Atalanta (*Met.* 8.322–23) in contrast to her *facies* (*talis erat cultus; facies, quam dicere uere / uirgineam in puero, puerilem in uirgine possis*, "such was she in accessory, in appearance—so that one could say truly there appeared a maiden in boyish form, boyishness in the maiden," 322–23; cf. also Iphis, *Met.* 9.712–13); cf. also Virgilian examples of *induo + vultus* (*Aen.* 1.683–84; 7.20; cf. also 7.415–16). *Cultus* refers to clothing at *Met.* 8.854; cf. also Mart. 8.48.2.

29. Hardie (2004, 13).

30. Callisto is identified by her status as a *uirgo*; cf. *uirgine*, 2.409; *uirgo*, 426; *uirgo*, 427.

31. As noted by Bergmann et al. (2012, 12). To a certain extent, a pair of Tibullan elegies (2.3 and 2.5) illustrate and juxtapose the "republican" versus "Augustan" aspect of Apollo, which lend precedent to the Ovidian treatment; Tibullus 2.3 gives a humorously deflationary picture of the god as a victim of love (2.3.11–27) that especially informs the Apolline self-hymn.

Notes to Pages 96–101

32. For the particulars of Aphrodite's progressive assimilation of Artemis' list of honors, see Turkeltaub (1993, 107–9). See also Cyrino (2013).

33. Turkeltaub (1993, 109).

34. The interpretation that hymns were preludes to epic performances (the "proem theory") was pioneered by Wolf (cf. 239n21). More recently, Petrovic (2012) reads hymns alongside the genre of *epyllia*.

35. Focus on the episode has largely been commanded by Ovid's use of *miles* in relation to a woman. This designator has led to discussion about how Ovid hints at an existing sexual relationship between Callisto and Diana that Jupiter capitalizes upon; cf. Oliver (2015). The archetype of the female huntress often borrows "masculine" characteristics; see, e.g., Stamatopoulou (2017, 84–86) on Cyrene's "masculinity" in Pindar. The evidence of Aesch. fr. 342 Radt (δέσποινα νύμφη, δυσχίμων ὀρῶν ἄναξ, "nymph queen, lord of dangerous hills") can also be noted here. It is possible that this line belongs to the *Toxotides* and comprises an address to Artemis, whereby the masculine ἄναξ is of especial relevance; cf. Manousakis (2020, 203n14).

36. Segal (1969) first popularized readings of the symbolic value of "virginal" landscapes in the *Metamorphoses*; cf. also Curran (1978) and Hinds (2002, 130–35).

37. See Ambühl (2005, 245–95) for the Callimachean modification of *Iliad* 21. On this scene as a case study for intertextuality, see Bonanno (1995).

38. Petrovic (2010, 221).

39. Cf. the commentary of Barchiesi ad loc. and Hardie (2004, 15).

40. Hardie (2004, 14–18, 54–55).

41. However, Artemis' desire also engages with the practice of the ancient worshipper attempting to cover all aspects of praise in their prayers, which results in the catch-all phrases that Versnel (2011, 49–60) calls "hesitative and dubitative formulas," such as found at Catull. 34.21–22, where the goddess is entreated by "whatever name pleases you." This is discussed below, but I read the Roman instances of this formula (or iterations of it) as additional literary tropes in awareness of the Callimachean demand.

42. For the textual dependency of the hymn to Artemis (*Hymn. Hom.* 27) on the hymn to Apollo, see Faulkner (2011a, 203).

43. Stephens ad 42–46. Cf. also Hunter (2003, 153) ad Theoc. *Id.* 17.75–76 and 110–11.

44. Text is Mynors (1958).

45. Cf. also the two similar hexameters that may be attributable to Valerius Cato's *Diana: Luna deum quae sola uides periuria uulgi / seu Cretaea magis seu tu Dictynna uocaris* (inc. fr. 35 Blänsdorf). Kronenberg (2018) reads Catullus 34 as an encoded literary critique of Valerius Cato's *Diana*, a poem perhaps indebted to Antimachus' *Artemis*.

46. Βοηθόον also reminds of Apollo's own specific role as "helper" designated by the epithet Βοηδρόμιος.

256   Notes to Pages 102–107

47. A lyric fragment (Sapph. fr. 44A Campbell = Alc. 304 L-P) also connects her oath of virginity with mountain peaks. On the importance of mountain peaks to Artemis, see also Konstantinou (2018, 41–42).

48. She is also associated with three mountains in Hor. *Carm.* 1.21 (Algidus, Erymanthus, and Gragus).

49. Text is Thomas (2011).

50. He addresses her as Luna at *CS* 36; on the necessary thematic suppression of her identity as Trivia within the context of the *Ludi Saeculares*, see Barchiesi (2002b) 123.

51. See Putnam (2000, 60) and the commentary of Thomas (2011) ad loc. Cf also the contrast between *Phoebus* and *alma nox* at Sen. *Med.* 874–76. Within the *Aeneid*, a text the *Carmen Saeculare* shows heightened awareness of, Diana is *alma Trivia* (7.774), *alma Phoebe* (10.215–16) and *alma . . . nemorum cultrix, Latonia uirgo* ("kind protectress of the groves, the maiden daughter of Leto," 11.557): the adjective is applied to each part of the tripartite nature that forms her especially Roman conception. For Roman Diana, see especially Green (2007).

52. Fratantuono (2015, 30), who points to Lucr. *DRN* 5.575–76 as textual precedent for the indebtedness of lunar light to the sun.

53. Cf. Bergmann et al. (2012, 9).

54. Pointed out by Bergmann et al. (2012, 10).

55. Fentress et al. (2003, 46). Cf. also Poulsen (2009, 411) on the *agyeius* on a wall painting in the House of Livia denoting a shrine to Diana; originally an Apolline monument, its use in a context of Diana's worship could mark Diana's new status as one of Augustus' "tutelary divinities."

56. The presentation of the Delian twins is also a focus of *Carm.* 4.6, a poem that ends with knowing self-reference to the *Carmen Saeculare* (4.6.41–44); see the commentary of Thomas (2011) ad loc.; Phillips (2019) 438–44; Gramps (2021, 131–34). On the Augustanism of the hymn, see also Marton (2022, 167–70).

57. She is also Latonia (*Met.* 1.696).

58. The Ovidian Apollo is not ever named as Pythius, for example, despite this being an Augustan epithet (cf. Prop. 2.31.16; Hor. *Carm.* 1.16.6).

59. Ovid here also integrates humorous awareness of Apollo's hair as his identifying feature within the Tibullan elegiac presentation of the myth of Apollo and Admetus: *quisquis inornatumque caput crinesque solutos / aspiceret, Phoebi quaererat ille comam* (2.3.25–26). Apollo's hair, unadorned, doesn't appear as Apollo's; the adornment, naturally, would be the laurel. Apollo speaking of Daphne's hair (the laurel itself, which will come to reflect Apollo's appearance) as *inornatus* is typically Ovidian humor.

60. See the discussion of Hardie (2002b, 47–48).

61. Cf. also *Aen.* 3.90–92, with the discussion of Barchiesi (1994). The motion (*agitasse*) could also reflect the less positive epiphany of Apollo at *Hymn. Hom. Ap.* 2–4, where the gods tremble (τρομέουσιν) when he comes near; in this light, *agitasse* can be read more closely with the laurel's initial fearful response to his touch (*trepidare*,

Notes to Pages 107–113   257

Met. 1.554; *refugit*, 1.556). However, *cacumen* can also mean "peak" with reference to mountains (*OLD* s.v. 1a); Artemis' presence is shown by trembling mountain peaks at *Hymn. Hom.* 27.6–7, recalling the Apolline epiphany in the presence of the gods.

62. Diana's presence on Delos bears the weight of Callimachean witness, as the *Aetia* specifically relates (*Aet.* fr. 26–28 Harder). On the importance of this myth for elegy, see Barchiesi (1993, 360–63).

63. The irony of the allusion is further underscored by the type of oath that Diana is marking: a binding oath of marriage, the same bond Apollo desired of Daphne. Acontius' success, ensured by Diana, further marks Apollo's erotic failure.

64. See Stephens ad loc.

65. In Homer, only used of Apollo; cf. *Il.* 4.101, 4.119, 15.55; *Od.* 17.494, 21.267. Its appearance in the Apellicon proem of the *Iliad* gives it further prominence as a defining Homeric epithet of Apollo. Bacchylides, however, applies it once to Apollo (1.147) and once to Artemis (11.39), contesting Apollo's sole ownership of the epithet. Propertius aligns the warlike appearance of Apollo in *Iliad* 1 with his slaying of the Python, giving the second deed a Homeric slant (Prop. 4.6.33–36).

66. Cf. also Naevius fr. 30 Morel.

67. Apollo's characterization of his arrow as a *certa sagitta* looks back not only to the programmatic *Amores* 1.1 (*me miserum! certas habuit puer ille sagittas*, "poor me! That boy has true arrows," *Am.* 1.1.25) but the Horatian ode where he is hailed as *metuende certa / Phoebe sagitta*, "Phoebus, rightfully feared for his true arrow," Hor. *Carm.* 1.12.23–24).

68. See Stephens ad loc.

69. Kampakoglou (2019, 266). The integration of Apollo's aspects as a healing god and city founder also features prominently in *Pythian* 4, where Apollo is addressed as Paean, and acts of civic leadership and healing are made analogous (*Pyth.* 4.270–74). See Marshall (2000, 16–18) for analysis of these overlaps, and their relationship to Callimachus' hymn; cf. also Kampakoglou (2019, 268). For paeans overcoming political discord, cf. Schol. Dion. Thrax P. 451.12 Hilgard.

70. On this omission, see Kampakoglou (2019, 267).

71. This trajectory gets epitomized for hymnic use in the Latin poets; cf. Hor. *Carm.* 2.10.18–20; Prop. 4.6.69–70; Sen. *Ag.* 322–27.

72. See Putnam (2000, 87–89). For comparison, cf. *Aen.* 12.391–97 with the discussion of Miller (2009a, 171).

73. Cf. Thomas (2011) ad loc.

74. Cf. Miller (2009a, 345–46). Horace also anticipates Apollo as a healer with the use of *mitis* at *CS* 33; cf. also the ending of *Carm.* 1.21 for Apollo in a role as warding off disease and pestilence.

75. Dedicated in 431 BC; restorations by the consul Gaius Sosius began in 32 BC.

76. Barchiesi (2002b, 117).

77. Cf. Breed (2004).

78. On Apollo's son Aesculapius as the *salutifer urbi/orbi* (cf. *Met.* 15.744), see Keith (1992b, 71–74). There is also a famous Arcadian healing sanctuary of Apollo Epikourios (mid-fifth BC) that would roughly translate as *opifer* (cf. Paus. 8.41.7).

79. The passage owes a great deal to a Tibullan couplet that explores the humor of the healer god not being able to heal his own love, capitalizing on the elegiac theme of love as sickness (*nec potuit curas sanare salubribus herbis: / quidquid erat medicae uicerat artis amor,* "nor was he able to heal his woes with health-bringing herbs; love had conquered whatever there was of healing art," Tib. 2.3.13–14).

80. Apollo's insistence that his healing arts avail all (*quae prosunt omnibus, Met.* 1.524) isn't just sweepingly dismissive of the elegiac perspective. It also underscores the "neotraditional," Augustan nature of *opifer*, calculated to recall (and build on) the god's role in the Ovidian *Remedia amoris* (76–78, 704–6). These two appearances of Apollo pair song and healing (*carmina*) and the bow and the lyre (ἔντεα), covering all areas of activity drawn upon in the *Metamorphoses*' self-hymn. Apollo of the *Remedia* as *repertor medicae opis* (76) is split into *inventor medicinae* and *opifer* in the *Metamorphoses*; the exclamation *ei mihi* is even more humorously self-reflexive, as it recalls these Apolline epiphanies.

81. See Wickkiser (2005) and Marton (2022, 160–61).

82. See Hopwood (2019, 72–75) for the significance and sources of these speeches.

83. Holzberg (1999, 324–25), who also points out that Apollo's rape would violate the Augustan *lex Iulia de adulteriis*.

84. See Thomas (2011) ad loc.

85. Green (2007, 140), yet cf. also the caveat issued by Zuchtriegel (2011, 12) about healing as a relatively undifferentiated divine responsibility in the mid-republic. Cf. also Strab. 14.1.6 for Apollo and Artemis both as healing divinities. Diana at Tibur is also called Diana Opifera Nemorensis.

86. In the reading of Petrovic (2010, 212). Apollo also fails to heal Aeneas in the *Aeneid*, posing a notable issue of interpretation; cf. Miller (2009a, 170–79). Artemis' status as the goddess of childbirth also brings her into contact with Apollo's sphere of healing. Her care for women at this medically perilous time allows her to additionally assume a healing aspect that leads to further overlap in the divine responsibilities of the siblings. Such an overlap not only provides another seam of contact exploitable for establishing a competitive relationship, but also reminds readers that in some versions of the siblings' birth, Artemis was born first and acted as midwife for Apollo's birth; for ancient sources, see Rutherford (2001, 368n18). This scenario also calls to mind the way Callimachus' Artemis claims the title of "helper" in childbirth, as ordained by the Fates (Callim. *Hymn* 3.21–25). Artemis' epithet Λοχία (λόχιος, "of/belonging to childbirth") also identifies her with Eileithyia as the goddess of childbirth; cf. Eur. *IT* 1097. In this capacity, we can also note that there was a shared sanctuary of Asclepius and Artemis Daphnaea (Paus. 3.24.9; cf. also Strab. 8.3.12 for Artemis Daphnia).

87. Although a call to a divinity to "bring help" appears generic, it is worth noting that the prayer to "bear help" occurs specifically as a plea to assist in childbirth. Twice

in Terence we observe women in labor calling out for Juno Lucina, an aspect of Diana as the goddess of childbirth (*Iuno Lucina, fer opem, serua me, obsecro*, "Juno Lucina, bear help, save me, I beseech," Ter. *An.* 473; *Iuno Lucina, fer opem! Serua me obsecro!*, Ter. *Ad.* 487). Plautus' *Amphitruo* provides a different formulation: when Alcumena begins to experience labor pains, she calls on the gods for help as women in childbirth do (*ut solent puerperae / inuocat deos immortalis ut sibi auxilium ferant*, "as laboring women are used to call upon the immortal gods, in order that they bring aid to them," Pluto *Amph.* 1092–93), echoing the statement that Jupiter makes about his assistance in the opening of Act III (*ueni ut auxilium feram*, "I come in order to bring aid," 870; *in tempore auxilium feram*, "I will bring aid in time," 877). Although it cannot be confirmed that the prayer *fer opem* would immediately recall a request for help in childbirth, the evidence suggests that Daphne's prayer may, in this way, further hint at healing language in an especially ironic fashion: it reconfigures the prayers of both father and daughter, one for descendants, and one for the preservation of virginity. A prayer uttered for safe deliverance instead of safe delivery acknowledges Peneus' desire for descendants at the same time it uncomfortably reflects a far different aspect of the goddess that Daphne wanted to emulate with virginity.

88. Notably, it physically literalizes the paralysis of the love Catullus laments in an elegiac prayer, a love he emphatically identifies as a disease (Catull. 76.20–22, 25; cf. esp. *torpor in artus*, 21). On the similarities in the Ovidian and Catullan language, see Vine (1993).

89. Within the descriptive confines of the hunting simile, Daphne is also seeking *salus* at 1.534, which has further resonance with Apollo as a practitioner of the *ars salutaris*; cf. also Cydippe's address to Diana, *parce laboranti, picta dea laeta pharetra / daque salutiferam iam mihi fratris opem* (Ov. *Her.* 21.173–74).

90. Phlegon of Tralles, *Macr.* 4 Keller = *FGrHist* 257 F 37.132–169 = Zosimus 2.6.1. See Thomas (2011, 277–78, trans. Dunning).

91. Barchiesi (2002b, 122).

92. On the *Ludi Saeculares*, see Davis (2001); Thomas (2011); Dunning (2016).

93. Miller (2009a, 148).

94. Curtis (2020, 195–200, quotation is from 199).

95. See also Proclus' definition (as a genre originally only used to supplicate Apollo and Artemis in times of plague, *ap. Bibl. Phot.* 320a20–24 Bekker); Rutherford (2001, 23–24); cf. also Barchiesi (2002b, 113–18).

96. Rutherford (1988, 72; 2001, 368). The Horatian pairing emphasizes that Diana, in bearing aid during times of childbirth, is equally critical to the continual propagation and regeneration of the social order and civic harmony generated and sustained in the healing dance; the paean enacts its own perfected harmony and order to uphold the civic and social sphere.

97. Ford (2006).

98. Cf. also the Ovidian description of the Python as *pestifer* (1.459), a description that casts Apollo's archery as an act of healing.

260 Notes to Pages 117–120

99. On Callimachus' hymn as a paean, see Lightfoot (2018); for the importance of the paean-cry within the hymn, see Kampakoglou (2019, 257–58, 288–90) and Gramps (2021, 10–11). An epigram of Theocritus (*Anth. Pal.* 6.336) offers "dark-leaved laurel" to "Pythian Paean" (3), further linking Apollo as Paean to Delphi.

100. On the ambiguity between the two, see Rutherford (2001, 121). Paeans are frequently addressed to the god, but the god himself is less commonly engaged with singing paeans. One example is Eur. *Ion* 905–6, within Creusa's monody, itself described as an anti-hymn; cf. Larue (1963); Swift (2010, see 94n86 for further bibliography, to which add Martin [2018, 370]). For Apollo singing paeans, cf. also Aesch. fr. 350.4 Radt.

101. Cf. also Foster (2017) on Horace 4.6 (which revisits the *Carmen Saeculare* with its depictions of Apollo and Diana, 4.6.31–44) and its reworking of Pindar's *Paean 6*.

102. For Cyrene's similarity with Daphne as an Apolline first love, see Ziogas (2013a, 67n46).

103. On the way the Pindaric Cyrene "revises" the Hesiodic tradition of *ehoie*, see Stamatopoulou (2017, 88–89). In Stamatopoulou's analysis, Apollo's praise characterizes Cyrene in a way that attracts her out of the limited sphere and agency of Hesiodic genealogical catalog poetry, forming part of *Pythian 9*'s set of Hesiodic revisions: the ode preserves all constituent elements of *ehoie* poetry but disrupts their structurally linear progression, thwarting expectations through its systematic reference to Hesiodic tradition. Hesiodic catalog poetry is also a concern in the structure of the Ovidian mythical narrative: the transformation of Apollo Pythoctonos to Apollo Philens mirrors the transitional seam from the *Theogony* to the *Catalogue*, an epic sequence that likewise sets up expectations for the Ovidian narrator to cleverly thwart; see Ziogas (2013a, 66–67). For further evidence on Ovidian engagements with Pindar where the god Apollo is concerned, see Philbrick (2018), who focuses on the Coronis myth.

104. Nonnus will later refer to her as a "second Artemis" (Nonnus, *Dion.* 13.300).

105. His spectatorship reviews everything the Pindaric Apollo does not dwell on in beholding Cyrene; see again Stamatopoulou (2017, 81–88).

106. Cf. Hardie (2002b, 46).

107. Peneus is probably part of Cyrene's Hesiodic genealogy, a view supported by the concerns of the Ovidian Peneus. In this role, the Ovidian Peneus props up the Augustan social agenda praised in the *Carmen Saeculare*, calling into question how the motivations of Ovid as epic *auctor* can align with Augustus as the *auctor* of family legislation.

108. Cf. Ap. Rhod. *Argon.* 2.500–507.

109. This is more notable if we consider the evidence that Thessaly was the original focal point for female genealogical poetry; see Skempis (2016, 52n23 for bibliography).

110. Plantinga (2004, 263–64) briefly mentions Cyrene as one example of rivalry.

111. In one etymology. The city's name is also linked to the spring Cyre (*Hymn* 2.88); cf. Williams (1978) ad loc. Cyrene as νύμφη ("bride" and "spring nymph,"

Notes to Pages 120–125 261

"water") hints at both derivations. Daphne's status as a river nymph also brings together both understandings of Cyrene's name: the eponymous nymph, or the spring Cyre. On the role of springs and nymphs in Callimachean poetry, see Depew (2007).

112. For this Libyan version, cf. Acesandros *FGrHist* 469 F4.

113. Atalanta defeated Peleus in wrestling at Pelias' funeral games, a popular vignette for vase painting; the hymn turns to her praises just a few lines later (*Hymn* 3.215–24).

114. See both Bornmann (1968) and Stephens ad loc.

115. The *Hymn to Delos* also seems to endorse the Thessalian version: Leto pleads that Mt. Pelion is even home to lionesses giving birth (*Hymn* 4.118–20). Stephens ad loc. notes the Pindaric reference but does not relate it to Cyrene's appearances within the other hymns.

116. ἀέθλου also hints at the Pindaric myth of Cyrene via allusion to Atalanta: in Pindar, Cyrene wrestles with the lion (as opposed to hunting it), and Atalanta is later metamorphosed into a lion. In one account this is by the will of Artemis (Nonnus, *Dion.* 12.87–89); on the closeness of Cyrene and Atalanta, cf. Howell and Howell (1989, 137–38); Stamatopoulou (2017, 82–84).

117. See Stephens ad loc. Delos is here identified as Ortygia, which is sometimes identified as a separate location (either the Syracusan Ortygia or an Ephesian Ortygia; see Stephens [2015, 102]); even within this image of collaboration there is a hint of rivalry, as Apollo takes the first step to "civilize" Ortygia.

118. On the temples of Apollo and Artemis, see Chamoux (1953, 311–20); Goodchild (1971, 109–128).

119. See the interpretation of Dobias-Lalou (2017).

120. Potentially anticipating the narrative of Syrinx, which is begun by an internal narrator (Mercury, 1.689–700) and finished by the omniscient Ovidian narrator (1.700–12).

121. As Traill (1998) reads Envy's reproach.

122. As analyzed by Fain (2004, see 147n14 for further bibliography).

123. Bing and Uhrmeister (1994, 26–28). For a parallel reading of the styles of Ovid and Callimachus' *Hymn to Artemis*, see Tissol (1997, 131–66).

124. Fain (2004, 54).

125. Her request for a chorus of sixty is ten more than usual, which reinforces the magnitude of Oceanus; cf. Bremmer (1999, 189) on fifty as the "characteristic number for adolescent choruses."

126. Petrovic (2007, 257–61) also explores the reasons for this textual modification, noting Caeratus as a prior name of Knossos, the city that boasts the famed sanctuary of Zeus. Her Cretan connection to Zeus is further emphasized when she asks the Cyclopes for a "Cydonian bow" (*Hymn* 3.81) and arrows, citing that she too is a child of Leto, like Apollo.

127. Homer mentions the Peneus briefly as a river that Titaressos, a branch of the Styx, does not mingle its waters with (*Il.* 2.751–55; cf. also Luc. 6.371–80). This Iliadic

262   Notes to Pages 126–128

passage is used by a scholiast to explain a phrase found among the fragments of Pindar's tenth *Paean* (Στυ[γὶ σύνδετον, 10a.4), which makes it plausible that the river in question refers to the Peneus; for the fragment see Rutherford (2001, 200–3).

128. Pelion also rejects the goddess in the *Homeric Hymn to Apollo* (33), but there is no parallel mention of the Peneus. McKay (1962a, 179) in discussing this crossing of communications—Leto's first appeal to Peneus, which goes unacknowledged, and her subsequent appeal to Pelion, which is then answered by the Peneus—suggests the reader "can only assume that literature told of an *agon* between the two geographical features, like that between Helikon and Kithairon described by Korinna." This seems quite a substantial assumptive leap to make. For the "cosmic disorder" caused by the flight of places from Leto, see Williams (1993, 221–23); for the difficulties posed by the imagining of this landscape in flight, see the analysis of Klooster (2012). For the historical aspects of the hymn, see most recently Giuseppetti (2012a; 2013, esp. 16–32 and 146–64).

129. Horace names the two locales together in hymning Apollo (*uos Tempe totidem tollite laudibus / natalemque, mares, Delon Apollonis*, "you boys, raise equal praises of Tempe and Delos, birthplace of Apollo," *Carm.* 1.21.9–10. Given the ritual relationship between Apollo and Tempe, it is possible here that *laudibus* summons the context of *laurus*, providing an additional pun to the "idea-play" observed by Cairns (1971, 440).

130. Wills (1990, 149).

131. In the words of Wills (1990, 150), "Like the story of Daphne, the *Hymn to Delos* is essentially a metamorphosis of flight into stability accompanied by Apollo's devotion."

132. Wills (1990, 150).

133. Which, as Wills recognizes, further integrates echoes of Callimachus' *Hymn*; Daphne, as Peneus' daughter, flees just as the river's flight is described by Leto, as if competing with the breezes (*Hymn* 4.112). The element of competition underscores both the Callimachean aetiological context of the Pythian games that Ovid has adaptively manipulated and a general spirit of poetic competition.

134. *Pigris* also looks back to Cupid as *impiger* when he flies to Parnassus (*Met.* 1.467).

135. On the Callimachean emphasis of Asteria's purity, see Bing (2008, 113).

136. Famously with respect to earthquakes; cf. Pind. fr. 33c.2 S-M, where the island is called ἀκίνητον τέρας; Virg. *Aen.* 3.75–77; Hdt. 6.98.3; Thuc. 2.8.3; Plin. *HN* 4.66; Sen. *QNat.* 6.26.2–4.

137. Immobility and lack of cultivation become integrated, defining concepts of the Delian land; see Nishimura-Jensen (2000, 292n15), and the overview of Stephens ad loc. Cf. also Barchiesi (1994, 441n15).

138. Plato connects Artemis' name with her love of virginity (*Cra.* 406b); van Windekens (1986, 19–20) attempts to connect ἀρτεμής ("healthy," "safe") as the root of Artemis' name to ἀτρεμής ("unmoved"), which bears interesting resonance to Delos'

Notes to Pages 128–132   263

naming and rootedness; Peters (2002, 371–72) also interprets ἀρτεμής as "intact" (i.e., virginal), making Artemis' purity the defining feature of both her name and being.

139. McKay (1962a, 184–85). As Richardson (2010, 90) notes of Delos in the *Homeric Hymn to Apollo*, "the dramatic personification of the eponymous nymph or deity of a place (with dialogue) occurs first here."

140. Bing (2008, 87). The image that gives way to the description of the poet as ploughman in the *Hymn to Artemis* is of the nymphs encircling the goddess in the dance, an image of dance and circling also applied to Delos as being surrounded by the Cyclades (*Hymn* 4.300–1). The idea of Delos as participating in the dance is also attested to in the visual tradition by a vase upon which Delos is depicted as a nymph dancing; cf. Constantakopoulou (2007, 26). Additionally, Apollo is also described as the center of the circle of the dancing immortals at *Hymn. Hom. Ap.* 194–203.

141. On the nature of Callimachus' relationship to Homer and especially Pindar, see Depew (1998).

142. Trans. Stephens.

143. Bing (2008, 126n57); Ukleja (2005, 300–301).

144. Hardie (2002b, 14).

145. Ukleja (2005, 286–301); see also Fantuzzi (2011, 451–53).

146. Cyra is also the Libyan name for asphodel, which renders Cyrene as the "city of asphodel"; Callimachus links Asteria to Cyrene by comparing her to an asphodel (*Hymn* 4.193), which further provides a botanical thread of connective tissue between Ovid's Daphne, Cyrene, and Callimachus' Delos. On this comparison, see Bing (2008, 121–22).

147. Pindar's ninth *Pythian* honors a Cyrenean winner of the hoplite race.

148. For the *Hymn to Delos* as emblematic of Callimachean poetry, cf. the metapoetic reading of Bing (2008, 110–28), esp. the sentiment of "the birth of Delos may thus be viewed as depicting the realization of Callimachean song" (121) and the allegorical reading of Slings (2004).

149. Fantuzzi (2011, 451–52); Petrovic (2016) identifies family dynamics as the uniting thread of the collection.

150. Manakidou (2020) reads *Hymns* 1 and 4 jointly through the theme of motherhood, packaging 1–4 together in a different way, as having complementary bookends.

151. The punishment Ares threatens, of overturning his streams (ἀποκρύψαι δὲ ῥέεθρα, *Hymn* 4.135) quotes the Homeric Apollo's punishment of Telphousa (ἀπέκρυψεν δὲ ῥέεθρα, *Hymn. Hom. Ap.* 383), the stream who tricks Apollo into changing his mind and establishing his oracle for mankind elsewhere, desirous as she is of keeping local fame for herself (*Hymn. Hom. Ap.* 244–76), which further implicates interplay of fame/praise/water in this passage.

152. As Mynors (1990) notes ad *Georg.* 4.317, "The wooded valley through which the Peneius flows eastwards between Olympus and Ossa to the sea, famous for its beauty . . . and hence in general any charming vale with woods and water, as in 2.469." Cf. also McKeown (1989) ad *Am.* 1.1.15–16. Hunter (1999, ad Theoc. *Id.* 1.67) identifies this usage

264 Notes to Pages 132–141

as the intermediate stage between Tempe and tempe, possibly the very appearance that inspired use in a generalizing sense by the later Roman poets. Schol. 67a Wendel shows "tempe" and "grove" to be fairly synonymous. For tempe, cf. also Hor. *Carm.* 3.1.24; App. Verg. *Cul.* 94; Virg. *Georg.* 2.469; Ov. *Fast.* 4.477; Stat. *Theb.* 1.485, [6.88], 10.119 and *Silv.* 5.3.209. Cf. also the usage of Τέμπη at Cic. *Att.* 4.15.5. Ael. *VH* 3.1 provides the most extensive description of Tempe. For Tempe in the Roman poets, cf. also *Met.* 7.222; Catull. 64.35 and 285–86; Hor. *Carm.* 1.7.4 and 1.21.9; Virg. *Georg.* 4.317; Columella, *Rust.* 10.1.1.265; Luc. 6.345 and 8.1; Stat. *Achil.* 1.237 and *Silv.* 1.2.215; Flaccus *Argon.* 8.452; Sen. *Herc. fur.* 286 and 980, *Tro.* 815 and *Med.* 457. The stratified existence of Tempe/tempe is similar to the case of Ida, as Ἴδα could mean a specific mountain (in Crete or the Troad) or simply "wood" (*LSJ* s.v. ἴδη) or later, any mountain.

153. On Delphi and Thessaly, see Mili (2014, 241–47). Delphi is also evoked via the aetiological knowledge of the first Delphic temple being constructed from Tempe's laurel, and the ritual knowledge of the Septerion.

154. Mili (2014, 246).

Chapter 4. Ovid's *Lavacrum Dianae*

1. On the basis of *Pont.* 4.16.34, Grattius is identified as a contemporary of Ovid; Ovid makes reference to *Cyn.* 23 here, which argues for his familiarity with the work. As such, this chapter presupposes Ovid's knowledge of Grattius' didactic. On the mutual influence of Grattius and Ovid's own didactic, the *Ars amatoria*, see Tsaknaki (2018), who does not commit to establishing a primacy of textual influence, allowing both texts to share collective insight. If Ovid is engaging with Grattius in the *Ars amatoria*, it would certainly speak to his ability to do so within the *Metamorphoses*.

2. Cf. Plantinga (2004, 273–75).

3. Cf. Steiner (2021, 245) on the suggestive nature of the similarity in sound.

4. Artemis is also part of the world of mythological exempla in the *Iliad*, in the myths of Meleager and Niobe.

5. Chariclo is the name of Chiron's wife and the mother of Ocyroe in the *Metamorphoses*.

6. Stephens (2015) ad 259–68; Plantinga (2004, 274).

7. On the mythological variants, see Fontenrose (1981, 5–32). Newlands (1995, 111–12) discusses Ovid's evasiveness toward Orion's sexual transgressions and boastfulness in the *Fasti*.

8. Fontenrose (1981, 33–47) traces the variations of the Actaeon myth; see also Schlam (1984) and Barchiesi (2007, 146–49).

9. Borthwick (1970); Valdés Guía (2021).

10. Cf. also *armigerae . . . Tritonidis* (Petron. *Sat.* 5.1.9).

11. Cf. Serv. ad *Aen.* 1.479–90.

12. Heath (1991, 241n21) likens her preparations to a "Roman matron's toilet," comparing it to Callimachus' hymn. In contrast, when Venus is disguised as a huntress (and Diana-type), she is described as *nuda genu* (Virg. *Aen.* 1.320), with her robes knotted up. On the *palla* and its significance, see Olson (2008, 33–36).

Notes to Pages 141–147

13. Manakidou (2020) focuses on motherhood as a leitmotif within the collection, but through the thematic union of *Hymns* 1 and 4.

14. As Michalopoulos (2001, 53–54) notes, Autonoe's name is etymologized from the Greek ἑαυτήν οὐ νοεῖ, "she who does not know herself," which links Actaeon to the prophecy about Narcissus that will cement Tiresias' reputation as a seer (*si se non nouerit*, "if he does not know himself," 3.348). Ovid therefore connects the Callimachean figures of Tiresias and Actaeon in a new way, via the further embedded figure of Narcissus. Actaeon's recognition of himself in the water is the beginning of Book 3's psychological drama of spectating and beholding that will prove Narcissus' undoing.

15. Hunter (1992, 19–22).

16. Van Tress (2004, 100–2).

17. Cf. the Virgilian model of Silvia's stag (*Aen.* 7.500–2), also using the language of supplication (*imploranti similis*, 502). The maddening of Ascanius' hounds by Allecto may derive inspiration from a version of the Actaeon myth (see the commentary of Horsfall [1999] ad loc.), rendering this another circular allusion completed by Ovid.

18. Rose (1931); Nagy (1973).

19. On the etymological play with *ceruus*, see Michalopoulos (2001, 51–53).

20. On poetic images of fawns with their mothers, see Wasdin (2018, 123–26).

21. *Varia* can be used substantively in this way; on reading *uarius* as *maculosus*, cf. Serv. ad *Aen* 1.323. Virgil also uses *uarius* to indicate a difference of opinion (*Aen.* 10.97), which further colors the multifaceted use of this adjective for the mythological episode, as it could also anticipates the debate over Diana's behavior that ends the narrative.

22. On the poetic implications of Actaeon's "dappled skin" in light of the νεβρὶς ποικιλόνωτος Nonnus receives from the Muses-Maenads, see Paschalis (2014, 112–14); the argument made here strengthens these specific inspirational ties between Ovid and Nonnus.

23. As in other Ovidian usages; cf. *Am.* 3.1.14, *Ars am* 3.272.

24. Rich (1860, s.v. *endromis*) argues that the ἐνδρομίς is open-toed, in contrast to the *cothurnus*; this is interesting to note in the case of Diana dipping her toe in the water before suggesting she and her nymphs undress to bathe, indicating open-toed footwear (*Met.* 2.457).

25. Faulkner (2013, 227) after O. Thomas (2011, 158n21).

26. On the connections between this episode and the *Homeric Hymn*, see Reckford (1995–96) and Olson (2011).

27. Cf. also *maculoso nebrida tergo* (Stat. *Silv.* 1.2.226).

28. This compound recalls the running boots from Artemis' hymn (ἐνδρομίς, *Hymn* 3.16).

29. All Grattian text and translations are Green (2018).

30. Green (2007, 126).

31. In contrast, Xenophon names Carthaginian or Colchian flax (*Cyn.* 2.4).

266 Notes to Pages 148–153

32. Yet cf. Pind. *Pyth.* 5.24, where a scholion records the Callimachean fragment as an explanation of the κᾶπον Ἀφροδίτας, which the poem places in Cyrene; on this question, see Phillips (2013, 160n32).

33. After Grattius, the only poets to use "Cinyphian" as an adjective are Ovid himself, Lucan, and Silius Italicus. In the exile poetry, Ovid mentions the land's fruitfulness, further attesting to the Herodotean account (*Pont.* 2.7.25); he also names Ibis' birthplace as "Cinyphian soil" (*Ib.* 222), which I would read as an additional Callimachean reference.

34. Larson (2007, 162). Cf. also the commentary of Barchiesi ad loc. for other appearances of Gargaphie.

35. Berenice II, one figure behind the poetic construction of Athena in the *Bath of Pallas*, is also named as a fourth Grace in a Callimachean poem (15 *GP* = 51 Pf. = *Anth. Pal.* 5.146) The overlap between Muses and Graces is also played out between Ptolemaic queens: Arsinoe was said to be labeled as a tenth Muse in the first edition of the *Aetia*, a label that perhaps passed to Berenice in the second edition; see Knox (1985, 63–64); the commentary of Harder ad *Aet.* 2a,1; Depew (2004, 129). For Callimachus' queens, see Prioux (2011). Arsinoe also unusually features in Posidippus as a water nymph, which also aligns her with the Muses (*SH* 978). As the commentary of Barchiesi ad loc. records, Pliny also lists Gargaphie alongside the famed Heliconian springs, the Hippocrene and Aganippe.

36. Cf. this same phrase at *Met.* 7.807; for knots as features in the nets, cf. also *plenisque . . . nodis* (Gratt. *Cyn.* 32). Heath (1991, 241n21) briefly notes the similarity in phrasing but is more focused on the sexual symbolism of Diana's bound hair.

37. Michalopoulos (2001, 134). Riley's translation (1893, 92n19) records a possible connection of Crocale to κεκρύφαλος, a woman's hair net; he does not note the additional meaning of "pouch/belly of a hunting net," as found in Xenophon (*Cyn.* 6.7).

38. Ovid's integration of weaving with hunting nets also brings Minerva and Diana closer together, creating another parallel between their spheres of power.

39. Cf. also Prop. 2.32.20 and Hor. *Epod.* 2.33.

40. As in the readings of Segal (1969), Curran (1978), and Heath (1991), which have set the interpretive tone for the episode. Cf. also the commentary of Barchiesi ad loc.

41. Cf. also Luc. 6.75; Mart. 13.19.1.

42. Cf. Pind. *Pyth.* 9.65; Ap. Rhod. *Argon.* 2.506–7. Aristaeus shares this title with Apollo and Pan.

43. *O felix* looks to the Virgilian *felix qui* (*Georg.* 2.490); *deus ille* similarly to the exclamation at Virg. *Ecl.* 5.64 (*deus, deus ille, Menalca!*).

44. See O'Rourke (2018, 203).

45. The designation of the landscape as a *lucus*, a space popularly etymologized via the concept of light (*lucus, a non lucendo*; cf. Serv. ad *Aen.* 1.22; Quint. *Inst.* 1.6.34) right before Actaeon enters (3.176) additionally plays upon Actaeon's connection with light.

46. Cf. Schiesaro (2019, 178–79 and esp. n. 10) on Nonnus' etymologizing of Actaeon, which can be aptly applied here.

Notes to Pages 154–165

47. See the argument of O'Rourke (2018).

48. Palaephatus *Peri Apiston* 6; see Hawes (2014, 71).

49. See Stephens (2015, 237).

50. Hopkinson (2020, 116).

51. Stephens ad loc.

52. On Dercylus as a source, see Bulloch (1985, 16–17); Stephens (2015, 35–36, 237) and ad *Hymn* 5.47–48 and 56. Ps-Plutarch also cites a "Dercyllus" as a source on a few occasions, interpreted by some scholars to be an invention, which lends another interesting example for playing with this name as a source text; see Cameron (2004, 133–34).

53. Cf. Varr. *Ling.* 5.178 on the derivation of *praemium* from *praeda*.

54. For a different interpretation, see Gale (2018, 93n38).

55. Whitlatch (2018, 183).

56. For Callimachus' use of the *Hippolytus*, see Bulloch (1985, 49–52); on the connections between Actaeon and Hippolytus in tragedy, see Manousakis (2020, 205–6). On tragedy more generally in the hymn, see Ypsilanti (2009, 109n2).

57. *Met.* 7. 753–55; Hyg. *Fab.* 189; Paus. 9.19.1.

58. One wonders if it appears in Aeschylus, given his love for neologism; on the tragic Actaeon, see Manousakis (2020).

59. Most recently, see Boyd (2017, 92).

60. On the variations, see Schlam (1984, 84n5).

61. The catalog exhibits some ring composition between the dogs named at 3.208 and the names and parentage of Melaneus (3.222) and Labros (3.224), who both have a Cretan father and Spartan mother. Hagnon also breeds the *thoes* (*Cyn.* 253–59); cf. the Ovidian Thoos (3.220).

62. On the poetic point of enumeration in the Callimachean catalog of dogs, see Henrichs (1993, 134–37).

63. Cf. Stephens (2015, 24).

64. Cf. the Ovidian dog Pterelas ("Wings," 3.212)

65. Stephens ad loc.

66. Stephens ad loc.

67. Sticte ("Spot," 3.217) also indicates markings, but without color specified.

68. According to Xenophon, dogs should have "small, delicate ears that are hairless behind" (*Cyn.* 4.1).

69. As an epithet of Heracles, the name also could relate to Artemis' first Arcadian hunt; she leaves one deer to escape for Heracles' labor (*Hymn* 3.107–9). Heracles reappears in her hymn in his role as a glutton (*Hymn* 3.144–61).

70. The other overlap between Xenophon's list and the Ovidian catalog is Alce (3.217). On name-sharing between dogs and centaurs, see Wachter (1991, 92–93, 97).

71. As mentioned previously, they are described as *famuli* (3.229); the catalog form itself is adopted from epic lists of warriors, underscoring the dogs' militant behavior as they hunt in an *agmen* (3.242). This military language also contrasts with the *nudae* ("unarmed," cf. *OLD*, s.v. 4) nymphs who surround Diana in a crowd to protect her (3.178).

268 Notes to Pages 165–175

72. Michalopoulos (2001, 134).

73. Thomas (1988) ad loc.; cf. also Serv. ad *Aen.* 1.500.

74. Like Ovid's myth, Claudian names seven nymphs, before adding a company of one hundred hailing from Taygetus, one hundred from Mt. Cynthus, and a hundred from "chaste" Ladon (*Cons. Stil.* 3.257–60).

75. Thomas (1988) ad loc.; Thomas (1986, 191–93).

76. Green (2007, 53; on the Grattian passage altogether, see 50–54).

77. Schlam (1984, 84–86); on the role Lyssa may have played in Aeschylus' tragedy, see Manousakis (2020, 212–15). On the connection between madness and *rabies* explored in Grattius, see Kayachev (2018, 110–13). The text of Tarrant prints *rapidum . . . agmen* to describe the dogs at 3.242 at the moment they close in on Actaeon, but he notes the alternate reading *rabidum* as conceivably right in the apparatus criticus. Both Lucan (2.491) and Silius (14.638) reprise *rapidum . . . agmen* in the same metrical sedes, while *rabidum . . . agmen* would be singular to Ovid. On the defense of *rabidum*, see de Verger (2008, 807–8).

78. For the "hymnic register" of this distancing, see the commentary of Barchiesi and Rosati ad loc.

79. Lowe (2013).

80. For a reading of Orion's relevance to the character of Actaeon in Aeschylus as well as mythological variants surrounding Orion, see Manousakis (2020, 203–5). On Orion as the archetype of the hunter, see Fontenrose (1981, 5–32); on the Aloads, see 112–20.

CHAPTER 5. THE HYMNIC BATTLE FOR HELICON

1. The fragmentary nature of the poem generates some interpretive issue about whether Helicon, as a participant, is understood here as a person (a man or hero) or personification; despite the contested nature of the text, scholarly opinion tends to identify Helicon here as the figure who will eventually give the mountain its name. See Berman (2015, 67–69) and Vergados (2012, 113).

2. Singing contests occupy a well-known place in the mytho-literary tradition, from the *certamen* of Homer and Hesiod to the competition between Aeschylus and Euripides in Aristophanes' *Frogs*, the recorded animus between Corinna and Pindar and the musical clashes between both Apollo and Marsyas and Pan and Tmolus. On the *agon* in Greek poetry, see the study of Collins (2004). The volume of Damon and Pieper (2018) assesses competition in antiquity more generally.

3. Even more radically, the Muses are only *invoked* in the epic's final book (*Met.* 15.622–25).

4. On reading them as a pair, see Heyworth (2004) and Ambühl (2005, 99–221).

5. Neither Cyane nor Arethusa are granted prominent roles in the parallel tales of Persephone's abduction in the *Homeric Hymn* or in the *Fasti*; Johnson (1996) and Zissos (1999), albeit approaching the issue from different angles, both see this discrepancy in narrative priority as justified by the selection of nymphs as judges for the contest.

Notes to Pages 175–178

6. For a literary occurrence of comparable narrative complexity, see Fernandelli (2012, 3–10) analyzing *Eclogue* 6. In terms of contemporary attitudes toward performance and writing, it seems apt to note Horace's recognition that poetic immortality is contingent not upon public performance but placing one's work upon shelves in the Palatine library (*Epist.* 2.1.214–18; cf. also Prop. 3.1.15–18). Even Virgil's pastoral privileges the act of writing in a genre that does not usually recognize the merits of such acts, given its traditional emphasis on performance and exchange of song, a point well discussed by Lowrie (2009, 144–50). Barchiesi (2002a, 187–95) explores the narratological complexity of this episode, including the question of what would appeal to Minerva as an audience (193).

7. The Hippocrene, created by the hoof-blow of Pegasus. This was not a unique event, as testified by the fact that a few "Hippocrenes" exist scattered across Greece, created in similar fashions (cf. Paus. 2.31.9; Strab. 8.6.21). For the creation of the Hippocrene, see esp. Aratus, *Phaen.* 205–24; Strab. 8.6.21; Paus. 9.31.3; Ant. Lib. *Met.* 9; Hyg. *Poet. astr.* 2.18; Nonnus, *Dion.* 7.234–36. Cf. also Prop. 3.3.1–2.

8. Hinds (1987, 21–24) contrasts this description with the *leuis . . . ungula* of the *Fasti*'s parallel narration of the act (*Fast.* 3.455–56) to make the case that these choices constitute conscious verbal signposts of each work's respective genre: *dura* for the epic *Metamorphoses*, and *leuis* for the elegiac *Fasti*. His valuable analysis of Helicon as a setting overall runs from 3–24, one largely echoed by Jouteur (2001, 76–78).

9. The goddess' awareness of the Hippocrene's creation stems from a particularly literary sort of *fama*; cf. Ov. *Fast.* 3. 455–56, where the spring is created when Bellerephon first bridles Pegasus. Cf. also Pind. *Ol.* 13.63 for his bridling by the Peirene; Strabo records that Pegasus was caught while drinking from this spring (8.6.21) before proceeding to relate the creation of the Hippocrene. Corinth, however, also had a bath that mimicked the Hippocrene, with the water flowing through Pegasus' hoof (Paus. 2.3.5). Persius links the two sites in his prologue (pr. 1.4–5); the two also find affiliation in a late epigram by the Corinthian poet Honestus (*Anth. Pal.* 9.225).

10. See note 8. The question of attributing generic significations to the springs of Helicon is complicated; for present purposes, it suffices to state that at some point Roman poets individually tied generic inspiration to the separate springs, an isolation of influence that led to Hippocrene's cementing as the acknowledged spring of epic, and the Permessus or Aganippe as the font of lighter genres, chiefly elegy. For the hierarchical distinction in the Heliconian springs, see Maass (1896, 388–428, esp. 423); Wilamowitz (1924, 93–95); Wimmel (1960, 233–38; Luck (1969, 139–40); Lyne (1998, 25–28); Waszink (1950, 1962); Quadlbauer (1968, 92–93). Ross (1975, 32–34) discusses the influence of the Propertian couplet on *Eclogue* 6, ultimately refusing to draw a distinction between the two water sources; he returns to this point at 119–20. Most recently, see Harder ad Callim. *Aet.* fr. 2, 1 and 2b, 1.

11. For analysis of Minerva's appearance within the episode, see Johnson (2008, 47–52).

270   Notes to Pages 178–179

12. These concerns are primarily achieved by careful reminiscence of the Judgement of Paris. See Bulloch (1985, 127–28, and further 19–20 and 132) for the nature of Athena's femininity and its Callimachean emphasis. See also Heath (1988, 74) and Hadjittofi (2008).

13. See chapter 4, p. 179. Cf. esp. *Met.* 2.454–59 and 3.163–64; *Fast.* 2.163–67. Artemis is also known for bathing in the Parthenius (Ap. Rhod. *Argon.* 2.936–39 and 3.876–77); cf. also Callim. *Aet.* fr. 75, 24 Harder and the notes ad loc. for the contextual suggestion of the river's name being linked to Ἄρτεμις Παρθενίη (Callim. *Hymn* 3.110).

14. See Bulloch (1985, 24) and Heath (1988, 82); cf. also Berman (2015, 128–30).

15. The activity of bathing and stillness of the hour receives immediate reemphasis and elaboration in the subsequent line, *Hymn* 5.72–73.

16. Crucially, the only other time Athena is pictured as sporting with nymphs is her play with the Oceanids, as Persephone narrates to Demeter; see *Hymn. Hom. Dem.* 424 with the notes of Richardson (1974) ad loc. For the connection of Artemis to nymphs, see Larson (1997), esp. for the identification of Artemis hunting and dancing with a chorus of nymphs as particularized to epic (249).

17. See Bulloch (1985, 179 ad 5.72 and n. 5 for reference and bibliography); Heath (1988, 76–77, 83); and Papanghelis (1989, 56–57). Midday inspirations are also ascribed to Archilochus and Epimenides; see Brillante (2004, 13–15). Additionally, a scholiast (cited in Fraser [1972] 721=Heath [1988, 83n39]) reports that Callimachus described himself at the time of his initiation just as the poet himself describes Tiresias, just with the first beginnings of a beard: ἄρτι γένεια/ περκάζων (*Hymn* 5.75–76). Tiresias' thirst is also a relevant detail (5.77); his desire to drink from the Hippocrene places him among the tradition of those inspired by drinking from the fountain, including Callimachus (for a good late example of the powers of the Heliconian spring water, cf. *Anth. Pal.* 9.364). For the connection of poetry and prophecy, see Heath (1988, 84n43).

18. Heath (1988, 85). However, Chariclo assigns of blame to Helicon itself (Callim. *Hymn* 5.89–92); Tiresias' desire to drink from the Hippocrene, instead of resolving into a poetic initiation, is cause for an "epic" punishment, and her complaint makes Helicon itself functionally write Tiresias into the epic corpus. For the hymn's reliance on Homeric epic, despite its meter, see Bulloch (1985, 29, 45).

19. The prophetic powers of the Muses are generally derived from their association with Apollo, and are part of their existence as figures of inspiration; Apollo is known as both Nymphagetes and Musagetes. Association of the Muses with Apollo are commonplace within Greek and Latin poetry; cf. Hes. *Theog.* 94–95; *Hymn. Hom. Ap.* 182–93; *Hymn. Hom.* 25; Alcm. fr. 46 *PMG*; Sappho fr. 208 L-P; Pind. *Pyth.* 1.1–13; Callim. *Hymn* 4.249–54 and *Ia.* 13 fr. 203 Pf.; Stat. *Theb.* 6.355–65; Strab. 10.3.10. Most specifically, the Muses were reported to have taught Aristaeus the art of prophecy (Ap. Rhod. *Argon.* 2.511–12). Athena acting with the power of a Muse in blinding Tiresias also relates to the Muses' punishment of Thamyris, who vied with them for primacy in song; cf. Apollod. *Bibl.* 1.3.3–4; Paus. 4.33.7.

20. Minerva's reservation for *opera . . . maiora* is also notable for *opus* as a generic tag; see Keith (1992a, 335) and Weinlich (2010, 139) on the programmatic *opus* of *Amores* 1.1.24. For other textual loci of import, cf. Prop. 2.10.11–12; Ov. *Am.* 3.1.24; and Virg. *Aen.* 7.45, as well as the less serious transitional usage at *Met.* 8.328, when Meleager turns his thoughts from love to the hunt.

21. Johnson (2008, 49) calls the suggestion that Minerva might have been a Muse "absurd," merely identifying it as an "unabashed bit of flattery."

22. See the commentary of Rosati ad loc.

23. Littlewood (2006, ad *Fast.* 6.655).

24. Fulg. *Myth.* 3.9; cf. also Luc. 9.352–54 for Minerva looking at herself in lake Tritonis. For Athena's birth near the river Triton, cf. Callim. *Aet.* fr. 37, 1 and the notes of Harder ad loc.; for the attendance of the nymphs at her birth, see Larson (2001) 190. Cf. also the flute's designation as *Tritoniaca . . . harundine* (*Met.* 6.384, with the notes of Rosati ad loc. Epicharmus (fr. 39 K-A) also lists Tritone as a Muse, which may add further (humorous) resonance to the Muse's choice of this designator (although not derived from Triton); see also n. 33.

25. For the Muses named Ardalides after Ardalus, the inventor of the flute, cf. Paus. 2.31.3 and Plut. *Conv. sept. sap.* 150b. According to Pindar's twelfth *Pythian* ode, Athena's invention of the flute is based upon the dirges of the Gorgons at Medusa's death; this timing coincides with the Ovidian chronology of her visit to Helicon, as she has just bid farewell to Perseus before proceeding onward to Helicon, a moment at which she also receives the epithet Tritonia (*Met.* 5.250).

26. See Richardson (1974) ad loc. and Foley (1993, 33). Diodorus also narrates a version that includes Athena (Diod. Sic. 5.3.4), closely tying her not only to the Sicilian landscape but to Artemis and Persephone.

27. For a summary of Minerva's treatment of women within the *Metamorphoses*, see Janan (1994, 430n9).

28. See *Met.* 4.798–803.

29. Cf. also the parallel uses of *uirgineumque Helicona* (*Met.* 5.254) and the *uirgineae mentes* of the Muses (*Met.* 5.274).

30. On the Muses as water nymphs in origin, see Meyer (1933, 692–93); Commager (1962, 11); Larson (2001, 7–8).

31. Cf. the view expressed by Socrates at Pl. *Phdr.* 238d. The best example of this connection is the existence of the Hamadryad, whose life is directly tied to the life of her tree; cf., e.g., Callim. *Hymn* 4.79–85. Kennedy (1982, 377–82) suggests that Hamadryads were presented as surrogate Muses in the poetry of Gallus. Places considered home to the nymphs were also often regarded as imbued with prophetic powers; see Larson (2001, 11–20) for nymphs and prophetic inspiration specifically.

32. Cf. also ps-Ov. *ES 27*. Oenone names herself as *Pegasis Oenone* (*Her.* 5.3), on which see the notes of Knox (1995) ad loc.

33. Note also Catullus' presentation of Aganippe as a nymph (*nympha . . . Aganippe*, 61.29–30), perhaps in the tradition that makes her a daughter of the Permessus;

272 Notes to Pages 184–187

cf. Harder ad Callim. *Aet.* fr. 2b, 2 and 3 and the ancient testimony of Paus. 9.29.5. Epicharmus (fr. 39 K-A) catalogs seven Muses, most of whom bear names derived from notable rivers: Neilo, Tritone, Asopo, Heptapore, Achelois, Titoplous, and Rhodia. Eumelus (fr. 35 West) names three Muses, also connected to rivers: Cephisso, Apollonis, and Borysthenis, which diverges from a different account in his corpus (fr. 34).

34. Cf. the similar thinking of Salzman-Mitchell (2005, 181–82) on Arethusa's simultaneous narrative bridging of "male" and "female," as her tale endorses the validity of both the male gaze and female victimhood.

35. Vergados (2020, 27, 30–38) most recently gives an overview of the ancient traditions surrounding the number and names of the Muses; on their importance to Hesiodic poetry see further 23–43.

36. According to Athenaeus (3.110b). A fragment (92 K-A) also gives us the information that Athena played the flute at the wedding, further underscoring her relationship to the Muses; cf. p. 181. On Epicharmus' Muses, see Cardin and Tribulato (2019).

37. The challenge of the Pierides is also specifically pitched as a battle (*et tali committit proelia uoce*, "and with such a proclamation, they begin the war," *Met.* 5.307).

38. Johnson and Malamud (1988, 33) briefly note Ovid's "doubling" of the Muses and Pierides.

39. E.g the *indocti . . . uulgi* of Prop. 2.23.1–2.

40. Cf. A. Hardie (2006, 58–59). Hardie differentiates the two epithets via ethnographic import: the Pierides try to disenfranchise the Muses by calling them by a cult title that would point to their recent establishment on Helicon, initiated only when Pieros came to Thespiae and changed the names of the Aload Muses, while Aonides, with its pre-Boeotian roots, nods to a "primordial, autochthonous character." Cf. also Virg. *Ecl.* 6.65 (*Aonas in montis*) with the notes of Cucchiarelli (2012) ad loc. For Aonia, cf. also Harder ad *Aet.* fr. 2b, 4. For this passage the crucial difference is created by the implicit reference to springs in Aonides, versus the urban referent of the Pierides: these differences are due to the influence of the Heliconian springs as the stakes of this contest. The Pierides wish to remove the Muses from their control over these springs, and so opportunistically refer to them as Thespiades.

41. Cf. Virg. *Georg.* 4.390. It refers to Thessaly at Catull. 64.324. Lachmann's emendation of Lucil. fr 41 M also gives an early example of the adjectival form *Emathius*. Pliny explicitly says that Emathia is an ancient name for Macedonia (*HN* 4.33). Emathia is paired with Pieria at Hom. *Il.* 14.226. Cassius Dio also records that Augustus resettled peasants in Dyrrachium and Philippi (and elsewhere) whose land had been redistributed to veterans, giving Macedonian land a further context of civil war here (51.4.6).

42. Either the two battles of Philippi, or both Philippi and Pharsalus.

43. For a summary of the arguments either condemning or justifying this choice of locales, given that Emathia is a West Macedonian district, while Haemus is a mountain in northern Thrace, see Doig (1965). For Pharsalus, Philippi, and Emathia cf. also *Met.* 15.822–24 and Prop. 3.11.37–38 with the notes of Heyworth (2007, 338).

Notes to Pages 187–193 273

44. Hendry (1997, 599), recapitulating Doig (1965).

45. See Hendry (1997) for examples and notes therewith.

46. For discussion of the Gigantomachic references in Book 1, see esp. Wheeler (2000, 24–26).

47. Prior to Ovid, this narrative analogy was poetically drawn upon to especially dramatic effect on the shield of Aeneas; see esp. Hardie (1986, 97–110, 125–43). On Gigantomachic imagery overall in the *Aeneid*, see Hardie (1983). See also Hor. *Carm.* 3.4, which begins with an invocation to Calliope, includes Philippi (26), describes Helicon (*Piero . . . antro*, 40), and has the Gigantomachy as its primary poetic focus. Augustus' victories are also informed by Gigantomachic comparisons at Prop. 2.1.19– 20 and 39–42. Lucan truly popularizes the connection; cf. the ecphrasis of Thessaly, which ends with the Gigantomachy (6.410–12), and esp. 7.144–50. Statius also talks of *Phlegraea . . . proelia* (*Silv.* 5.3.196–97).

48. For the Campanian plains, see Plin. *HN* 18.29; Diod. Sic. 4.21.5 and 5.71.4; Strab. 5.4.4, 5.4.6 and 6.3.5; Sil. *Pun.* 8.538; also alluded to in Prop.1.11.3, with the notes of Enk (1946) ad loc. On Thessaly as a landscape of civil war, see Ambühl (2016).

49. Cf. esp. Quint. *Inst.* 10.2.16, 12.10.12, 17, 73 and 80. The epic poet Antimachus (Catull. 95.10) provides a classic example. On writing styles, see Gell. *NA* 6.14.3–4 and Plin. *Ep.* 7.12.4 and 9.26.5; for literary bombast and its failure to reach the sublime, see Longinus *Subl.* 3 with the notes of Russell (1965) ad loc.

50. E.g. Prop. 3.9.35–36. See Ingleheart (2006, 87–88) for Ovid's use of *tumidus* at *Tr.* 1.2.24 and its reference to epic. For *arma* as an epic tag, see Barchiesi (1997, 16–17) and Conte (1994, 108–9).

51. This is partially glossed by *diues* in the following qualification *diues in aruis*.

52. Cardin and Tribulato (2019, 181). Cf. also the bibliography and different renderings of their names listed by Vergados (2020, 32n45).

53. See Johnson (2008, 52–63) for an analysis of the Gigantomachic themes of the Pierid song.

54. Perhaps echoing a Propertian foray into epic territory (*bella canam*, Prop. 2.10.8); cf. also 2.1, where Propertius denies he'd sing of a Gigantomachy or the civil war, even with the requisite poetic fortitude (Prop. 2.1.19–20, 27–36; *canerem . . . bella* appears at 2.1.28). At the midpoint of his celebration of Actium, he will declare *bella satis cecini* ("I have sung to satisfaction of war," Prop. 4.6.69).

55. See the statement of Goslin (2010, 371) that Zeus' defeat of Typhon was a "necessary act of violence that paves the way for the birth of the Muses."

56. For the myth and its variants, see Griffiths (1960); cf. also Pind. fr. 91 S-M and Ant. Lib. *Met.* 28.3, who reports that Nicander tells this tale in the fourth book of the *Heteroeumena*. For further sources, see Robinson (2011) ad *Fast.* 2.461.

57. Virg. *Aen.* 8.711–13; cf. also Hor. *Carm.* 1.37.12–21.

58. As McKay (1962a, 91) notes, there are other moments of amplification; Erysichthon consumes a heifer that was being fattened for Hestia, whose customary offering was the (smaller) sow. In Ovid's tale, the tree itself is amplified so as to be as forest unto itself; cf. *Met.* 8.743–44.

274   Notes to Pages 193–196

59. As noted by Stephens ad loc.

60. Bing (1996, 31).

61. McKay (1962a, 92); Hopkinson (1984b ad loc.); Bornmann (1992); Ambühl (2005, 164n291, 201n447); Stephens ad loc.

62. Bornmann (1992, 16); Ambühl (2005, 201n447).

63. See McKay (1962a, 94) and Ambühl (2005, 201n447).

64. As Giuseppetti (2012b, 107) formulates, "the theme of fasting . . . serves as a countermelody to Erysichthon's supernatural hunger."

65. Enumerated by Faulkner (2011b, 78 and n. 17); cf. also Kazantzidis (2021, 146–47, esp. n. 85 and 88).

66. Faulkner (2011b).

67. See Faulkner (2011b, 83–84) for the unusual features of the transition.

68. Murray (2019, 258). Iambe's role in Philicus' *Hymn to Demeter* is also humorous, further adding to the drama of Callimachus' tonal substitution; on Iambe in Philicus, see Giuseppetti (2012b, 122–24) and Danielewicz (2015, 147–48). On Iambe's jesting as the *aetion* for the ritual breaking of the fast, see Rotstein (2010, 167–70, 182).

69. As noted by Danielewicz (2015, 147–48).

70. Murray (2004, 214).

71. Murray (2019, 259–60).

72. For an interpretation of this point, see Faraone (2012). Erysichthon's targeted carnivorous appetite contrasts throughout the hymn with Demeter's role as an agricultural goddess. Although Thessaly was also renowned for its grain production, her anger does not target the natural world, instead attacking the other defining Thessalian pride: its animal flocks and herds.

73. Wilkins (2000, 71).

74. See Wilkins (2000, 98) and Mili (2015, 263). Further ancient evidence is collected by Athenaeus (10.418b–e).

75. Cf. Wilkins (2000, 111–12).

76. On the *mattye*, see Dalby (1996, 155–57).

77. Callimachus sets his myth in the Thessalian plain of Dotium (*Hymn* 6.24), the first detail that introduces Erysichthon's tale. When Lycophron's Cassandra briefly catalogs the mourning of Greece, she uses "the impassable Leibethrian gates of Dotion" as a boundary (*Alex.* 410). Previously, "Leibethrian" is used in the context of the Muses' territory, both Heliconian and Pierian (*Alex.* 274–75). Lycophron's transfer of the clearly Pierian geographical descriptor to the Thessalian plain begs some questions about a perceived relationship between Pieria and Thessaly. The Thessalian region Larisa borders the southern part of Pieria; their contiguous geographical relationship is one easy justification for Lycophron's descriptor. However, there is a fifth/fourth-century votive inscription dedicated to the Muses as the Pierides from Larisa that could point to the presence of a Mouseion and cult of the Muses in Thessaly; see Santin and Tziafalias (2020). Demeter therefore has potentially a greater connection to the Muses within Callimachus' hymn.

Notes to Pages 197–209

78. Van Tress (2004) gives a detailed exploration.

79. D'Alessio (2004, 31–33).

80. D'Alessio (2004, 31).

81. Ingleheart (2010, 169). On the Callimacheanism of Achelous as a narrator, see Boyd (2006, 200–202); Barchiesi (2011, 523); Kirstein (2019, 200).

82. Murray (2004, 236–38) reads an identification of the Ovidian Achelous with the Callimachean Erysichthon.

83. Cf. Virg. *Ecl.* 3.58–59. On the Pierides' following of proper contest decorum, see Johnson (2008, 44).

84. The scholion to Apollonius ad loc. comments that this was the former name of the Nile (p. 277 Wendel). Cf. also Plin. *HN* 5.10.

85. Guillén (2012, 83); on this fragment of Epicharmus, see also Olson (2007, 54). On Pallas and Athena, see also Valdes Guía (2021).

86. Bosher (2021, 34–79).

Chapter 6. Calliope's Hymn

1. The *exordium* of *Met.* 5.341–45 shows its generic allegiance as a hymn. Additionally, marking Calliope's song as a hymn, belonging to an inherited linguistic tradition of showing praise, is the collocation of *carmen dicere* (cf. 5.344–45); see Nikolaev (2014, 556–59).

2. For the etymological connection, cf. Varro, *Ling.* 6.96. For the affiliated passage describing her "taming" powers (*Hymn. Hom. Ven.* 69–74) as reliant on a description of Poseidon's powers (*Il.* 13.18–19, 27–29), see Schein (2013, 303).

3. On these adjectives, see the commentary of Olson (2012) ad loc.

4. On Aphrodite's speech mannerisms, see Bergren (1989).

5. See Coughanowr (1997) for discussion.

6. Cf. Sen. *Thy.* 21–22, *regione quidquid impia cessat loci / complebo* with the note of Tarrant (1985) ad loc.

7. Ceres is later described as *non cessans* in the search for her daughter (5.440–41).

8. As this relates negatively to her presentation in Cicero's *Verrines*, see Johnson (1996, 135–38).

9. Spaeth (1994). On the identification as Venus, see 67n7.

10. See Spaeth (1996, 1, 33–34). Isidore also notes this etymology; cf. *Etym.* 8.11.59.

11. O'Hara (1996, 253).

12. Spaeth (1996, 22); Fantham (2002, 39–40).

13. Johnson (1996); Zissos (1999); Johnson (2008, 64–71). More diffusely, Salzman-Mitchell (2005, 166–84).

14. On Calliope's "rewriting of, and specifically her politicization of, the Lucretian Venus," see Ham (2022); quotation is from 171.

15. See Gale (1994, 67–68). For Lucretius' choice of Venus as Muse, see also Asmis (2015). Plutarch lists Eros as the companion of the Muses; cf. Plut. *Amat.* 758c.

16. A. Hardie (2013, 214).

17. Gale (1994, 68); O'Hara (1998, 71).

18. See Ham (2022, 167–70).

19. McPhee (2019, 772). For the present context, this is especially relevant in the case of Triptolemus, who is said to be the son of Polyhymnia (cf. Tzet. ad Hes. *Op.* 1); the song of Calliope concludes with Triptolemus.

20. This episode is largely untreated; see recently Cowan (2020). Salzman-Mitchell (2005, 168) briefly mentions how it anticipates themes in Calliope's song.

21. For a reading of this pairing and its interpretive consequences, see McPhee (2019).

22. A tradition beginning with Hesiod; cf. *Theog.* 79–80 and Vergados (2020, 24–25).

23. McPhee (2019, 772–73).

24. Johnson (1996, 140n39).

25. Johnson (1996, 140).

26. See the reading of Zissos (1999, 105–7).

27. See especially Zissos (1999).

28. Text is Fränkel (1961).

29. In a review of Callimachean influences upon Calliope's song, Sampson (2012, 88n14) reads Ovid's stated genealogy of the Sirens as an anticipation of Achelous' role in narrating the Erysichthon myth. See additionally 91–92, which suggests an allusion Callimachus makes to the Sirens in the opening of the *Hymn to Demeter* via wordplay on the Achelous and Callichorus (cf. *Hymn* 6.7–15).

30. A. Hardie (2009, 36).

31. For the Muses as *doctae*, cf. also Catull. 65.2; Manilius 2.49; Ov. *Fast.* 6.811, *Tr.* 2.1.13. For a reading of the Sirens as drawing men in due to their knowledge, cf. Cic. *Fin.* 5.18. On the similarity of Muses and Sirens, see Pollard (1952). Montiglio (2018) explores the resonances and powers of the Sirens' song.

32. For a different reading of the significance of these flowers, see Hinds (1987, 78–80). Salzman-Mitchell (2005, 171) notes the color symbolism. On the trope of meadows and virginity, see Deacy (2013).

33. A. Hardie (2009, 36) also notes that Molpe is the name of a Siren, which, as reminiscent of Melpomene, further brings together the Muses, Sirens, and Oceanids. The Oceanids and the daughters of Achelous are also connected by the identification of Achelous with Oceanus; see again pp. 197–98.

34. The positive favor shown toward the Sirens can also be read as a rehabilitation of a previous encounter: Pausanias records that Hera persuaded the Sirens to compete with the Muses; when they lost, the Muses plucked their feathers to fashion crowns (9.34.3–4); cf. also Steph. Byz. s.v. Ἄπτερα; Schol. in Lyc. *Alex.* 653. A sarcophagus relief depicts three Sirens engaged in a contest with Euterpe, Clio, and Erato; *LIMC* VIII.1, 1102 s.v. *Seirenes* 119. This naturally invites comparison to the contest between the Muses and Pierides.

Notes to Pages 214–220

35. See Murray (2002, 35–36) on the differences between the Muses and Sirens based on sexuality. See Lowe (2015, 90–96) on the allegorizing of the Sirens.

36. Cf. also the description of Scylla (*Met.* 13.733–34) with Tissol (1997, 111–12). Lowe (2015, 74–75) tackles the Ovidian originality of this tale.

37. Hinds (1987, 87, 91–92); Johnson (1996, 143–44); Zissos (1999, 102–5).

38. On the narratological complexities of her tale, see Barchiesi (2002a, 188–92). On Arethusa as a (male/self-conscious/metapoetic) narrator, see also Ntanou (2020a, 99–102).

39. Arethusa is also directly addressed in the *Aeneid*; cf. 3.694–96. Arethusa and Aeneas are also united by rare uses of the verb *renarro* (Virg. *Aen.* 3.717; *Met.* 5.635.)

40. The similarities between the description of Arethusa and the ecphrasis of the Sun's palace could also entail a subtle way of acknowledging Arethusa's replacement of the role Helios plays in the *Homeric Hymn to Demeter*, acting as a visual footnote of sorts.

41. See Thomas (1986, 190–93).

42. For the influence of pastoral on this episode, see Johnson (2008, 42–47); Ntanou (2020a, 90–94; 2020b). The interaction between Muse and goddess also looks back to the pastoral invitation Argus makes to the disguised Mercury at *Met.* 1.678–81.

43. Hinds (2002, 131); the tales of Daphne and Arethusa are especially similar, as has been often noted; see the commentary of Rosati (2009, 230–31). In Sicily, Arethusa is worshipped alongside Artemis; see Lewis (2019, 66). For the mythological versions of Alpheus pursuing Artemis, see Paus. 5.14.6; 6.22.9. Salzman-Mitchell (2005, 181) sees Arethusa as constructing her story most similarly to Actaeon's myth.

44. This is also hinted at by the Arethusa of the *Georgics*, who has "set aside her arrows" (Virg. *Georg.* 4.344), indicating a relinquishing of her identity as a virgin huntress.

45. Hinds (1987, 72–74).

46. Cf. Ceres' speech to Jupiter in the *Fasti* (4.589–90).

47. On etymology as the science of "true names," see Sluiter (2015, 906–9).

48. Jupiter's formulation looks back to Calliope's initial description: *paene simul uisa est dilectaque raptaque Diti; / usque adeo est properatus amor*, "all at once she was espied and loved and seized by Dis; such it is with the hastiness of love," 5.395–96).

49. Cf. also *OLD*, s.v. 1c, d for the meaning of "kidnapping," and attested usages with *mors* within the epigraphic tradition.

50. Inachus' conclusions about his missing daughter's whereabouts (*Met.* 1.585–87) also cohere with Ceres' sentiments about her discovery of Proserpina's own location (5.518–20).

51. Ziogas (2016, 2–3), citing the inspiration of Ahl (1985, 144–45) on Io's role in etymologizing Io-vis.

52. On *umor* and *amor*, see Friedlander (1941, 18); Snyder (1980, 94–95); Gale (1991, 419); Taylor (2020, 128–29).

278 Notes to Pages 220–232

53. All Lucretian text is Leonard and Smith (1942). On the ambiguity of *misceat*, see Zissos (1999, 104).

54. Hardie (1988; 2002b, 150–65).

55. Cf. the Catullan use of *alebat amor* at 68A.24, B.96.

56. See again Wheeler (2000, 35–36).

57. The text of Goold (1977) also prints *lacus* at 5.634 instead of Tarrant's *locus*.

58. Cf. also the ring composition provided by the echoing *guttas* at *DRN* 4.1286.

59. This is especially the case in the tales of Narcissus and Salmacis and Hermaphroditus, where water becomes the medium of experiencing love; on the similarities between these myths, see Salzman-Mitchell (2005, 178–79).

60. See Maltby, s.v. *amnis* and Michalopoulos (2001, 25).

61. See Hinds (2002, 131) for the relevance of this etymology to the narrative thread of erotic pursuit in an idyllic landscape.

62. Reading Arethusa's tale within Calliope's hymn as a metapoetic review of the first pentad modifies the view of Holzberg (1997, 126, 133–35) who identifies the Muse's mythological narration as a poetically self-conscious epilogue to the first portion of the epic. For further bibliography on Calliope's tale as a microcosm of the *Metamorphoses*, see Ntanou (2020b, 88n32).

63. Stephens ad 3.82, noting Petrovic; cf. the commentary of Adjordáni (2021) ad loc.

64. Adjordáni (2021) ad loc.

65. The first in the epic; cf. Narcissus' query of *meministis* to the "witnessing" trees at 3.445.

66. A. Hardie (2009, 50–51; 2013, 232–33). Aphrodite receives this epithet in the *Orphic Hymn* (*Hymn. Orph.* 55.1).

67. The other interpretation is "much wooed," or "much courted"; cf. A. Hardie (2013, 232–33).

68. A. Hardie (2013, 233). For a joint play on Erato and Polymnia, see *Hymn. Orph.* 76.12

69. Barchiesi (1991, 10). The fact that it is instead the Pierides in *Metamorphoses* 5 who sing a hymn reminiscent of the *Theogony* (by attempting to supplant its divine order) further underscores the way that hymnic praise of Zeus is bypassed or distorted in the world of the *Metamorphoses*.

70. Polyhymnia's interest in etymology is also observable in the *Ciris*; as he prepares for a proemial digression, the poet offers the aside *nam uerum fateamur: amat Polyhymnia uerum* ("for let us speak the truth: Polyhymnia loves the truth," *Ciris* 55). Kayachev (2016, 49) notes how *uerum fateri* is effectively a translation of ἐτυμολογεῖν and the further etymological play Polyhymnia's name makes for the wider passage, justifying the singling out of this particular Muse.

CONCLUSION

1. On *Tristia* 1.7 systematically unwriting the completeness of the *Metamorphoses*, see Hinds (1985).

Notes to Pages 233–235

2. Cf. also the opening of the *Ciris, etsi me uario iactatum laudis amore.*

3. For further overlap and analysis, see Wheeler (1995).

4. On how both tapestries can equally be understood as bearing Callimachean affiliation, and for their relationship to the proem, see Klein (2022, 21–25).

5. Cf. also Virg. *Ecl.* 3.60. Even Orpheus' staging of a hymn to Jupiter can be juxtaposed with the Orpheus of the *Argonautica*, who sings a hymn to Apollo (Ap. Rhod. *Argon.* 2.703–13).

6. On the relationship between the poem's sphragis and the epic as a whole, see Wickkiser (1999).

WORKS CITED

Ackermann, H., and J. R. Gisler, eds. 1981–97. *Lexicon Iconographicum Mythologiae Classicae.* Zurich.

Acosta-Hughes, B. 2009. "Ovid and Callimachus: Rewriting the Master." In Knox 2009, 236–51.

Acosta-Hughes, B., and S. A. Stephens. 2012. *Callimachus in Context: From Plato to the Augustan Poets.* Cambridge.

Acosta-Hughes, B., L. Lehnus, and S. A. Stephens, eds. 2011. *Brill's Companion to Callimachus.* Leiden.

Adorjáni, Z. 2021. *Der Artemis-Hymnos des Kallimachos: Einleitung, Text, Übersetzung und Kommentar.* Berlin.

Ahl, F. M. 1982. "Amber, Avallon, and Apollo's Singing Swan." *AJP* 103 (4): 373–411.

Ahl, F. M. 1985. *Metaformations: Soundplay and Wordplay in Ovid and Other Classical Poets.* Ithaca.

Algra, K. 2009. "Stoic Philosophical Theology and Greco-Roman Religion." In *God and Cosmos in Stoicism*, edited by R. Salles, 224–52. Oxford.

Allen, T. W., ed. 1912. *Homeri Opera* V. Oxford.

Allen, T. W., W. R. Halliday, and E. E. Sikes, eds. 1936. *The Homeric Hymns.* 2nd ed. Oxford.

Allen, R. E. 1991. *The Dialogues of Plato.* Vol. 2, *The Symposium.* New Haven.

Ambühl, A. 2005. *Kinder und junge Helden: Innovative Aspekte des Umgangs mit der literarischen Tradition bei Kallimachos.* Leuven.

Ambühl, A. 2016. "Thessaly as an Intertextual Landscape of Civil War in Latin Poetry." In *Valuing Landscape in Classical Antiquity*, edited by J. McInerney and I. Sluiter, 297–322. Mnemosyne Supplements 393. Leiden.

Anagnostou-Laoutides, E. 2017. "Eros and the Poetics of Violence in Plato and Apollonius." In *Cultural Perceptions of Violence in the Hellenistic World*, edited by M. Champion, L. Sullivan, and L. Asmonti, 174–90. London.

Works Cited

Anderson, W. S. 1972. *Ovid's "Metamorphoses": Books 6–10.* Norman.

Anderson, W. S. 1989. "Lycaon: Ovid's Deceptive Paradigm in *Metamorphoses* 1." *ICS* 14:91–101.

Andolfi, I. 2019. *Acusilaus of Argos' Rhapsody in Prose: Introduction, Text, and Commentary.* Trends in Classics Supplementary Volumes 70. Berlin.

Angeli Bernardini, P. 2009. "L'Inno primo di Pindaro e la sua destinazione cultuale." *Paideia* 64:73–89.

Asmis, E. 1982. "Lucretius' Venus and Stoic Zeus." *Hermes* 110 (4): 458–70.

Asmis, E. 2015. "Venus and the Passion for Renewal in Lucretius's *On the Nature of Things.*" In *Venus as Muse: From Lucretius to Michel Serres*, edited by H. Berressem, G. Blamberger, and S. Goth, 41–54. Leiden.

Asper, M. 2011. "Dimensions of Power: Callimachean Geopoetics and the Ptolemaic Empire." In Acosta-Hughes, Lehnus, and Stephens 2011, 153–77. Leiden.

Barbantani, S. 2011. "Callimachus on Kings and Kingship." In Acosta-Hughes, Lehnus, and Stephens 2011, 178–200.

Barchiesi, A. 1989. "Voci e istanze narrative nelle *Metamorfosi* di Ovidio." *MD* 23:55–97. (= Barchiesi 2001: 49–78 and Knox 2006: 274–319.)

Barchiesi, A. 1991. "Discordant Muses." *PCPhS* 37:1–21.

Barchiesi, A. 1993. "Future Reflexive: Two Modes of Allusion and Ovid's *Heroides.*" *HSCP* 95:333–65.

Barchiesi, A. 1994. "Immovable Delos: *Aeneid* 3.73–98 and the Hymns of Callimachus." *CQ* 44 (2): 438–43.

Barchiesi, A. 1997. *The Poet and the Prince: Ovid and Augustan Discourse.* Berkeley.

Barchiesi, A. 1999. "Venus' Masterplot: Ovid and the *Homeric Hymns.*" In Hardie, Barchiesi, and Hinds 1999, 112–26.

Barchiesi, A. 2001. *Speaking Volumes: Narrative and Intertext in Ovid and Other Latin Poets.* London.

Barchiesi, A. 2002a. "Narrative Technique and Narratology in the *Metamorphoses.*" In P. R. Hardie 2002a, 180–99.

Barchiesi, A. 2002b. "The Uniqueness of the *Carmen Saeculare* and Its Tradition." In *Traditions and Contexts in the Poetry of Horace*, edited by T. Woodman and D. Feeney, 107–23. Cambridge.

Barchiesi, A. 2005. *Ovidio: Metamorfosi.* Vol. 1, *Libri I–II.* Translated by L. Koch. Rome.

Barchiesi, A. 2007. *Ovidio: Metamorfosi.* Vol. 2, *Libri III–IV.* Translated by L. Koch. Rome.

Barchiesi, A. 2009. "Senatus consultum de Lycaone: Concili degli dei e immaginazione politica nelle *Metamorfosi* di Ovidio." *MD* 61:117–45.

Barchiesi, A. 2011. "Roman Callimachus." In Acosta-Hughes, Lehnus, and Stephens 2011, 509–33.

Barchiesi, A. 2017. "Colonial Readings in Vergilian Geopoetics: The Trojans at Buthrotum." In *Imagining Empire: Political Space in Hellenistic and Roman Literature*, edited by V. Rimell, 151–66. Heidelberg.

Works Cited

Bekker, I. ed. 1824. *Photii Bibliotheca*. 2 vols. Berlin.

Belayche, N., P. Brulé, G. Freyburger, Y. Lehmann, L. Pernot, and P. Frost, eds. 2006. *Nommer les dieux: Théonymes, épithètes, épiclèses dans l'Antiquité*. Recherches sur les Rhétoriques Religieuses 5. Turnhout.

Bénatouïl, T. 2009. "How Industrious Can Zeus Be? The Extent and Objects of Divine Activity in Stoicism." In *God and Cosmos in Stoicism*, edited by R. Salles, 23–45. Oxford.

Bergmann, B., J. Farrell, D. Feeney, J. Ker, D. Nelis, and C. Schultz. 2012. "An Exciting Provocation: John F. Miller's *Apollo, Augustus, and the Poets*." *Vergilius* 58:3–20.

Bergren, A. T. 1989. "*The Homeric Hymn to Aphrodite*: Tradition and Rhetoric, Praise and Blame." *CA* 8 (1): 1–41.

Berman, D. W. 2015. *Myth, Literature and the Creation of the Topography of Thebes*. Cambridge.

Bernabé, A. O., ed. 2004. *Orphicorum et Orphicis similium testimonia et fragmenta: Poetae Epici Graeci*. Pars II. Fasc. 1. Leipzig.

Bing, P. 1996. "Callimachus and the *Hymn to Demeter*." *Syllecta Classica* 6:29–42.

Bing, P. 2008. *The Well-Read Muse: Present and Past in Callimachus and the Hellenistic Poets*. Rev. ed. Ann Arbor.

Bing, P., and V. Uhrmeister. 1994. "The Unity of Callimachus' *Hymn to Artemis*." *JHS* 114:19–34.

Blänsdorf, J., ed. 2011. *Fragmenta poetarum Latinorum epicorum et lyricorum: Praeter Enni Annales et Ciceronis Germanicique Aratea post W. Morel et K. Büchner editionem quartam auctam*. New York.

Bömer, F. 1969–86. *P. Ovidius Naso, "Metamorphosen": Kommentar*. Heidelberg.

Bonanno, M. G. 1995. "L'Artemide bambina di Callimaco (a proposito di intertestualità)." *Lexis* 13:23–47.

Bornmann, F. 1968. *Callimachi Hymnus in Dianam*. Florence.

Bornmann, F. 1992. "Der Text der Phönissen des Euripides und der Demeterhymnus des Kallimachos." *ZPE* 91:15–17.

Borthwick, E. 1970. "P. Oxy. 2738: Athena and the Pyrrhic Dance." *Hermes* 98 (3): 318–31.

Bosher, K. G. 2021. *Greek Theater in Ancient Sicily*. Cambridge.

Bowra, C.M. 1964. *Pindar*. Oxford.

Boyd, B. W. 1992. "Virgil's Camilla and the Traditions of Catalogue and Ecphrasis (*Aeneid* 7.803–17)." *AJP* 113 (2): 213–34.

Boyd, B. W. ed. 2002. *Brill's Companion to Ovid*. Leiden.

Boyd, B. W. 2006. "Two Rivers and the Reader in Ovid, *Metamorphoses* 8." *TAPA* 136 (1): 171–206.

Boyd, B. W. 2012. "On Starting an Epic (Journey): Telemachus, Phaethon, and the Beginning of the *Metamorphoses*." *MD* 69:101–18.

Boyd, B. W. 2017. *Ovid's Homer: Authority, Repetition, and Reception*. Oxford.

Boys-Stones, G.R. 1998. "Eros in Government: Zeno and the Virtuous City." *CQ* 48 (1): 168–74.

Boys-Stones, G. R., and J. H. Haubold, eds. 2010. *Plato & Hesiod.* Oxford.

Breed, B. W. 2004. "Tua, Caesar, Aetas: Horace *Ode* 4.15 and the Augustan Age." *AJP* 125 (2): 245–53.

Bremmer, J. N. 1999. "Transvestite Dionysos." *Bucknell Review* 43:183–200.

Bremmer, J. N. 2009. "Zeus' Own Country: Cult and Myth in the *Pride of Halicarnassus.*" In *Antike Mythen: Medien, Transformationen und Konstruktionen,* edited by U. Dill and C. Walde, 292–312. Berlin.

Bremmer, J. N. 2013. "Local Mythography: The Pride of Halicarnassus." In *Writing Myth: Mythography in the Ancient World,* edited by S. M. Trzaskoma and R. S. Smith, 55–73. Leuven.

Brillante, C. 2004. "Il sogno di Epimenide." *QUCC* 77:11–39.

Brody, L. R. 2001. "The Cult of Aphrodite at Aphrodisias in Caria." *Kernos* 14:93–109.

Brumbaugh, M. 2019. *The New Politics of Olympos: Kingship in Kallimachos' "Hymns."* Oxford.

Bulloch, A. W. 1985. *Callimachus: The Fifth Hymn.* Cambridge.

Bulloch, A. W. 2010. "Hymns and Encomia." In *A Companion to Hellenistic Literature,* edited by J. J. Clauss and M. Cuypers, 166–80. Chichester.

Cairns, F. 1971. "Five 'Religious' Odes of Horace. (I, 10; I, 21 and IV, 6; I, 30; I, 15)." *AJP* 92 (3): 433–52.

Cairns, F. 1996. "Ancient 'Etymology' and Tibullus: on the Classification of 'Etymologies' and on 'Etymological Markers.'" *PCPhS* 42:24–59.

Calame, C. 1999. *The Poetics of Eros in Ancient Greece.* Translated by J. Lloyd. Princeton.

Cameron, A. 2004. *Greek Mythography in the Roman World.* Oxford.

Campbell, B. 1996. "Shaping the Rural Environment: Surveyors in Ancient Rome." *JRS* 86:74–99.

Campbell, C. 2018. "(Poetic) License to Kill: Apollo, the Python, and Nicander's *Theriaca* in Ovid, *Metamorphoses* 1." *G&R* 65 (1): 155–74.

Campbell, D. A. 1982. *Greek Lyric.* Vol. 1, *Sappho, Alcaeus.* Cambridge.

Campbell, J. B. 1995. "Sharing out Land: Two Passages in the *Corpus Agrimensorum Romanorum.*" *CQ* 45:540–6.

Caneva, S. G. 2010. "Raccontare Zeus: Poesia e cultura di corte ad Alessandria, a partire dall'*Inno* I di Callimaco." *Pallas* 83:295–311.

Cardin, M., and O. Tribulato. 2019. "Enumerating the Muses: Tzetzes *in Hes. Op.* 1 and the Parody of Catalogic Poetry in Epicharmus." In *Approaches to Greek Poetry: Homer, Hesiod, Pindar, and Aeschylus in Ancient Exegesis,* edited by M. M. Ercoles, L. Pagani, F. Pontani, and G. Ucciardello, 161–92. Trends in Classics Supplementary Volumes 73. Berlin.

Casali, S. 2020. "Evander and the Invention of the Prehistory of Latium in Virgil's *Aeneid.*" In *Nos Sumus Romani Qui Fuimus Ante . . . : Memory of Ancient Italy,* edited by M. Aberson, M. C. Biella, M. Di Fazio, and M. Wullschleger, 145–68. Berne.

Works Cited

Chamoux, M. F. 1953. *Cyrène sous la Monarchie des Battiades*. Paris.

Chaniotis, A. 2010. "Aphrodite's Rivals: Devotion to Local and Other Gods at Aphrodisias." *Cahiers du Centre Gustave Glotz* 21:235–48.

Cheshire, K. 2016. "Neither Beast nor Woman: Reconstructing Callisto in Callimachus' *Hymn to Zeus*." In *Resemblance and Reality in Greek Thought: Essays in Honor of Peter M. Smith*, edited by A. Park, 80–94. London.

Clarke, W. M. 1974. "The God in the Dew." *L'Antiquité Classique* 43 (1): 57–73.

Clay, J. S. 1989. *The Politics of Olympus: Form and Meaning in the Major Homeric Hymns*. Princeton.

Cole, T. 2004. "Ovid, Varro, and Castor of Rhodes: The Chronological Architecture of the *Metamorphoses*." *HSCP* 102:355–422.

Cole, T. 2008. *Ovidius Mythisthoricus: Legendary Time in the "Metamorphoses."* Studien zur klassischen Philologie Band 160. Frankfurt.

Collins, D. 2004. *Master of the Game: Competition and Performance in Greek Poetry*. Washington, DC.

Commager, S. 1962. *The Odes of Horace: A Critical Study*. New Haven.

Constantakopoulou, C. 2007. *The Dance of the Islands: Insularity, Networks, the Athenian Empire and the Aegean World*. Oxford.

Conte, G. B. 1994. *Genres and Readers*. Translated by G. Most. Baltimore.

Cooley, A. E. 2009. *Res Gestae Divi Augustii: Text, Translation, and Commentary*. Cambridge.

Coughanowr, E. 1997. "Φυσίζοος Αἶα and Death in Homer." *Euphrosyne* 25:365–68.

Cowan, R. 2020. "A Brutal Hack: Tyranny, Rape, and the Barbarism of Bad Poetry in Ovid's Pyreneus Episode." *Antichthon* 54:80–102.

Cucchiarelli, A. 2012. *Publio Virgilio Marone, "Le Bucoliche": Introduzione e commento*. Translated by Alfonso Traina. Rome.

Curley, D. 2013. *Tragedy in Ovid: Theater, Metatheater, and the Transformation of a Genre*. Cambridge.

Curran, L. 1978. "Rape and Rape Victims in Ovid's Metamorphoses." *Arethusa* 11:213–41.

Curtis, L. 2017. "Ovid's Io and the Aetiology of Lament." *Phoenix* 41:301–20.

Curtis, L. 2020. "Paradise and Performance in Vergil's Underworld and Horace's *Carmen Saeculare*." In *Walking through Elysium: Vergil's Underworld and the Poetics of Tradition*, edited by B. Gladhill and M. Y. Myers, 187–205. Toronto.

Cuypers, M. 2004. "Prince and Principle: The Philosophy of Callimachus' *Hymn to Zeus*." *Hellenistica Groningana* 7:95–116.

Cyrino, M. S. 2013. "Bow and Eros: Hunt as Seduction in the *Homeric Hymn to Aphrodite*." *Arethusa* 46 (3): 375–93.

Dalby, A. 1996. *Siren Feasts: A History of Food and Gastronomy in Greece*. London.

D'Alessio, G.-B. 2004. "Textual Fluctuations and Cosmic Streams: Ocean and Acheloios." *JHS* 124:16–37.

D'Alessio, G.-B. 2009. "Re-constructing Pindar's First Hymn: The Theban 'Theogony' and the Birth of Apollo." In *Apolline Politics and Poetics*, edited by L. Athanassaki, R. P. Martin, and J. F. Miller, 128–47. Athens.

Damen, M. L., and R. A. Richards. 2012. "'Sing the Dionysus': Euripides' *Bacchae* as Dramatic Hymn." *AJP* 133 (3): 343–69.

Damon, C., and C. Pieper. 2018. *Eris vs. Aemulatio: Valuing Competition in Classical Antiquity*. Mnemosyne Supplements 423. Leiden.

Danielewicz, J. 1990. "Ovid's Hymn to Bacchus (*Met.* 4.11ff.): Tradition and Originality." *Euphrosyne* 18:73–84.

Danielewicz, J. 2015. "Philicus' 'Novel Composition' for the Alexandrian Grammarians: Initial Lines and Iambe's Speech." *Classica Cracoviensia* 18:137–49.

Davis, P. 2001. "The Fabrication of Tradition: Horace, Augustus and the Secular Games." *Ramus* 30:111–27.

Deacy, S. 2013. "From 'Flowery Tales' to 'Heroic Rapes': Virginal Subjectivity in the Mythological Meadow." *Arethusa* 46:395–413.

Depew, M. 1993. "Mimesis and Aetiology in Callimachus' *Hymns*." *Hellenistica Groningana* 1:57–78.

Depew, M. 1994. "POxy 2509 and Callimachus' *Lavacrum Palladis*: αἰγιόχοιο Διὸς κούρη μεγάλοιο." *CQ* 44 (2): 410–26.

Depew, M. 1998. "Delian Hymns and Callimachean Allusion." *HSCP* 98:155–82.

Depew, M. 2004. "Gender, Power, and Poetics in Callimachus' Book of *Hymns*." *Hellenistica Groningana* 2:117–38.

Depew, M. 2007. "Springs, Nymphs, and Rivers: Models of Origination in Third-Century Alexandrian Poetry." In *Literatur und Religion: Wege zu einer mythisch-rituellen Poetik bei den Griechen*, vol. 2, edited by A. Bierl, R. Lämmle, and K. Wesselmann, 141–71. Berlin.

Diels, H., and W. Kranz, eds. 1952. *Die Fragmente der Vorsokratiker*. 6th ed. Berlin.

Dobias-Lalou, C. 2017. *Greek Verse Inscriptions of Cyrenaica* in collaboration with Alice Bencivenni, with help from Joyce M. Reynolds and Charlotte Roueché. Bologna. http://doi.org/10.6092/UNIBO/IGCYRGVCYR.

Doig, G. 1965. "Vergil, *Georgics*, I, 491–2." *AJP* 86 (1): 85–88.

Due, O. S. 1974. *Changing Forms: Studies in the "Metamorphoses" of Ovid*. Copenhagen.

Dueck, D. 2020. "A Lunar People: The Meaning of an Arcadian Epithet, or, Who Is the Most Ancient of Them All?" *Philologus* 164 (1): 133–47.

Dunning, S. 2016. "Roman Ludi Saeculares from the Republic to Empire." PhD diss., University of Toronto.

Eckerman, C. 2017. "Pindar's Olympian 1, 1–7 and Its Relation to Bacchylides 3, 85–87." *Wiener Studien* 130:7–32.

Enk, P. J., ed. 1946. *Sex. Propertii Elegiarum Liber I (Monobiblos)*. Leiden.

Fain, G. L. 2004. "Callimachus' *Hymn to Artemis* and the Tradition of Rhapsodic Hymn." *BICS* 47:45–56.

Works Cited 287

Fantham, E. 2002. "The *Fasti* as a Source for Women's Participation in Roman Cult." In *Ovid's* Fasti: *Historical Readings at Its Bimillennium*, edited by G. Herbert-Brown, 23–46. Oxford.

Fantham, E. 2004. *Ovid's "Metamorphoses."* Oxford.

Fantuzzi, M. 2011. "Speaking with Authority: Polyphony in Callimachus' *Hymns*." In Acosta-Hughes, Lehnus, and Stephens 2011, 429–53.

Faraone, C. A. 2012. "*Boubrôstis*, Meat Eating and Comedy: Erysichthon as Famine Demon in Callimachus' *Hymn to Demeter*." *Hellenistica Groningana* 16:61–80.

Faraone, C. A. 2021. *Hexametrical Genres from Homer to Theocritus*. Oxford.

Farrell, J. 2013. "Complementarity and Contradiction in Ovidian Mythography." In *Writing Myth: Mythography in the Ancient World*, edited by S. M. Trzaskoma and R. Scott Smith, 223–52. Leuven.

Faulkner, A. 2011a. "The Collection of *Homeric Hymns*: From the Seventh Centuries to the Third Centuries BC." In Faulkner 2011c, 175–205. Oxford.

Faulkner, A. 2011b. "Fast, Famine, and Feast: Food for Thought in Callimachus' *Hymn to Demeter*." *HSCP* 106: 75–95.

Faulkner, A., ed. 2011c. *The Homeric Hymns: Interpretive Essays*. Oxford.

Faulkner, A. 2013. "*Et in Arcadia Diana*: An Encounter with Pan in Callimachus' *Hymn to Artemis*." *CP* 108 (3): 223–34.

Faulkner, A., A. Vergados, and A. Schwab, eds. 2016. *The Reception of the "Homeric Hymns."* Oxford.

Feeney, D. C. 1991. *The Gods in Epic: Poets and Critics of the Classical Tradition*. Oxford.

Feldherr, A. 2010. *Playing Gods: Ovid's "Metamorphoses" and the Politics of Fiction*. Princeton.

Felson, N. 2011. "Children of Zeus in the *Homeric Hymns*: Generational Succession." In Faulkner 2011, 254–79. Oxford.

Fentress, E., et al. 2003. *Cosa V: An Intermittent Town; Excavations 1991–1997.* Supplements to the Memoirs of the American Academy in Rome 2. Ann Arbor.

Fernandelli, M. 2012. *Via Latina: Studi su Virgilio e sulla sua fortuna*. Polymnia 15. Trieste.

Ferrari, F. 2006. "*Poietes kai pater*: Esegesi medioplatoniche di *Timeo*, 28C3." In *Tradizione, ecdotica, esegesi*, edited by G. Di Gregorio and S. Medaglia, 43–58. Naples.

Ferrari, F. 2014. "Gott als Vater und Schöpfer: Zur Rezeption von *Timaios* 28c3–5 bei einigen Platonikern." In *The Divine Father: Religious and Philosophical Conceptions of Divine Parenthood*, edited by F. Albrecht and R. Feldmeier, 57–69. Leiden.

Fischer-Hansen, T., and B. Poulsen, eds. 2009. *From Artemis to Diana: The Goddess of Man and Beast*. Acta Hyperborea 12. Copenhagen.

Fitzgerald, W. 2018. "Claiming Inferiority: Weakness into Strength." In *Complex Inferiorities: The Poetics of the Weaker Voice in Latin Literature*, edited by S. Matzner and S. Harrison, 13–28. Oxford.

Floridi, L. 2004. "Mendacità del mito e strategie encomiastiche nell' *Inno a Zeus* di Callimaco." In *La cultura ellenistica: L'opera letteraria e l'esegesi antica*, edited by R. R. Pretagostini and E. Dettori, 65–75. Rome.

Foerster, R., and E. Richtsteig, eds. 1972. *Choricii Gazaei opera*. Stuttgart.

Foley, H., ed. 1993. *The Homeric "Hymn to Demeter": Translation, Commentary, and Interpretive Essays*. Princeton.

Fontenrose, J. 1981. *Orion: The Myth of the Hunter and the Huntress*. Berkeley.

Ford, A. 2006. "Genre of Genres: Paeans and Paian in Early Greek Poetry." *Poetica* 38:277–96.

Ford, A. 2019. "Mythographic Discourse among non-Mythographers: Pindar's *Ol.* 1, Plato's *Phaedrus* and Callimachus' *Hymn to Zeus*." In *Host or Parasite? Mythographers and Their Contemporaries in Classical and Hellenistic Periods*, edited by A. J. Romano and J. Marincola, 5–27. Berlin.

Foster, M. 2017. "*Poeta Loquens*: Poetic Voices in Pindar's *Paean* 6 and Horace's *Odes* 4.6." In *Voice and Voices in Antiquity: Orality and Literacy in the Ancient World*, vol. 2, edited by N. Slater, 149–65. Leiden.

Francese, C. 2004. "Daphne, Honor, and Aetiological Action in Ovid's *Metamorphoses*." *CW* 97 (2): 153–57.

Fränkel, H. 1945. *Ovid: A Poet between Two Worlds*. Berkeley.

Fränkel, H., ed. 1961. *Apollonii Rhodii Argonautica*. Oxford.

Fraser, P. M. 1972. *Ptolemaic Alexandria*. Oxford.

Fratantuono, L. 2015. "*Montium Domina*: Catullus' Diana, Rome and the Moon's Bastard Light." *Acta Classica* 58:27–46.

Friedlander, P. 1941. "Pattern of Sound and Atomistic Theory in Lucretius." *AJP* 62 (1): 16–34.

Fuhrer, T. 1988. "A Pindaric Feature in the Poems of Callimachus." *AJP* 109 (1): 53–68.

Fuhrer, T. 1999. "Der Götterhymnus als Prahlrede: Zum Spiel mit einer literarischen Form in Ovids *Metamorphoses*." *Hermes* 127:356–67.

Fulkerson, L., and T. Stover, eds. 2016. *Repeat Performances: Ovidian Repetition and the "Metamorphoses."* Madison.

Furley, W. D. 1995. "Praise and Persuasion in Greek Hymns." *JHS* 115:29–46.

Furley, W. D., and J. M. Bremer. 2001. *Greek Hymns: Selected Cult Songs from the Archaic to the Hellenistic Period*. Vol. 1, *The Texts in Translation*; Vol. 2, *Greek Texts and Commentary*. Tübingen.

Gagné, R. 2006. "What Is the Pride of Halicarnassus?" *CA* 25:1–33.

Gale, M. R. 1991. "Man and Beast in Lucretius and the *Georgics*." *CQ* 41 (2): 414–26.

Gale, M. R. 1994. *Myth and Poetry in Lucretius*. Cambridge.

Gale, M. R. 2018. "'te sociam, Ratio . . .': Hunting as Paradigm in the *Cynegetica*." In S. Green 2018, 77–96.

Galinsky, G. K. 1975. *Ovid's "Metamorphoses": An Introduction to the Basic Aspects*. Oxford.

Gigante Lanzara, V. 1990. *Callimacho: Inno a Delo*. Pisa.

Giuseppetti, M. 2012a. "Mito e storia nell'*Inno a Delo* di Callimaco." *Hellenistica Groningana* 18:469–94.

Giuseppetti, M. 2012b. "Two Poets for a Goddess: Callimachus' and Philicus' Hymns to Demeter." *Hellenistica Groningana* 16:103–30.

Giuseppetti, M. 2013. *L'Isola esile: Studi sull' "Inno a Delo" di Callimacho.* Rome.

Glare, P. G. W., and C. Stray, eds. 2012. *Oxford Latin Dictionary.* 2nd ed. Oxford.

Goodchild, R. G. 1971. *Kyrene und Apollonia.* Zurich.

Goold, G., ed. 1977. *Ovid: "Metamorphoses," Vol. 1: Books 1–8.* Cambridge.

Goslin, O. 2010. "Hesiod's Typhonomachy and the Ordering of Sound." *TAPA* 140 (2): 351–73.

Gow, A. S. F., and D. L. Page, eds. 1968. *The Greek Anthology: The Garland of Philip and Some Contemporary Epigrams.* 2 vols. Cambridge.

Grafton, A., G. W. Most, and J. E. G. Zetzel, eds. 1985. *F.A. Wolf: Prolegomena to Homer, 1975.* Princeton.

Gramps, A. 2021. *The Fiction of Occasion in Hellenistic and Roman Poetry.* Berlin.

Granger, H. 2007. "The Theologian Pherecydes of Syros and the Early Days of Natural Philosophy." *HSCP* 103:135–63.

Graziosi, B. 2016. "Theologies of the Family in Hesiod and Homer." In *Theologies of Ancient Greek Religion*, edited by E. Eidinow, J. Kindt, and R. Osborne, 35–61. Cambridge.

Green, C. M. C. 2007. *Roman Religion and the Cult of Diana at Aricia.* Cambridge.

Green, P. 2008. *The Argonautica: Apollonios Rhodios.* Berkeley.

Green, S. J., ed. 2018. *Grattius: Hunting an Augustan Poet.* Oxford.

Griffiths, J. G. 1960. "The Flight of the Gods before Typhon: An Unrecognized Myth." *Hermes* 88 (3): 374–76.

Guillén, L. R-N. 2012. "On Epicharmus' Literary and Philosophical Background." In *Theater Outside Athens: Drama in Greek Sicily and South Italy*, edited by K. Bosher, 76–96. Oxford.

Hadjittofi, F. 2008. "Callimachus' Sexy Athena: The *Hymn to Athena* and the *Homeric Hymn to Aphrodite*." *MD* 60:9–37.

Ham, C. T. 2018. "The Poetics of Strife and Competition in Hesiod and Ovid." In *Eris vs. Aemulatio: Valuing Competition in Classical Antiquity*, edited by C. Damon and C. Pieper, 281–99. Mnemosyne Supplements 423. Leiden.

Ham, C. T. 2022. "*Venus discors*: The Empedocleo-Lucretian Background of Venus and Calliope's Song in *Metamorphoses* 5." In Volk and Williams 2022, 164–83.

Hanses, M. 2020. "*Naso Deus*: Ovid's Hidden Signature in the *Metamorphoses*." In *Metamorphic Readings: Transformation, Language, and Gender in the Interpretation of Ovid's "Metamorphoses,"* edited by A. Sharrock, D. Möller, and M. Malm, 126–44. Oxford.

Harden, S., and A. Kelly. 2013. "Proemic Convention and Character Construction in Early Greek Epic." *HSCP* 107:1–34.

Harder, A. M. 1992. "Insubstantial Voices: Some Observations on the Hymns of Callimachus." *CQ* 42 (2): 384–94.

Harder, A. M. 2012. *Callimachus: "Aetia." Introduction, Text, and Translation; Commentary.* 2 vols. Oxford.

Hardie, A. 2006. "The Aloades on Helicon: Music, Territory, and Cosmic Order." *A&A* 52:42–71.

Hardie, A. 2009. "Etymologising the Muse." *MD* 62:9–57.

Hardie, A. 2013. "Empedocles and the Muse of the *Agathos Logos*." *AJP* 134 (2): 209–46.

Hardie, P. R. 1983. "Some Themes from Gigantomachy in the 'Aeneid.'" *Hermes* 111 (3): 311–26.

Hardie, P. R. 1986. *Virgil's "Aeneid": Cosmos and Imperium.* Oxford.

Hardie, P. R. 1988. "Lucretius and the Delusions of Narcissus." *MD* 20/21:71–89.

Hardie, P. R., ed. 2002a. *The Cambridge Companion to Ovid.* Cambridge.

Hardie, P. R. 2002b. *Ovid's Poetics of Illusion.* Cambridge.

Hardie, P. R. 2004. "Approximative Similes in Ovid: Incest and Doubling." *Dictynna* 1. https://doi.org/10.4000/dictynna.166.

Hardie, P. R. 2022. "Philosophizing and Theologizing Reincarnations of Ovid: Lucan to Alexander Pope." In Volk and Williams 2022, 335–50.

Hardie, P. R., A. Barchiesi, and S. E Hinds, eds. 1999. *Ovidian Transformations: Essays on Ovid's "Metamorphoses" and Its Reception.* Cambridge Philological Society Supplement 23. Cambridge.

Haslam, M. W. 1993. "Callimachus' *Hymns*." *Hellenistica Groningana* 1:111–25.

Hawes, G. 2014. *Rationalizing Myth in Antiquity.* Oxford.

Heath, J. R. 1988. "The Blessings of Epiphany in Callimachus' *Bath of Pallas*." *CA* 7:72–90

Heath, J. R. 1991. "Diana's Understanding of Ovid's *Metamorphoses*." *CJ* 86:233–43.

Heath, J. R. 2011–12. "Poetic Simultaneity and Genre in Ovid's *Metamorphoses*." *CW* 107 (2): 189–211.

Hejduk, J. 2020. *The God of Rome: Jupiter in Augustan Poetry.* Oxford.

Hendry, M. 1997. "Three Propertian Puns." *CQ* 47:599–603.

Henrichs, A. 1993. "Gods in Action: The Poetics of Divine Performance in the *Hymns* of Callimachus." *Hellenistica Groningana* 1:129–47.

Heyworth, S. J. 2004. "Looking into the River: Literary History and Interpretation in Callimachus, *Hymns* 5 and 6." *Hellenistica Groningana* 7:139–59.

Heyworth, S. J. 2007. *Cynthia: A Companion to the Text of Propertius.* Oxford.

Hilgard, A., ed. 1901. *Scholia in Dionysii Thracis Artem Grammaticam.* Leipzig.

Hilton, J. 1992. "Azania—Some Etymological Considerations." *Acta Classica* 35:151–59.

Hinds, S. E. 1985. "Booking the Return Trip: Ovid and *Tristia* 1." *PCPhS* 31:13–32.

Hinds, S. E. 1987. *The Metamorphosis of Persephone: Ovid and the Self-Conscious Muse.* Cambridge.

Hinds, S. E. 1992. "*Arma* in Ovid's *Fasti*. Part I: Genre and Mannerism." *Arethusa* 25 (1): 81–112.

Hinds, S. E. 1998. *Allusion and Intertext: Dynamics of Appropriation in Roman Poetry.* Cambridge.

Works Cited

Hinds, S. E. 2002. "Landscape with Figures: Aesthetics of Place in the *Metamorphoses* and Its Tradition." In Hardie 2002a, 122–49.

Hinds, S. E. 2006. "Venus, Varro and the *Vates*: Toward the Limits of Etymologizing Interpretation." *Dictynna* 3. https://doi.org/10.4000/dictynna.206

Hladký, V. 2020. "God's Many Names." In *Pseudo-Aristotle: "De Mundo (On the Cosmos)*," edited by P. Gregorić and G. Karamanoulis, 213–30. Cambridge.

Hoenig, C. 2018. *Plato's "Timaeus" and the Latin Tradition*. Cambridge.

Hollis, A. S. 1996. "Ovid, *Metamorphoses* 1, 445ff.: Apollo, Daphne, and the Pythian Crown." *ZPE* 112:69–73.

Holzberg, N. 1997. *Ovid: Dichter und Werk*. Munich.

Holzberg, N. 1999. "Apollos erste Liebe und die Folgen: Ovids Daphne-Erzählung als Programm für Werk und Wirkung." *Gymnasium* 106:317–34.

Holzberg, N. 2007. *Ovids Metamorphosen*. Munich.

Hopkinson, N. 1984a. "Callimachus' *Hymn to Zeus*." *CQ* 34:139–48.

Hopkinson, N. 1984b. *Callimachus: Hymn to Demeter*. Cambridge.

Hopkinson, N. 1984c. "Rhea in Callimachus' *Hymn to Zeus*." *JHS* 104:176–77.

Hopkinson, N. 2020. *A Hellenistic Anthology*. 2nd ed. Cambridge.

Hopwood, B. 2019. "The Good Wife: Fate, Fortune, and *Familia* in Augustan Rome." In *The Alternative Augustan Age*, edited by K. Morrell, J. Osgood, and K. Welch, 63–77. Oxford.

Horsfall, N. 1999. *Virgil, "Aeneid" 7: A Commentary*. Leiden.

Howell, R. A., and M. L. Howell. 1989. "The Atalanta Legend in Art and Literature." *Journal of Sport History* 16 (2): 127–39.

Hunter, R. L. 1992. "Writing the God: Form and Meaning in Callimachus, *Hymn to Athena*." *MD* 29:9–34.

Hunter, R. L. 1999. *Theocritus: A Selection; Idylls 1, 3, 4, 6, 7, 10, 11 and 13*. Cambridge.

Hunter, R. L. 2003. *Theocritus: Encomium of Ptolemy Philadelphus*. Cambridge.

Hunter, R., and T. Fuhrer. 2002. "Imaginary Gods? Poetic Theology in the *Hymns of Callimachus*." In Montanari and Lehnus 2002, 143–87.

Hunter, R., and R. Laemmle. 2020. "Pulling Apollo Apart." *Mnemosyne* 73:377–404.

Ingleheart, J. 2006. "Ovid, *Tristia* 1.2: High Drama on the High Seas." *G&R* 53 (1): 73–90.

Ingleheart, J. 2010. "The Literary 'Successor': Ovidian Metapoetry and Metaphor." *CQ* 60 (1): 167–72.

Isager, S. 1998. "The Pride of Halikarnassos: Editio Princeps of an Inscription from Salmakis." *ZPE* 123:1–23.

Italiano, F. 2008. "Defining Geopoetics." *TRANS-* (6). http://journals.openedition.org/trans/299.

Jacoby, F., ed. 1923–69. *Die Fragmente der Griechischen Historiker*. Leiden.

Janan, M. 1994. "'There beneath the Roman Ruin Where the Purple Flowers Grow'; Ovid's Minyeides and the Feminine Imagination." *AJP* 115 (3): 427–48.

Johnson, P., and M. Malamud. 1988. "Ovid's 'Musomachia.'" *Pacific Coast Philology* 23 (1/2): 30–38.

Johnson, P. J. 1996. "Constructions of Venus in Ovid's *Metamorphoses V.*" *Arethusa* 29:125–49.

Johnson, P. J. 2008. *Ovid before Exile: Art and Punishment in the "Metamorphoses."* Madison.

Johnston, P. A. 2021. "Catullus, Horace, and Diana Tifana's Sacred Choir." In *Artemis and Diana in Ancient Greece and Italy: At the Crossroads between the Civic and the Wild*, edited by G. Casadio and P. A. Johnston, 276–86. Newcastle.

Jouteur, I. 2001. *Jeux de genre dans les "Métamorphoses" d'Ovide.* Louvain.

Kaczyńska, E. 2016. "Epimenides' Tale of the Birth of Zeus." *Graeco-Latina Brunensia* 21:157–67.

Kampakoglou, A. 2019. *Studies in the Reception of Pindar in Ptolemaic Poetry.* Trends in Classics Supplementary Volumes 76. Berlin.

Kassel, R., and C. Austin, eds. 1983–. *Poetae Comici Graeci.* Berlin.

Kayachev, B. 2016. *Allusion and Allegory: Studies in the "Ciris."* Berlin.

Kayachev, B. 2018. "Hunt as War and War as Hunt: Grattius' *Cynegetica* and Virgil's *Aeneid.*" In Green 2018, 97–114.

Kazantzidis, G. 2021. *Lucretius on Disease: The Poetics of Morbidity in "De rerum natura."* Trends in Classics Supplementary Volumes 117. Berlin.

Keith, A. 1992a. "Amores 1.1: Propertius and the Ovidian Programme." In *Studies in Latin Literature and Roman History VI*, edited by C. Deroux, 327–44. Collection Latomus. Brussels.

Keith, A. 1992b. *The Play of Fictions: Studies in Ovid's "Metamorphoses" Book 2.* Ann Arbor.

Keith, A. 2010. "Dionysiac Theme and Dramatic Allusion in Ovid's *Metamorphoses 4.*" In *Beyond the Fifth Century: Interactions with Greek Tragedy from the Fourth Century BCE to the Middle Ages*, edited by I. Gildenhard and M. Revermann, 187–218. Berlin.

Keith, A. 2016. "The *Homeric Hymn to Aphrodite* in Ovid and Augustan Literature." In Faulkner, Vergados, and Schwab 2016, 109–26.

Keller, O., ed. 1877. *Rerum Naturalium Scriptores Graeci Minores.* Vol. 1, *Paradoxographi Antigonus, Apollonius, Phlegon, Anonymus Vaticanus.* Leipzig.

Kelly, P. 2021. "Crafting *Chaos*: Intelligent Design in Ovid, *Metamorphoses* Book 1 and Plato's *Timaeus.*" *CQ* 70 (2): 734–48.

Kelly, P. 2022. "Cosmic Artistry in Ovid and Plato." In Volk and Williams 2022, 207–25.

Kennedy, D. F. 1982. "Gallus and the Culex." *CQ* 32:371–89.

Kinkel, G., ed. 1877. *Epicorum Graecorum Fragmenta.* Leipzig.

Kirichenko, A. 2012. "Nothing to Do with Zeus? The Old and New in Callimachus' First Hymn." *Hellenistica Groningana* 16:181–202.

Kirstein, R. 2019. "New Borders of Fiction? Callimachaean Aetiology as a Narrative Device in Ovid's *Metamorphoses.*" *Hellenistica Groningana* 24:193–220.

Klein, F. 2022. *"Carmen perpetuum deducere?* Retour sur le 'programme callimachéen' du proème des *Métamorphoses."* *Dictynna* 19. https://journals.openedition.org/dictynna/3061.

Klooster, J. 2012. "Visualizing the Impossible: The Wandering Landscape in the *Delos Hymn* of Callimachus." *Aetia* 2. https://doi.org/10.4000/aitia.420.

Knox, P. E. 1985. "The Epilogue to the *Aetia."* *GRBS* 26 (1): 59–65.

Knox, P. E. 1986. *Ovid's "Metamorphoses" and the Traditions of Augustan Poetry.* Proceedings of the Cambridge Philological Society Supplement 11. Cambridge.

Knox, P. E. 1988. "Phaethon in Ovid and Nonnus." *CQ* 38 (2): 536–51.

Knox, P. E. 1990. "In Pursuit of Daphne." *TAPA* 120:183–202, 385–86.

Knox, P. E. 1995. *Ovid: "Heroides": Select Epistles.* Oxford.

Knox, P. E., ed. 2006. *Oxford Readings in Ovid.* Oxford.

Knox, P. E., ed. 2009. *A Companion to Ovid.* Chichester.

Konstantinou, A. 2018. *Female Mobility and Gendered Space in Ancient Greek Myth.* London.

Kronenberg, L. 2018. "Catullus 34 and Valerius Cato's *Diana."* *Paideia* 73:157–73.

Kyriakidis, S. 2007. *Catalogues of Proper Names in Latin Epic Poetry: Lucretius, Vergil, Ovid.* Newcastle.

Lang, C., ed. 1881. *Cornuti Theologiae Graecae Compendium.* Leipzig.

Larson, J. L. 1997. "Handmaidens of Artemis?" *CJ* 92:249–57.

Larson, J. L. 2001. *Greek Nymphs: Myth, Cult, Lore.* Oxford.

Larson, J. L. 2007. *Ancient Greek Cults: A Guide.* Abingdon.

Larue, J. 1963. "Creusa's Monody: *Ion* 859–922." *TAPA* 94:126–36.

Lather, A. 2019. "Pindar's Water Music: The Acoustics and Dynamics of the *Kelados."* *CP* 114 (3): 468–81.

Lentz, A., ed. 1867–70. *Herodiani technici reliquiae.* 2 vols. Leipzig.

Lenzi, S. 2015. *Giove e il potere delle parola nelle "Metamorfosi" di Ovidio: Tradizione letteraria e realtà romana.* Padova.

Leonard, W. E., and S. B. Smith, eds. 1942. *De Rerum Natura: The Latin Text of Lucretius.* Madison.

Lewis, V. M. 2019. *Myth, Locality, and Identity in Pindar's Sicilian Odes.* Oxford.

Lightfoot, J., ed. 2010. *Hellenistic Collection: Philitas. Alexander of Aetolia. Hermesianax. Euphorion. Parthenius.* Cambridge.

Lightfoot, J. 2018. "Callimachus, *Hymn* 2 and the Genre of Paean." *Aetia* 8 (1). https://doi.org/10.4000/aitia.2156

Littlewood, R. J. 2006. *A Commentary on Ovid's "Fasti," Book 6.* Oxford.

Lloyd-Jones, H. 1999. "The Pride of Halicarnassus." *ZPE* 124:1–14.

Lloyd-Jones, H., and P. Parsons, eds. 1983. *Supplementum Hellenisticum.* New York.

Lobel, E., and D. Page, eds. 1955. *Poetarum Lesbiorum fragmenta.* Oxford.

Lowe, D. 2013. "Chasing (Most) of the Giants out of Grattius' *Cynegetica."* *QUCC* 104 (2): 183–88.

Lowe, D. 2015. *Monsters and Monstrosity in Augustan Poetry.* Ann Arbor.

Lowrie, M. 2009. *Writing, Performance, and Authority in Augustan Rome.* Oxford.

Luck, G. 1969. *The Latin Love Elegy.* 2nd ed. London.

Lüddecke, K. 1998. "Contextualizing the Voice in Callimachus' 'Hymn to Zeus.'" *MD* 41:9–33.

Lyne, R. O. A. M. 1998. "Propertius 2.10 and 11 and the Structure of Books '2A' and '2B.'" *JRS* 1998:21–36.

Maass, E. 1896. "Untersuchungen zu Properz und seinen griechischen Vorbildern." *Hermes* 31 (2): 375–434.

Maltby, R. 1991. *A Lexicon of Ancient Latin Etymologies.* Leeds.

Manakidou, F. 2020. "Maternity in Callimachus' *Hymns* 1 and 4: Interweaving Poetics and Politics." *Hellenistica Groningana* 25:195–222.

Manousakis, N. 2020. "Aeschylus' Actaeon: A Playboy on the Greek Tragic Stage?" In *Fragmentation in Ancient Greek Drama*, edited by A. A. Lamari, F. Montanari, and A. Novokhatko, 201–34. Berlin.

Marshall, E. 2000. "Death and Disease in Cyrene: A Case Study." In *Death and Disease in the Ancient City*, edited by V. M. Hope and E. Marshall, 8–23. London.

Martin, G. 2018. *Euripides, "Ion": Edition and Commentary.* Berlin.

Marton, M. 2022. "The Case of Apollo and the Sibylline Books." *Sapiens ubique civis* 3:147–76.

Mayor, J. M. B. 2017. *Power Play in Latin Love Elegy and Its Multiple Forms of Continuity in Ovid's "Metamorphoses."* Trends in Classics Supplementary Volumes 42. Berlin.

McKay, K. J. 1962a. *Erysichthon: A Callimachean Comedy.* Mnemosyne Supplement 7. Leiden.

McKay, K. J. 1962b. *The Poet at Play: Kallimachos, The Bath of Pallas.* Mnemosyne Supplement 6. Leiden.

McKeown, J. C. 1989. *Ovid, Amores: Text, Prolegomena and Commentary in Four Volumes.* Vol. 2, *A Commentary on Book One.* Leeds.

McKim, R. 1984–85. "Myth against Philosophy in Ovid's Account of Creation." *CJ* 80 (2): 97–108.

McLennan, G. R. 1977. *Callimachus: "Hymn to Zeus": Introduction and Commentary.* Rome.

McPhee, B. 2019. "*(Adhuc) Virgineusque Helicon*: A Subtextual Rape in Ovid's Catalogue of Mountains (*Met.* 2.219)." *CQ* 69 (2): 769–75.

Meijer, P. A. 2007. *Stoic Theology: Proofs for the Existence of the Cosmic God and of the Traditional Gods.* Delft.

Meisner, D. A. 2018. *Orphic Tradition and the Birth of the Gods.* Oxford.

Mejer, J. 2009. "Artemis in Athens." In Fischer-Hansen and Poulsen 2009, 61–78.

Merkelbach, R., and M. L. West, eds. 1967. *Fragmenta Hesiodea.* Oxford.

Meyer, M. 1933. "Musai." *RE* 16.1: 679–757.

Michalopoulos, A. 2001. *Ancient Etymologies in Ovid's "Metamorphoses": A Commented Lexicon.* ARCA 40. Leeds.

Mili, M. 2015. *Religion and Society in Ancient Thessaly*. Oxford.

Miller, J. F. 2009a. *Apollo, Augustus, and the Poets*. Cambridge.

Miller, J. F. 2009b. "Primus Amor Phoebi." *CW* 102 (2): 168–72.

Miller, J. F. 2014. "Virgil's Salian Hymn to Hercules." *CJ* 109 (4): 439–63.

Miller, J. F. 2016. "Ovid's Bacchic Helmsman and *Homeric Hymn 7*." In Faulkner, Vergados, and Schwab 2016, 95–108.

Mineur, W. H. 1984. *Callimachus, "Hymn to Delos": Introduction and Commentary*. Leiden.

Montanari, F., and L. Lehnus, eds. 2002. *Callimaque: Sept exposés suivis de discussions*. Entretiens sur l'antiquité Classique 48. Vandoeuvres.

Montiglio, S. 2018. "The Song of the Sirens between Sound and Sense." In *Sound and the Ancient Senses*, edited by S. Butler and S. Nooter, 171–83. Senses in Antiquity 6. Abingdon.

Morel, W., ed. 1927. *Fragmenta Poetarum Latinorum Epicorum et Lyricorum praeter Ennium et Lucilium*. Leipzig.

Murray, J. 2004. "The Metamorphoses of Erysichthon: Callimachus, Apollonius, and Ovid." *Hellenistica Groningana* 7:207–41.

Murray, J. 2019. "Poetically Erect: The Female Oriented Humor in Callimachus' *Hymn to Demeter*." *Hellenistica Groningana* 24:249–64.

Murray, P. 2002. "Plato's Muses: The Goddesses that Endure." In *Cultivating the Muse: Struggles for Power and Inspiration in Classical Literature*, edited by E. Spentzou and D. Fowler, 29–46. Oxford.

Myers, K. S. 1994. *Ovid's Causes: Cosmogony and Aetiology in the "Metamorphoses."* Ann Arbor.

Myers, K. S. 1999. "The Metamorphosis of a Poet: Recent Work on Ovid." *JRS* 89: 190–204.

Myers, M. Y. 2019. "Lascivus Puer: Cupid, Hermes, and Hymns in Ovid's *Metamorphoses*." In *Tracking Hermes, Pursuing Mercury*, edited by J. F. Miller and J. Strauss Clay, 141–56. Oxford.

Mynors, R. A. B., ed. 1958. *C. Valerii Catulli Carmina*. Oxford.

Mynors, R. A. B., ed. 1969. *P. Vergili Maronis Opera*. Oxford.

Mynors, R. A. B. 1990. *Virgil: Georgics*. Oxford.

Nagy, G. 1973. "On the Death of Actaeon." *HSCP* 77:179–80.

Nagy, G. 2004. *Homer's Text and Language*. Champaign.

Nethercut, J. S. 2016. "Hercules and Apollo in Ovid's *Metamorphoses*." In Faulkner, Vergados, and Schwab 2016, 127–44.

Newlands, C. 1995. *Playing with Time: Ovid and the "Fasti."* Ithaca.

Nielson, T. H. 1999. "The Concept of Arkadia—The People, Their Land, Their Organisation." In *Defining Ancient Arkadia*, edited by T. H. Nielson and J. Roy, 16–79. Acts of the Copenhagen Polis Centre 6. Copenhagen.

Nielson, T. H., and J. Roy. 1998. "The Azanians of Northern Arkadia." *Classica et Medievalia* 49:5–44.

Nikolaev, A. 2014. "Showing Praise in Greek Choral Lyric and Beyond." *AJP* 133 (4): 543–72.

Nishimura-Jensen, J. 2000. "Unstable Geographies: The Moving Landscape in Apollonius' *Argonautica* and Callimachus' *Hymn to Delos*." *TAPA* 130:287–317.

Ntanou, E. 2020a. "*HAC Arethusa TENUS* (*Met.* 5.642): Geography and Poetics in Ovid's Arethusa." In *Metamorphic Readings: Transformation, Language, and Gender in the Interpretation of Ovid's "Metamorphoses,"* edited by A. Sharrock, D. Möller, and M. Malm, 84–103. Oxford.

Ntanou, E. 2020b. "*Musae Ambo*: Pastoral Poetry in the Contest between Muses and Pierides." *Journal of Greco-Roman Studies* 59 (3): 77–94.

O'Hara, J. J. 1996. *True Names: Vergil and the Alexandrian Tradition of Etymological Wordplay*. Ann Arbor.

O'Hara, J. J. 1998. "Venus or the Muse as 'Ally' (Lucr. 1.24, Simon. Frag. Eleg. 11.20–22 W)." *CP* 93 (1): 69–74.

O'Hara, J. J. 2004–5. "'Some God . . . or His Own Heart': Two Kinds of Epic Motivation in the Proem to Ovid's *Metamorphoses*." *CJ* 100 (2): 149–61.

O'Hara, J. J. 2007. *Inconsistency in Roman Epic: Studies in Catullus, Lucretius, Vergil, Ovid and Lucan*. Cambridge.

Oliver, J. H. 2015. "*Oscula iungit nec moderata satis nec sic a virgine danda*: Ovid's Callisto Episode, Female Homoeroticism, and the Study of Ancient Sexuality." *AJP* 136 (2): 281–312.

Olson, K. 2008. "*Dress and the Roman Woman: Self-Presentation and Society*. Abingdon.

Olson, S. D. 2007. *Broken Laughter: Select Fragments of Greek Comedy*. Oxford.

Olson, S. D. 2011. "Immortal Encounters: *Aeneid* 1 and the *Homeric Hymn to Aphrodite*." *Vergilius* 57:55–61.

Olson, S. D. 2012. *The Homeric Hymn to Aphrodite and Related Texts: Text, Translation and Commentary*. Texte und Kommentare 39. Berlin.

O'Meara, D. 2012. "Who Is the Demiurge in Plato's *Timaeus*?" In "Demiurge: The World-Maker in the Platonic Tradition," edited by E. Song, special issue, *Horizons: Seoul Journal of Humanities* 3 (1–2): 3–18.

O'Rourke, D. 2018. "Authorial Surrogates in Grattius' *Cynegetica*." In S. Green 2018, 193–212.

Otis, B. 1966. *Ovid as an Epic Poet*. Cambridge.

Pandey, N. B. 2018. "Blood beneath the Laurels: Pyrrhus, Apollo, and the Ethics of Augustan Victory." *CP* 113 (3): 279–304.

Papaioannou, S. 2003. "Founder, Civilizer, and Leader: Vergil's Evander and his Role in the Origins of Rome." *Mnemosyne* 56 (6): 680–702.

Papaioannou, S. 2007. *Redesigning Achilles: "Recycling" the Epic Cycle in the "Little Iliad": (Ovid, "Metamorphoses" 12.1–13.622)*. Untersuchungen zur antiken Literatur und Geschichte 89. Berlin.

Papanghelis, T. D. 1989. "About the Hour of Noon: Ovid, *Amores* 1,5." *Mnemosyne* 42 (1/2): 54–61.

Works Cited

Park, A. 2009. "Two Types of Ovidian Personification." *CJ* 104 (3): 225–40.

Parker, R. 2003. "The Problem of the Greek Cult Epithet." *Opuscula Atheniensia* 28:173–83.

Parker, R. 2017. *Greek Gods Abroad: Names, Natures, and Transformations.* Sather Classical Lecture Series 72. Berlin.

Parry, H. 1964. "Ovid's *Metamorphoses*: Violence in a Pastoral Landscape." *TAPA* 95:268–82

Paschalis, M. 2014. "Ovidian Metamorphosis and Nonnian *poikilon eidos.*" In *Nonnus of Panopolis in Context: Poetry and Cultural Milieu in Late Antiquity*, edited by K. Spanoudakis, 97–140. Berlin.

Pavlock, B. 2009. *The Image of the Poet in Ovid's "Metamorphoses."* Madison.

Pender, E. E. 2007. "Poetic Allusion in Plato's *Timaeus* and *Phaedrus.*" *Göttinger Forum für Altertumswissenschhaft* 10:21–57.

Pender, E. E. 2010. "Chaos Corrected: Hesiod in Plato's Creation Myth." In Boys-Stones and Haubold 2010, 219–45.

Pendergraft, M. L. B. 1991. "Eros Ludens: Apollonius' Argonautica 3, 132–41." *MD* 26:95–108.

Peraki-Kyriakidou, H. 2002. "Aspects of Ancient Etymologizing." *CQ* 52 (2): 478–93.

Peters, M. 2002. "Aus der Vergangenheit von Heroen und Ehegöttinnen." In *Novalis Indogermanica: Festschrift für Günter Neumann zum 80. Geburtstag*, edited by M. Fritz and S. Zeil-Felder, 357–80. Graz.

Petrovic, I. 2007. *Von den Toren des Hades zu den Hallen des Olymp: Artemiskult bei Theokrit und Kallimachos.* Mnemosyne Supplement 281. Leiden.

Petrovic, I. 2010. "Transforming Artemis: From the Goddess of the Outdoors to City Goddess." In *The Gods of Ancient Greece: Identities and Transformations*, edited by J. Bremmer and A. Erskine, 209–27. Edinburgh.

Petrovic, I. 2012. "Rhapsodic Hymns and Epyllia." In *Brill's Companion to Greek and Latin "Epyllion" and Its Reception*, edited by M. Baumbach and S. Bär, 149–76. Leiden.

Petrovic, I. 2016. "Gods in Callimachus' *Hymns.*" In *The Gods of Greek Hexameter Poetry: From the Archaic Age to Late Antiquity and Beyond*, edited by J. J. Clauss, M. Cuypers, and A. Kahane, 164–79. Potsdamer Altertumswissenschaftliche Beiträge 56. Berlin.

Pfeiffer, R., ed. 1949–53. *Callimachus.* Vol. 1, *Fragmenta*; Vol. 2, *Hymni et epigrammata.* Oxford.

Philbrick, R. 2018. "Coronis and the Metamorphosis of Apollo: Ovidian Re-Formations of Pindar's Third *Pythian.*" *AJP* 139 (3): 451–82.

Phillips, T. 2013. "Callimachus in the Pindar Scholia." *CCJ* 59:152–77.

Phillips, T. 2019. "Sublime Measures: Horace *Odes* 4.6." *CP* 114:430–45.

Plantinga, M. 2004. "A Parade of Learning: Callimachus' *Hymn to Artemis* (lines 170–268)." *Hellenistica Groningana* 7:257–77.

Pollard, J. R. T. 1952. "Muses and Sirens." *Classical Review* 2 (2): 60–63.

Postgate, J. P. 1924. *Tibulli Aliorumque Carminum Libri Tres*. Oxford.

Poulsen, B. 2009. "The Sanctuaries of the Goddess of the Hunt." In Fischer-Hansen and Poulsen 2009, 401–26.

Powell, J. U., ed. 1925. *Collectanea Alexandrina: Reliquiae minores poetarum Graecorum aetatis Ptolemaicae, 323–146 A.C.: Epicorum, elegiacorum, lyricorum, ethicorum*. Oxford.

Prioux, É. 2011. "Callimachus' Queens." In Acosta-Hughes, Lehnus, and Stephens 2011, 201–24.

Prodi, E. 2017. "Text as Paratext: Pindar, Sappho, and Alexandrian Editions." *GRBS* 57:547–82.

Putnam, M. C. J. 2000. *Horace's "Carmen Saeculare": Ritual Magic and the Poet's Art*. New Haven.

Quadlbauer, F. 1968. "Properz 3,1." *Philologus* 112 (1): 83–118.

Race, W. H. 1982. "Aspects of Rhetoric and Form in Greek Hymns." *GRBS* 23:5–14.

Race, W. H. 1997. *Pindar: Olympian Odes. Pythian Odes*. Cambridge.

Radt, S., ed. 1985. *Tragicorum Graecorum Fragmenta*. Vol. 3, *Aeschylus*. Göttingen.

Radt, S., ed. 1999. *Tragicorum Graecorum Fragmenta*. Vol. 4, *Sophocles*. Göttingen.

Ramirez de Verger, A. 2008. "Seven Critical Notes on Ovid's 'Metamorphoses.'" *Athenaeum* 2:807–12.

Reckford, K. 1995–96. "Recognizing Venus (I): Aeneas Meets His Mother." *Arion* 3 (2/3): 1–42.

Regali, M. 2010. "Hesiod in the *Timaeus*: The Demiurge Addresses the Gods." In Boys-Stones and Haubold 2010, 259–75.

Rich, A. 1860. *A Dictionary of Roman and Greek Antiquities*. Edinburgh.

Richardson, J. 2008. *The Language of Empire: Rome and the Idea of Empire from the Third Century BC to the Second Century AD*. Cambridge.

Richardson, N. J. 1974. *The Homeric Hymn to Demeter*. Oxford.

Richardson, N. J. 2010. *Three Homeric Hymns: To Apollo, Hermes, and Aphrodite*. Cambridge

Richlin, A. 1992. "Reading Ovid's Rapes." In *Pornography and Representation in Greece and Rome*, edited by A. Richlin, 158–79. New York.

Riley, H. T. 1893. *The "Metamorphoses" of Ovid*. Vol. 1, *Books I–VII*. London.

Robbins, F. E. 1913. "The Creation Story in Ovid *Met*. i." *CP* 8:401–14.

Robinson, D. M. 1936. "A New Lebes Gamikos with a Possible Representation of Apollo and Daphne." *AJA* 40 (4): 507–19.

Robinson, M. J. 2011. *A Commentary on Ovid's "Fasti," Book 2*. Oxford.

Romano, A. 2009. "The Invention of Marriage: Hermaphroditus and Salmacis at Halicarnassus and in Ovid." *CQ* 59 (2): 543–61.

Rosati, G. 2009. *Ovidio: Metamorfosi*. Vol. 3, *Libri V–VI*. Translated by G. Chiarini. Rome.

Rose, H. J. 1931. "De Actaeone Stesichoreo." *Mnemosyne* 59:431–32.

Works Cited

Ross, D. O., Jr. 1975. *Backgrounds to Augustan Poetry: Gallus, Elegy, and Rome.* Cambridge.

Rotstein, A. 2010. *The Idea of Iambos.* Oxford.

Russell, D. A. 1965. *"Longinus": On the Sublime.* Oxford.

Rutherford, I. 1988. "Pindar on the Birth of Apollo." *CQ* 38:65–75.

Rutherford, I. 2001. *Pindar's "Paeans": A Reading of the Fragments with a Survey on the Genre.* Oxford.

Salzman-Mitchell, P. B. 2005. *A Web of Fantasies: Gaze, Image, and Gender in Ovid's "Metamorphoses."* Columbus.

Sampson, C. M. 2012. "Callimachean Tradition and the Muse's *Hymn to Ceres* (Ov. *Met.* 5.341–661')." *TAPA* 142 (1): 83–103.

Santamaría, M. A. 2016. "Did Plato Know of the Orphic God Protogonos?" In *Greek Philosophy and Mystery Cults*, edited by M. J. Martín-Velasco and M. J. García Blanco, 205–31. Newcastle.

Santin, E., and A. Tziafalias. 2020. "Les Muses de Larissa: Une nouvelle inscription votive thessalienne d'époque hellénistique sur la fondation d'un sanctuaire." *BCH* 144 (1). https://doi.org/10.4000/bch.1090.

Schachter, A. 1981. *Cults of Boiotia.* 2 vols. BICS Supplement 38. London.

Schachter, A. 2016. *Boiotia in Antiquity: Selected Papers.* Cambridge.

Schein, S. L. 2013. "Divine and Human in the *Homeric Hymn to Aphrodite.*" In *Hymnes de la Grèce antique: approches littéraires et historiques. Actes du colloque international de Lyon, 19–21 juin 2008*, edited by R. Bouchon, P. Brillet-Dubois, and N. Le Meur-Weissmann, 295–312. Collection de la Maison de l'Orient méditerranéen ancien. Série littéraire et philosophique 50. Lyon.

Schiesaro, A. 2019. "Nonnus' Actaeon: Destiny in a Name." *Philologus* 163 (1): 177–83.

Schlam, C. C. 1984. "Diana and Actaeon: Metamorphoses of a Myth." *CA* 3 (1): 82–110.

Schmidt, E. A. 1991. *Ovids poetische Menschenwelt: Die "Metamorphosen" als Metapher und Symphonie.* Heidelberg.

Schmitzer, U. 2002. "Neue Forschungen zu Ovid." *Gymnasium* 109:143–66.

Scully, S. 2015. *Hesiod's "Theogony": From Near Eastern Creation Myths to "Paradise Lost."* Oxford.

Sedley, D. N. 2010. "Hesiod's *Theogony* and Plato's *Timaeus.*" In Boys-Stones and Haubold 2010, 246–58.

Segal, C. P. 1969. *Landscape in Ovid's Metamorphoses: A Study in the Transformations of a Literary Symbol.* Hermes Einzelschrift 23. Wiesbaden.

Segal, C. P. 1999. "Ovid's Arcadia and the Characterization of Jupiter in the *Metamorphoses.*" In *Ovid: Werk und Wirkung; Festgabe für Michael von Albrecht zum 65. Geburtstag*, part I, edited by W. Schubert, 402–7. Frankfurt.

Sharrock, A. R. 2002. "Gender and Sexuality." In Hardie 2002a, 95–107.

Sider, D. 2017. "The Salmacis Inscription." In *Hellenistic Poetry: A Selection*, edited by D. Sider, 32–39. Ann Arbor.

Skafte Jensen, M. 2009. "Artemis in Homer." In Fischer-Hansen and Poulsen 2009, 51–60.

Skempis, M. 2016. "Erysichthon in Thessaly: Lament, False Stories, and Locality in Callimachus' *Hymn to Demeter*." *Scripta Classica Israelica* 35:35–57.

Skutsch, O. 1985. *The Annals of Quintus Ennius*. Oxford.

Slings, S. R. 2004. "The *Hymn to Delos* as a Partial Allegory of Callimachus' Poetry." *Hellenistica Groningana* 7:279–98.

Sluiter, I. 2015. "Ancient Etymology: A Tool for Thinking." In *Brill's Companion to Ancient Greek Scholarship*, edited by F. Montanari, S. Matthaios, and A. Rengakos, 896–921. Leiden.

Snell, B., and H. Maehler, eds. 1975. *Fragments of Pindar*. 2 vols. 4th ed. Leipzig.

Snyder, J. M. I. 1980. *Puns and Poetry in Lucretius' "De rerum natura."* Amsterdam.

Solodow, J. B. 1988. *The World of Ovid's "Metamorphoses."* Chapel Hill.

Spaeth, B. S. 1994. "The Goddess Ceres in the Ara Pacis Augustae and the Carthage Relief." *AJA* 98 (1): 65–100.

Spaeth, B. S. 1996. *The Roman Goddess Ceres*. Austin.

Spanakis, M. 2018. "Images of the Hellenistic Peloponnese in Rhianus' Ἀχαϊκά and Ἠλιακά." *Eikasmos* 29:313–34.

Stephens, S. A. 2002. "Egyptian Callimachus." In Montanari and Lehnus 2002, 235–70.

Stephens, S. A. 2003. *Seeing Double: Intercultural Poetics in Ptolemaic Alexandria*. Berkeley.

Stephens, S. A. 2015. *Callimachus: The Hymns*. Oxford.

Stamatopoulou, Z. 2017. *Hesiod and Classical Greek Poetry: Reception and Transformation in the Fifth Century BCE*. Cambridge.

Steiner, D. T. 2021. *Choral Constructions in Greek Culture: The Idea of the Chorus in the Poetry, Art and Social Practices of the Archaic and Early Classical Period*. Cambridge.

Swift, L. A. 2010. *The Hidden Chorus: Echoes of Genre in Tragic Lyric*. Oxford.

Syed, Y. 2004. "Ovid's Use of the Hymnic Genre in the Metamorphoses." In *Rituals in Ink: A Conference on Religion and Literary Production in Ancient Rome*, edited by A. Barchiesi, J. Rüpke, and S. Stephens, 99–114. Munich.

Tarrant, R. J. 1985. *Seneca's "Thyestes."* Atlanta.

Tarrant, R. J., ed. 2004. *P. Ovidi Nasonis. Metamorphoses*. Oxford.

Taylor, B. 2020. *Lucretius and the Language of Nature*. Oxford.

Thomas, R. F. 1986. "Virgil's *Georgics* and the Art of Reference." *HSCP* 90:171–98.

Thomas, R. F. 1988. *Virgil: "Georgics."* Vols. 1 and 2. Cambridge.

Thomas, R. F. 2011. *Horace: "Odes" Book IV and "Carmen Saeculare."* Cambridge.

Thomas, O. 2011. "The *Homeric Hymn to Pan*." In Faulkner 2011, 151–72. Oxford.

Tissol, G. 1997. *The Face of Nature: Wit, Narrative, and Cosmic Origins in Ovid's "Metamorphoses."* Princeton.

Traill, D. A. 1998. "Callimachus' Singing Sea (*Hymn* 2.106)." *CP* 93 (3): 215–22.

Tsaknaki, C. 2018. "*Ars Venandi*: The Art of Hunting in Grattius' *Cynegetica* and Ovid's *Ars Amatoria*." In S. Green 2018, 115–32.

Turkeltaub, D. 1993. "The Three Virgin Goddesses in the Homeric *Hymn to Aphrodite*." *Lexis* 21:101–16.

Works Cited

Ukleja, K. 2005. *Der "Delos-Hymnus" des Kallimachos innerhalb seines Hymnensextetts.* Münster.

Usener, H. 1948. *Götternamen.* 3rd ed. Frankfurt.

Valdés Guía, M. 2021. "Pallas and a Female Pyrrhic Dance for Athena in Attica." *Mnemosyne* 74 (6): 913–34.

Vamvouri Ruffy, M. 2004. *La fabrique du divin: Les Hymnes de Callimaque à la lumière des "Hymnes homériques" et des "Hymnes épigraphiques."* Liège.

Vanhaegendoren, K. 2005. "Ovid, *Metamorphoses* 1.258: Textual Criticism and Ovidian Mockery." *L'antiquité Classique* 74:199–206.

Van Tress, H. 2004. *Poetic Memory: Allusion in the Poetry of Callimachus and the "Metamorphoses" of Ovid.* Leiden.

Van Windekens, A. J. 1986. *Dictionnaire étymologique complementaire de la langue grecque.* Leuven.

Vergados, A. 2012. "Corinna's Poetic Mountains: *PMG* 654 col i 1–34 and Hesiodic Reception." *CP* 107 (2): 101–18.

Vergados, A. 2020. *Hesiod's Verbal Craft: Studies in Hesiod's Conception of Language and Its Ancient Reception.* Oxford.

Versnel, H. S. 2011. *Coping with the Gods.* Leiden.

Vine, B. 1993. "Catullus 76.21: *Ut Torpor in Artus.*" *RhM* 136:292–97.

Volk, K., and G. Williams, eds. 2022. *Philosophy in Ovid, Ovid as Philosopher.* Oxford.

Volk, K., and J. E. G. Zetzel. 2015. "Laurel, Tongue and Glory (Cicero, *de Consulato Suo* fr. 6 Soubiran)." *CQ* 65 (1): 204–23.

von Arnim, H., ed. 1903–5. *Stoicorum veterum fragmenta.* Stuttgart.

von Glinski, M. L. 2012. *Simile and Identity in Ovid's "Metamorphoses."* Cambridge.

von Glinski, M. L. 2018. "Squaring the Epic Cycle: Ovid's Rewriting of the Epic Tradition in the *Metamorphoses.*" In *Brill's Companion to Prequels, Sequels, and Retellings of Classical Epic,* edited by R. Simms, 227–47. Leiden.

Wachter, R. 1991. "The Inscriptions on the François Vase." *Museum Helveticum* 48 (2): 86–113.

Walker, A. 2006. *Coins of Peloponnesos: The BCD Collection.* Auktion LHS 96. Zurich.

Wallensten, J. 2008. "Personal Protection and Tailor-Made Deities: The Use of Individual Epithets." *Kernos* 21:81–95.

Warmington, E. H., ed. *Remains of Old Latin.* Vol. 3, *Lucilius, The Twelve Tables.* Cambridge.

Wasdin, K. 2018. *Eros at Dusk: Ancient Wedding and Love Poetry.* Oxford.

Waszink, J. H. 1950. "The Proem of the *Annales* of Ennius." *Mnemosyne* 3 (3): 215–40.

Waszink, J. H. 1962. "Retractatio Enniana." *Mnemosyne* 15 (2): 113–32.

Weinlich, B. 2010. "The Story of a Poet's Apologetic Emancipation: The *Recusatio*-Narratives in Propertius 3.3, *Amores* 1.1, 2.1, and 3.1." *Helios* 2:129–52.

Wendel, C., ed. 1935. *Scholia in Apollonium Rhodium vetera.* Berlin.

West, M. L. 1983. *The Orphic Poems.* Oxford.

Works Cited

West, M. L., ed. 1989–92. *Iambi et elegi Graeci ante Alexandrum cantati.* 2 vols. 2nd ed. Oxford.

Wheeler, S. 1995. "*Imago Mundi*: Another View of the Creation in Ovid's *Metamorphoses.*" *AJP* 116 (1): 95–121.

Wheeler, S. 1999. *A Discourse of Wonders: Audience and Performance in Ovid's "Metamorphoses."* Philadelphia.

Wheeler, S. 2000. *Narrative Dynamics in Ovid's "Metamorphoses."* Tübingen.

Whitlatch, L. 2018. "The Conditions of Poetic Immortality: Epicurus, Daphnis, and Hagnon." In Green 2018, 179–92.

Wickkiser, B. L. 2005. "Augustus, Apollo, and an Ailing Rome: Images of Augustus as a Healer of State." In *Studies in Latin Literature and Roman History*, edited by C. Deroux, 12:267–89. Brussels.

Wickkiser, B. L. 1999. "Famous Last Words: Putting Ovid's Sphragis Back into the *Metamorphoses.*" *MD* 42:113–42.

Wilamowitz, U. von. 1924. *Hellenistische Dichtung in der Zeit des Kallimachos.* Vol 2, *Interpretationen.* Berlin.

Wilkins, J. 1988. "Ovid and the Erymanthian Bear." *Mnemosyne* 41:379–81.

Wilkins, J. 2000. *The Boastful Chef: The Discourse of Food in Ancient Greek Comedy.* Oxford.

Williams, F. 1978. *Callimachus: Hymn to Apollo. A Commentary.* Oxford.

Williams, F. 1981. "Augustus and Daphne: Ovid *Metamorphoses* 1, 560–63 and Phylarchus FGrH81 F 32 (b)." *PLLS* 3:249–57.

Williams, F. 1993. "Callimachus and the Supranormal." *Hellenistica Groningana* 1:217–25.

Wills, J. 1990. "Callimachean Models for Ovid's Apollo-Daphne." *MD* 24:143–56.

Wimmel, W. 1960. *Kallimachos in Rom: Die Nachfolge seines apologetischen Dichtens in der Augusterzeit.* Wiesbaden.

Ypsilanti, M. 2009. "Callimachus' Use of the Story of Melanippe in His Bath of Pallas." *QUCC* 92 (2): 105–17.

Ziogas, I. 2013a. *Ovid and Hesiod: The Metamorphosis of the "Catalogue of Women."* Cambridge.

Ziogas, I. 2013b. "The Topography of Epic Narrative in Ovid's *Metamorphoses.*" In *Geography, Topography, Landscape: Configurations of Space in Greek and Roman Epic*, edited by M. Skempis and I. Ziogas, 325–48. Berlin.

Ziogas, I. 2016. "Introduction: Power, Puns and Politics from Horace to Silius Italicus." In *Wordplay and Powerplay in Latin Poetry*, edited by P. Mitsis and I. Ziogas, 1–12. Leiden. Trends in Classics Supplementary Volumes 36.

Zissos, A. 1999. "The Rape of Proserpina in Ovid *Met.* 5.341–661: Internal Audience and Narrative Distortion." *Phoenix* 53:97–113.

Zuchtriegel, G. 2011. "An Open-Air Sanctuary on an Amphora by the *Pittore delle Gru* and the Cult of Artemis in Early Etruria." *MEFRA* 123:5–11. https://doi.org/10.4000/mefra.472.

INDEX

Achaia (Argos), 86, 252n89, 252n90

Achelous, 7, 197–98, 211, 212, 214, 248n39, 275n81, 275n82, 276n29

Acontius, 107, 253n17

acorns, 31, 53, 55, 246n26, 257n63

Actaeon, 7, 134–39, 140, 141, 142–43, 144, 146–47, 148–50, 152–60, 161, 164–65, 167–68, 169–72, 178, 179, 224, 225, 231, 238n11, 264n8, 265n14, 265n17, 266n45, 267n56, 267n58, 268n77, 268n80, 277n43

Acusilaus, 18

Admetus, 67, 108

Aeneas, 53, 114, 146, 216, 258n86, 277n39; shield of, 273n47

Aeschylus, 143, 159, 160, 246n12, 267n58, 268n77, 268n80

aetiology, 4, 12, 32, 57, 74–75, 77, 87, 98, 119, 121, 177, 184, 207, 217, 219, 221, 249n55, 250n74, 254n17, 262n133, 264n153

Agamemnon, 138, 169, 171

Aganippe, 269n10

Alcithoe, 31–32, 33, 34, 35

Alexander the Great, 191

Alexandria, 6, 66, 67, 191

Allecto, 265n17

allusion, 3, 5, 6, 7, 11, 12, 15, 22, 23, 27, 32, 37, 43, 48, 64, 78, 103, 107, 123, 126, 127, 129, 131, 132, 135, 142, 143, 145–46, 152, 155, 158, 160–64, 189, 192, 199, 209–10, 215, 225, 230, 239n15, 240n29, 257n63, 261n116, 265n17, 276n29; antiphrastic, 195; geographical, 252n94

Alpheus, 216, 218, 220, 221–22, 223, 277n43; river, 248n45

Amnisus, river, 124

Amor. *See* Cupid

Amphis, 97

Anchises, 41, 96–97, 204, 235

Antagoras, 22–23, 41

Anticlea, 121

Antiope, 185

Antiphanes, 196

Aphrodisias (Caria), 32, 33–34

Aphrodite, 10, 34, 37, 40–43, 96–98, 158, 193, 203–6, 210, 214, 220, 235, 243n65, 244n76, 255n32, 275n4, 278n66. *See also* Venus

Apidanus, river, 55, 57, 62, 64, 65, 67, 83, 86, 248n42, 249n52, 249n53, 252n94

Apis, 86, 252n90

Apollo: and Artemis, 88–133; Apollo Citharoedus, 94, 132; Apollo Epikourios, 258n78; Apollo Galaxios, 48–49; Apollo Medicus, 112; Apollo Philens, 260n103; Apollo Pythoctonos, 260n103; as Cynthius, 92, 254n21; and Daphne, 46, 49, 59–60, 61, 64, 73–74, 78, 83, 85, 87, 88–89, 94–98, 105–6, 107–8, 111–12, 113–15, 118–19, 122–23, 125, 126–27, 130–33, 223, 231, 249n54, 256n59, 257n63, 259n87; defeat of the Python, 59, 73, 84, 90, 115, 117, 257n65, 259n98; as Delius, 48, 92, 105; identities of, 107–11; as Nomios, 108, 110; as *opifer*, 111–15, 258n78, 258n80; as Paean, 74, 105, 115–17, 257n69; as Phoebus, 48, 73, 92, 94, 100, 105, 108, 110, 112, 113, 180, 190, 245n11, 256n51, 257n67; as Sol, 51, 52, 103, 216, 245n11; bow of, 71, 73, 90–93, 100, 109, 110–12

Apollonius of Rhodes, 42–43, 55, 119, 199, 212–13, 232, 245n81, 252n94, 275n84

Arachne, 233

Arcadia, 37, 46, 52–53, 55–56, 57, 59–60, 64, 66–67, 68, 72, 76, 77, 78–84, 85–86, 121, 129, 131, 132, 145, 160, 162, 163, 246n13, 247n33, 247n34, 248n45, 252n90

Archimedes, 43, 245n81

Ares, 41, 126, 131, 242n41, 263n151

Arethusa, 176, 202, 206, 212, 227, 268n5, 272n34, 277n38, 277n39, 277n42, 277n43, 277n44, 278n62; as Muse, 214–18; and nature of love, 218–25

Argus, 83, 277n42

Aricia, 104, 114, 151, 152

Aristaeus, 119, 152, 154, 165, 216, 248n40, 249n53, 266n42, 270n19

Aristophanes, 18, 19, 268n2

armillary sphere, 43, 245n81

Artemis, 61, 89, 90–91, 95, 96, 97–98, 99, 100, 101, 102, 103, 105, 107, 108, 109, 114, 117, 118, 119–20, 121–22, 123–24, 125, 128–29, 130, 131, 132, 133, 135–41, 144–46, 158–60, 161, 162, 163–64, 165, 167, 169, 170–71, 173, 175, 178–79, 181, 203, 208, 212, 224, 225, 231. *See also* Diana

Ascalaphus, 211

Ascanius, 265n17

Asteria, 89, 126–29, 262n135, 263n146

Atalanta, 121, 159, 163–64, 235, 254n28, 261n113, 261n116

Athena, 41, 42, 137, 139–40, 141, 144, 146, 148, 151, 154, 159, 173, 175, 178–79, 180, 181, 199, 203, 208, 266n35, 270n12, 270n16, 271n24, 271n25, 271n26, 272n36. *See also* Minerva

Athenaeus, 272n36

Augustan age, 8–9, 33, 45, 74, 87, 88, 92, 94, 95, 104, 108, 112–17, 130, 133, 147, 163, 170, 191–92, 206, 229, 230

Augustus (Octavian), emperor, 45, 47, 48, 49, 53, 78, 87, 93, 113, 243n65, 244n62, 246n17, 260n107, 272n41, 273n47

Aulus Gellius, 29

authority, cosmic, 14, 42

Autonoe, 141, 265n14

Azenis, 57, 69

Bacchus, 32, 239n17

Battus, 111

Berenice, 173, 266n35

Beroe, 165

Bion, 217

Brauron, 167

Britomartis, 121

Brumbaugh, Michael, 6, 68–69

Brutus, 233

Cadmus, 184

Caeratus, river, 124, 131, 261n126

Calchas, 110

Index

305

Callimachus: *Aetia*, 6, 193, 244n75, 257n62, 266n35; *Bath of Pallas*, 6, 7, 134–35, 138, 139–41, 146, 148, 150, 151–52, 154, 158, 159, 161, 171–72, 174, 175, 178–84, 199, 200, 231, 238n11, 266n35; epigrams of, 6; *Hecale*, 6; *Hymn to Apollo*, 6, 10, 48, 67, 71–72, 84, 89, 107, 109–10, 117, 119–22, 123–24, 125, 126, 128, 132, 133, 198; *Hymn to Artemis*, 6, 10, 61, 89, 94, 101, 103, 107–8, 119, 120–21, 123–25, 128–29, 133, 134, 135–39, 140, 144, 146, 147, 159, 161, 163, 165, 171, 172, 208, 224, 231; *Hymn to Delos*, 6, 7, 10, 89, 125–30, 131, 132, 133, 230, 238n5; *Hymn to Demeter*, 6, 7, 41, 174, 192–98, 200, 231, 238n5; *Hymn to Zeus*, 6, 21, 22, 35, 39, 40–41, 46, 54, 59, 64–65, 66, 68, 72, 77, 78, 80, 82–83, 85, 87, 129, 131, 230; *Iambs*, 6; *Ibis*, 6

Calliope, 8, 9, 10, 35, 40, 174, 175, 176, 181, 182, 184, 185, 192, 201–28, 232, 233, 234, 273n47, 275n1, 276n19, 276n20, 276n29, 277n48, 278n62

Callisto, 46, 59, 78–79, 82, 83, 84, 95, 96, 97, 105, 135–36, 137, 251n82, 254n27, 254n30, 255n35; as constellation of the Bear, 80

Campania, 188, 273n48

Canopus, 191

Capaneus, 193

Carneia (festival), 120

Catullus, 95, 101, 102, 103, 142, 210, 253n8, 255n45, 259n88, 271n33

Celmis, 31–32

Centauromachy, 195

centaurs, 163, 267n70

Cephalus, 163

Ceres, 9, 35, 36, 37, 40, 181, 185, 192, 199, 201–2, 203, 205, 206, 207–8, 209, 215, 216, 218, 219, 227, 275n7, 277n46, 277n50

Cerialia (festival), 207

Chaos (personification), 58, 245n82, 247n32

Chariclo, 137, 140, 141, 142, 178–79, 264n5, 270n18

childbirth, 82, 102, 258–59n86

Chios, 171

Chiron, 118, 264n5

Choricius of Gaza, 70

Chryses, 8, 110

Cicero, 17, 43, 75, 185, 241n10, 251n76, 251n77, 253n15, 275n8

Cinyps, river, 147, 148

Cithaeron, 173

Claudian, 165, 243, 268n74

Cleanthes, 22–23, 241n8, 242n38

Cleopatra, 191

Clio, 165, 216, 276n34

coins, 103, 246n26

Cole, Thomas, 86

comedy, 96, 97, 184, 195, 196, 197, 199, 200, 230; New Comedy, 95

Corinna, 165, 173, 216, 268n2

Cornificius, Lucius, 104

Coronis, 260n103

Corydon, 165

cosmogony, 16, 17–18, 19, 21, 24, 25, 28, 43, 44, 64, 73, 77, 184, 220, 221, 226, 231, 234, 241n7, 242n30, 242n34, 242n38

craftsmanship, metaphor of, 17, 19, 20, 43. *See also* demiurge

Crete, 33, 55, 66–67, 124, 129, 132, 160, 248n48, 264n152

Crocale, 148–49, 164, 266n37

Cupid (Amor), 10, 14, 16, 20, 23–24, 30, 34, 35–36, 37, 42, 43, 44, 46, 73, 90, 91–92, 93, 109, 201, 203, 208, 209, 210, 214, 218, 219, 233, 235, 240n1, 240n5, 241n6, 243n47, 251n79, 252n4, 253n9, 253n12, 254n22, 262n134. *See also* Eros

Curetes, 31–32, 33

Cyane, 176, 212, 268n5

Index

Cyclopes, 261n126

Cydippe, 107, 216, 253n17, 254n17, 259n89

Cyllene, mount, 59, 163, 190

Cyrene, 89, 111, 118–22, 125, 129–30, 132, 133, 148, 159, 165, 255n35, 260n102, 260n103, 260n105, 260n107, 261n111, 261n115, 261n116, 263n146, 266n32

dance, 96, 120, 138, 139–40, 198, 259n96, 263n140, 270n16

Daphne, 46, 49, 59–60, 61, 62, 64, 65–66, 73, 74, 75, 76, 77, 78, 83, 85, 86, 87, 88–89, 94–98, 99, 100, 104–7, 108, 111, 112, 113–15, 122–25, 131, 132–33, 168, 223, 231, 235, 242n32, 243n47, 249n54, 251n80, 256n59, 257n63, 259n87, 259n89, 260n102, 261n111, 263n146, 277n43; and Asteria, 125–30; and Cyrene, 117–22

Daphnephoria (festival), 49, 245n7

deer, 90, 135, 138, 140, 143, 144, 145, 146, 154, 161, 162, 168, 170, 267n69

Delos, 71, 92, 121, 126–28, 129, 130, 132, 257n62, 261n117, 262n129, 263n139, 263n140, 263n146, 263n148

Delphi, 48, 109, 122, 132, 260n99, 264n153

Demeter, 37, 38, 41, 143, 192, 193–94, 195, 196, 197–98, 199, 205, 206, 212, 231, 247n38, 270n16, 274n72

demiurge, 17–18, 20, 21, 23, 25, 27, 30, 43, 235, 240n5, 241n13

Dercylus, 152, 153, 154, 158, 267n52

Dia, 96

Diana: as a Muse, 134–72; as Augusta, 104; as Cynthia, 92, 105; as Delia, 92; as Dictynna, 105, 145; as Eileithyia, 258n86; as Genitalis, 102; grotto of, 12, 150; as Ilythia, 102; as Juno Lucina, 101, 102, 186, 189, 259n87; as Luna, 101, 103, 256n50; *Lavacrum Dianae*, 134–72; "manynamedness" of, 100, 103,

104; as *opifera*, 114, 258n85; as Phoebe, 76, 92, 93, 94, 97, 99–100, 104–5, 106, 118, 254n20, 256n51; torch of, 92, 104; as Trivia, 80, 101, 105, 256n50; virginity of, 93, 95, 97, 98, 104, 106–7, 169, 208, 256n47. *See also* Artemis

Dio Cassius, 113, 272n41

Dionysus, cult of, 32

Dis, 209

disguise, 94–98, 199, 204, 205, 206, 214, 235, 254n27, 264n12, 277n42

Doris, 216

doublets, divine, 83, 86

earthquakes, 262n136

ecphrasis, 46, 47, 50, 52, 62, 63, 64, 67, 72, 76, 84, 150, 216, 246n12, 273n47, 277n40

ecpyrosis, 26

Egypt, 66, 132, 190, 191, 252n94

elegiac, 4, 18, 26, 32, 34, 45, 67, 75, 76, 77, 92, 106, 142, 173, 231, 233, 235, 239n15, 241n6, 243n57, 249n54, 251n79, 256n60, 258n79, 258n80, 269n8

Emathia. *See* Macedonia

Empedocles, 18, 209–10, 225, 227, 242n30

Ennius, 235

Ephesus, 243n65

epic (genre), 8, 9, 14, 35, 77, 92, 116, 124, 169, 179, 180, 226, 227, 230

Epicharmus, 184, 189, 198–99, 271n24, 272n33, 275n85

Epimenides, 66, 248n49, 270n17

epinician, 21, 69, 71

Epirus, 67

epthets, divine, 12, 34, 55, 66, 90, 91, 94, 104, 108, 135, 141, 152, 180, 181, 185, 187, 206, 224, 225, 226

Eridanus, river, 67, 248n45, 249n51

Eris, 22, 193

Eros, 14, 18–20, 21–27, 34, 42–43, 44, 231, 241n17, 242n29, 243n56, 245n80,

275n15; as demiurge, 18, 20, 23, 25, 27. *See also* Cupid

Erymanthus, river, 57, 65, 79–80, 251n81

Erysichthon, 7, 192–93, 194, 195, 196, 197, 200, 238n11, 273n58, 274n64, 275n82

etymology, 12, 20, 28–29, 57–58, 65, 75, 76, 114, 148, 153, 165, 187, 188, 198, 199, 206, 207, 219, 220, 222, 223, 225, 226, 243n44, 244n61, 246n12, 247n32, 251n76, 253n11, 260n111, 265n14, 265n19, 266n45, 266n46, 275n2

Euphrates, river, 198

Euripides, 193, 268n2

Europa, 27, 28

Eurypylus, 120

Evander, 53

Faraone, Christopher, 8

fates, 164, 167, 258n86

fertility, 108, 205, 206

Gaia, 33, 57, 58, 69, 247n31

Gallus, 173, 180, 217, 271n31

Gargaphie (Argaphia), 148, 149–50, 151, 158, 266n34, 266n35

genealogy, 30, 59, 60, 84, 86, 119, 130, 252n93, 260n103, 276n29

genre, 8, 9, 11, 14, 35, 74, 77, 92, 116–17, 124, 169, 179, 180, 185, 217, 226, 227, 230, 255n34

geography, 4, 12, 13, 22, 32, 46, 53, 55, 56, 59–80, 61, 64, 66, 67, 73, 77, 78, 80, 82, 125, 130, 132, 133, 141, 187, 188, 191, 192, 193, 210, 230

giants (Titans), 10, 28, 29, 84, 85, 170, 171, 188, 190, 193, 194, 195, 196, 199, 234

Gigantomachy, 26, 28, 169–70, 175, 188, 190, 191, 193, 195, 196–97, 198, 200, 226

gluttony, 196

gods, council of the, 27, 46, 53, 62, 78, 84

Golden Age, 31, 55, 108

Graces, the, 148, 149, 266n35

Grattius, 135, 146–49, 151, 152, 153, 154, 156, 157, 158, 160, 161, 162, 163, 164, 166, 167, 168, 169–70, 171, 172, 229, 231, 264n1, 266n33, 268n77

Hades, 38, 39, 40, 41, 205

Haemus, mount, 126, 187, 188, 210, 272n43

Hagnon, 152, 154, 155, 156, 157, 158, 160, 267n61

hairstyles, 94, 95, 105–6

Halicarnassus inscription, 32–33, 34

Harmonia, 184

healing, 108, 110, 111, 112, 114, 115, 117, 257n69, 258n78, 258n79, 258n80, 258n85, 259n87

Hebe, 184, 189, 247n38

Helicon, mount, 68, 137, 138, 140, 141, 171, 201, 210, 211, 213, 215, 227, 249n59, 268n1, 269n17, 271n25, 272n40, 273n47, 274n77; hymnic battle for, 173–200

Helios. *See* Sol

Hera, 42, 91, 98, 100, 125, 129, 224, 253n12, 254n27, 276n34. *See also* Juno

Heracles, 184, 267n69

Hermaphroditus, 32, 33, 34, 35, 243n53, 278n59

Hermes, 9–10, 91, 204–5 *See also* Mercury

Hesiod, 17, 21, 22, 23, 33, 38, 54, 58, 118, 119, 128, 130, 173, 186, 190–91, 199, 204, 213, 226, 241n12, 242n31, 244n70, 248n42, 252n90, 260n103, 268n2, 272n35, 276n22

Hestia, 41, 203, 273n58

hexameter, 8, 9, 21, 54, 93, 109, 231, 232, 233

Hippo, 138, 140, 169

Hippocrene, 175, 176, 178, 179, 182, 186, 188, 217, 218, 225, 249n59, 266n35, 269n7, 269n9, 270n17, 270n18

308 Index

Hippolytus, 158–59, 267n56
Homer, 38, 51, 90, 91, 98, 100, 173, 212, 217, 232, 252n89, 253n10, 257n65, 261n127, 263n140, 268n2
Homeric Hymns: to Apollo, 68, 69, 71; *to Artemis*, 90, 96, 100, 145, 169; *to Demeter*, 35, 37, 38, 40, 41, 181, 185, 201, 203, 205–6, 208, 212, 218; *to Hermes*, 9, 244n70, 252n4; *to Zeus*, 10, 72
Honestus, 269n9
Horace, 96, 253n16, 262n129, 269n6; *Carmen Saeculare*, 95, 102–3, 104, 112–13, 114, 116, 117, 133, 229, 257n74, 260n101
hunting, 81, 90, 94, 105, 118, 124, 137, 138, 141, 144–45, 146, 147, 148–49, 152–53, 154–55, 156, 158–69, 170, 171, 259n89, 266n38, 270n16
hunting dogs, 120–21, 145, 146, 154, 156, 158–59, 160–69, 172; names of, 164–68
Hyacinthus, 235
Hyale, 164
hymnic tradition, 3, 4, 5, 7–9, 10, 11–12, 13, 14–15, 21, 22–23, 24, 26, 27, 30, 32, 34, 35, 37, 40, 41–42, 44, 46, 48, 59, 68, 70, 71, 72, 74, 75, 76, 77, 87, 88, 89, 91, 94–95, 96, 97–99, 101, 103, 104, 107, 108, 109, 114, 115, 117, 119, 122, 123, 124, 125, 129–30, 132, 133, 135, 139, 146, 147, 154, 162, 169, 171, 172, 174, 178, 179, 184–85, 191, 192, 193, 194, 196, 197, 199, 200, 201, 202, 203, 206, 207, 208, 209, 214, 225, 226, 227, 228, 229, 230, 231, 232, 234, 235. See also Callimachus; *Homeric Hymns*
Hypseus, 120, 121

Ibis, 266n33
Ida, mount, 33, 151, 264n152
imperialism, 38, 40, 205
Inachus, 24, 85–86, 114, 247n38, 252n90, 277n50

intertextuality, 7, 11, 12, 63, 67–68, 72, 76, 145, 146, 216, 237n4, 240n29, 251n79, 255n37
Io, 24–25, 27, 28, 59, 77, 83, 86, 114, 123, 219, 235, 242n33, 247n38, 251n80, 252n90, 252n94, 277n51
Ismenus, river, 79, 251n81

Jason, 42
Julio-Claudian dynasty, 3
Julius Caesar, 243n65
Juno, 24, 25. *See also* Hera
Jupiter, 10, 12, 14, 15, 16, 19, 23, 24, 25–27, 28, 29, 30–34, 35, 36, 37, 38, 42, 43, 44, 45–52, 72–73, 74, 76, 77–78, 79, 80, 82, 83–84, 85, 86, 87, 88, 95, 97, 109, 131, 184, 190, 191, 203, 218–19, 220, 230, 231, 234–35; and Arcadia, 52–64. *See also* Zeus

Kalliopeia, 225
Katabasis, 205
kingship, 22, 41, 54, 244n63
kleos, Homeric, 43, 232
Knossos, 261n126

Ladon, river, 57, 60, 62, 65, 79, 81, 83, 126, 163, 247n35, 248n47, 251n81, 268n74
landscape, 12, 46, 47, 50, 52, 56, 58, 59, 62, 64, 66, 69, 72, 74, 76, 78, 79, 80, 82, 87, 97, 121, 130, 131–32, 135, 143, 144, 147, 149–50, 151, 152, 158, 176, 178, 182, 183, 184, 186, 204, 205, 223, 230, 240n34, 249n59, 251n85, 262n128, 266n45, 271n26, 273n48, 278n61
Latona. *See* Leto
laurel, symbolism of, 46, 48, 49, 74–75, 76, 87, 88, 90, 106–7, 115, 116, 117, 122, 123, 125, 127, 130, 132, 251n79, 256n59, 256n61, 260n99, 264n153
Leda, 96

Index

309

Leto (Latona), 7, 71, 93, 94, 104, 108, 114, 124, 125–26, 128, 129, 130–31, 132, 136, 137, 261n115, 262n128

Libya, 118, 120, 121, 122, 147, 148, 190, 214

Ligea, 216

Lucan, 248n47, 249n53, 261n127, 266n33, 268n77, 271n24, 273n47

Lucretius, 206, 209–10, 220, 221–22, 232–33, 242n39, 242n41, 275n14, 275n15, 278n53

Ludi Saeculares, 116, 256n50, 258n92

Lupercalia (festival), 55

Lycaeus, mount, 59, 165

Lycaon, 53–55, 59, 63, 73, 78, 80, 84, 246n18

Lycophron, 199, 274n7

Lycorias, 216

lynxes, 144–45, 146, 163

Lyssa, 268n77

Macedonia, 185, 187, 188, 191, 196, 272n41, 272

Maenalus, mount, 59, 80, 105, 145, 153, 163

Maiestas (personification), 27, 28, 29, 30

Mark Antony, 191

Mars. *See* Ares

Marsyas, 268n2

Medea, 42, 232

Medusa, 177, 182, 186, 188, 271n25

Melpomene, 213, 276n33

memory, 183, 225

Menelaus, 50, 51

Mercury, 83, 277n42. *See also* Hermes

Merope, 171

Metamorphoses. *See* Ovid

metaphor, 10, 17, 20, 42, 43, 56, 68, 69, 72, 74, 78, 91, 92, 97, 117, 123, 128, 130, 131, 144, 145, 148, 153, 156, 162, 188, 189, 194, 195, 205

metapoetics, 68, 69, 71, 72, 82, 124, 128, 131, 133, 148, 149, 186, 192, 198, 200,

202, 210, 211, 223, 227, 228, 230, 232, 234, 249n59, 250n61, 277n38, 278n62

Milky Way, 47, 48, 49, 50, 52, 62, 67

Minerva, 134, 139, 171, 174, 175, 176, 177–78, 183, 184, 186, 187, 198–99, 200, 201, 208, 213, 215, 217, 218, 225, 226, 227, 228, 233, 266n38, 269n6, 271n20, 271n21, 271n24; and Diana, 139–41; as Muse, 178–82. *See also* Athena

Minyeides, 31

Mnemosyne, 185

Muses, 5, 40, 70, 71, 111, 153, 173, 176, 178, 179, 180–81, 190–91, 197, 198, 201, 202, 215, 217, 218, 225, 226, 227, 233, 244n70, 266n35, 268n3, 270n19, 272n33, 272n35, 272n36, 272n37, 272n38, 272n40, 273n55, 274n77, 275n15, 276n31, 276n33, 276n34, 277n35; as Aloads, 170–71, 268n80, 272n40; as *Aonides*, 186, 217, 272n40; as *Ardalides*, 271n25; contest with the Pierides, 10, 12, 174–75, 184–89, 192, 199, 200, 231; as *Emathides*, 187; and Helicon, 182–84; and love, 208–14; as *Maenads*, 265n22; as *Pegasides*, 183; as *Thespiades*, 186, 272n40; virginity of, 208, 210

Nape, 165

Narcissus, 137, 220, 221, 265n14, 278n59

narratology, 11, 124, 230, 232, 240n29, 277n38

Nausicaa, 136

Nebrophone, 165

Nemi, 152, 166, 167

Nephele, 164

Neptune, 63. *See also* Poseidon

Nile, river, 66, 190, 191, 199, 248n45, 248n47, 252n94, 275n84

Niobe, 86, 252n92, 264n4

Nisus and Euryalus, 1n

nymphs, 25, 33, 62, 81, 120, 121, 124–25, 126, 136, 140, 144, 145, 151, 175, 176, 186,

310 Index

nymphs (*continued*)
202, 208, 224, 261n111, 263n140, 265n24, 267n71, 268n74, 270n16, 271n24; huntress, 135, 137, 164–69; Muses as, 182–84

Oceanids, 124, 144, 165, 181, 212, 213, 216, 270n16, 276n33
Oceanus, 197–98, 261n125, 276n33
Ocyroe, 264n5
Oeagrus, 210
Oeneus, 138
Olympus, mount, 39, 40, 170, 193, 194, 263n152
Orion, 138, 139, 140, 169, 170–71, 264n7, 268n80
Orpheus, 142, 210, 211, 232, 235, 279n5
Orphism, 18–19, 20, 21, 23, 44, 241n15, 242n34, 245n80
Otis, Brooks, 7
Otus, 138, 169, 170–71
Ourania (Urania), 177, 213, 225, 226, 227
Ovid, *Metamorphoses* of: and Callimachus, 5–6; cosmic authority in, 14–44; Diana in, 134–72; hymnic influence on, 12–13; narrative matrix of, 4; theme of love in, 3, 8, 10, 13, 14–44. *See also* Ovid, other works of
Ovid, other works of: *Amores*, 16, 23, 24, 26, 27, 67, 73, 91, 216, 223; *Ars amatoria*, 48, 92, 95, 106, 214, 232; Callimacheanism of, 5, 6–7, 197; *Fasti*, 6, 28, 29, 43, 53, 55, 56, 92, 143, 206, 207–8, 219, 225, 226, 227; *Remedia amoris*, 92, 232; *Tristia*, 232. *See also* Ovid, *Metamorphoses* of

paean (genre), 77, 128, 239n19, 250n72, 257n69, 259n96, 260n99, 260n100, 260n101, 262n127
Paeonia, 187, 188

Pallas. *See* Athena; Minerva
Pan, 121, 145, 146, 159, 160, 162, 163, 266n42, 268n2
Paris (hero), 151, 270n12
Parmenides, 18
Parthenius, mount, 148, 163, 270n13
Pausanias, 132, 251n81, 276n34
Pegasus, 176, 177, 188, 269n7, 269n9. *See also* Hippocrene
Peleus, 184, 261n113
Pelias, 121, 261n113
Pelion, mount, 126, 128, 261n115
Peneus, 60–61, 62, 63, 64, 76, 77, 114, 119, 124, 125–26, 130, 131, 223, 242n35, 247n38, 248n39, 248n40, 259n87, 260n107, 261n127, 262n128
Permessus, 269n10, 271n33
Persephone. *See* Proserpina
Perseus, 175, 177, 178, 271n25
personification, divine, 15, 22, 263n139, 268n1
Phaethon, 25, 37, 50, 59, 67, 78, 79, 246n23, 252n88
Pharsalus, 188, 272n42, 272n43
Pherecydes of Syros, 18, 19, 21, 23, 58, 247n32
Phiale, 164
Philicus, 195, 274n68
Philippi, 187, 188, 272n41, 272n42, 272n43, 273n47
Philomela, 141, 143
Phlegraea, 188, 234
Phoroneus, 86
Phrygia, 33
Pieria, 185, 196, 272n41, 274n77
Pierides, 10, 12, 173–74, 175, 176, 184–85, 186, 187, 188, 189–92, 195, 196–97, 198, 199, 200, 201, 215, 226, 226, 231, 233, 272n37, 272n40, 273n53, 274n77, 275n83, 276n34, 278n69
Pierus, 185, 186
Pimpleias, 189

Index

311

Pindar, 21, 69, 70–71, 72, 110, 111, 112, 116, 117, 118, 119, 120, 121, 128, 130, 184, 226, 244n69, 249n58, 250n61, 255n35, 260n101, 260n103, 261n115, 261n116, 262n127, 263n141, 263n147, 268n2, 271n25

Plato, 17–18, 19, 21, 44, 241n13, 252n92, 262n138

Plautus, 75, 259n87

Pliny, 113, 248n42, 266n35, 272n41

Polyhymnia (Polymnia), 28, 225–27, 228, 232, 276n19, 278n68, 278n70

Poseidon, 37, 90–91, 275n2. *See also* Neptune

primacy, poetic, 30, 37, 45–72, 87, 180, 234

Proclus, 18, 259n95

Procris, 121, 159, 163

Propertius, 95, 104, 173, 183, 210, 247n52, 257n65, 269n10, 273n54

prophecy, 9, 74, 88, 106, 108, 110, 112, 116, 117, 127, 130, 178–79, 265n14, 270n17, 270n19, 271n31

Proserpina (Persephone), 37, 41, 175, 181, 184, 196, 197, 200, 205, 206, 207, 208, 211, 212, 213, 214, 215, 216, 219, 247n38, 268n5, 270n16, 271n26, 277n50

Protogonos (Phanes), 18–19, 241n15

Psecas, 164

Pyreneus, 210, 227

rape, 12, 175, 181, 184, 192, 196, 197, 206, 207, 210, 213, 218, 219, 258n83

Rhanis, 164

Rhea, 33, 57, 58, 68, 69, 71, 72, 83, 131, 247n31, 247n32, 249n58

Rhianus, 86

rivalry, divine, 3, 10, 12–13, 15, 16, 35, 41, 44, 45–46, 52, 72, 82, 90, 98, 104, 120, 122, 125, 129, 132, 133, 139, 201, 203, 208, 215, 230, 231, 233

rivers, 25, 60, 62, 64–67, 69, 72–73, 74, 76–77, 79, 80, 81, 82, 83, 85, 124,

125–26, 131, 147, 148, 163, 168, 190, 191, 197, 198, 218, 221, 222, 223, 247n33, 247n35, 248n39, 248n40, 248n41, 248n42, 248n45, 249n52, 250n59, 250n61, 251n81, 252n89, 261n111, 262n127, 270n13, 271n24, 272n33

Rome, 6, 9, 50, 53, 102, 104, 112, 117; Ara Pacis, 206; Aventine, 104; Capitoline, 28, 29, 47; House of Livia, 256n55; Jupiter Tonans, temple of, 47–48; Palatine Hill, 46–48, 51, 52, 54, 59, 104, 112, 132, 269n6

sacrifice, 53, 138, 196, 197

Salian Hymn to Hercules, 8

Salmacis, 32, 33, 34, 35, 220, 221, 243n56, 278n59

Sappho, 93, 112

Seneca, 75, 245n6

Servius, 116, 207

Sibylline books, 112, 116Sicily, 199, 206, 217, 218, 271n26, 277n42

Silius Italicus, 266n33

Sirens, 211–14, 216, 276n29, 276n31, 276n33, 276n34, 277n35

Sol (Helios), 38, 51–52, 85, 103, 216, 218, 245n11, 277n40

springs, 32, 63, 79, 121, 140, 141, 148, 176, 177–78, 179, 183, 186, 187, 191, 207, 215, 217, 260n111, 266n35, 269n9, 270n17, 272n40

Stesichorus, 143

Stoics, 17, 22, 23, 26, 241n8, 242n38, 242n39, 245n80

Syrinx, 59, 83, 86, 93, 95, 105, 135, 261n120

Tartarus, 36, 38, 203, 205

Telemachus, 50, 51, 52

Tempe, grove of, 62, 64, 76, 122, 124, 132, 262n129, 264n152

Tenedos, 110

Terpsichore, 212–13

Index

territory, divine, 11, 12, 35–42, 51, 52, 72, 84, 149, 201, 230, 231,
Tethys, 124, 131
Thamyris, 270n19
Thebes, 70
Theocritus, 185
theogony, 19, 21, 23, 30, 44, 185
theomachy, 90, 98
Thespiae, 186, 272n40
Thessaly, 61, 64, 74, 76, 78, 84, 118, 122, 130, 132, 188, 193, 248n42, 252n94, 260n109, 264n153, 272n41, 273n47, 274n72
Thetis, 184
Thyrsus, 165
Tibullus, 75–76, 95, 106, 108, 173
Tiresias, 137, 138, 139, 142, 154, 161, 171, 173, 178, 179, 180, 265n14, 270n17
Titanomachy, 195, 199
Titans. *See* giants
Tmolus, 268n2
tragedy, 134, 169, 179, 200, 230, 267n56
Triptolemus, 276n19
Tritonis, lake
Typhoeus, 190, 191, 198

Urania. *See* Ourania

Valgius Rufus, 113
Varro, 147, 173, 222–23
Veiovis, 28–29
Velleius Paterculus, 17

Venus, 3, 8, 14, 35–42, 43, 73, 146, 181, 201, 202, 203, 205–6, 207, 208, 209, 210, 211, 213, 214, 215, 218, 220, 222, 227, 232, 233, 235, 240n3, 242n39, 242n41, 243n57, 244n59, 244n62, 244n63, 264n12, 275n15
Virgil: *Aeneid*, 8, 15, 114, 116, 146, 185, 206, 216, 232–33; *Eclogues*, 185, 217; *Georgics*, 146, 154, 165, 187, 191, 207, 216
virginity, 60, 93, 95, 97, 98, 99, 104, 106–7, 124, 129, 149, 169, 202, 208, 210, 213, 214, 256n47, 259n87, 262n138, 276n32

warfare, 84, 92, 167, 174, 179, 185, 187, 188, 191, 192, 200, 209, 231, 233
weddings, 184, 189, 272n36

Xenophanes, 195
Xenophon, 162–63, 265n31, 266n37, 267n68, 267n70

Zeno of Citium, 17
Zeus, 9–10, 14, 17, 18–19, 24, 26, 33, 34, 37, 39, 42, 43, 44, 51, 52, 61, 62, 71–72, 76, 77, 78, 84, 85, 86, 95, 96, 97, 124, 126, 129, 131, 132, 138, 144, 185, 191, 199, 220, 230, 235; as Ammon, 190, 191; birth of, 56–59, 64, 66, 68, 69, 74, 83; as demiurge, 20–23, 27; kingship of, 40–41, 54; Orphic hymn to, 19; primacy of, 70–74, 231. *See also* Jupiter

INDEX LOCORUM

Acesander
 F4, 121, 261n112
Achilles Tatius
 Isagoges excerpta
  3 [b1a], 247n31
Aelian
 Varia Historia
  3.1, 264n152
Aeschylus
 Agamemnon
  1147, 143
 Fragments
  fr. 44, 244n60
  fr. 342, 255n35
  fr. 350.4, 260n100
 Memnon
  fr. 300.4, 246n12
 Prometheus vinctus
  667, 246n12
  667–68, 242n37
 Supplices
  117, 252n94
  128, 252n94
  260–70, 252n90, 252n94
Alciphron
 1.11.3, 148

Alcmaeon
 fr. 46, 270n19
Amphis
 fr. 46, 95
Antagoras
 fr. 1.1, 22
Anthologia Palatina
 5.146, 266n35
 6.336, 260n99
 9.225, 269n9
 9.364, 270n17
Antiphanes
 fr. 249, 196
Antoninus Liberalis
 Metamorphoses
  9, 269n7
  28.3, 273n56
Aphthonius
 Progymnasmata
  5, 247n35
Apollodorus
 Bibliotheca
  1.3.3–4, 270n19
  1.7.4, 170
  2.1.1, 252n94
  3.8.2, 96

313

Index Locorum

Apollonius of Rhodes
  Argonautica
    1.580, 252n94
    2.500–507, 260n108
    2.506–7, 266n42
    2.511–12, 270n19
    2.513–15, 249n53
    2.703–13, 279n5
    2.936–39, 270n13
    3.91–99, 42
    3.131–44, 42
    3.876–77, 270n13
    4.263–65, 55
    4.267, 252n94
    4.269, 199
    4.891–99, 212
    4.893, 212
    4.896, 213
    4.898, 213
    4.903, 213
  Appendix Vergiliana
    Cul. 94, 264n152
Aratus
  Phaenomena
    1.1, 235
    205–24, 269n7
Aristophanes
  Birds
    692–99, 18
Aristotle
  [*De mundo*]
    401a13–15, 246n28
Athenaeus
    3.110b, 272n36
    10.418b–e, 274n74
    534e, 242n39
Augustine
  De civitate Dei
    18.5, 252n94
Augustus
  Res Gestae
    13, 38

Aulus Gellius
  Attic Nights
    5.12.11, 29
    6.14.3–4, 273n49
Bacchylides
    1.147, 257n65
    11.39, 257n65
Callimachus
  Aetia
    fr. 1, 23–24, 189, 269n10
    fr. 2, 1, 269n10
    fr. 2, 2, 244n75
    fr. 2b, 1, 269n10
    fr. 2b, 2–3, 272n33
    fr. 2b, 4, 272n40
    fr. 24, 270n13
    fr. 26–28, 257n62
    fr. 37, 1, 271n24
    fr. 75, 270n13
  Fragments
    fr. 29 Pf., 250n62
    fr. 673 Pf., 248n49
  Hymn to Apollo
    2.1, 107
    2.4–5, 48
    2.6, 122
    2.19, 111
    2.21, 117
    2.29, 72
    2.29–31, 129
    2.42–46, 110
    2.44, 111
    2.47–49, 108
    2.47–54, 249n54
    2.50–54, 108
    2.58–63, 121
    2.65–96, 120
    2.69–71, 100
    2.88, 260n111
    2.90–95, 120
    2.91, 121
    2.97–104, 117

Index Locorum

2.105–6, 123

2.108–12, 250n59

2.141, 123

2.225, 123

Hymn to Artemis

3.2, 162

3.4–6, 98

3.6, 61

3.7, 100

3.11, 254n19

3.11–12, 141

3.13, 144

3.13–17, 124

3.15–17, 144

3.16, 145, 265n28

3.18, 145, 149

3.20–22, 101

3.21–25, 258n86

3.29–31, 254n27

3.42–43, 165

3.44–45, 124

3.68, 245n10

3.81–83, 224

3.82, 278n63

3.86–87, 162

3.88–89, 145

3.90–91, 121

3.91, 162

3.91–93, 121

3.93–94, 161

3.95, 145, 161, 163

3.95–97, 162

3.96, 145

3.97, 145, 161

3.98, 162

3.98–106, 145

3.107–9, 267n69

3.110, 270n13

3.144–61, 267n69

3.146–47, 141

3.161, 141

3.162–67, 145

3.166, 140

3.175–82, 128

3.189–224, 124

3.200–203, 121

3.205, 254n19

3.206–8, 120, 159

3.209–10, 159

3.212–13, 253n14

3.215–17, 159

3.215–24, 261n113

3.217, 159

3.221, 163

3.223, 159

3.239, 140

3.240–45, 139

3.259–68, 138

3.264–65, 170

Hymn to Athena (Bath of Pallas)

5.5–12, 179

5.7–8, 199

5.17–28, 178

5.18–20, 151

5.47–48, 267n52

5.56, 267n52

5.57–131, 137, 178

5.66–67, 140

5.70, 141

5.72–73, 270n15

5.75–76, 270n17

5.77, 270n17

5.89–92, 270n18

5.90, 140

5.94–95, 141

5.110–11, 146

5.111–15, 159

5.115–16, 140

5.119–26, 179

Hymn to Delos

4.11, 128

4.37–41, 126

4.51–54, 127

4.54, 127

Index Locorum

Callim., *Hymn to Delos* (*continued*)
  4.79–85, 271n31
  4.98, 127
  4.105–52, 126
  4.112, 262n133
  4.118–20, 261n115
  4.124–27, 131
  4.129–31, 131
  4.135, 263n151
  4.152, 130
  4.193, 263n146
  4.229, 128
  4.240–48, 129
  4.244–48, 126
  4.249–54, 270n19
  4.251, 126
  4.256, 126
  4.268, 128
  4.268–69, 126
  4.268–70, 128
  4.268–73, 129
  4.292, 128
  4.300–301, 263n140
  4.325–26, 128, 131
Hymn to Demeter
  6.7–15, 276n29
  6.9, 197
  6.13–14, 197
  6.15, 198
  6.17, 192
  6.18–23, 192
  6.24, 274n77
  6.34, 193
  6.37, 193
  6.39, 195
  6.55, 196
  6.57–58, 193
Hymn to Zeus
  1.1–2, 68
  1.1–7, 69
  1.1–9, 56
  1.3, 84

  1.4–5, 22, 56
  1.8, 247n49
  1.10–14, 83
  1.10–32, 57, 68
  1.14, 57, 67
  1.16, 58
  1.18, 58, 65, 79
  1.19, 66
  1.20, 57, 68
  1.22, 251n81
  1.27, 69, 79
  1.28, 149n58
  1.29, 58
  1.32, 58, 68
  1.38–41, 78
  1.42, 66
  1.50, 40
  1.57–67, 39
  1.61, 40
  1.65, 40
  1.66, 40
  1.79, 54
  1.92–93, 40
Iambics
  fr. 202 Pf., 248n49
  fr. 202.35–39 Pf., 247n38
  fr. 203, 270n19
Cassianus Bassius
  Geoponica
    11.2, 247n35
Catullus
  34, 95, 103, 255n45
  34.2, 103
  34.9, 102, 103
  34.13–16, 101, 102
  34.15–16, 103
  34.21–24, 101
  61.29–30, 271n33
  64.35, 264n152
  64.285–86, 264n152
  65.2, 210, 276n31
  65.12, 142

65.14, 142
68A.24, 278n55
68B.96, 278n55
76.20–22, 259n88
76.21, 259n88
76.25, 259n88
95.10, 273n49
Choeroboscus
   Epimerismi in Psalmos
   183.9, 246n28
Choricius of Gaza
   13.1, 70
Cicero
   De finibus
      5.18, 276n31
   De natura deorum
      1.18.5–6, 17
      2.57.3, 17
      2.58.2, 17
      3.54, 185
      3.58.2, 253n15
   De officiis
      1.77.3, 75
   Epistulae ad Atticum
      4.15.5, 264n152
   Epistulae ad familiares
      15.6.1, 75
   In Pisonem
      74.4, 75
   Timaeus (Latin translation)
      6.3, 17
      6.7, 17
   Tusculan Disputations
      1.63.1–5, 43
Claudian
   De consolatu Stilichonis
      3.250, 165
      3.257–60, 268n74
      3.314–15, 165
Clement of Alexandria
   Stromateis
      1.21.6, 252n91

Columella
   De re rustica
      10.1.1.265, 264n152
Cornutus
   Theologia Graeca
      2.6–8, 246n28
      48.5–9, 242n39
Dio Cassius
   51.4.6, 272n41
   56.6, 113
Diodorus Siculus
   4.21.5, 274n48
   5.3.4, 271n26
   5.71.4, 274n48
Dionysius Periegeta
   415, 247n29
   415–17, 248n47
   916, 247n35
Dionysius Thrax
   P. 451.12, 257n69
Empedocles
   B 3.3 D–K, 209, 210, 225
   B 131 D–K, 209
Ennius
   Annales
      fr. 81, 245n6
Epicharmus
   fr. 39, 271n24, 272n33
   fr. 135, 199
Epimenides
   fr. 202, 248n49
Eumelus
   fr. 35, 272n33
Euripides
   Hippolytus
      17–19, 158
      447–48, 244n60
      1268–82, 244n60
   Ion
      905–6, 260n100
   Iphigenia Taurica
      1097, 258n86

Index Locorum

Euripedes (*continued*)
  Phoenissae
    1131–32, 193
    1182–86, 193
Fulgentius
  Mythologiae
    3.9, 271n24
Grattius
  Cynegetica
    1–9, 157
    1–23, 147
    4, 167
    23, 147, 264n1
    24–25, 147
    32, 266n36
    34–35, 147
    61–66, 169–70
    95–107, 152
    108–9, 153
    199–204, 161
    212, 160
    213–52, 154
    218, 156
    221, 157
    246–52, 155
    251–52, 157
    253–59, 267n61
    269, 163
    271, 163
    483–96, 166
    484, 151
    494–95, 167
Greek Verse Inscriptions of Cyrenaica
  028, 122
Heraclitus
  fr. B64 D–K, 242n38
Herodian
  Περὶ παθῶν
    p. *187.24*, 148
Herodotus
  1.66.2, 55
  4.175, 148

  4.198, 148
  6.98.3, 262n136
  7.129.2, 248n42
Hesiod
  Fragments
    fr. *128*, 252n90
    fr. *215*, 118
  Theogony
    5–6, 179
    11, 226
    27–28, 244n70
    37, 226
    40–41, 213
    48, 226
    50–52, 191
    51, 226
    79–80, 276n22
    94–95, 270n19
    96, 54
    111–13, 38
    140, 244n7, 245n10
    337–38, 248n47
    367, 248n42
    376, 199
    383, 199
    881–85, 38
    912–14, 243n58
Homer
  Iliad
    1.38, 110
    1.44–52, 111
    1.70, 110
    1.601–4, 111
    2.751–55, 261n127
    4.101, 257n65
    4.119, 257n65
    4.171, 252n89
    4.442–43, 193
    5.447–48, 114
    12.164, 244n75
    12.167–72, 244n75

Index Locorum

13.18–19, 275n2
13.27–29, 275n2
14.226, 272n41
14.317, 96
14.342–52, 24
15.5, 257n65
15.187–93, 38
15.443–44, 253n14
21.470–77, 90
21.485–88, 253n12
21.489–92, 91
21.505–10, 98

Odyssey
4.71–75, 51
4.73, 51
4.75, 52
6.106–9, 136
12.159, 214
17.494, 257n65
21.59–60, 253n14
21.267, 257n65

Homeric Hymn to Aphrodite
1, 41
1–6, 244n60
3, 203
6, 41
7, 40
7–35, 203
9, 41
10, 41
12–15, 41
16–20, 96, 169
19, 165
21, 41
26, 247n36
33, 40
69–74, 275n2
93, 96
121, 205
121–25, 204
126–30, 205

133, 204
136, 204
173–74, 193

Homeric Hymn to Apollo
1–12, 71
2–4, 256n61
19, 69
33, 262n128
53–55, 128
67–69, 71
72, 128
91, 121
119–20, 68
131, 93
132, 71
182–93, 270n19
194–203, 263n140
199, 100
207, 69
244–76, 263n151
383, 263n151

Homeric Hymn to Artemis (9)
2, 100

Homeric Hymn to Artemis (27)
2, 90, 169
3, 100
6–7, 257n61

Homeric Hymn to Demeter
3, 205
5, 212
83–87, 38
86, 40
131, 194
188–89, 193
189, 193
202–5, 194
423, 213
424, 181, 212, 270n16

Homeric Hymn to Dionysius
1–9, 246n27
5, 244n70

Index Locorum

Homeric Hymn to Pan (19)
  24, 145
Homeric Hymn to the Muses and Apollo
  (25)
  4, 246n19
Horace
  Carmen Saeculare
    2, 103
    9, 103
    13–16, 102
    17–20, 113, 114
    33, 257n74
    36, 456n50
    45–46, 4
    61–62, 92
    61–64, 112
    63–64, 115
    74, 114
  Epistulae
    2.1.214–18, 269n6
  Epodes
    2.33, 266n39
  Odes
    1.2.32, 92
    1.7.4, 264n152
    1.12.23–24, 257n67
    1.16.6, 256n58
    1.21, 95, 256n48, 257n74
    1.21.9, 264n152
    1.21.9–10, 262n129
    1.37.12–21, 273n57
    2.10.18–20, 257n71
    3.1.24, 264n152
    3.4, 274n47
    3.4.26, 274n47
    3.4.35, 253n16
    3.4.40, 274n47
    4, 113
    4.2, 250n61
    4.6, 256n56, 260n101
    4.6.31–44, 260n101
    4.6.41–44, 256n56

Hyginus
  Fabulae
    141.1, 212
    145.1.3–4, 252n92
    189, 267n57
  Poetica astronomica
    2.18, 269n7
Isidore of Seville
  Etymologies
    8.11.59, 275n10
    13.21.3, 223
    14.8.33, 223
    17.7.2, 75
Longinus
  De sublimitate
    3, 273n49
Lucan
  Pharsalia
    2.491, 268n77
    6.75, 266n41
    6.345, 264n152
    6.371–80, 261n127
    6.374, 248n47
    6.398, 249n53
    6.410–12, 274n47
    7.144–50, 274n47
    8.1, 264n152
    9.352–54, 271n24
Lucilius
  fr. 41, 272n41
Lucretius
  De rerum natura
    1.1, 209
    1.1–43, 209
    1.1–49, 244n60
    1.2, 206
    1.24, 209
    1.31–43, 242n41
    1.921–27, 232
    4.1058–1140, 221
    4.1060, 221
    4.1105–14, 220

Index Locorum

4.1114, 221
4.1128, 221
5.575–76, 256n52
6.94, 209
Lycophron
  Alexandra
    119, 199
    274–75, 274n77
    410, 274n77
    576, 199
Manilius
  2.49, 276n31
Martial
  8.48.2, 254n28
  13.19.1, 266n41
Marullus
  Hymns to Nature
    1.60–100, 245n82
    1.100, 245n82
    3.13–20, 245n82
    3.21–22, 245n82
Moschus
  Epitaphios Bionis
    76–77, 217
Naevius
  fr. 30, 257n66
Nonnus
  Dionysiaca
    7.234–36, 269n7
    12.87–89, 261n116
    13.300, 260n104
    18.266, 252n88
Orphic Fragments
  12, 18
  14.1–2b, 18
  31, 18
  64, 18
  120–43b, 18
  147–49, 18
  153–58, 18
  168, 18
  171–73, 18

240–41, 18
243.1–2, 18
Orphic Hymns
  55.1, 278n66
  76.12, 278n68
Ovid
  Amores
    1.1, 24, 26, 201, 243n57, 253n9, 257n67
    1.1.1–4, 16
    1.1.3–4, 219
    1.1.5, 23
    1.1.5–10, 201
    1.1.10, 91
    1.1.13–14, 243n57
    1.1.15–16, 263n152
    1.1.23, 253n9
    1.1.25, 257n67
    1.5.1, 216
    1.8.69, 149
    1.11, 165
    1.12, 165
    2.1, 26
    2.1.15–20, 26
    2.1.22, 249n54
    2.5, 27
    2.5.1, 92
    2.5.51–52, 27
    2.17.32, 67
    3.1.14, 265n23
    3.1.24, 271n20
    3.2, 92
    3.2.51, 92
    3.2.55, 254n22
    3.2.56, 240n3
    3.10.20, 246n24
  Ars amatoria
    1.45, 249
    1.259, 151
    2.239, 92
    2.493–94, 48
    2.495–96, 48

Ovid, *Ars amatoria (continued)*

3.141–44, 94
3.272, 265n23
3.311–12, 214

Epistulae ex Ponto

2.7.25, 266n33
4.16.34, 264n1

Fasti

2.91, 92
2.159, 92
2.163–67, 270n13
2.289–90, 55
2.461, 273n56
2.465, 249n51
2.492, 248n39
3.346, 92
3.353, 92
3.437–48, 28
3.438, 29
3.440, 29
3.447, 29
3.455–56, 269n8, 269n9
4.85–90, 207
4.93, 207
4.95, 207
4.96, 207
4.172, 245n10
4.288, 245n10
4.447, 264n152
4.469, 249n54
4.481–82, 143
4.482, 143
4.547, 207
4.589–90, 277n46
4.597, 219
5.9, 226
5.9–10, 226
5.11–12, 226
5.25–46, 28
5.29, 28
5.45–46, 28, 29
5.55, 226

5.79–80, 226
5.90, 55
5.111–28, 246n24
5.342, 207
6.59, 151
6.665, 271n23
6.811, 276n31

Heroides

4.40, 92
5.3, 271n32
15.23, 48, 93
18.74, 92
20.19–20, 107
20.95, 92
20.204, 91
20.229–32, 253n17
21.173–74, 259n89
21.206, 149

Ibis

222, 266n33

Metamorphoses

1.2, 3, 15
1.2–3, 4
1.4, 4, 63
1.6, 24
1.9, 25
1.17, 24
1.18, 60
1.21, 16, 23, 233
1.29–32, 240n5
1.32, 16
1.35, 24, 223
1.37–41, 126
1.38–42, 63
1.57, 16
1.79, 16
1.106, 31, 53
1.113–14, 31, 53
1.149–51, 116
1.151–55, 28
1.151–62, 84, 188
1.160, 149

Index Locorum

1.163–252, 27
1.166, 73
1.168–76, 47, 54
1.170, 47
1.173, 63
1.175–76, 47
1.178, 28, 54, 197
1.192–95, 63, 184
1.216, 80
1.216–17, 59
1.218, 55
1.230–31, 55
1.240, 55
1.244–48, 126
1.251, 126
1.253–58, 25
1.256, 58, 126
1.259, 25
1.268–69, 126
1.276, 63
1.291–92, 25
1.330, 73
1.378, 73
1.409, 242n32
1.416–37, 25
1.417, 25
1.430–33, 221
1.433, 25
1.434–37, 85
1.438–49, 84
1.441–42, 90
1.444, 115
1.449–50, 75
1.451, 105, 245n11
1.452, 60, 73, 92, 105, 119, 245n11
1.453, 73, 245n11
1.454, 92, 105
1.454–55, 105
1.455, 453n7
1.459, 259n98
1.461, 92
1.461–62, 73, 74

1.463, 92, 105, 245n11
1.463–65, 253n12
1.467, 262n134
1.468, 253n14
1.468–69, 243n47
1.472, 60, 119
1.473, 105
1.474–77, 99
1.475–76, 105, 118
1.476, 104
1.477, 105, 106
1.481–82, 114
1.481–87, 60
1.483–87, 99
1.486, 106
1.486–87, 61
1.490, 105, 113, 245n11
1.491, 114
1.492–96, 242n35
1.496, 114
1.497, 105, 106
1.497–502, 118
1.498, 105
1.498–99, 126
1.500, 123
1.500–502, 74
1.502, 127
1.504, 60, 119
1.512–14, 107
1.512–24, 95
1.513–14, 249n54
1.514–22, 109
1.520–31, 123
1.521–22, 113
1.521–24, 113
1.524, 258n80
1.525, 60, 119, 123
1.526, 123
1.527, 127
1.527–30, 123
1.534, 259n89
1.536, 114

Index Locorum

Ovid, *Metamorphoses* (*continued*)

1.539, 114
1.544, 223
1.546, 224
1.546–47, 115
1.548, 115
1.551, 127
1.553, 105, 245n11
1.554, 257n61
1.556, 257n61
1.557, 114
1.557–65, 49
1.558–59, 74
1.560–61, 75
1.564, 76
1.564–67, 106
1.565–66, 75
1.566, 105, 116
1.568–82, 61
1.574–75, 64
1.577–78, 64, 65, 77
1.578, 124
1.579, 65
1.580, 65
1.583–85, 252n90
1.585–87, 277n50
1.588–600, 27
1.595–96, 28, 243n43
1.599–600, 24, 219
1.612, 24
1.612–13, 24
1.615, 25
1.659, 114
1.668, 86
1.689–700, 261n120
1.694–98, 93
1.696, 256n57
1.700–712, 83, 261n120
1.702, 82
1.704, 83
1.741, 42
1.752, 245n11

2.1–4, 50
2.5–7, 246n12
2.11–12, 216
2.24, 245n11
2.36, 245n11
2.110, 245n11
2.215, 249n51
2.219, 210
2.236, 249n51
2.239–59, 67, 79
2.244, 79
2.272, 206
2.319, 249n51
2.340–66, 67
2.354, 42
2.370, 249n51
2.399, 245n11
2.401–8, 37
2.405–6, 246n23
2.405–10, 79
2.409, 254n30
2.415, 97, 105
2.415–16, 80
2.416, 105
2.425, 80, 95, 105
2.426, 254n30
2.427, 254n30
2.427–29, 82
2.429–30, 82
2.441, 105
2.441–42, 105, 145
2.442, 80
2.443–44, 80
2.451, 105
2.453–64, 81
2.454, 245n11
2.454–59, 270n13
2.457, 265n24
2.460, 83
2.463, 82
2.464, 82
2.465, 92, 105

Index Locorum

2.499, 80
2.524, 86
2.846–47, 27
2.847, 28
2.847–49, 243n43
3.1, 135
3.2, 135
3.17, 135
3.81–83, 224
3.85–87, 250n61
3.100–106, 135
3.133, 105
3.139, 144
3.142, 157, 167
3.143, 144, 146, 150
3.146–47, 157
3.148, 147, 154
3.153, 147, 148
3.155–62, 12
3.155–64, 150
3.156, 148
3.157, 151
3.160, 149
3.163–64, 270n13
3.165–66, 224
3.165–72, 164
3.166, 149, 150
3.168, 145
3.168–70, 148
3.175–76, 167
3.175–82, 164
3.176, 266n45
3.177–85, 136
3.178, 267n71
3.183–84, 153
3.183–85, 150
3.186, 165
3.194, 144
3.197, 143
3.198, 141
3.200–201, 144
3.206, 160, 162

3.207, 160
3.208, 160
3.209–11, 160
3.210, 163
3.211, 160, 165
3.212, 267n64
3.213, 164
3.216, 163
3.217, 267n67, 267n70
3.218, 162
3.219, 160
3.220, 267n61
3.221–22, 162
3.222, 267n61
3.224, 160, 267n61
3.225, 165
3.225–31, 155
3.227, 157
3.229, 267n71
3.232, 162
3.236, 165
3.237–41, 142
3.242, 267n71, 268n77
3.242–46, 155
3.249, 165
3.249–52, 168
3.252, 92, 168
3.253–55, 168–69
3.305, 243n47
3.307, 243n47
3.348, 265n14
3.411, 220
3.445, 278n65
4.11–30, 32
4.274–84, 31
4.289, 33
4.298–99, 34
4.304, 243n56
4.308–15, 34
4.315, 243n56
4.320–21, 34
4.323, 34

Ovid, *Metamorphoses (continued)*

4.324, 34
4.513, 149
4.592, 42
4.658, 42
4.785–86, 177
4.798–803, 271n28
5.250, 199, 271n25
5.254, 210, 271n29
5.254–59, 177
5.255, 213
5.257, 178
5.260, 213, 225
5.260–63, 177
5.262, 177
5.262–63, 177
5.263, 199
5.263–72, 182
5.268, 225
5.268–70, 180
5.270, 180, 184, 199
5.273–74, 210
5.274, 271n29
5.280, 225
5.302, 189
5.302–14, 186
5.304, 189
5.305, 189, 195
5.306, 189
5.307, 189, 272n37
5.311–14, 187
5.312, 141, 188, 191
5.313, 188
5.313–14, 188
5.314, 175
5.319–31, 190
5.320, 195
5.332–37, 217
5.333, 186
5.333–34, 215
5.336, 199
5.337, 211
5.337–39, 226

5.341–45, 203, 275n1
5.342, 207
5.343, 207
5.344–45, 275n1
5.356–63, 37
5.365–79, 36, 202
5.368, 38, 205
5.369, 37
5.371, 205
5.371–72, 244n62
5.373–74, 38
5.375, 199
5.375–76, 181
5.376–77, 209
5.378–79, 209
5.390, 213
5.390–95, 213
5.391, 213
5.392, 213
5.394, 213
5.395–96, 277n48
5.440–41, 275n7
5.487, 220
5.487–88, 216
5.487–508, 215
5.490, 206
5.498–501, 215
5.518–20, 277n50
5.520, 218
5.521, 218
5.524–26, 219
5.552, 212
5.552–53, 214
5.552–55, 211
5.555, 213
5.556–60, 212
5.559, 221
5.572, 206
5.572–73, 216
5.574, 216
5.574–75, 216
5.585, 225
5.586, 216

Index Locorum

5.587, 221
5.595, 221
5.597, 221
5.608, 79
5.618–20, 223
5.622–24, 222
5.632, 221
5.634, 278n57
5.635, 221, 277n39
5.636, 221
5.636–37, 218, 220
5.636–38, 222
5.637, 221
5.638, 220, 221
5.669, 187
6.2, 187
6.19, 233
6.69, 234
6.71, 233
6.103–28, 233
6.384, 271n24
7.222, 264n152
7.701, 149
7.753–55, 163, 267n57
7.755, 92
7.771, 163
7.807, 266n36
8.322–23, 254n28
8.328, 271n20
8.331, 149
8.585–89, 198
8.587, 198
8.738–878, 197
8.743–44, 273n58
8.835–36, 198
8.854, 254n28
9.712–13, 254n28
10.148, 210
10.148–54, 233
10.155–61, 235
10.162–219, 235
10.202–17, 235
10.230, 206

10.515–18, 254n23
10.525, 92
10.533–36, 233
13.733–34, 277n36
13.759, 206
14.331, 150
14.719–20, 250n72
14.806, 248n39
15.537, 92
15.622–25, 268n3
15.744, 258n78
15.822–24, 272n43
15.844, 206
15.875–76, 235

Remedia amoris
76–78, 258n80
202, 149
379, 92
704–6, 258n80

Tristia
1.2.24, 273n50
1.4.1, 80
1.7, 278n1
2.1.13, 276n31
3.4b.1, 80
4.2.49, 251n79
4.2.51–52, 251n79

Palaephatus
Progymnasmata
17, 247n35
50, 247n35

Parthenius
Fragments
fr. 56, 148
Narrationum amatoriarum libellus
15.1–3, 247n35

Pausanias
2.3.5, 269n9
2.25.3, 85
2.31.3, 271n25
2.31.9, 269n7
3.24.9, 258n86
4.33.7, 270n19

328 — Index Locorum

Pausanias (*continued*)
  5.14.6, 277n43
  6.22.9, 277n43
  8.6.6, 85
  8.6.21, 269n9
  8.24.2, 251n81
  8.41.7, 258n78
  9.2.3, 143
  9.10.6, 251n81
  9.19.1, 267n57
  9.29.3, 185
  9.29.5, 272n33
  9.31.3, 269n7
  9.34.3, 276n34
  10.16.8, 132
Persius
 Satires
  1.70, 76
Petronius
 Satyricon
  5.1.9, 264n10
  109.9–10, 254n25
  126.18.1–3, 242n41
Philicus
 Hymn to Demeter
  SH 680.55, 195
  SH 680.57, 195
Pindar
 Fragments
  fr. 29, 250n62
  fr. 33c. 2, 262n136
  fr. 91, 273n56
 Olympian Odes
  1, 69
  1.1, 250n61
  1.24–27, 250n61
  13.63, 269n9
 Paeans
  10(a).4, 262n127
 Pythian Odes
  1.1–2, 213
  1.1–13, 270n19

  4.270–74, 257n69
  5.24, 266n32
  5.63–69, 111
  9.6, 120
  9.14–17, 119
  9.17–25, 118
  9.26–37, 118
  9.65, 266n42
 Threnoi
  3, fr. 128c, 117
Plato
 Cratylus
  396a–b, 20, 246n28
  404e–406a, 253n11
  406b, 262n138
 Laws
  715e–716a, 241n14
 Phaedrus
  238d, 271n31
 Symposium
  177a–d, 19
  178b, 19
  187d–e, 227
  195a, 19
  197a, 20
  197e, 20
 Timaeus
  22a, 252n92
  28c, 17
Plautus
 Amphitruo
  870, 259n87
  877, 259n87
  1092–93, 259n87
 Cistellaria
  201, 75
Pliny the Elder
 Natural History
  4.30.6, 248n42
  4.33, 272n41
  4.66, 262n136
  5.10, 275n84

Index Locorum

18.29, 274n48
25.4.2, 113
31.30, 248n48
Pliny the Younger
  Epistulae
    7.12.4, 274n49
    9.26.5, 274n49
Plotinus
  Commentary on Plato's Timaeus
    32c [B3], 18
Plutarch
  Agis
    9.2, 247n35
  Alcibiades
    16.1–2, 242n39
  Amatorius
    758c, 275n15
  Convivium septem sapientium
    150b, 271n25
  De mulierum virtutibus
    244e, 253n8
  De Pythiae oraculis
    29 [409A], 245n7
Posidippus
  fr. 113 A–B, 266n35
Propertius
  1.3.6, 249n52
  1.9.12, 249n54
  1.11.3, 274n48
  2.1.19–20, 274n47, 273n54
  2.1.27–36, 273n54
  2.1.39–42, 274n47
  2.10.8, 273n54
  2.10.11–12, 271n20
  2.23.1–2, 272n39
  2.30.33–36, 210
  2.31.16, 256n58
  2.32.20, 266n39
  2.34.80, 254n21
  3.1.15–18, 269n6
  3.1.19, 183

3.3.1–2, 269n7
3.9.35–36, 273n50
3.11.37, 272n43
4.6, 95
4.6.25, 253n9
4.6.33–36, 257n65
4.6.69, 273n54
4.6.69–70, 257n71
Pseudo-Ovid
  Epistula Sapphus
    27, 271n32
Pseudo-Plutarch
  De fluviis
    16, 66
Quintilian
  Institutio oratoria
    1.6.34, 266n45
    3.7.27, 76
    9.3.69–70, 249n51
    10.2.16, 274n49
    12.10.12, 274n49
    12.10.17, 274n49
    12.10.73, 274n49
    12.10.80, 274n49
Sappho
  fr. 44A, 256n47
  fr. 208, 270n19
Scholia Danielis
  On the Eclogues
    5.64, 266n43
    8.12, 75
Seneca
  Agamemnon
    322–27, 257n71
  Hercules furens
    286, 264n152
    828–29, 75
    980, 264n152
  Medea
    457, 264n152
    874–76, 456n51

330 Index Locorum

Seneca (*continued*)
  Natural Questions
    2.18.1, 245n6
    6.26.2–4, 262n136
  Thyestes
    21–22, 275n6
  Troades
    815, 264n152
Servius
  Commentary on Virgil's Aeneid
    1.22, 266n45
    1.479–90, 264n11
    1.500, 268n73
    3.91, 247n35
Silius Italicus
  Punica
    8.538, 274n48
    14.638, 268n77
Simonides
  fr. 11.16, 213
  fr. 11.21, 209
Sophocles
  Fragments
    fr. 941, 244n60
  Trachiniae
    99, 246n12
    213, 253n8
Statius
  Achilleis
    1.237, 264n152
  Silvae
    1.1.4, 245n10
    1.2.215, 264n152
    1.2.226, 265n27
    3.1.131, 245n10
    5.3.196–97, 274n47
    5.3.209, 264n152
  Thebais
    1.485, 264n152
    6.355–65, 270n19
    10.119, 264n152
Strabo
  5.4.4, 274n48

5.4.6, 274n48
6.3.5, 274n48
8.3.12, 258n86
8.6.21, 269n7
10.3.10, 270n19
Suetonius
  Augustus
    91.2, 47
Teleclides
  fr. 1.15, 196
Terence
  Andria
    473, 259n87
    487, 259n87
Theocritus
  Idylls
    1.67, 263n152
    10.24, 185
    11.3, 185
    17.75–76, 455n43
    17.110–11, 455n43
Thucydides
  2.8.3, 262n136
Tibullus
  2.3, 108, 254n31
  2.3.11–32, 249n54
  2.3.11–27, 254n31
  2.3.13, 258n79
  2.3.23, 108
  2.3.25–26, 265n59
  2.5, 95, 254n31
  2.5.4–5, 75
  2.5.64, 247n36
  2.5.105–6, 251n79
  2.5.115–20, 76
  2.5.120, 251n79
  2.5.121, 76
  2.5.121–22, 106
Tzetzes
  On Hesiod's Works and Days
    1, 276n19

Index Locorum

On Lycophron
  6, 247n35
Valerius Cato
  fr. 35, 255n45
Valerius Flaccus
  Argonautica
    8.452, 264n152
Varro
  De lingua Latina
    5.28.1–2, 222
    5.178, 267n53
    6.96, 275n2
  Satirae Menippeae
    385.2, 147, 149
Virgil
  Aeneid
    1.293, 248n39
    1.315, 214
    1.320, 264n12
    1.323, 146, 265n21
    1.329, 146
    1.507, 248n39
    1.556, 114
    1.618, 206
    1.683–84, 254n28
    1.731, 248n39
    2.1, 216
    2.257–96, 243n57
    3.75–77, 262n136
    3.90–92, 256n61
    3.694–96, 277n39
    3.717, 277n39
    4.274, 114
    4.376, 92
    6.364, 114
    6.398, 249n53
    6.657–58, 116
    6.791, 244n62
    6.794–95, 244n62
    6.823, 233
    7.20, 254n28
    7.45, 271n20

7.415–16, 254n28
7.496, 233
7.500–502, 265n17
7.502, 265n17
7.774, 255n51
8.285–305, 8
8.349–54, 246n13
8.425, 245n10
8.711–13, 273n57
8.720, 48
9.184–85, 15
9.630–31, 245n82, 245n6
10.132, 233
10.332, 206
10.524, 114
11.557, 255n51
11.649, 253n16
11.650, 253n16
11.652, 140
12.391–97, 257n72
Eclogues
  3.58–59, 275n83
  3.60, 279n5
  6.3, 254n21
  6.13, 185
  6.65, 180, 272n40
  6.66, 180
  7.4, 165
  7.66, 248n50
  8.63, 185
  9.33, 185
  10.1, 217
  10.72, 185
Georgics
  1.7, 206
  1.13, 240n4
  1.36–39, 244n63
  1.431, 254n20
  1.489–92, 187
  2.469, 263n152, 264n152
  2.490, 266n43
  3.2, 249n53

332 Index Locorum

Virgil, *Georgics (continued)*
  3.6, 254n21
  3.264, 146
  4.287, 191
  4.290, 253n16
  4.317, 263n152, 264n152
  4.334–44, 216
  4.336, 216
  4.339–40, 217
  4.341, 216
  4.341–42, 165
  4.344, 277n44
  4.351, 216
  4.351–52, 216
  4.355, 119
  4.363–73, 248n40

  4.367, 248n40
  4.390, 272n41
  4.511, 142
  4.515, 143
  4.535, 165
Xenophanes
  fr. 1.19–24, 195
Xenophon
  Cynegeticus
    2.4, 265n31
    4.1, 267n68
    4.7, 162
    4.7–8, 162
    6.7, 266n37
    7.5, 163